RANDOM HOUSE WEBSTER'S
AMERICAN SIGN LANGUAGE
LEGAL DICTIONARY

Elaine Costello, Ph.D.

Illustrated by
Linda C. Tom

Random House Reference
New York

Copyright © 2003 by Elaine Costello

All rights reserved under International and Pan-American Copyright Conventions. No part of this book may be reproduced in any form or by any means, electronic or mechanical, including photocopying, without the written permission of the publisher. All inquiries should be addressed to Random House Reference, Random House, Inc., New York, NY. Published in the United States by Random House, Inc., New York and simultaneously in Canada by Random House of Canada Limited.

Random House is a trademark of Random House, Inc.

This book is available for special purchases in bulk by organizations and institutions, not for resale, at special discounts. Please direct your inquiries to the Random House Premium Sales, fax 212-572-4961.

Please address inquiries about electronic licensing of reference products, for use on a network or in software or on CD-ROM, to the Subsidiary Rights Department, Random House Reference, fax 212-940-7352.

Visit the Random House Reference Web site: www.randomwords.com

Typeset and printed in the United States of America.

Library of Congress Cataloging-in-Publication Data is available.

First Edition
0 9 8 7 6 5 4 3 2 1
April 2003

ISBN 0-375-71943-1

New York   Toronto   London   Sydney   Auckland

Deep appreciation goes to three wonderful people who, despite conflicting schedules, came through, providing the valuable core vocabulary included in this book. Shirley Herald of the Arkansas Judicial Department, Little Rock, AR, graciously and willingly shared from her legal interpreting experience and coordinated the invaluable sign contributions of Raphael (Ray) James and Pamela Harrison, instructors in the Interpreter Education Program at the University of Arkansas at Little Rock. Without their tireless involvement, this book would not have come to fruition.

My gratitude also goes to Linda C. Tom, a woman of incredible talent, who served both as photographer and illustrator of the signs in this book. And finally, I am indebted to Richard Newman, whose good humor during endless hours of modeling the signs provided the morale boost necessary to stay on task to completion.

Contents

Introduction: Why This Dictionary?   iv

Guide: How to Use This Dictionary   vi

    How to Find a Sign   vi

    How to Make a Sign   vii

American Manual Alphabet Used in Fingerspelling   ix

Handshapes   x

Numbers   x

Legal Dictionary: A-Z   1–422

Introduction

Why This Dictionary?

Except for the skilled intervention of a legal interpreter, most Deaf defendants would not understand the charges against them nor would they be able to participate effectively in their own defense. Although considerable progress has been made in recent years to make courts more accessible to Deaf people, it remains the task of practiced interpreters, knowledgeable of the judicial system and legal concepts, to accurately communicate legal proceedings, whether between the Deaf person and the arresting officer, the Deaf person and the attorney, or the Deaf person in the context of a courtroom hearing or trial.

The task of using sign language in a legal setting is far more complex than in any other circumstance. The meanings of otherwise ordinary terms have unique meanings when used in the legal arena. For example, damages in legal sense refers to a monetary consideration, not to something that is destroyed or otherwise marred. A person who would use the more common sign for damages would fail to give the Deaf person accurate information, and may in fact, cause harm to the Deaf person and to the outcome of the proceedings.

Because of the unique nature of legal terminology, a book such as the Random House Webster's American Sign Language Legal Dictionary becomes a necessary resource. A great many of the signs in the book are strings of signs that conceptually define the legal term. Though strings of signs may seem to be cumbersome for conveying an English term, the signs serve to provide a clear meaning of the term reducing the possibility of miscommunication.

The Americans with Disabilities Act (ADA) requires all state and local courts to be accessible to Deaf individuals and requires the provision of interpreters, transcription, or other appropriate auxiliary aids for Deaf people in court. What is not mandated by the ADA is the requirement of the courts to provide qualified interpreters for Deaf persons who initiate legal actions. Qualified interpreters are often not present at the time of arrest so Deaf people may not know the charges against them, understand the Miranda warning, be aware of their right to counsel and to post bail, and other such constitutional rights. This book, with more than 1,000 defined and described signs, is intended to be available as an essential resource. Though it is not intended to replace a qualified interpreter, it can serve as a stop-gap until the interpreter arrives.

It is hoped not only that this book can serve as an introductory vocabulary resource for interpreters and the legal community, but that Deaf people themselves can benefit from having a source for legal terms and definitions. The signs in this book are used by interpreters in legal settings nationwide. However, the nuances of interpreting in a legal setting only is achieved by practice and knowledge of legal concepts and protocol. By enabling and enhancing communication in such settings, use of these signs can sharply reduce the kinds of misunderstanding that English words alone might convey.

Guide

How to Use This Dictionary

How to Find a Sign
Alphabetization

All the entries in this book, whether complete entries, entries for alternate signs, or cross-reference entries, are shown in **large boldface type** in a single alphabetical listing—e.g., **capital, capital asset, caption, care, case1, case2, casebook.**

Complete Entries

Each complete entry has at least one *definition*, a description of *how to make the sign,* and one *illustration.* However, many of the entries are more complex than that. It is not unusual for a legal term to be constructed of several signs put together, just as a term in English can be composed of more than one word. The entry for **contract,** for example, is made up of the two signs: **agree | sign,** and the word **polygraph** of the three sequential signs: **lie | test | machine.** These component words are shown in **small boldface type** and each has an appropriate illustration and description of its sign.

Multiple Entries for the Same Word

When several entries are spelled the same way, each is marked with a small identifying superscript number. See, for example, the two entries for **conviction.** Note that the second of these is labeled "alternate sign." That is because it shares the meaning of the first, **conviction**[1], which contains the definition. Although the second therefore lacks a definition of its own, it has descriptions and illustrations for *alternate signs* that can be used instead of those shown at the earlier entry.

When identically spelled entries do have different meanings, each is defined, as at the two entries for **closing,** the first of which refers to the completion of a real estate transaction.

Any group of these entries may include one that is simply a cross reference to one or more other signs elsewhere in the alphabet—e.g., **handicap,** which says, "See signs for DISABILITY[1,2]."

Cross References

Many entries include a list of other terms, shown in **smaller boldface,** for which the same sign (or compound sign) is applicable. Because the signs of ASL tend to represent broad concepts rather than specific English words, these additional terms are not always precise synonyms of the main entry. Often, their English equivalents do not even share a part of speech. However, they share the entry's concept in some way, and their meanings can all be conveyed with the same sign. The sign at **mandatory,** for example, is also used to express **demand.**

Where appropriate, these additional words are given usage labels (e.g., *informal, slang*) to indicate that in the context of certain social situations, the sign should be used with some caution.

A cross-reference entry at its own alphabetical listing does not show either a description or a sign. It may, however, give a definition when its meaning is not quite the same as that given for the main entry. A referential entry of this sort sends the reader to one or more complete entries by using small capital letters to point to the referent, where signs and descriptions will be found. Typical examples are the entry for **supra,** which says only "See sign for ABOVE," and the entry for **perjury,** which first defines and explains the word at length and then directs the reader to the appropriate main entry with the instruction, "See sign for FRAUD[1,2]."

How to Make a Sign

Illustrations

Every complete entry and every entry labeled "alternate sign" contains at least one illustration. All the line drawings demonstrate how a right-handed signer would execute each sign as seen by the listener. The model's right hand is on the reader's left. A left-handed signer should transpose the hands, treating the picture as if it were a mirror image.

Descriptions

Each illustration is accompanied by a description. Within the description, italicized terms such as *A hand* and *C hand* refer to handshapes shown in the chart of the Manual Alphabet (p. xi). Terms such as *one hand* or *10 hand* refer to handshapes for numbers (p. xii). Other special handshapes, such as *bent hand, open hand,* and *flattened C hand,* are also shown on page 00.

An initialized sign (see, e.g., the entry for **discrimination**) is formed with one of the handshapes from the American Manual Alphabet (p. xi), and fingerspelled signs use the Manual Alphabet to spell out shortened forms, such as initialisms and acronyms, as at **driving while intoxicated,** where the instruction reads, "Fingerspell acronym: D-W-I."

Using the above conventions, descriptions give detailed instructions on how to make the sign. Typically included in the description are a sign's four standard component parts: (1) handshape, (2) location in relation to the body, (3) movement of the hands, and (4) orientation of the palms. A component can appear more than once. The instructions at **bar,** for example, in the description for **group,** are as follows, with the components numbered to correspond with the descriptions just given:

(1) Beginning with both C hands

(2) in front of the chest,

(4) palms facing each other,

(3) bring the hands away from each other in outward arcs

(4) while turning the palms in, ending with the little fingers near each other.

Note that because the orientation of the palms changes during the course of making this sign, it is accounted for more than once.

American Manual Alphabet

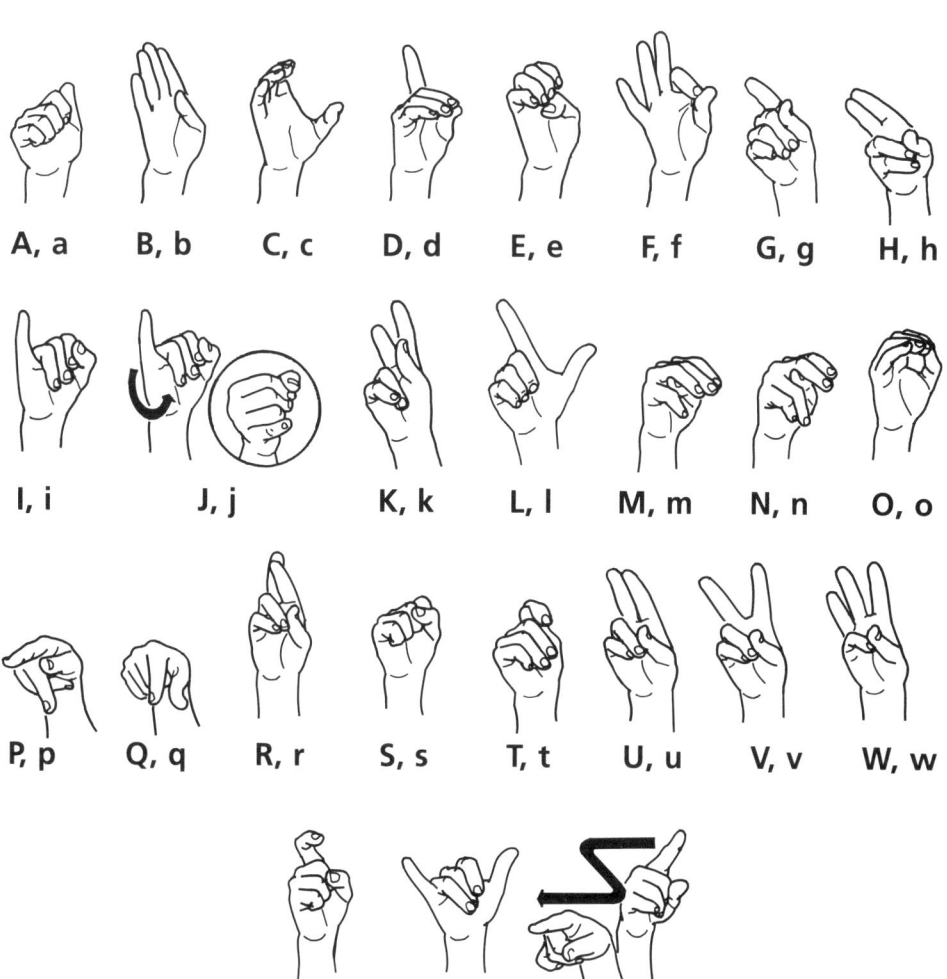

Handshapes

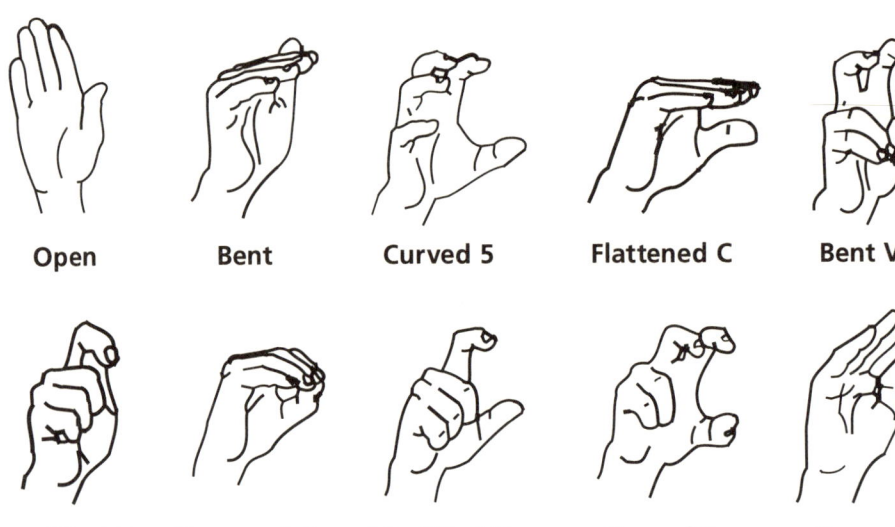

Numbers

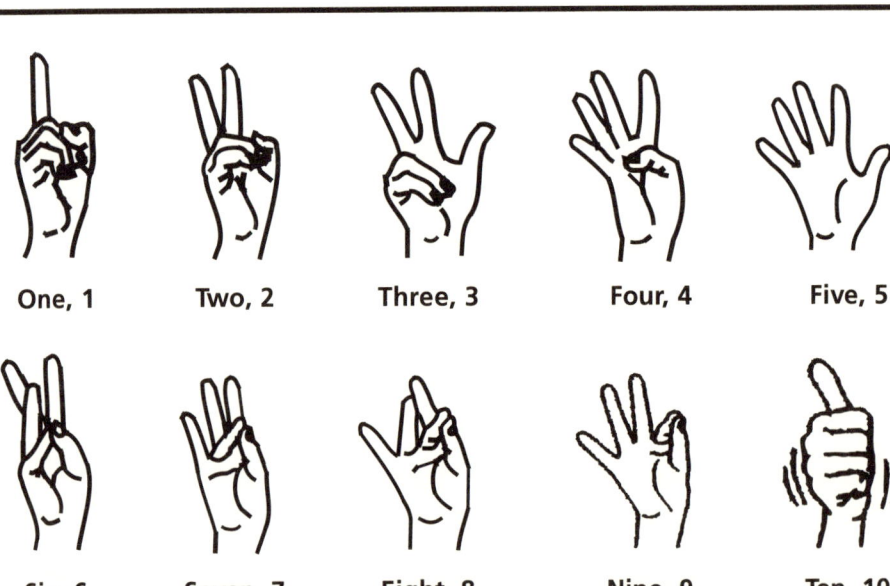

abate[1] To reduce or eliminate.
- **end** Beginning with the palm side of the right *B hand,* near the fingertips of the left *B hand,* palm in, bring the right hand deliberately down.

abate[2] See sign for ENJOIN[1].

abate[3] See sign for TRUST.

abduction See signs for KIDNAPPING.

abet See sign for AID AND ABET.

abortion[1] The intentional termination of pregnancy.
- **baby** With the right bent arm resting on the left bent arm, swing the arms from side to side with a double movement.

- **remove** Beginning with the fingers of the right *curved hand* on the right side of the abdomen, move the right hand outward while changing to an *A hand* and then opening to a *5 hand.*

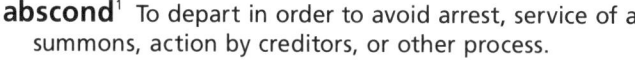

abscond[1] To depart in order to avoid arrest, service of a summons, action by creditors, or other process.
- **escape** Beginning with the extended right index finger, palm facing left, pointing up between the index and middle fingers of the left *5 hand,* palm facing down, pull the right hand to the right with a deliberate movement.

abscond

abscond[2] (alternate sign)
- **disappear** Beginning with the extended right index finger, palm facing left, pointing up between the index and middle fingers of the left *5 hand*, palm facing down, pull the right hand straight down a short distance.

absolute An unqualified right or privilege.
- **true** Beginning with the thumb side of the right *one hand* in front of the mouth, palm left, move the extended index finger forward.

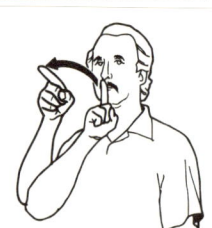

- **rights** Slide the little-finger side of the right *open hand*, palm facing left, in an upward arc across the upturned left palm held in front of the body.

- **can** Move both *S hands*, palms facing down, downward simultaneously in front of each side of the body.

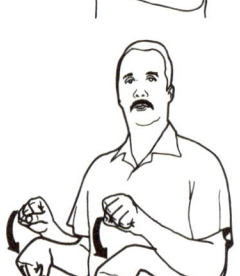

absolute immunity An unqualified exemption from civil suit or criminal prosecution.
- **accuse** Push the little-finger side of the right *A hand*, palm facing left, forward across the back of the left *open hand*, palm facing down.

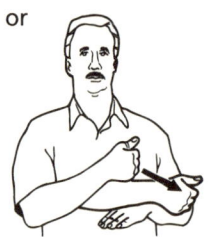

- **sue** Hit the fingertips of the right *bent hand* into the left *open hand*, palm right and fingers pointing forward.

---- [sign continues] ---->

abuse

- **can't** With a negative head shake, bring the extended index finger of the right *one hand* downward, hitting the extended index finger of the left *one hand* as it moves.

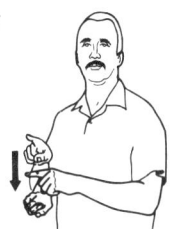

absolute privilege A special right or exemption that prohibits some privileges from being taken away from a person under any circumstances.

- **true** Beginning with the thumb side of the right *one hand* in front of the mouth, palm left, move the extended index finger forward.

- **rights** Slide the little-finger side of the right *open hand*, palm facing left, in an upward arc across the upturned left palm held in front of the body.

- **remove** Beginning with the palm side of the right *A hand* on the palm of the left *open hand*, move the right hand upward to the right and then down while opening to a *5 hand*.

- **can't** With a negative head shake, bring the extended index finger of the right *one hand* downward, hitting the extended index finger of the left *one hand* as it moves.

abuse Mistreatment of a person.

- **decide** Move the extended right index finger from the right side of the forehead, palm left, down in front of the chest while changing into an *F hand*, ending with both *F hands* moving downward in front of the body, palms facing each other.

 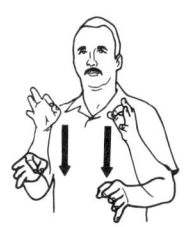

---- [sign continues] -->

abuse

- **cruel** Beginning with the right *curved 5 hand* near the face and the left *curved 5 hand* in front of the body, close the right hand into an *A hand* while moving it quickly down and close the left hand into an *A hand* while moving it quickly up, brushing the knuckles of the hands together as they pass each other.

accelerate To cause a legal right that was to arise in the future to do so immediately.

- **go-ahead** Beginning with both *open hands* in front of the body, palms facing in and fingers pointing toward each other, move the hands forward a short distance simultaneously.

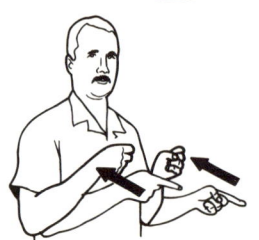

- **fast** Beginning with the extended index fingers of both *one hands* pointing forward in front of the chest, pull the hands back toward the chest while changing to *S hands*.

acceleration clause A clause in a credit agreement that allows the creditor to declare that the entire balance is due immediately if specific events occur.

- **paper** Brush the heel of the right *open hand* with a double movement on the heel of the left *open hand*, palms facing each other.

- **paragraph** Tap the fingertips of the right *C hand*, palm facing left, against the palm of the left *open hand*, palm facing right and fingers pointing up, with a double movement.

- **quote** Beginning with both bent index fingers near each side of the head, palms facing each other and fingers pointing up, twist the hands back.

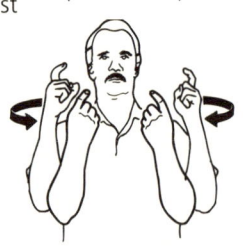

---- [sign continues] -->

accept

- **avoid** Beginning with the knuckles of the right *A hand*, palm left, near the base heel of the left *A hand*, palm right, bring the right hand back toward the body with a wavy movement.

- **must** Move the bent index finger of the right *X hand* downward with a deliberate movement in front of the right side of the body by bending the wrist down.

- **pay**[1] Beginning with the extended right index finger touching the palm of the left *open hand,* palms facing each other, move the right finger forward and off the left fingertips.

- **all** Move the right *open hand* from near the left shoulder in a large circle in front of the chest, ending with the back of the right hand in the left *open hand* held in front of the body, palms facing up.

- **now** Bring both *Y hands,* palms facing up, downward in front of each side of the body.

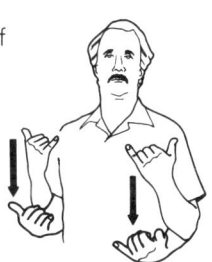

accept To agree to an offer, transaction, or proposal. Related form: **acceptance.**
- **accept** Beginning with both *5 hands* in front of the body, fingers pointing forward and palms down, pull both hands back to the chest while changing to *flattened O hands.*

accessory

accessory A person who assists a criminal.

- **person** Move both *P hands*, palms facing each other, downward along the sides of the body.

- **crime** Place the palm side of the right *L hand*, palm facing left, first on the fingers and then on the heel of the left *open hand,* palm facing right and fingers pointing up. Then beginning with both *S hands* in front of the body, index fingers touching and palms down, move the hands away from each other while twisting the wrists with a deliberate movement, ending with the palms facing each other.

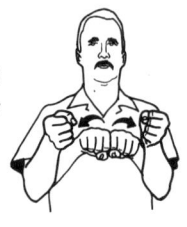

- **with** Beginning with both *A hands* in front of the chest, palms facing each other, bring the hands together.

accessory after the fact A person who knowingly assists a felon avoid capture or prosecution.

- **person** Move both *P hands*, palms facing each other, downward along the sides of the body.

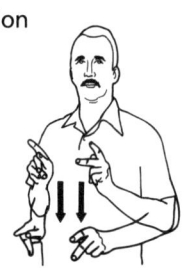

- **crime** Place the palm side of the right *L hand*, palm facing left, first on the fingers and then on the heel of the left *open hand,* palm facing right and fingers pointing up. Then beginning with both *S hands* in front of the body, index fingers touching and palms down, move the hands away from each other while twisting the wrists with a deliberate movement, ending with the palms facing each other.

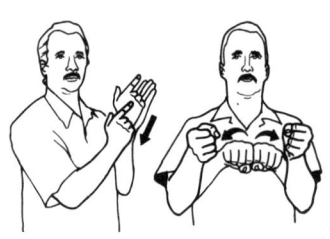

- **help** With the little-finger side of the right *A hand* in the upturned left *open hand,* move both hands upward in front of the chest.

---- [sign continues] ---->

accomplice

- **escape** Move the extended right index finger, palm left and finger pointing up, from between the index and middle fingers of the left *5 hand*, palm down in front of the chest, forward to the right with a deliberate movement.

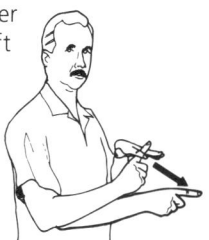

accessory before the fact See sign for AID AND ABET.

accommodation or **surety** Something done as a favor rather than for consideration.
- **do** Move both *C hands*, palms facing down, simultaneously back and forth in front of the body with a swinging movement.

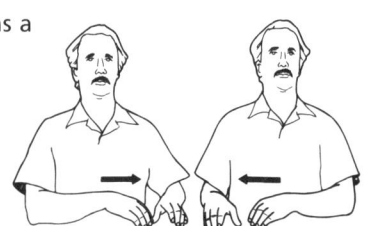

- **for** Beginning with the extended right index finger touching the right side of the forehead, twist the hand forward, ending with the index finger pointing forward.

accomplice A person who assists another in planning or committing a crime.
- **person-person** Move both *P hands*, palms facing each other, downward along the sides of the body. Repeat by shifting the body to the side.

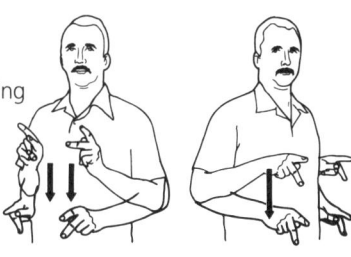

- **two-of-them** Swing the right *2 hand*, palm up, from side to side in front of the body.

- **plan** Move both *open hands* from in front of the left side of the body, palms facing each other and fingers pointing forward, in a long smooth movement to in front of the right side of the body.

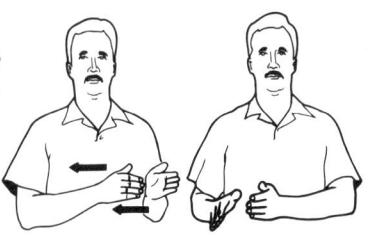

---- [sign continues] -->

accomplice

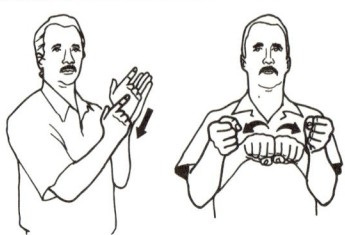

- **crime** Place the palm side of the right *L hand*, palm facing left, first on the fingers and then on the heel of the left *open hand*, palm facing right and fingers pointing up. Then beginning with both *S hands* in front of the body, index fingers touching and palms down, move the hands away from each other while twisting the wrists with a deliberate movement, ending with the palms facing each other.

accounting A detailed description of how the assets of an estate or trust fund have been managed.

- **count** Move the fingertips of the right *F hand*, palm down, across the upturned palm of the left *open hand* from the heel to the fingers with a repeated movement.

accrue[1] (financial) To come into existence and accumulate.

- **earn** Bring the little-finger side of the right *curved hand*, palm facing left, across the upturned left *open hand* from fingertips to heel while changing into an *S hand*.

accrue[2] (alternate sign)

- **add-to** Swing the right *5 hand* upward from the right side of the body while changing into a *flattened O hand*, ending with the right index finger touching the little-finger side of the left *flattened O hand* in front of the chest, both palms facing in.

accusation See sign for ALLEGATION.

accusatorial system See sign for ADVERSARY SYSTEM.

accused A person formally charged with a crime.

- **accuse** Push the little-finger side of the right *A hand*, palm facing left, forward across the back of the left *open hand*, palm facing down.

---- [sign continues] -->

act

- **person marker** Move both *open hands*, palms facing each other, downward along the sides of the body.

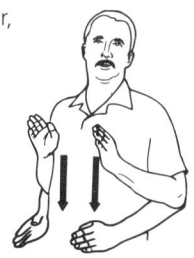

acknowledgment An admission of the truth or the existence of an obligation. See sign for CONFESSION.

acquaintance rape Rape committed by someone known to the victim. See signs for DATE RAPE[1,2].

acquit[1] To release a criminal defendant from a charge. Same sign used for **dismiss, dismissal, discharge, release**.

- **excuse** Wipe the fingertips of the right *open hand* across the upturned left *open hand* from the heel off the fingertips.

acquit[2] (alternate sign) Same sign used for **dismiss, dismissal, discharge, release**.

- **court** Move both *F hands*, palms facing each other, up and down in front of each side of the chest with a repeated alternating movement.

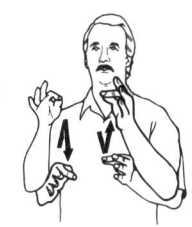

- **decide** Move the extended right index finger from the right side of the forehead, palm left, down in front of the chest while changing into an *F hand*, ending with both *F hands* moving downward in front of the body, palms facing each other.

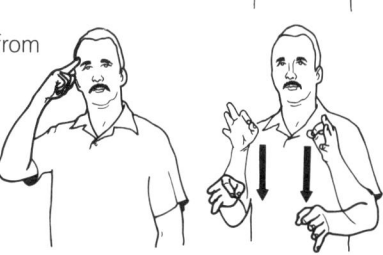

- **excuse** Wipe the fingertips of the right *open hand* across the upturned left *open hand* from the heel off the fingertips.

act See sign for LAW.

action

action See sign for HEARING. See sign for LEGAL ACTION.

act of God A natural event (such as an earthquake) beyond human control.

- **natural** Move the right *N hand* in a small circle and then straight down to land on the back of the left *open hand*.

- **happen** Beginning with both extended index fingers in front of the body, palms facing up and fingers pointing forward, flip the hands over toward each other, ending with the palms facing down.

actual or **bona fide** Real; known to have happened.

- **true** Beginning with the thumb side of the right *one hand* in front of the mouth, palm left, move the extended index finger forward.

actual damages See sign for COMPENSATORY DAMAGES.

actual knowledge See sign for KNOWLEDGE.

adjourn¹ or **adjournment in contemplation of dismissal**
To suspend or postpone a proceeding, either temporarily or indefinitely.

- **hold** Move the right *S hand*, palm facing up, in a circular movement in front of the right side of the chest.

- **during** Beginning with both extended index fingers in front of each side of the body, palms down, move them forward and upward in parallel arcs.

---- [sign continues] -->

10

adjudge

- **consider** Beginning with both extended index fingers in front of each side of the forehead, palms facing in and fingers angled up, move the fingers in repeated alternating circular movements toward each other in front of the face.

- **maybe** Beginning with both *open hands*, palms up and fingers pointing forward, in front of each side of the chest, one hand higher than the other, alternately move the hands up and down with a double movement.

- **excuse** Wipe the fingertips of the right *open hand* across the upturned left *open hand* from the heel off the fingertips.

adjourn[2] or adjournment in contemplation of dismissal (alternate sign)
- Fingerspell: A-C-D

adjournment in contemplation of dismissal See signs for ADJOURN[1,2].

adjudge To render a judicial decision to certain effect.
- **decide** Move the extended right index finger from the right side of the forehead, palm left, down in front of the chest while changing into an *F hand*, ending with both *F hands* moving downward in front of the body, palms facing each other.

- **order** Move the extended right index finger, palm forward and finger pointing up, from in front of the mouth forward and down, ending with the finger pointing forward and the palm down.

11

administer

administer To manage the estate of a decedent by paying debts and taxes and distributing the assets according to a will.
- **manage** Beginning with both *modified X hands* in front of each side of the body, right hand forward of the left hand and palms facing each other, move the hands forward and back with a repeated movement.

administrator or **executor** The person appointed by a court to manage the estate of a person who dies without a will.
- **manage** Beginning with both *modified X hands* in front of each side of the body, right hand forward of the left hand and palms facing each other, move the hands forward and back with a repeated movement.

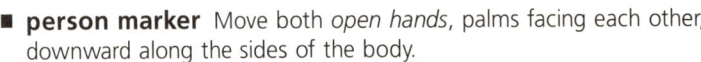

- **person marker** Move both *open hands*, palms facing each other, downward along the sides of the body.

- Fingerspell: W-I-L-L

admissible Evidence that is permitted to be considered by the judge and jury in a trial. Related form: **admissibility**.
- **accept** Beginning with both *5 hands* in front of the body, fingers pointing forward and palms down, pull both hands back to the chest while changing to *flattened O hands*.

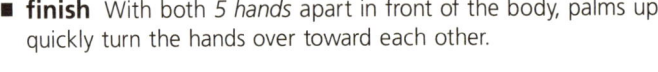

- **finish** With both *5 hands* apart in front of the body, palms up, quickly turn the hands over toward each other.

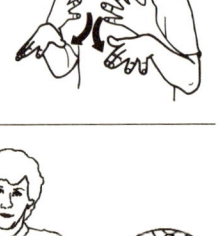

admonition[1] The judge's direction or warning to a jury, witness, or lawyer regarding any matter during a case. Related form: **admonish**. Same sign used for **censure**, **warning**.
- **warn** Pat the fingers of the right *open hand* on the back of the left *open hand*, palm facing down, with a repeated movement.

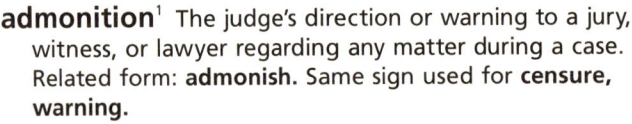

advance directive

admonition[2] (alternate sign) Related form: **admonish**. Same sign used for **censure, warning**.

- **scold** Shake the extended right index finger, palm left, with a repeated movement in front of the chest.

adoption[1] To take on in accordance with a policy. Related form: **adopt**. Same sign used for **attachment, ratify**.

- **take-up** Beginning with both 5 hands in front of the body, fingers pointing down and palms down, pull both hands up toward the chest while changing to S hands.

adoption[2] (alternate sign) Related form: **adopt**. Same sign used for **ratify**.

- **certify** Beginning with the right S hand in front of the right shoulder, palm facing down, twist the wrist to hit the upturned left open hand with the little-finger side of the right hand with a deliberate movement.

adultery[1] Sexual intercourse by a married person with someone other than that person's spouse.

- **adultery**[1] Slide the palm of the right open hand, fingers pointing left, around the little-finger side of the left open hand, palm facing right and fingers pointing up.

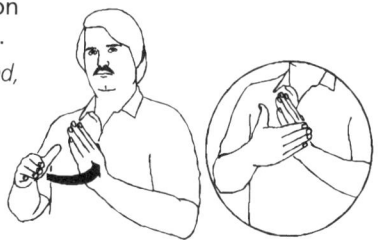

adultery[2] (alternate sign)

- **adultery**[2] Slide the extended right index finger around the little-finger side of the left open hand, palm facing right and fingers pointing up.

advance directive See sign for LIVING WILL.

13

advancement

advancement An advance payment or transfer of part of one's estate to an heir while the person is still alive.

- **before** Beginning with the back of the right *open hand*, palm in and fingers pointing left, touching the back of the left *open hand*, palm forward, move the right hand in toward the chest.

- **gift** Move both *X hands* from in front of the body, palms facing each other, forward in simultaneous arcs.

adversary system or **accusatorial system** The American method of trial in which the burden of proof is the responsibility of those bringing the accusation.

- **you** Point the right extended index finger forward toward the referent.

- **accuse** Push the little-finger side of the right *A hand*, palm facing left, forward across the back of the left *open hand*, palm facing down.

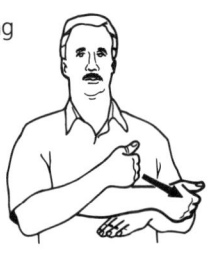

- **show** With the extended right index finger touching the palm of the left *open hand*, palm right and fingers pointing forward, move both hands forward a short distance.

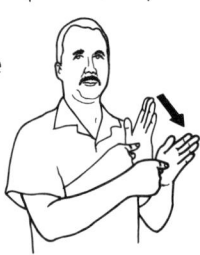

- **proof** Move the right *open hand* downward, ending with the back of the right hand on the palm of the left *open hand*, both palms facing up in front of the chest.

---- [sign continues] ---->

adverse witness

- **must** Move the bent index finger of the right *X hand* downward with a deliberate movement in front of the right side of the body by bending the wrist down.

adverse possession A method of acquiring title to real estate by openly occupying the property for a period of time set by statue.

- **use** With the heel of the right *U hand* on the back of the left *S hand*, move the right hand in a small circle.

- **land** Beginning with both *flattened O hands* in front of each side of the body, palms facing up, move the thumb of both hands smoothly with a double movement across each fingertip, starting with the little fingers and ending as *A hands* each time.

- **later**[1] With the thumb of the right *L hand*, palm facing forward, on the palm of the left *open hand*, palm facing right and fingers pointing forward, twist the right hand forward, keeping the thumb in place and ending with the right palm facing down.

- Fingerspell: O-W-N

adverse witness[1] or **hostile witness** A witness called by one side although known to be friendly with the other side.

- **witness** With the index finger of the right *X hand* pull down slightly on the cheek near the outside corner of the right eye.

- **person marker** Move both *open hands*, palms facing each other, downward along the sides of the body.

---- [sign continues] -->

adverse witness

- **grumbling** Move the fingertips of the right *curved 5 hand* in a circular movement on the center of the chest.

- **answer** Beginning with both extended index fingers pointing up in front of the mouth, right hand nearer the mouth than the left and palms forward, bend the wrists down simultaneously, ending with the fingers pointing forward and the palms down.

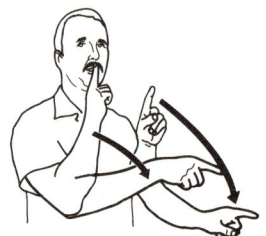

- **must** Move the bent index finger of the right *X hand* downward with a deliberate movement in front of the right side of the body by bending the wrist down.

---

adverse witness[2] or **hostile witness** A witness called by one side in a case but known to be friendly with the other side.
  - **witness** With the index finger of the right *X hand* pull down slightly on the cheek near the outside corner of the right eye.

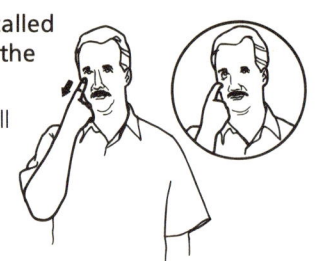

- **appoint** Move the right *S hand*, palm in, from in front of the left side of the body with a deliberate movement to the right, ending with the palm facing left.

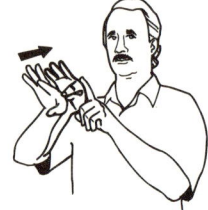

- **story** Beginning with the fingertips of both *F hands* touching in front of the chest, pull the hands apart to in front of each side of the chest. Repeat.

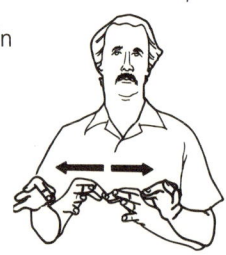

---- [sign continues] ---------→

affidavit

- **must** Move the bent index finger of the right *X hand* downward with a deliberate movement in front of the right side of the body by bending the wrist down.

- **don't-want-to** Beginning with both *curved 5 hands* in front of the body, palms up, swing the hands downward by twisting the wrists, ending with the palms facing down.

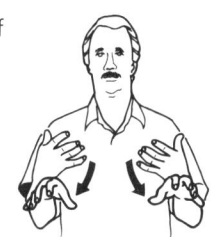

affidavit A formal written statement swearing to the truth of stated facts.

- **promise** Bring the extended right index finger, palm facing left and finger pointing up, from in front of the lips downward, changing into an *open hand* and placing the palm of the right hand on the index-finger side of the left *open hand* held in front of the body, palm facing right.

- **honest**[1] Slide the extended fingers of the right *H hand*, palm facing left, forward from the heel to the fingers of the upturned left *open hand*.

- **signature** Place the extended fingers of the right *H hand*, palm down, down on the upturned palm of the left *open hand* held in front of the chest with a double movement.

- **paper** Brush the heel of the right *open hand* with a double movement on the heel of the left *open hand*, palms facing each other.

affirm

affirm, affirmation, oath, swear, or swear or affirm
To swear solemnly that statements are true. Same sign used for **guarantee, guaranty, warranty.**

- **promise** Bring the extended right index finger, palm facing left and finger pointing up, from in front of the lips downward, changing into an *open hand* and placing the palm of the right hand on the index-finger side of the left *S hand* held in front of the body, palm facing right.

affirmative action
Steps taken to promote diversity and prohibit discrimination.

- **support** Push the knuckles of the right *S hand* upward under the little-finger side of the left *S hand*, both palms in, pushing the left hand upward a short distance in front of the chest.

- **different-different** Beginning with both extended index fingers crossed in front of the chest, palms forward, bring the hands apart from each other with a double movement. Repeat in a different direction.

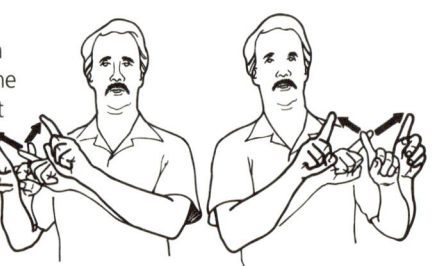

against the law
See signs for ILLEGAL[1,2].

agent, agency, or attorney-in-fact
The relationship between two people where one is authorized to act on behalf of the other.

- **person** Move both *P hands*, palms facing each other, downward along the sides of the body.

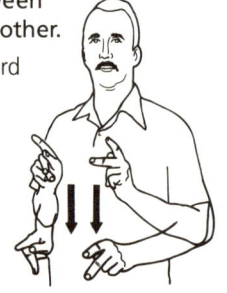

- **give-power** Beginning with the fingertips of the right *bent 5 hand* touching the left upper arm, twist the wrist and move the right hand forward, ending with the palm forward.

agreement

agency See sign for AGENT.

aggravated An offense (such as assault or rape) that is more serious than usual because of its severity of injury or use of weapons.

- **crime** Place the palm side of the right *L hand*, palm facing left, first on the fingers and then on the heel of the left *open hand*, palm facing right and fingers pointing up. Then beginning with both *S hands* in front of the body, index fingers touching and palms down, move the hands away from each other while twisting the wrists with a deliberate movement, ending with the palms facing each other.

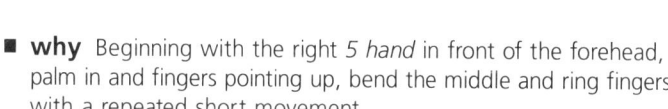

- **worse** Brush the back of the right *V hand* across the index-finger side of the left *V hand*, both palms facing in, as the hands cross with a double movement in front of the chest.

- **why** Beginning with the right *5 hand* in front of the forehead, palm in and fingers pointing up, bend the middle and ring fingers with a repeated short movement.

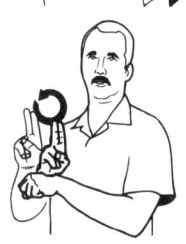

- **use** With the heel of the right *U hand* on the back of the left *S hand*, move the right hand in a small circle.

- **something** Move the right *one hand* in a small circle in front of the right shoulder, palm facing back.

agreement or **contract** An enforceable document of assent between parties.

- **paper** Brush the heel of the right *open hand* with a double movement on the heel of the left *open hand*, palms facing each other.

---- [sign continues] ----

agreement

- **agree** Beginning with both extended index fingers pointing forward in front of each side of the body, both palms facing up, flip the hands toward each other, turning the palms down.

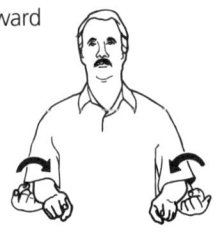

aid and abet, abet, or **accessory before the fact** To knowingly encourage or assist someone committing a crime.

- **person** Move both *P hands*, palms facing each other, downward along the sides of the body.

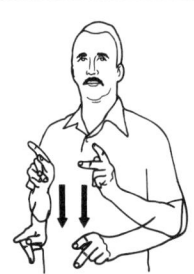

- **crime** Place the palm side of the right *L hand*, palm facing left, first on the fingers and then on the heel of the left *open hand*, palm facing right and fingers pointing up. Then beginning with both *S hands* in front of the body, index fingers touching and palms down, move the hands away from each other while twisting the wrists with a deliberate movement, ending with the palms facing each other.

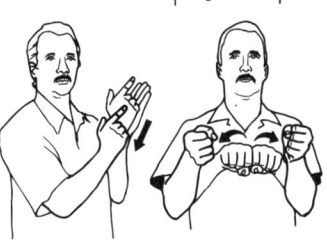

- **you** Point the right extended index finger forward toward the referent.

- **with** Beginning with both *A hands* in front of the chest, palms facing each other, bring the hands together.

alibi In a criminal case, a defense that the accused was somewhere else when a crime was committed.

- **proof** Move the right *open hand* downward, ending with the back of the right hand on the palm of the left *open hand*, both palms facing up in front of the chest.

---- [sign continues] -->

alimony

- **person** Move both *P hands*, palms facing each other, downward along the sides of the body.

- **different** Beginning with both extended index fingers crossed in front of the chest, palms forward, bring the hands apart from each other with a deliberate movement.

alien A person who is not a citizen or national of the United States.
- **foreign** Move the thumb side of the right *F hand*, palm facing left, in a double circular movement near the bent left elbow.

- **not** Bring the thumb of the right *10 hand* forward from under the chin with a deliberate movement.

- Fingerspell abbreviation: U-S

alimony, maintenance, or spousal support
Money that one divorced spouse must pay as support to the other person during or after a divorce.

- **divorce**² Beginning with the right *curved hand*, palm facing down, clasping the left *curved hand*, palm facing up, bring the hands apart while opening into *5 hands*, fingers pointing up and palms forward.

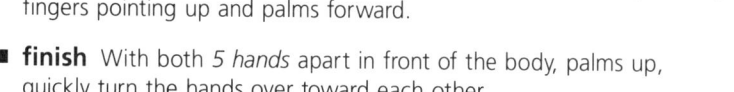

- **finish** With both *5 hands* apart in front of the body, palms up, quickly turn the hands over toward each other.

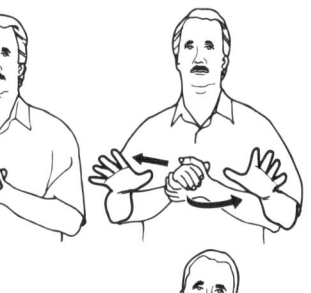

---- [sign continues] ---------------------------------→

21

alimony

- **pay**[1] Beginning with the extended right index finger touching the palm of the left *open hand,* palms facing each other, move the right finger forward with a double movement off the left fingertips.

- **support** Push the knuckles of the right *S hand* upward under the little-finger side of the left *S hand*, both palms in, pushing the left hand upward a short distance in front of the chest.

allegation, accusation, or **charge** An assertion that one intends to prove at trial. Related form: **allege.**

- **accuse** Push the little-finger side of the right *A hand,* palm facing left, forward across the back of the left *open hand*, palm facing down.

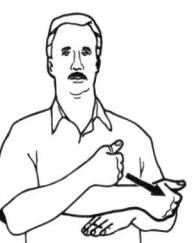

amend To revise, add to, or subtract from a legal document by proper means. Related form: **amendment**. See sign for RIDER.

amicus curiae *Latin.* See sign for FRIEND OF THE COURT.

amnesty A government's forgiveness of past offenses for a class of people or an individual.

- **government** Beginning with the extended right index finger pointing upward near the right side of the head, palm facing forward, twist the wrist to touch the finger to the right temple.

- **excuse-excuse** Wipe the fingertips of the left *open hand* across the upturned palm of the right *open hand* from the heel off the fingertips. Repeat by wiping the fingers of the right *open hand* across the upturned palm of the left *open hand*.

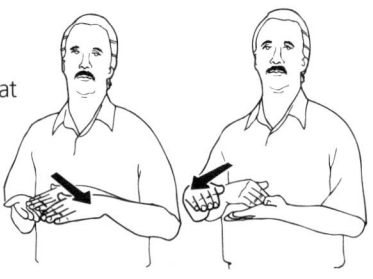

---- [sign continues] ---->

annulment

- **finish** With both 5 hands apart in front of the body, palms up, quickly turn the hands over toward each other.

amortize To pay a debt in regular installments over a specific period of time.

- **owe** With a double movement, tap the extended right index finger against the palm of the left *open hand*, palm facing right.

- **excuse-excuse** Wipe the fingertips of the left *open hand* across the upturned palm of the right *open hand* from the heel off the fingertips. Repeat by wiping the fingers of the right *open hand* across the upturned palm of the left *open hand*.

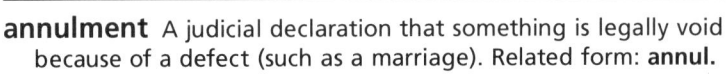

- **installment** Move the little-finger side of the right *open hand*, palm left, with repeated short movements across palm of the upturned left *open hand*.

annulment A judicial declaration that something is legally void because of a defect (such as a marriage). Related form: **annul**.

- **marry** Bring the right *curved hand*, palm facing down, downward in front of the chest to clasp the left *curved hand*, palm facing up.

- **cancel** With the extended right index finger, draw a large X across the upturned left *open hand*.

answer

answer¹ or reply To respond to a complaint, motion, or other procedural step in a case. Same sign used for **plea, plead.**

- **answer** Beginning with both extended index fingers pointing up in front of the mouth, right hand nearer the mouth than the left and palms forward, bend the wrists down simultaneously, ending with the fingers pointing forward and the palms down.

answer² or reply (alternate sign)

- **rectangle** With both extended index fingers, palms down, trace a square in the air, beginning together in front of the chest, moving apart to each side, moving straight down, and then together again at the bottom.

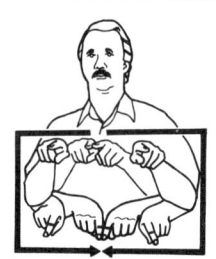

- **sentence** Beginning with the thumbs and index fingers of both *F hands* touching in front of the chest, palms facing each other, pull the hands apart, ending in front of each side of the chest.

antitrust Federal laws intended to foster vigorous competition by outlawing price fixing and monopolization.

- **government** Beginning with the extended right index finger pointing upward near the right side of the head, palm facing forward, twist the wrist to touch the finger to the right temple.

- **law** Place the palm side of the right *L hand*, palm facing left, first on the fingers and then on the heel of the left *open hand*, palm facing right and fingers pointing up.

- **support** Push the knuckles of the right *S hand* upward under the little-finger side of the left *S hand*, both palms in, pushing the left hand upward a short distance in front of the chest.

---- [sign continues] -->

appeal

- **compete** With an alternating movement, move both *A hands* forward and back past each other quickly, palms facing each other in front of the body.

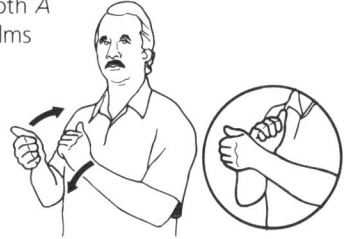

apparent Obvious; seemingly true. See sign for IMPLIED.

appeal¹, appellate review, or review

- **file** Move the fingers of the right *V hand*, palm facing forward, downward on each side of the extended left index finger, which is pointing up in front of the chest.

- **advance** Move both *bent hands*, palms facing each other, from near each side of the head upward a short distance.

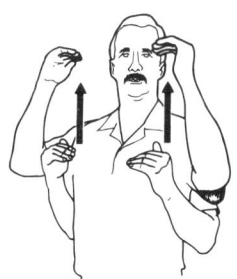

- **court** Move both *F hands*, palms facing each other, up and down in front of each side of the chest with a repeated alternating movement.

appeal², appellate review, or review (alternate sign)

- **ask** Bring the palms of both *open hands* together, fingers angled upward, while moving the hands down and in toward the chest.

---- [sign continues] -->

appeal

- **higher** Move the right *10 hand*, thumb up and palm left, upward with a deliberate movement.

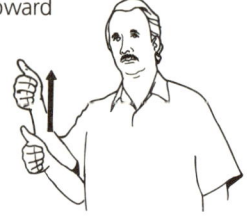

- **court** Move both *F hands*, palms facing each other, up and down in front of each side of the chest with a repeated alternating movement.

appear To come before a court in person. Related form: **appearance**. See sign for HEARING.

appellate court or **higher court** (alternate sign) Same sign used for **Supreme Court**.

- **court** Move both *F hands*, palms facing each other, up and down in front of each side of the chest with a repeated alternating movement.

- **advance** Move both *bent hands*, palms facing each other, from near each side of the head upward a short distance.

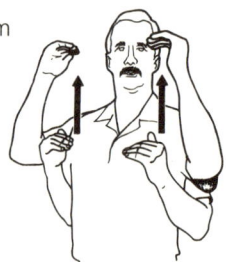

appellate review See signs for APPEAL[1].

approach the bench A request by a lawyer asking the judge if he or she can come close to present a document or to confer with the judge.

- **can** Move both *S hands*, palms facing down, downward simultaneously in front of each side of the body.

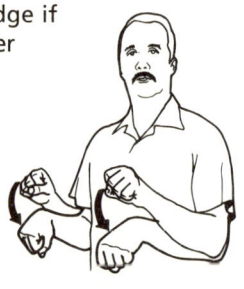

---- [sign continues] ---------------------------------→

argue

- **face-to-face** Beginning with both *open hands* in front of the chest, palms facing each other and fingers pointing up, move the right hand forward in a smooth movement toward the left hand while moving both hands upward.

arbitration¹ The process of resolving disputes without resorting to the courts.

- **meeting** Beginning with both *open hands* in front of the chest, palms facing forward and fingers pointing up, close the fingers with a double movement into *flattened O hands* while moving the hands together.

- **solve** Beginning with both *flattened O hands* in front of each side of the body, palms facing up, move the thumb of each hand smoothly across each fingertip, starting with the little fingers and ending as *10 hands* while moving the hands outward to each side.

- **problem** Beginning with the knuckles of both *bent V hands* touching in front of the chest, twist the hands in opposite directions with a deliberate movement, rubbing the knuckles against each other.

arbitration² (alternate sign)

- **discuss–discuss** Tap the side of the extended right index finger, palm facing in, on the upturned left *open hand* with a repeated movement while moving the hands to and from the body with a double movement.

argue To present reasons supporting a conclusion on a matter. Related form: **argument**.

- **discuss** Tap the side of the extended right index finger, palm facing in, on the upturned left *open hand* with a double movement.

---- [sign continues] ---→

argue

- **offer** Beginning with both *open hands* in front of each side of the body, palms up, move the hands upward and forward in simultaneous arcs.

arraignment[1] The proceeding in which a defendant is brought before a court.

- **first** Touch the extended right index finger, palm facing in, against the extended thumb of the left *10 hand*, palm facing right.

- **time** Tap the bent index finger of the right *X hand*, palm down, with a double movement on the wrist of the downturned left hand.

- **face-to-face** Beginning with both *open hands* in front of the chest, palms facing each other and fingers pointing up, move the right hand forward in a smooth movement toward the left hand while moving both hands upward.

- **court** Move both *F hands*, palms facing each other, up and down in front of each side of the chest with a repeated alternating movement.

arraignment[2] (alternate sign)

- **face-to-face** Beginning with both *open hands* in front of the chest, palms facing each other and fingers pointing up, move the right hand forward in a smooth movement toward the left hand while moving both hands upward.

---- [sign continues] -->

arrest

- **court** Move both *F hands,* palms facing each other, up and down in front of each side of the chest with a repeated alternating movement.

- **for-for** With a questioning expression and beginning with the extended right index finger touching the right side of the forehead, twist the hand forward with a double movement, turning the index finger forward each time.

- **answer** Beginning with both extended index fingers pointing up in front of the mouth, right hand nearer the mouth than the left and palms forward, bend the wrists down simultaneously, ending with the fingers pointing forward and the palms down.

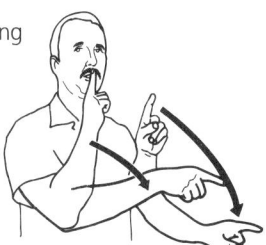

arrest[1] or **under arrest** Taking an individual into custody for the purpose of charging him or her for a crime.

- **arrest** Move the right *C hand* from in front of the right side of the chest, palm facing left, to the left to close around the extended left index finger held up in front of the chest, palm facing right.

arrest[2] or **under arrest** alternate sign

- **police** Tap the thumb side of the right *modified C hand,* palm facing left, against the left side of the chest with a double movement.

- **seize** Beginning with both *curved 5 hands* in front of each shoulder, palms facing forward, move the hands downward while closing into *S hands.*

arrest

arrest[3] or **under arrest** (alternate sign)

- **police** Tap the thumb side of the right *modified C hand*, palm facing left, against the left side of the chest with a double movement.

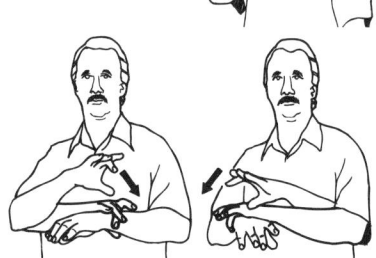

- **handcuffs** With the curved thumb and index finger of the left hand, palm facing down, grasp the wrist of the right *open hand.* Then repeat with the right hand on the wrist of the left hand. Then, beginning with the wrists of both *A hands* near each other in front of the chest, move the hands forward with a short deliberate movement.

arrest warrant See sign for WARRANT.

arson The crime of intentionally causing a fire for the purpose of destroying property.

- **mean** Touch the fingertips of the right *V hand*, palm facing down, in the palm of the left *open hand,* palm facing up and fingers pointing forward, and then twist the right wrist and touch the fingertips down again.

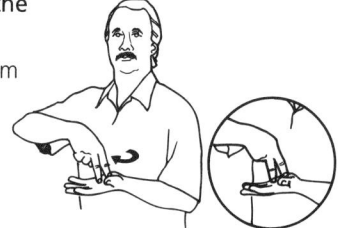

- **plan** Move both *open hands* from in front of the left side of the body, palms facing each other and fingers pointing forward, in a long smooth movement to in front of the right side of the body.

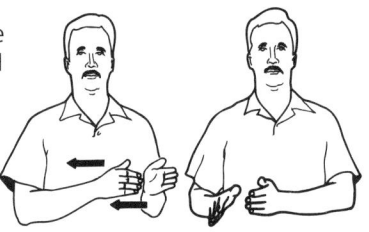

- **strike-match** With the palm side of the right *modified X hand* touching the palm of the left *open hand*, palm facing right, in front of the chest, move the right hand upward with a quick movement.

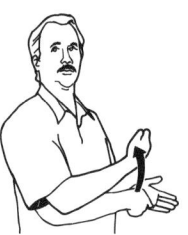

- **fire** Move both *5 hands,* palms facing up, from in front of the waist upward in front of the chest while wiggling the fingers.

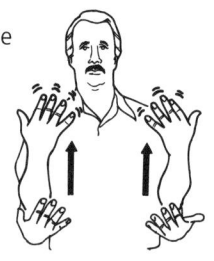

as a matter of law

as a matter of law[1] Compelled by principles of law, a court makes a finding without the use of a jury.

- **law** Place the palm side of the right *L hand*, palm facing left, first on the fingers and then on the heel of the left *open hand*, palm facing right and fingers pointing up.

- **court** Move both *F hands*, palms facing each other, up and down in front of each side of the chest with a repeated alternating movement.

- **follow** With the knuckles of the right *10 hand*, palm facing left, near the wrist of the left *10 hand*, palm facing right, move both hands forward a short distance.

as a matter of law[2] (alternate sign)

- **law** Place the palm side of the right *L hand*, palm facing left, first on the fingers and then on the heel of the left *open hand*, palm facing right and fingers pointing up.

- **court** Move both *F hands*, palms facing each other, up and down in front of each side of the chest with a repeated alternating movement.

- **decide** Move the extended right index finger from the right side of the forehead, palm left, down in front of the chest while changing into an *F hand*, ending with both *F hands* moving downward in front of the body, palms facing each other.

 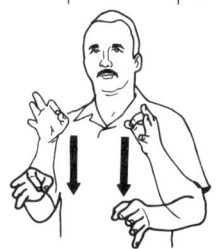

as is

as is The sale of goods in which the buyer assumes the risk of any defects.

- **stay** Move the right *Y hand*, palm facing down, downward in front of the right side of the body with a deliberate movement.

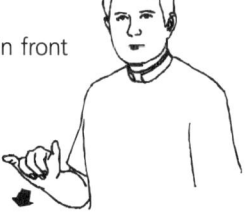

asked and answered An objection raised during a trial, when the other side asks the same question again after it has already been answered by the witness.

- **ask-me**[1] Beginning with the right extended index finger pointing up, palm facing back, move the right hand toward the body while bending into an *X hand*.

- **answer** (from right side) Beginning with both extended index fingers pointing up in front of the mouth, right hand nearer the mouth than the left and palms forward, bend the wrists down simultaneously, ending with the fingers pointing forward and the palms down.

- **finish** With both *5 hands* apart in front of the body, palms up, quickly turn the hands over toward each other.

assault[1]**, assault and battery,** or **battery** Used in criminal law to refer to harm by physical contact as well as fear of immediate bodily harm.

- Fingerspell: A-S-S-A-U-L-T
- Fingerspell: B-A-T-T-E-R-Y

assault[2]**, assault and battery,** or **battery**
(alternate sign)

- **hurt** Beginning with the extended index fingers of both *one hands* pointing toward each other, right palm down and left palm up, twist the wrists in opposite directions, ending with the right palm up and the left palm down.

assess

assault³, assault and battery, or battery
(alternate sign)

- **hurt** Beginning with the extended index fingers of both *one hands* pointing toward each other, right palm down and left palm up, twist the wrists in opposite directions, ending with the right palm up and the left palm down.

- **accuse** Push the little-finger side of the right *A hand*, palm facing left, forward across the back of the left *open hand*, palm facing down.

assault and battery See signs for ASSAULT¹,²,³.

assault with a deadly weapon The use of a gun, knife, or other weapon in a crime intended for the purpose of maiming or killing.

- Fingerspell: A-S-S-A-U-L-T

- **kill** Push the side of the extended right index finger, palm down, across the palm of the left *open hand*, palm right, with a deliberate movement.

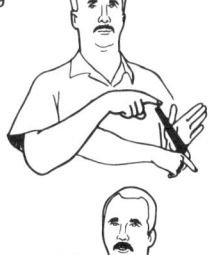

- **use** With the heel of the right *U hand* on the back of the left *S hand*, move the right hand in a small circle.

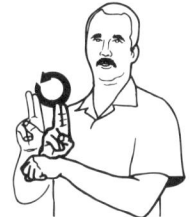

- Fingerspell: W-E-A-P-O-N

assess To set an amount of a tax, fine, or damages.

- **cost** Strike the knuckle of the right *X hand*, palm facing in, down on the palm of the left *open hand*, palm facing right and fingers pointing forward.

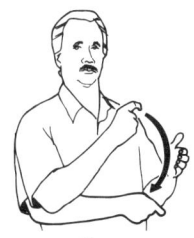

- **how-much** Beginning with the right *S hand* in front of the right side of the chest, palm facing up, flick the fingers open quickly into a *5 hand*.

---- [sign continues] ---→

33

assess

- **set-up**[1] Beginning with the right *10 hand* in front of the right shoulder, palm down, twist the wrist up with a circular movement and then move the right hand straight down to land on the little-finger side of the back of the left *open hand*, palm down.

asset Any property of a person that has monetary value, such as land, money, automobile, etc.

- **important** Beginning with the fingertips of both *F hands* touching, palms facing down, bring the hands upward in a circular movement, ending with the index-finger sides of the *F hands* touching in front of the chest.

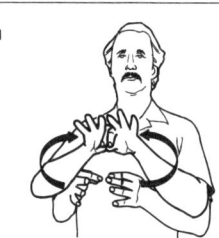

- **things** Beginning with both *open hands* in front of the body, palms facing up, move the hand to the sides away from each other in a double arc.

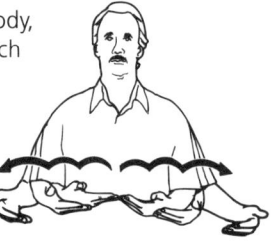

assign To transfer an interest or right, or to substitute another person for oneself in a contract. Related forms: **assignable, assignment**.

- **give-give-give** Move both *flattened O hands*, palms facing up, from left to right in front of the body.

assigned counsel[1] Attorney appointed by a court to represent a defendant who cannot afford to hire one.

- **lawyer** Place the palm side of the right *L hand*, palm facing left, first on the fingers and then on the heel of the left *open hand*, palm facing right and fingers pointing up. Move both *open hands*, palms facing each other, downward along the sides of the body.

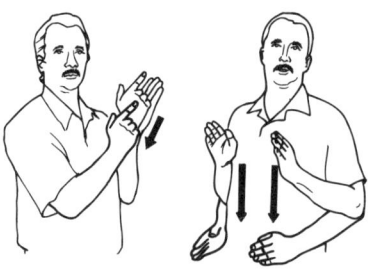

- **choose**[1] Bring the back of the right *5 hand*, palm forward, back against the palm of the left *open hand*, palm forward, while pinching the thumb and index finger together.

associate

assigned counsel[2] (alternate sign)

- **lawyer** Place the palm side of the right *L hand*, palm facing left, first on the fingers and then on the heel of the left *open hand*, palm facing right and fingers pointing up. Move both *open hands*, palms facing each other, downward along the sides of the body.

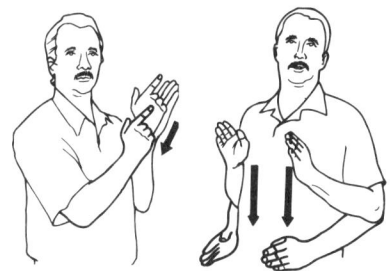

- **gift** Move both *X hands* from in front of the body, palms facing each other, forward in simultaneous arcs.

assisted suicide Aiding a person to commit suicide.

- **help-me** With the little-finger side of the right *A hand* in the upturned left *open hand*, move both hands in an arc back toward the chest.

- **kill** Push the side of the extended right index finger, palm down, across the palm of the left *open hand*, palm right, with a deliberate movement.

- **myself** Bring the thumb side of the right *A hand*, palm left, against the chest with a double movement.

associate An attorney working on salary in a law firm (as opposed to a partner).

- **lawyer** Place the palm side of the right *L hand*, palm facing left, first on the fingers and then on the heel of the left *open hand*, palm facing right and fingers pointing up. Move both *open hands*, palms facing each other, downward along the sides of the body.

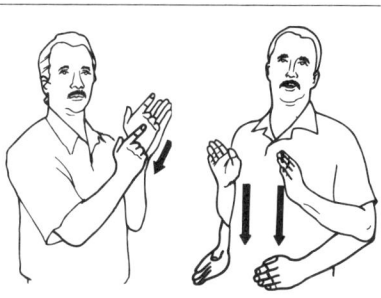

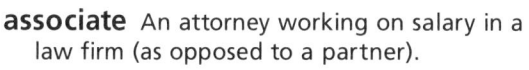
[sign continues]

associate

- **work** Tap the heel of the right *S hand*, palm forward, with a double movement on the back of the left *S hand* held in front of the body, palm down.

- **for** Beginning with the extended right index finger touching the right side of the forehead, twist the hand forward, ending with the index finger pointing forward.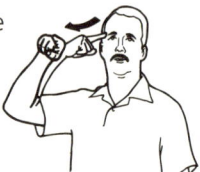

- **you** Point the right extended index finger forward toward the referent.

assume To take over responsibility or obligation for another. Related form: **assumption**.

- **accept** Beginning with both *5 hands* in front of the body, fingers pointing forward and palms down, pull both hands back to the chest while changing to *flattened O hands*.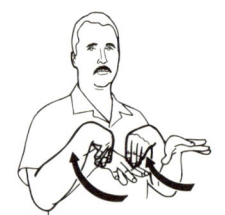

- **for** Beginning with the extended right index finger touching the right side of the forehead, twist the hand forward, ending with the index finger pointing forward.

asylum Refuge granted by a country to a person wanted for prosecution in another country.

- **offer** Beginning with both *open hands* in front of each side of the body, palms up, move the hands forward in simultaneous arcs.

- **protect** With the wrists of both *S hands* crossed in front of the chest, palms facing in opposite directions, move the hands forward with a short double movement.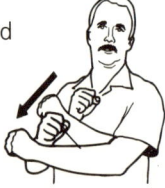

attorney

at hand see sign for INSTANT.

attachment[1] The seizing or freezing of property by court order so a dispute as to ownership of it can be resolved.

- **court** Move both *F hands*, palms facing each other, up and down in front of each side of the chest with a repeated alternating movement.

- **order** Move the extended right index finger, palm forward and finger pointing up, from in front of the mouth forward and down, ending with the finger pointing forward and the palm down.

- **take-up** Beginning with both *5 hands* in front of the body, fingers pointing down and palms down, pull both hands up toward the chest while changing to *S hands*.

attachment[2] See sign for ADOPTION[1].

attempt The substantial step toward the commission of a crime (like attempted murder). Related form: **attempted**.

- **try** Beginning with both *T hands* in front of the chest, palms in, simultaneously twist the wrists forward, ending with the palms facing forward.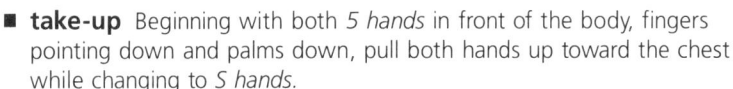

attorney, attorney at law, counsel, counselor, counselor at law, or **lawyer** A person whose profession is to advise or act for clients in legal matters.

- **law** Place the palm side of the right *L hand*, palm facing left, first on the fingers and then on the heel of the left *open hand*, palm facing right and fingers pointing up.

- **person marker** Move both *open hands*, palms facing each other, downward along the sides of the body.

attorney at law

attorney at law See sign for ATTORNEY.

attorney-client privilege The privilege of a client to prevent disclosure of confidential communication to his or her lawyer.

- **law** Place the palm side of the right *L hand*, palm facing left, first on the fingers and then on the heel of the left *open hand*, palm facing right and fingers pointing up.

- **person-person** Move both *P hands*, palms facing each other, downward along the sides of the body. Repeat by shifting the body to the side.

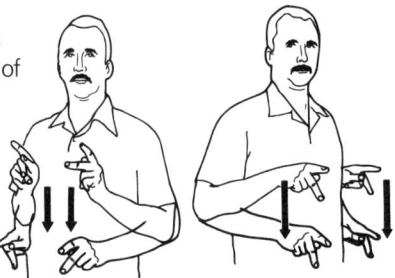

- **discuss-discuss** Tap the side of the extended right index finger, palm facing in, on the upturned left *open hand* with a repeated movement while moving the hands to and from the body with a double movement.

- **secret** Tap the thumb side of the right *A hand*, palm left, against the mouth with a repeated movement.

Attorney General[1] or **United States Attorney** The chief legal officer of the federal government.

- Fingerspell: U-S-A-G

Attorney General[2] or **United States Attorney** (alternate sign)

- **government** Beginning with the extended right index finger pointing upward near the right side of the head, palm facing forward, twist the wrist to touch the finger to the right temple.

---- [sign continues] ---→

38

award

- **law** Place the palm side of the right *L hand*, palm facing left, first on the fingers and then on the heel of the left *open hand*, palm facing right and fingers pointing up.

- **person marker** Move both *open hands*, palms facing each other, downward along the sides of the body.

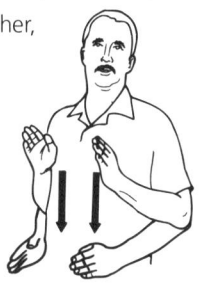

- **higher** Move the right *10 hand*, thumb up and palm left, upward with a deliberate movement.

attorney in fact See sign for AGENT.

authority[1] The legal power of a public official to act in an official capacity.

- **power** Touch the fingertips of the right *claw hand* to the left upper arm.

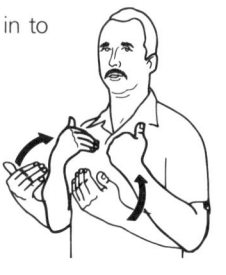

- **have** Bring the fingertips of both *bent hands*, palms facing in, in to touch each side of the chest.

authority[2] A source of information on how to apply the law in a particular situation. See sign for EVIDENCE[1].

award The grant of damages by a court. See signs for BEQUEATH[1,2].

bad check See signs for KITE[1,2,3].

bad faith Lacking overall fairness in a transaction.

- **fair** Beginning with the fingertips of both *bent hands* together, palms facing down, bring the hands apart a short distance.

- **not** Bring the thumb of the right *10 hand* forward from under the chin with a deliberate movement.

badge A special device worn as a sign of membership on the police force. See signs for POLICE[1,2].

bail The money or goods, such as bonds, mortgages, titles, etc., pledged to a court on behalf of a person accused of a crime to assure court appearance.

- **money** Tap the back of the right *flattened O hand,* palm facing up, with a double movement against the palm of the left *open hand,* palm facing up.

- **deposit** Beginning with the thumbs of both *10 hands* touching in front of the chest, both palms facing down, bring the hands downward and apart by twisting the wrists.

- **for-for** With a questioning expression and beginning with the extended right index finger touching the right side of the forehead, twist the hand forward with a double movement, turning the index finger forward each time.

---- [sign continues] ---➤

bailiff

- **out** Beginning with the right *5 hand,* palm facing down, in front of the right shoulder bring the hand outward to the right, closing the fingers and thumb together into a *flattened O hand.*

- **jail**[1] Bring the back of the right *4 hand* from near the chest forward with a double movement while bringing the left *4 hand* in to meet the right hand, ending with the fingers crossed at an angle, both palms facing in.

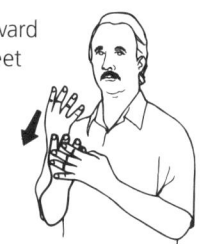

- **understand** Beginning with the right *modified X hand*, palm in, near the right side of the forehead, flick the index finger upward with a deliberate movement.

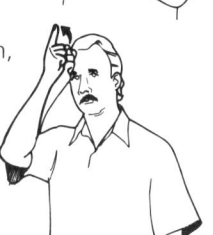

- **must** Move the bent index finger of the right *X hand* downward with a deliberate movement in front of the right side of the body by bending the wrist down.

- **come-back** Beginning with both extended index fingers pointing up in front of the body, palms facing in, bring the fingers back toward the chest.

bailiff The court officer charged with managing the courtroom.
- **court** Move both *F hands,* palms facing each other, up and down in front of each side of the chest with a repeated alternating movement.

---- [sign continues] ---------------------------------->

bailiff

- **police** Tap the thumb side of the right *modified C hand*, palm facing left, against the left side of the chest with a double movement.

bait and switch See signs for FALSE ADVERTISING[1,2].

bankrupt A judicial proceeding by which a person unable to pay debts can have the debts adjusted to get a fresh start. Related form: **bankruptcy**.

- **penniless** Hit the little-finger side of the right *open hand*, palm down and fingers pointing back, against the right side of the neck with a deliberate movement.

bar A general term used for the legal profession.

- **lawyer** Place the palm side of the right *L hand*, palm facing left, first on the fingers and then on the heel of the left *open hand*, palm facing right and fingers pointing up. Move both *open hands*, palms facing each other, downward along the sides of the body.

- **group** Beginning with both *claw hands* in front of the chest, palms facing each other, bring the hands away from each other in outward arcs while turning the palms in, ending with the little fingers near each other.

bargain To negotiate terms of a contract. See sign for NEGOTIATE[2].

barter An exchange of goods or services without using money.

- **switch** Beginning with both *F hands* in front of the chest, right hand somewhat higher than the left hand, palms facing in, and fingers pointing in opposite directions, move the hands in an arc around each other to reverse positions.

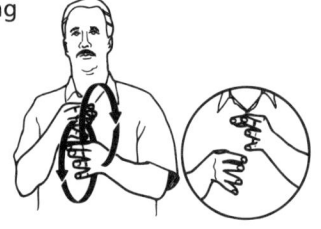

basis The amount of money that one has invested in a piece of property.

- **pay**[1] Beginning with the extended right index finger touching the palm of the left *open hand*, palms facing each other, move the right finger forward and off the left fingertips.

---- [sign continues] ---------------->

bench conference

- **how-much** Beginning with the right *S hand* in front of the right side of the chest, palm facing up, flick the fingers open quickly into a *5 hand*.

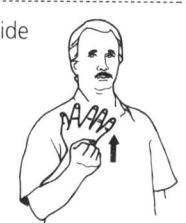

battery See signs for ASSAULT[1,2,3].

bearer A person in possession of a negotiable document made out to "bearer."

- **paper** Brush the heel of the right *open hand* with a double movement on the heel of the left *open hand*, palms facing each other.

- **hold** Move the right *S hand*, palm facing up, in a circular movement in front of the right side of the chest.

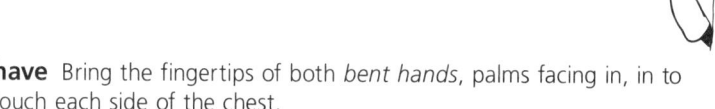

- **have** Bring the fingertips of both *bent hands*, palms facing in, in to touch each side of the chest.

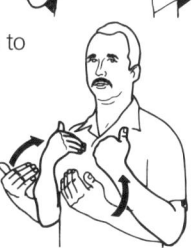

bench The judge's seat in a courtroom.

- **judge** Move the right *modified X hand*, palm left, with a double up-and-down movement.

- **sit** Place the fingers of the right *H hand*, palm facing down, across the extended fingers of the left *H hand* held in front of the chest, palm facing down and fingers pointing right.

bench conference See sign for SIDEBAR.

bench trial

bench trial A trial in which no jury is present and all factual issues are decided by the judge. See sign for JUDGMENT.

bench warrant See sign for WARRANT.

beneficiary or **distributee** A person for whom a trust is established, or who is to receive benefits under an insurance policy.

- **receive** Beginning with both *curved 5 hands* in front of the body, right hand higher than the left hand and both palms facing back, bring the hands back toward the chest while closing into *S hands*, ending with the right little finger on the index-finger side of the left hand.

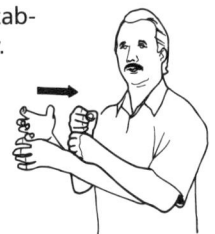

- **person** Move both *P hands*, palms facing each other, downward along the sides of the body.

bequeath[1] or **devise** To give personal property by a will. Same sign used for **award, bequest, gift, grant, legacy**.

- **gift** Move both *X hands* from in front of the body, palms facing each other, forward in simultaneous arcs.

bequeath[2] or **devise** (alternate sign) Same sign used for **award, bequest, gift, grant, legacy**.

- **donate** Beginning with the right *X hand* in front of the right shoulder and the left *X hand* in front of the left side of the body, palms facing in opposite directions, move the right hand downward in an arc and the left hand upward with a double alternating movement.

bequest The personal property given by a will. See signs for BEQUEATH[1,2].

best interests of the child Court decisions based on circumstances that positively affect a child's rearing rather than on genetics.

- **best** Bring the right *open hand*, palm facing in and fingers pointing left, from in front of the mouth upward in a large arc to the right side of the head, changing to a *10 hand* as the hand moves.

---- [sign continues] ---->

44

beyond the scope

- **for** Beginning with the extended right index finger touching the right side of the forehead, twist the hand forward, ending with the index finger pointing forward.

- **child** Move the right *open hand* downward in front of the right side of the body, palm facing down.

beyond a reasonable doubt or **standard of proof** The degree of certainty necessary to convict a defendant of a crime.

- **include** Swing the right *5 hand*, palm down, in a circular movement over the left *S hand*, palm in, while changing into a *flattened O hand*, ending with the fingertips of the right hand inserted in the center of the thumb side of the left hand.

- **doubt** Beginning with both *S hands* in front of the body, one hand higher than the other, both palms down, move the hands up and down with a short alternating movement.

- **more** Tap the fingertips of both *flattened O hands*, palms facing down, together in front of the chest with a double movement.

beyond the scope An objection raised in a trial for questioning that attempts to go into matters that were not asked about in the immediately preceding examination.

- **deviate** Move the extended right index finger toward the extended left index finger held up in front of the chest and then move quickly off to the right.

bill

bill A formal document containing a list of items.

- **paper** Brush the heel of the right *open hand* with a double movement on the heel of the left *open hand*, palms facing each other.

- **formal** Move the thumb of the right *5 hand*, palm facing left, upward and forward in a double circular movement in the center of the chest.

- **list**[1] Touch the fingertips of the right *flattened O hand*, several times on the palm of the left *open hand*, palm right and fingers pointing up, as it moves from the fingers downward to the heel.

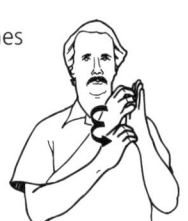

bill of lading A document identifying goods received for shipment and designating who is entitled to delivery.

- **paper** Brush the heel of the right *open hand* with a double movement on the heel of the left *open hand*, palms facing each other.

- **name** Tap the middle-finger side of the right *H hand* across the index-finger side of the left *H hand* with a double movement.

- **receive** Beginning with both *curved 5 hands* in front of the body, right hand higher than the left hand and both palms facing back, bring the hands back toward the chest while closing into *S hands*, ending with the right little finger on the index-finger side of the left hand.

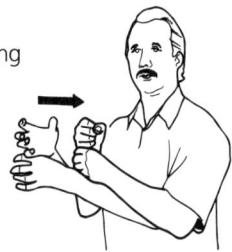

---- [sign continues]

bill of particulars

- **who** With the extended right index finger, palm down, draw a little circle around the mouth.

bill of particulars¹ A written statement setting forth the details of a civil claim or a criminal charge.

- **paper** Brush the heel of the right *open hand* with a double movement on the heel of the left *open hand*, palms facing each other.

- **put-down-put-down** Touch the fingertips of the right *flattened O hand*, palm down, to the palm of the left *open hand*, palm up. Then slap the palm of the right *open hand* against the left palm. Repeat.

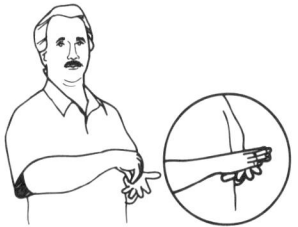

bill of particulars² (alternate sign)

- **paper** Brush the heel of the right *open hand* with a double movement on the heel of the left *open hand*, palms facing each other.

- **write** With the thumb and index finger of the right hand pinched together, move the right hand with a wiggling movement across the palm of the left *open hand* held in front of the body, palm up.

- **itemize** Move the right extended index finger downward in a series of small arcs pointing to each finger of the left *5 hand*, both palms in.

47

bill of sale

bill of sale A document transferring title in a personal property from seller to buyer.

- **paper** Brush the heel of the right *open hand* with a double movement on the heel of the left *open hand*, palms facing each other.

- **proof** Move the right *open hand* downward, ending with the back of the right hand on the palm of the left *open hand,* both palms facing up in front of the chest.

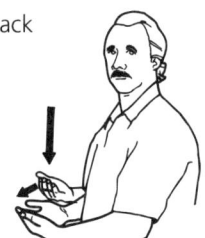

- **sell** Beginning with both *flattened O hands* held in front of each side of the chest, palms down and fingers pointing down, swing the fingertips forward and back by twisting the wrists upward with a double movement.

- **finish** With both *5 hands* apart in front of the body, palms up, quickly turn the hands over toward each other.

bind over To order a person accused of a crime be subjected to trial.

- **person** Move both *P hands*, palms facing each other, downward along the sides of the body.

- **accuse** Push the little-finger side of the right *open hand*, palm facing left, forward across the back of the left *open hand*, palm facing down.

---- [sign continues] -->

48

binder

- **answer** Beginning with both extended index fingers pointing up in front of the mouth, right hand nearer the mouth than the left and palms forward, bend the wrists down simultaneously, ending with the fingers pointing forward and the palms down.

- **court** Move both *F hands*, palms facing each other, up and down in front of each side of the chest with a repeated alternating movement.

binder A document granting a person who has applied for insurance temporary coverage.

- **paper** Brush the heel of the right *open hand* with a double movement on the heel of the left *open hand*, palms facing each other.

- **show** With the extended right index finger touching the palm of the left *open hand*, palm right and fingers pointing forward, move both hands forward a short distance.

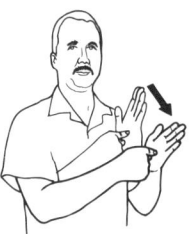

- **short** Rub the middle-finger side of the right *H hand*, palm angled left, back and forth with a repeated movement on the index-finger side of the left *H hand*, palm angled right.

- **insurance** Move the right *I hand*, palm forward, from side to side with a repeated movement in front of the right shoulder.

blackmail

blackmail or **extortion** To obtain money from a person through intimidation, such as threatening to reveal an injurious truth.

- **pay**[2] Beginning with the right *flattened O hand* in front of the right side of the body, palm facing up, move the hand forward while quickly sliding the thumb off each finger.

- **shut-up** Beginning with the thumb of the *flattened C hand* touching the chin, palm facing in, close the fingers to the thumb, forming a *flattened O hand*.

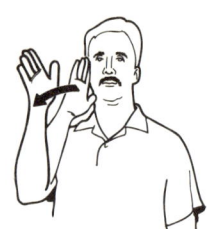

- **will** Move the right *open hand*, palm left and fingers pointing up, from the right side of the chin forward while tipping the fingers down.

- **me** Point the extended right index finger to the center of the chest.

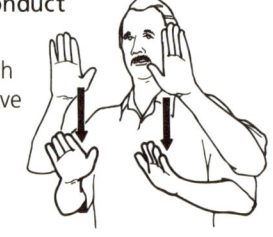

blue law[1] or **Sunday closing law** A law regulating conduct of business on Sunday.

- **Sundays** Beginning with both *open hands* in front of each shoulder, palms facing forward and fingers pointing up, move the hands downward with a smooth movement.

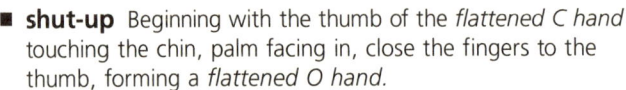

- **business** Brush the base of the right *B hand*, palm forward, with a repeated rocking movement on the back of the left *open hand*, palm down.

---- [sign continues] ---------→

board of directors

- **law** Place the palm side of the right L hand, palm facing left, first on the fingers and then on the heel of the left open hand, palm facing right and fingers pointing up.

blue law[2] or Sunday closing law A law forbidding on Sunday certain otherwise legal activities.

- **Sundays** Beginning with both open hands in front of each shoulder, palms facing forward and fingers pointing up, move the hands downward with a smooth movement.

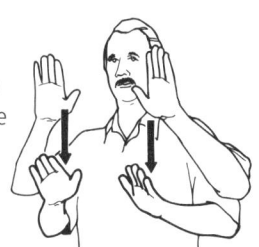

- **business** Brush the base of the right B hand, palm forward, with a repeated rocking movement on the back of the left open hand, palm down.

- **illegal** Hit the palm side of the right L hand, palm left, sharply on the palm of the left open hand, palm right, and off again.

board of directors A governing body of a corporation elected by shareholders to set policy.

- **board of directors** Touch the index-finger side of the right B hand to the left side of the chest, and then move the hand in an arc while changing to a D hand to touch again on the right side of the chest.

- **manage** Beginning with both modified X hands in front of each side of the body, right hand forward of the left hand and palms facing each other, move the hands forward and back with a repeated movement.

---- [sign continues] ---->

board of directors

- **person marker** Move both *open hands*, palms facing each other, downward along the sides of the body.

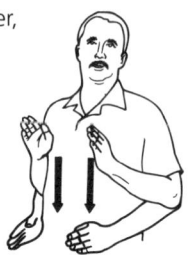

boilerplate Standardized language usually included in legal documents, such as contracts, wills, and deeds.

- **law** Place the palm side of the right *L hand*, palm facing left, first on the fingers and then on the heel of the left *open hand*, palm facing right and fingers pointing up.

- **language** Beginning with the thumbs of both *L hands* near each other in front of the chest, palms angled down, bring the hands outward with a wavy movement to in front of each side of the chest.

- **standard** Beginning with both *Y hands* in front of the body, palms facing down, move the hands in a large flat circle.

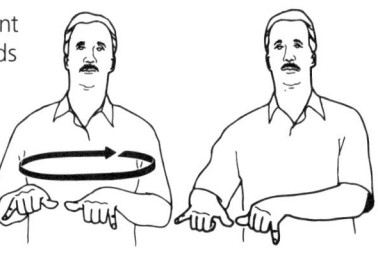

bona fide *Latin.* See sign for ACTUAL.

bond or **note** A written obligation to pay or forfeit a sum of money upon the occurrence of a specified event.

- **paper** Brush the heel of the right *open hand* with a double movement on the heel of the left *open hand*, palms facing each other.

- **promise** Bring the extended right index finger, palm facing left and finger pointing up, from in front of the lips downward, changing into an *open hand* and placing the palm of the right hand on the index-finger side of the left *S hand* held in front of the body, palm facing right.

---- [sign continues] ---->

breach

- **pay**[1] Beginning with the extended right index finger touching the palm of the left *open hand*, palms facing each other, move the right finger forward and off the left fingertips.

boycott A deliberate action not to buy from, sell to, work for, or deal with a company as a means of protest or coercion.

- **go-go-go** Move both extended right index fingers from pointing up in front of the body, palms facing forward, deliberately forward while bending the wrists so the fingers point forward. Repeat sign in two other directions.

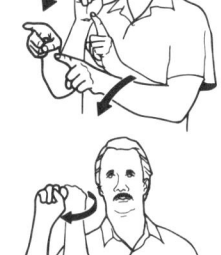

- **protest** Beginning with the right *S hand* in front of the right shoulder, palm facing back, twist the hand sharply forward.

brain dead Irreversible cessation of brain functioning when heart and lung may continue to function by machines.

- **mind** Tap the extended right index finger, palm facing in, against the right side of the forehead with a double movement.

- **die** Beginning with both *open hands* in front of the body, right palm up and left palm down, flip the hands to the right, turning the right palm down and the left palm up.

breach or **breach of contract** Violation of a legal duty or obligation, usually civil.

- **agree** Move the extended right index finger from touching the right side of the forehead downward to beside the extended left index finger, ending with both fingers pointing forward in front of the body, palms down.

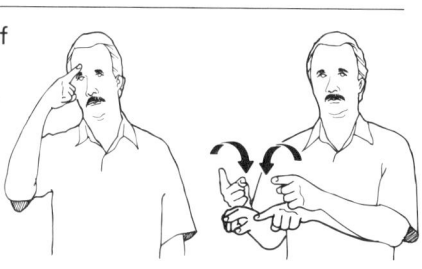

[sign continues]

breach

- **break** Beginning with both *S hands* in front of the body, index fingers touching and palms down, move the hands away from each other while twisting the wrists with a deliberate movement, ending with the palms facing each other.

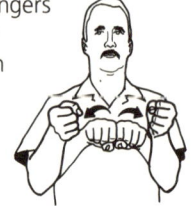

breach of contract See sign for BREACH.

breaking and entering Forcible entry into the home or office of another.

- **enter** Move the back of the right *open hand* forward in a downward arc under the palm of the left *open hand*, both palms down.

- **illegal** Hit the palm side of the right *L hand*, palm left, sharply on the palm of the left *open hand*, palm right, and off again.

bribery[1] The crime of giving or promising something of value with the view of corrupting the behavior of a person, such as a public official. Related form: **bribe**.

- **pay-me** Move the right *flattened O hand*, palm facing up and fingers pointing back, back under the downturned palm of the left *open hand* while quickly sliding the thumb off each finger.

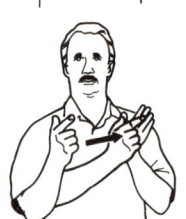

bribery[2] (alternate sign)

- **bribe** Move the right *B hand*, palm facing up and fingers pointing forward, forward under the downturned palm of the left *open hand*.

brief A written argument submitted to a court, outlining the facts and legal basis for a case.

- Fingerspell: C-A-S-E
- **summary** Beginning with both *5 hands* in front of the chest, right hand above the left hand and fingers pointing in opposite directions, bring the hands toward each other while squeezing the fingers together, ending with the little-finger side of the right *S hand* on top of the thumb side of the left *S hand*.

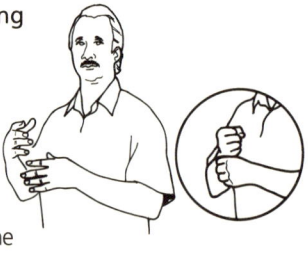

burglary

bring See sign for FILE.

broad construction See LIBERAL CONSTRUCTION.

burden or **burden of proof** The obligation to produce evidence in support of an accusation.

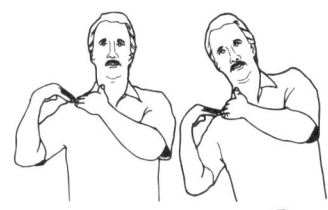

- **burden** With the fingertips of both *bent hands* on the right shoulder, push the shoulder down slightly.

- **proof** Move the right *open hand* downward, ending with the back of the right hand on the palm of the left *open hand*, both palms facing up in front of the chest.

- **must** Move the bent index finger of the right *X hand* downward with a deliberate movement in front of the right side of the body by bending the wrist down.

burden of proof See sign for BURDEN.

burglary The crime of breaking and entering for the purpose of stealing.

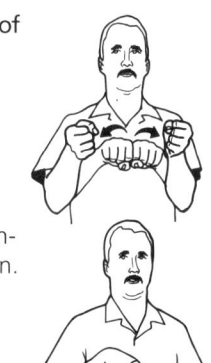

- **break** Beginning with both *S hands* in front of the body, index fingers touching and palms down, move the hands away from each other while twisting the wrists with a deliberate movement, ending with the palms facing each other.

- **enter** Move the back of the right *open hand* forward in a downward arc under the palm of the left *open hand*, both palms down.

- **steal**[1] Beginning with the index-finger side of the right *V hand*, palm facing down, on the elbow of the bent left arm, held at an upward angle across the chest, pull the right hand upward toward the left wrist while bending the fingers in tightly.

55

by the entirety

by the entirety See sign for COMMUNITY PROPERTY.

bylaw[1] Any rule in a set of rules adopted collectively by a group to govern itself.
- Fingerspell acronym: B-L

bylaw[2] (alternate sign)
- **bylaw** Place first the index-finger side of the right *B hand,* palm forward, on the fingers of the left *open hand,* palm facing right and fingers pointing up, followed by placing the index-finger side of the right *L hand* on the heel of the left hand.

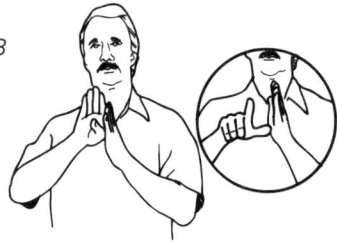

calendar A court's list of cases scheduled to be heard on a particular day or time period.
- **court** Move both *F hands*, palms facing each other, up and down in front of each side of the chest with a repeated alternating movement.

- **schedule** Beginning with the left *open hand* held in front of the left shoulder, palm facing right and fingers pointing forward, bring the fingers of the right *4 hand*, palm facing left, down the heel of the left hand, and then drag the back of the right fingers across the length of the left palm from the heel to the fingertips.

call[1] To ask a witness to come forward to testify.
- **call** Slap the fingers of the right *open hand* on the back of the left *open hand*, palm facing down, dragging the right fingers upward and closing them into an *A hand* in front of the right shoulder.

call[2] To demand payment.
- **require** With the extended index finger of the right *X hand* touching the palm of the left *open hand* bring both hands back toward the chest.

- **pay**[1] Beginning with the extended right index finger touching the palm of the left *open hand*, palms facing each other, move the right finger forward and off the left fingertips.

57

canon

canon A fundamental rule or principle.

- **base** Move the right *B hand*, palm facing forward, in a flat circle under the left *open hand*, palm facing down.

- **rule** Touch the fingertips of the right *R hand* first on the fingers and then on the heel of the left *open hand*, palms facing each other.

capacity or **legal capacity** The legal ability to perform an act that has legal consequences, like making a will or entering into a contract.

- **law** Place the palm side of the right *L hand*, palm facing left, first on the fingers and then on the heel of the left *open hand*, palm facing right and fingers pointing up.

- **can** Move both *S hands*, palms facing down, downward simultaneously in front of each side of the body.

- **decide** Move the extended right index finger from the right side of the forehead, palm left, down in front of the chest while changing into an *F hand*, ending with both *F hands* moving downward in front of the body, palms facing each other.

capital or **capital asset** Any form of wealth used for the production of more wealth.

- **money** Tap the back of the right *flattened O hand*, palm facing up, with a double movement against the palm of the left *open hand*, palm facing up.

---- [sign continues] ---->

- **deposit** Beginning with the thumbs of both *10 hands* touching in front of the chest, both palms facing down, bring the hands downward and apart by twisting the wrists.

capital asset See sign for CAPITAL.

capital punishment or **death penalty** The killing of a person by the government as punishment for a crime.
- **punish** Strike the extended right index finger, palm facing left, downward across the elbow of the left bent arm.

- **die** Beginning with both *open hands* in front of the body, right palm up and left palm down, flip the hands to the right, turning the right palm down and the left palm up.

caption The heading on a court paper containing such information as the name and number of the case, etc.
- **court** Move both *F hands*, palms facing each other, up and down in front of each side of the chest with a repeated alternating movement.

- **paper** Brush the heel of the right *open hand* with a double movement on the heel of the left *open hand*, palms facing each other.

- **caption** Beginning with the fingers of both *G hands* together in front of the face, pull the hands apart to the sides.

59

care

care, due care, or **reasonable care** The exercise of caution in one's conduct so as to avoid causing injury or loss.

- **rights** Slide the little-finger side of the right *open hand,* palm facing left, in an upward arc across the upturned left palm held in front of the body.

- **take-care-of** With the little-finger side of the right *K hand* across the index-finger side of the left *K hand,* move the hands in a repeated flat circle in front of the body.

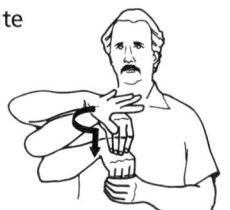

case[1] All proceedings with respect to a charge, claim, or dispute filed with a court.

- Fingerspell: C-A-S-E
- **include** Swing the right *5 hand,* palm down, in a circular movement over the left *S hand,* palm in, while changing into a *flattened O hand,* ending with the fingertips of the right hand inserted in the center of the thumb side of the left hand.

case[2] The totality of evidence presented by a party in support of its position in a case.

- **proof-proof-proof** Move the fingertips of the right *open hand,* palm facing in, from in front of the mouth downward, ending by placing the back of the right hand on the palm of the left *open hand,* both palms facing up, moving downward in front of the chest each time.

casebook A collection of judicial opinions in a particular area of law, supplemented with questions and commentary.

- **decide** Move the extended right index finger from the right side of the forehead, palm left, down in front of the chest while changing into an *F hand,* ending with both *F hands* moving downward in front of the body, palms facing each other. Repeat sign toward another direction.

- **include** Swing the right *5 hand,* palm down, in a circular movement over the left *S hand,* palm in, while changing into a *flattened O hand,* ending with the fingertips of the right hand inserted in the center of the thumb side of the left hand.

---- [sign continues] -->

case law

- **print** Bring the thumb side of the right *G hand*, palm down, against the left *open hand*, palm up, and pinch the right thumb and index finger together with a double movement.

case law[1] Law created by judicial decision and interpretation of statutes rather than by statute.
- Fingerspell: C-A-S-E
- Fingerspell: L-A-W

case law[2] (alternate sign)
- **court** Move both *F hands*, palms facing each other, up and down in front of each side of the chest with a repeated alternating movement.

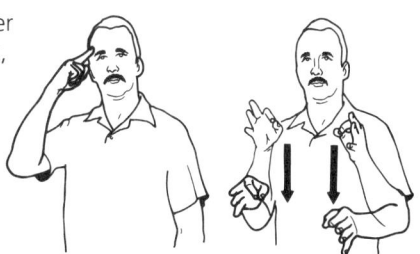

- **decide** Move the extended right index finger from the right side of the forehead, palm left, down in front of the chest while changing into an *F hand*, ending with both *F hands* moving downward in front of the body, palms facing each other.

- **interpret** With the fingertips of both *F hands* touching in front of the chest, palms facing each other, twist the hands in opposite directions to reverse positions.

- **become** Beginning with the palm of the right *open hand* laying across the upturned palm of the left *open hand*, rotate the hands, exchanging positions while keeping the palms together.

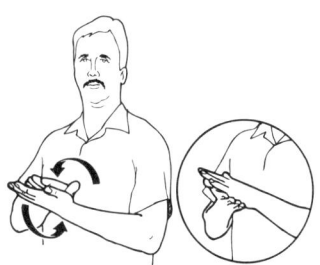

---- [sign continues] ---->

case law

- **law** Place the palm side of the right *L hand,* palm facing left, first on the fingers and then on the heel of the left *open hand,* palm facing right and fingers pointing up.

casualty Harm to a person or property caused by sudden or unusual event, such as a car accident or natural disaster.

- **terrible** Beginning with both *8 hands* near each side of the head, palms facing forward, flip the fingers open to *5 hands* with a deliberate movement.

- **happen** Beginning with both extended index fingers in front of the body, palms facing up and fingers pointing forward, flip the hands over toward each other, ending with the palms facing down.

cause or **for cause** A legally sufficient reason for taking certain action.

- **law** Place the palm side of the right *L hand,* palm facing left, first on the fingers and then on the heel of the left *open hand,* palm facing right and fingers pointing up.

- **decide** Move the extended right index finger from the right side of the forehead, palm left, down in front of the chest while changing into an *F hand*, ending with both *F hands* moving downward in front of the body, palms facing each other.

cease and desist order or **injunction** An order of the court directing a person to refrain from specified unlawful conduct.

- **order** Move the extended right index finger, palm forward and finger pointing up, from in front of the mouth forward and down, ending with the finger pointing forward and the palm down.

---- [sign continues] -->

chain of custody

- **stop** Hit the little-finger side of the right *open hand* on the palm of the left *open hand*.

censure A formal statement issued by a disciplinary committee condemning the behavior of one of its own members. See signs for ADMONITION[1,2].

certificate A formal document declaring some right, interest, or permission granted to the person to whom it was issued. Related form: **certification**. See sign for LICENSE.

certified check A check on which the bank has written a notice signifying that the funds for payment have been set aside.

- Fingerspell: B-A-N-K
- **your** Push the palm of the right *open hand*, palm forward and fingers pointing up, toward the person being talked to.
- **check** Beginning with the fingertips of both *L hands* touching in front of the chest, palms facing forward, bring the hands apart to in front of each shoulder, and then pinch each thumb and index finger together.

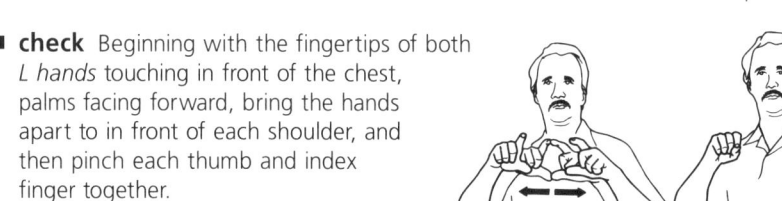

chain of custody The sequence of places where a piece of physical evidence was located from the time of its gathering until trial.

- **proof** Move the right *open hand* downward, ending with the back of the right hand on the palm of the left *open hand,* both palms facing up in front of the chest.

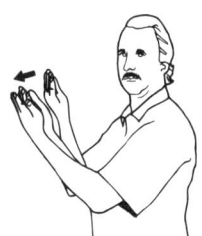

- **pick-up** Bring the right *5 hand*, palm down, upward in front of the right side of the body while pinching the thumb and index finger together.

---- [sign continues] ---->

chain of custody

- **hold** Move the right *S hand*, palm facing up, in a circular movement in front of the right side of the chest.

- **paper** Brush the heel of the right *open hand* with a double movement on the heel of the left *open hand*, palms facing each other.

- **sign** Place the extended fingers of the right *H hand*, palm down, firmly down on the upturned palm of the left *open hand* held in front of the chest.

- **hold** Move the right *S hand*, palm facing up, in a circular movement in front of the right side of the chest.

- **happen** Beginning with both extended index fingers in front of the body, palms facing up and fingers pointing forward, flip the hands over toward each other, ending with the palms facing down.

chain of title The sequence of owners and transfers of property.
- **paper** Brush the heel of the right *open hand* with a double movement on the heel of the left *open hand*, palms facing each other.

---- [sign continues] ---------→

chambers

- **name** Hit the middle-finger side of the right *H hand* across the index-finger side of the left *H hand*.

- **your** Push the palm of the right *open hand*, palm forward and fingers pointing up, toward the person being talked to.

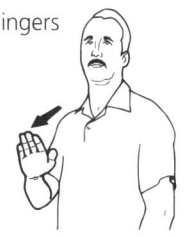

- **sell** Beginning with both *flattened O hands* held in front of each side of the chest, palms down and fingers pointing down, swing the fingertips forward and back by twisting the wrists upward with a double movement.

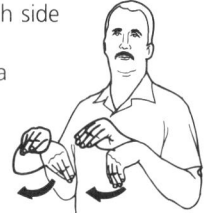

- **name** Tap the middle-finger side of the right *H hand* across the index-finger side of the left *H hand*.

- **sell** Beginning with both *flattened O hands* held in front of each side of the chest, palms down and fingers pointing down, swing the fingertips forward and back by twisting the wrists upward with a double movement.

challenge The rejection of a potential juror with or without reason. See sign for RECALL^2.

chambers A judge's office. Same sign used for **court, courtroom**.

- **court** Move both *F hands,* palms facing each other, up and down in front of each side of the chest with a repeated alternating movement.

---- [sign continues] ---->

65

chambers

- **room** Beginning with both *R hands* in front of each side of the chest, palms facing each other and fingers pointing forward, move the hands in opposite directions by bending the wrists, ending with the left hand near the chest and the right hand several inches forward of the left hand, both palms facing in.

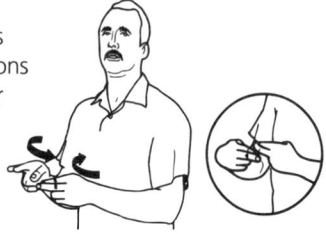

---

chancery, chancery court, or **court of chancery** The traditional name for a court.

- Fingerspell: C-I-V-I-L

- **court** Move both *F hands*, palms facing each other, up and down in front of each side of the chest with a repeated alternating movement.

---

chancery court See sign for CHANCERY.

---

character The general disposition of a person in respect to some trait that is relevant in a case.

- **character** Move the right *C hand*, palm facing left, in a small circle and then back against the left side of the chest.

- **your** Push the palm of the right *open hand*, palm forward and fingers pointing up, toward the person being talked to.

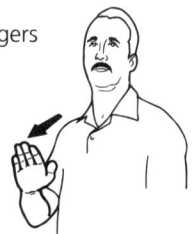

---

character witness A witness called to testify about another's character.

- **witness** With the index finger of the right *X hand*, pull down slightly on the cheek near the outside corner of the right eye.

- **proof** Move the right *open hand* downward, ending with the back of the right hand on the palm of the left *open hand*, both palms facing up in front of the chest.

[sign continues] ──▶

child abuse

- **support** Push the knuckles of the right *S hand* upward under the little-finger side of the left *S hand*, both palms in, pushing the left hand upward a short distance in front of the chest.

- **character** Move the right *C hand*, palm facing left, in a small circle and then back against the left side of the chest.

charge A formal allegation that a person has violated a criminal law. See signs for ALLEGATION, LITIGATE[1,2,3].

charter[1] or **corporate charter** A legislative grant of rights and powers establishing a corporation and setting forth its purposes and structure.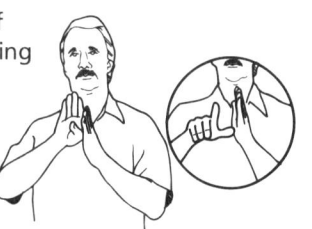
- Fingerspell: C-O
- **bylaw** Place first the index-finger side of the right *B hand*, palm forward, on the fingers of the left *open hand*, palm facing right and fingers pointing up, followed by placing the index-finger side of the right *L hand* on the heel of the left hand.

charter[2] or **corporate charter** (alternate sign)
- Fingerspell abbreviation for *company*: C-O
- Fingerspell abbreviation for *bylaw*: B-L

check A document by which a person directs a bank to pay a specified sum of money to another person.
- **check** Beginning with the fingertips of both *L hands* touching in front of the chest, palms facing forward, bring the hands apart to in front of each shoulder, and then pinch each thumb and index finger together.

child abuse Wrongful exercise of power or mistreatment of a child.
- **wrong** Bring the middle fingers of the right *Y hand*, palm in, back against the chin with a deliberate movement.

---- [sign continues] ---➤

67

child abuse

- **use** With the heel of the right *U hand* on the back of the left *S hand*, move the right hand in a small circle.

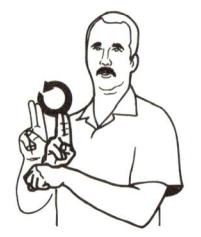

- **children** Beginning with the index fingers of both *B hands* touching in front of the body, palms down and fingers pointing forward, move the hands outward to each side with a bouncing movement.

child custody or **custody** The determination of the residence, care, and education of a minor child.

- **responsible** With the fingertips of both *bent hands* on the right shoulder, push the shoulder down slightly.

- **take-care-of** With the little-finger side of the right *K hand* across the index-finger side of the left *K hand*, move the hands in a repeated flat circle in front of the body.

- **child** Move the right *open hand* downward in front of the right side of the body, palm facing down.

child neglect or **parental neglect** Failure of a parent to support or to safeguard a child's health and well-being.

- **children** Beginning with the index fingers of both *B hands* touching in front of the body, palms down and fingers pointing forward, move the hands outward to each side with a bouncing movement.

---- [sign continues] -->

child pornography

- **ignore** Beginning with the index-finger side of the right *4 hand* touching the nose, palm facing down and fingers pointing left, bring the hand downward in an arc, ending with the little-finger side of the hand touching the chest, palm facing up.

child pornography[1] Any sexually explicit visual depiction of a person under age 18.

- **dirty** With the back of the right *open hand* under the chin, palm facing down, wiggle the fingers.

- **picture** Move the right *C hand*, palm facing forward, from near the right side of the face, downward, ending with the index-finger side of the right *C hand* against the palm of the left *open hand*, palm facing right.

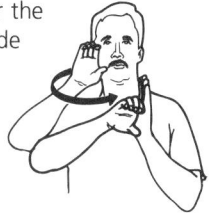

- **what** Beginning with the right *5 hand* in front of the right side of the body, palm up, shake the hand loosely from side to side from the wrist with a double movement.

- **child** Move the right *open hand* downward in front of the right side of the body, palm facing down.

child pornography[2] (alternate sign)

- **children** Beginning with the index fingers of both *B hands* touching in front of the body, palms down and fingers pointing forward, move the hands outward to each side with a bouncing movement.
- Fingerspell: P-O-R-N-O

child support

child support Money paid by a noncustodial parent as directed by the court to the custodial parent after a divorce.

- **child** Move the right *open hand* downward in front of the right side of the body, palm facing down.

- **pay**² Beginning with the right *flattened O hand* in front of the right side of the body, palm facing up, move the hand forward while quickly sliding the thumb off each finger.

- **support** Push the knuckles of the right *S hand* upward under the little-finger side of the left *S hand*, both palms in, pushing the left hand upward a short distance in front of the chest.

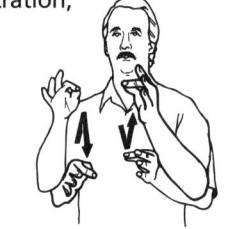

circuit A geographic division for purposes of judicial administration, with a court in each circuit.

- **court** Move both *F hands,* palms facing each other, up and down in front of each side of the chest with a repeated alternating movement.

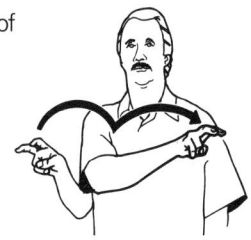

- **travel** Move the right *bent V hand,* palm down, in a series of repeated arcs in a random pattern.

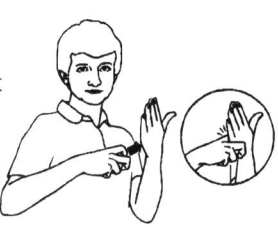

citation A written notice to appear in court to answer a charge.

- **ticket** Push the bent index and middle fingers of the right *bent V hand*, palm down, with a repeated movement around the little-finger side of the left *open hand* held in front of the chest, palm in and fingers pointing up.

civil

citizen or **national** A person who owes allegiance to a government and is entitled to its protection.

- Fingerspell abbreviation: U-S
- **person** Move both *P hands*, palms facing each other, downward along the sides of the body.

---

citizen's arrest An arrest made by a private citizen rather than by a police officer.

- **regular** With the right index finger extended, brush the little-finger side of the right hand, palm facing in, across the extended left index finger, palm facing in, as the right hand moves toward the chest in a double circular movement.

- **person** Move both *P hands*, palms facing each other, downward along the sides of the body.

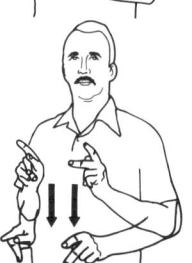

- **seize** Beginning with both *curved 5 hands* in front of each shoulder, palms facing forward, move the hands downward while closing into *S hands*.

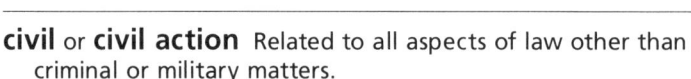

---

civil or **civil action** Related to all aspects of law other than criminal or military matters.

- **everyday** Move the palm side of the right *A hand* forward on the right side of the chin with a repeated movement.

- **law** Place the palm side of the right *L hand*, palm facing left, first on the fingers and then on the heel of the left *open hand*, palm facing right and fingers pointing up.

---- [sign continues] ---------->

civil

- **army** Tap the palm side of both *A hands* against the right side of the chest, right hand above the left hand, with a repeated movement.

- **not** Bring the thumb of the right *10 hand* forward from under the chin with a deliberate movement.

civil action See sign for CIVIL.

civil disobedience Open and nonviolent refusal to obey certain laws for the purpose of influencing legislation or policy.

- **everyday** Move the palm side of the right *A hand* forward on the right side of the chin with a repeated movement.

- **law** Place the palm side of the right *L hand*, palm facing left, first on the fingers and then on the heel of the left *open hand*, palm facing right and fingers pointing up.

- **protest** Beginning with the right *S hand* in front of the right shoulder, palm facing back, twist the hand sharply forward.

civil liberties See sign for CIVIL RIGHTS.

civil rights or **civil liberties** Political and personal liberties protected by the constitution; freedom from discrimination.

- **constitution** Place the little-finger side of the right *C hand*, palm facing left, first on the fingers and then the heel of the left *open hand*, palm facing right and fingers pointing up.

---- [sign continues] ---->

class action

- **law** Place the palm side of the right *L hand*, palm facing left, first on the fingers and then on the heel of the left *open hand*, palm facing right and fingers pointing up.

claim or **claim for relief** An assertion of facts presented in the court that, if true, would result in a favorable judgment.

- **offer** Beginning with both *open hands* in front of each side of the body, palms up, move the hands forward in simultaneous arcs.

claim for relief See sign for CLAIM.

claimant A person who asserts a claim.

- **offer** Beginning with both *open hands* in front of each side of the body, palms up, move the hands upward and forward in simultaneous arcs.

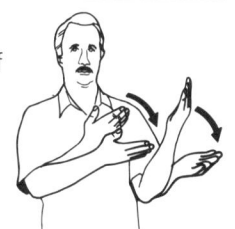

- **person marker** Move both *open hands*, palms facing each other, downward along the sides of the body.

class action An action brought on behalf of a class of persons having a common interest.

- **group** Beginning with both *claw hands* in front of the chest, palms facing each other, bring the hands away from each other in outward arcs while turning the palms in, ending with the little fingers near each other.

- **file** Move the fingers of the right *V hand*, palm facing forward, downward on each side of the extended left index finger, which is pointing up in front of the chest.

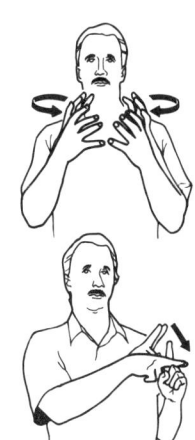

73

clean hands

clean hands The quality of having acted fairly and properly in a matter over which one is suing someone else.

- **honest**[1] Slide the extended fingers of the right *H hand,* palm facing left, forward from the heel to the fingers of the upturned left *open hand.*

- **law** Place the palm side of the right *L hand,* palm facing left, first on the fingers and then on the heel of the left *open hand,* palm facing right and fingers pointing up.

- **follow** With the knuckles of the right *10 hand,* palm facing left, near the wrist of the left *10 hand,* palm facing right, move both hands forward a short distance.

clear and convincing evidence Evidence presented that persuades the court that the facts are highly probable.

- **proof** Move the right *open hand* downward, ending with the back of the right hand on the palm of the left *open hand,* both palms facing up in front of the chest.

clear title[1] or **marketable title** Title to property that is free from someone else claiming a right to the same property.

- Fingerspell: T-I-T-L-E
- **only** Beginning with the extended right index finger pointing up in front of the right shoulder, palm facing forward, twist the wrist in, ending with the palm facing in near the right side of the chest.

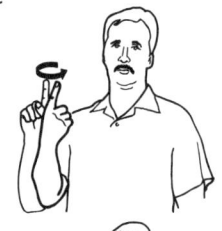

- **name** Tap the middle-finger side of the right *H hand* across the index-finger side of the left *H hand* with a double movement.

clemency

clear title[2] or marketable title (alternate sign)

- **paper** Brush the heel of the right *open hand* with a double movement on the heel of the left *open hand*, palms facing each other.

- **proof** Move the right *open hand* downward, ending with the back of the right hand on the palm of the left *open hand*, both palms facing up in front of the chest.
- Fingerspell: O-W-N

- **yourself** Push the thumb of the right *10 hand*, palm facing left, toward the person being talked to with a small double movement.

clemency, executive clemency, commute,

or **pardon** The exercise by a president or governor to grant pardon or to reduce a sentence of a convicted criminal.

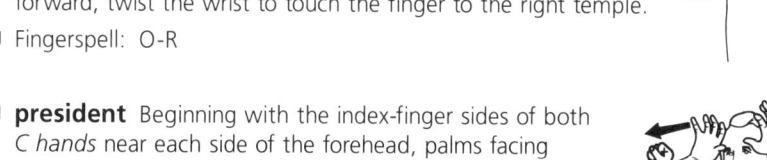

- **government** Beginning with the extended right index finger pointing upward near the right side of the head, palm facing forward, twist the wrist to touch the finger to the right temple.
- Fingerspell: O-R

- **president** Beginning with the index-finger sides of both *C hands* near each side of the forehead, palms facing forward, move the hands outward to above each shoulder while closing into *S hands*.

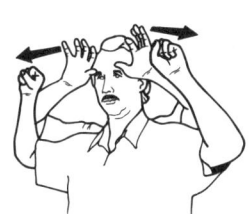

- **excuse** Wipe the fingertips of the right *open hand* across the upturned left *open hand* from the heel off the fingertips.

75

clerk

clerk or **court clerk** A court official charged with the administration of the court's operations, particularly maintenance of the court's records.

- **decide** Move the extended right index finger from the right side of the forehead, palm left, down in front of the chest while changing into an *F hand*, ending with both *F hands* moving downward in front of the body, palms facing each other.

- **manage** Beginning with both *modified X hands* in front of each side of the body, right hand forward of the left hand and palms facing each other, move the hands forward and back with a repeated movement.

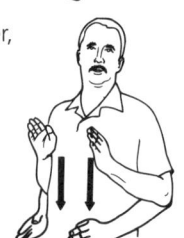

- **person marker** Move both *open hands*, palms facing each other, downward along the sides of the body.

closing¹, closing statement, closing argument, or summation A lawyer's address to the judge or jury after all evidence has been presented summarizing the case. Related form: **close**.

- **summary** Beginning with both *5 hands* in front of the chest, right hand above the left hand and fingers pointing in opposite directions, bring the hands toward each other while squeezing the fingers together, ending with the little-finger side of the right *S hand* on top of the thumb side of the left *S hand*.

- **sentences** Beginning with the thumbs and index fingers of both *F hands* touching in front of the chest, palms facing each other, with a double movement pull the hands apart to in front of each side of the chest.

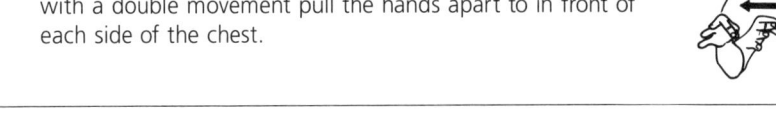

closing² or **settlement** The completion of a real estate transaction. Related form: **close**.

- **close** Beginning with both *B hands* in front of each side of the chest, palms facing back, twist the wrists and bring them sharply toward each other until the index fingers touch, ending with palms facing forward.

cohabit

closing argument See signs for CLOSING[1].

closing statement See signs for CLOSING[1].

code An organized compilation of statutes or rules. See sign for LAW. See sign for REGULATION.

coerce[1] To compel by force or intimidation. Same sign used for **involuntary**.

- **force** Beginning with the right *C hand* in front of the right shoulder, palm forward, and the left arm bent across the body, move the right hand downward and forward, ending with the right wrist across the left wrist, both palms down.

coerce[2] (alternate sign) Same sign used for **involuntary**.

- **prod** With the left *modified X hand* somewhat more forward than the right *modified X hand*, palms facing each other, move the hands forward with a double short jabbing movement.

cohabit An unmarried couple living together in an intimate relationship similar to that of husband and wife. Same sign used for **common-law marriage, domestic partnership, palimony**.

- **sleep-together** With both *S hands*, palms down, near each other in front of the chest, flick the index and middle fingers forward with a double movement, forming *U hands* each time.

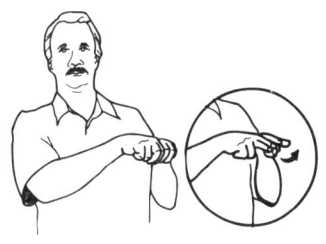

- **looks-like** Move the right extended index finger in a circle around the face. Then move the right *Y hand*, palm facing forward, from side to side with a double movement in front of the right side of the body.

- **husband** Move the right *C hand* from the right side of the forehead, palm left, down to clasp the left *curved hand* held in front of the chest, palm up.

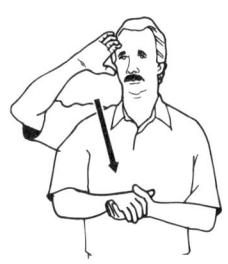

---- [sign continues] -->

77

cohabit

- **wife** Move the right *C hand* from near the right side of the chin, palm left, down to clasp the left *curved hand* held in front of the chest, palm up.

collateral or **security interest** Property pledged as security for a loan.

- **money** Tap the back of the right *flattened O hand*, palm facing up, with a double movement against the palm of the left *open hand*, palm facing up.

- **borrow** With the little-finger side of the right *V hand* across the index-finger side of the left *V hand,* bring the hands back, ending with the right index finger against the chest.

- **pay**² Beginning with the right *flattened O hand* in front of the right side of the body, palm facing up, move the hand forward while quickly sliding the thumb off each finger.

- **hold** Move the right *S hand,* palm facing up, in a circular movement in front of the right side of the chest.

collective bargaining Negotiation regarding wages and working conditions between an employer and a union representing employees.

- Fingerspell: U-N-I-O-N

- **boss** Tap the fingertips of the right *curved 5 hand* on the right shoulder with a repeated movement.

---- [sign continues] -->

78

common carrier

- **come-together** Beginning with both *curved 5 hands* in front of each side of the body, palms facing each other, bring the fingers together in front of the body.

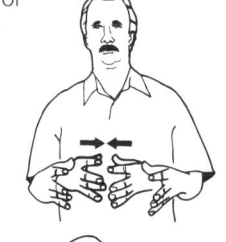

- **discuss** Tap the side of the extended right index finger, palm facing in, on the upturned left *open hand* with a double movement.

color See sign for RACE².

commerce An interchange of goods or commodities between countries or between areas of the same country; trade.

- **business** Brush the base of the right *B hand,* palm forward, with a repeated movement on the back of the left *open hand,* palm down.

commit¹ To do something wrong.
Related form: **commission**.

- **do** Move both *C hands*, palms facing down, simultaneously back and forth in front of the body with a swinging movement.

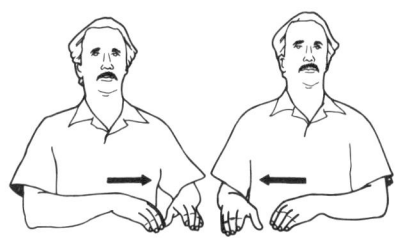

- **wrong** Bring the middle fingers of the right *Y hand*, palm in, back against the chin with a deliberate movement.

commit² See signs for JAIL³,⁴,⁵.

common carrier A company in the business of transporting people or goods, offering its services to the public.

- Fingerspell: T-R-A-N-S-I-T

common-law marriage

common-law marriage A marraige entered into without the usual ceremony, but effected by a mutual agreement between the parties. See signs for COHABIT, DOMESTIC PARTNERSHIP.

community property or **by the entirety** Words used to describe ownership of property granted to a married couple as a unit, by the entirety.

- **things** Beginning with both *open hands* in front of the body, palms facing up, move the hands to the sides away from each other in a double arc.

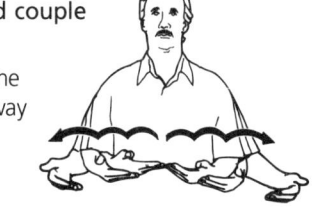

- **buy** Beginning with the back of the right *flattened O hand*, palm facing up, in the upturned palm of left *open hand*, move the right hand forward in an arc.

- **during** Beginning with both extended index fingers in front of each side of the body, palms down, move them forward and upward in parallel arcs.

- **marry** Bring the right *curved hand*, palm facing down, downward in front of the chest to clasp the left *curved hand*, palm facing up.

commute See sign for CLEMENCY.

company A business enterprise.
- Fingerspell abbreviation: C-O

compensation Payment for services rendered.
- **pay**[2] Beginning with the right *flattened O hand* in front of the right side of the body, palm facing up, with a double movement, move the hand forward while quickly sliding the thumb off each finger.

complaint

compensatory damages, actual damages, or **just compensation** Payment awarded to compensate for harm that results from the defendant's wrongdoing.

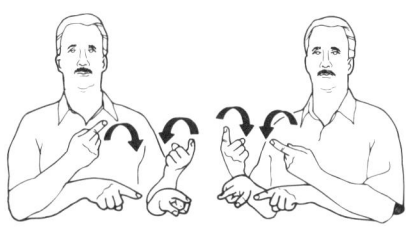

- **happen-happen** Beginning with both extended index fingers in front of the body, palms facing up and fingers pointing forward, flip the hands over toward each other, ending with the palms facing down. Repeat sign in a different location.

- **now** Bring both *Y hands,* palms facing up, downward in front of each side of the body.

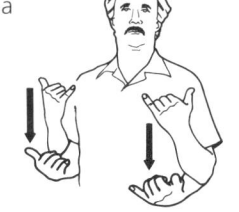

- **pay**[1] Beginning with the extended right index finger touching the palm of the left *open hand,* palms facing each other, move the right finger forward and off the left fingertips.

competent Possessing sufficient mental capacity to make rational decisions about legal matters.

- **can** Move both *S hands,* palms facing down, downward simultaneously in front of each side of the body.

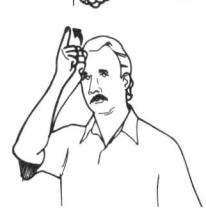

- **understand** Beginning with the right *modified X hand,* palm in, near the right side of the forehead, flick the index finger upward with a deliberate movement.

complaint[1] The initial document in a civil matter wherein the plaintiff states the facts and what relief is sought.

- **document** Brush the heel of the right *open hand* with a double movement on the heel of the left *open hand,* palms facing each other. Then with both extended index fingers, palms down, trace a square in the air, beginning together in front of the chest, moving apart to each side, moving straight down, and then together again at the bottom.

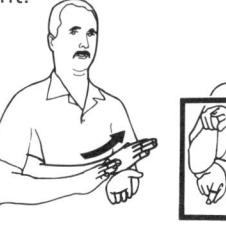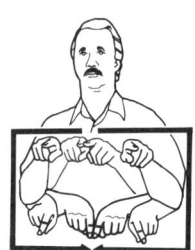

---- [sign continues] ---→

81

complaint

- **complain** Tap the fingertips of the right *curved 5 hand* against the center of the chest.

- **against** Hit the fingertips of the right *bent hand* into the left *open hand*, palm right and fingers pointing forward.

complaint[2] See sign for GRIEVANCE.

compounding a crime Accepting a bribe from someone who has committed a crime in return for not prosecuting the person.

- **bribe** Move the right *flattened O hand*, palm facing up, forward under the downturned palm of the left *open hand*.

- **myself** Bring the thumb side of the right *A hand*, palm left, against the chest with a double movement.

- **cover-up** With the heel of the right *S hand* on the palm of the left *5 hand*, twist the right hand to the left.

concur To agree with the decision being made by the court. Same sign used for **meeting of the minds, settle,** and **stipulation.**

- **agree** Move the extended right index finger from touching the right side of the forehead downward to beside the extended left index finger, ending with both fingers pointing forward in front of the body, palms down.

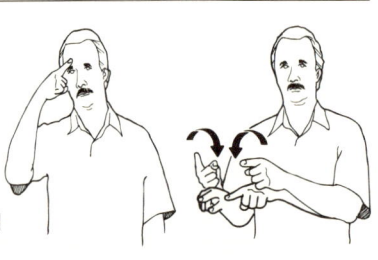

condemn

concurrent sentences Sentences on different charges to be served simultaneously.

- **punish-punish** Strike the extended right index finger, palm facing left, downward across the elbow of the left bent arm. Repeat sign in a different location.

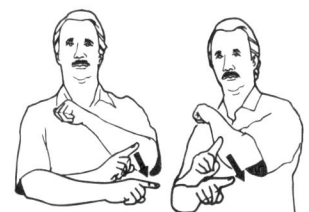

- **time** Tap the bent index finger of the right *X hand*, palm down, with a double movement on the wrist of the downturned left hand.

- **same-as** Move the right *Y hand*, palm down, from side to side in front of the body.

- **during** Beginning with both extended index fingers in front of each side of the body, palms down, move them forward and upward in parallel arcs.

condemn To order something destroyed because it is illegal or poses a hazard to the public.

- **order** Move the extended right index finger, palm forward and finger pointing up, from in front of the mouth forward and down, ending with the finger pointing forward and the palm down.

- **destroy** Beginning with both *curved 5 hands* in front of the chest, right hand over the left, right palm facing down and left palm facing up, bring the right hand in a circular movement over the left. Then close both hands into *A hands* and bring the knuckles of the right hand past the left knuckles as the right hand moves forward to the right with a deliberate movement.

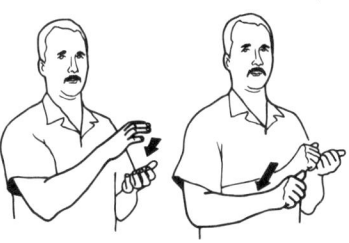

83

condition

condition A future event which, upon its occurrence, a right or interest under a contract depends. Related form: **conditional**.

- **paper** Brush the heel of the right *open hand* with a double movement on the heel of the left *open hand*, palms facing each other.

- **sign** Place the extended fingers of the right *H hand*, palm down, firmly down on the upturned palm of the left *open hand* held in front of the chest.

- **itemize** Move the right extended index finger downward in a series of small arcs, pointing to each finger of the left *5 hand*, both palms in.

- **include** Swing the right *5 hand*, palm down, in a circular movement over the left *S hand*, palm in, while changing into a *flattened O hand*, ending with the fingertips of the right hand inserted in the center of the thumb side of the left hand.

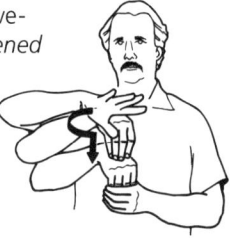

confession[1] A statement admitting that one has committed a crime. Same sign used for **acknowledgement**.

- **admit** Move the right *open hand*, palm facing in, from the chest forward in an arc while turning the palm slightly outward.

confession[2] (alternate sign) Same sign used for **acknowledgement**.

- **confess** Beginning with the fingers of both *5 hands* on the chest, move the hands forward in an arc.

conscientious objector

conflict of interest A situation where one's personal interest could potentially influence the way one carries out a duty.

- **myself** Bring the thumb side of the right *A hand*, palm left, against the chest with a double movement.

- **conflict** Beginning with both extended index fingers in front of each side of the body, palms facing in and fingers angled toward each other, move the hands toward each other, ending with the fingers crossed.

confrontation The right of a defendant, under the sixth amendment, to be confronted in open court by witnesses against him so they can be cross-examined.

- **face-to-face** Beginning with both *open hands* in front of the chest, palms facing each other and fingers pointing up, move the right hand forward in a deliberate movement toward the left hand while both hands move upward.

conscientious objector A person whose religion or personal belief system forbids participation as a combatant in a war.

- **inside** Move the fingers of the right *flattened O hand* downward with a short double movement in the palm side of the left *C hand* held in front of the chest.

- **believe** Move the extended right index finger from touching the right side of the forehead downward while opening the hand, ending with the right hand clasping the left *open hand*, palm facing up, in front of the body.

- **war** Beginning with both *5 hands* held apart in front of the body, palms in, swing the hands simultaneously from side to side.

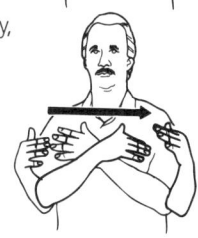

---- [sign continues] -->

conscientious objector

- **not-responsible** Beginning with the bent middle finger of both *5 hands* touching each shoulder, flick the fingers quickly upward while moving the head back.

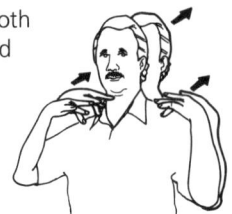

consecutive sentences Sentences on different charges to be served one after the other.

- **punish-punish** Strike the extended right index finger, palm facing left, downward across the elbow of the left bent arm. Repeat sign in a different location.

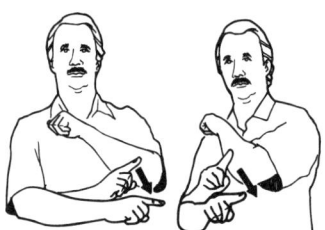

- **not** Bring the thumb of the right *10 hand* forward from under the chin with a deliberate movement.

- **same** Move the right *Y hand*, palm down, from side to side in front of the body.

- **not** Bring the thumb of the right *10 hand* forward from under the chin with a deliberate movement.

- **follow** With the knuckles of the right *10 hand*, palm facing left, near the wrist of the left *10 hand*, palm facing right, move both hands forward a short distance.

conservator

consent or **informed consent** Giving agreement after receiving sufficient information about the proposed course of action.

- **paper** Brush the heel of the right *open hand* with a double movement on the heel of the left *open hand*, palms facing each other.

- **sign** Place the extended fingers of the right *H hand*, palm down, firmly down on the upturned palm of the left *open hand* held in front of the chest.

- **allow** Beginning with both *open hands* in front of the waist, palms facing each other and fingers pointing down, bring the fingers forward and upward by bending the wrists.

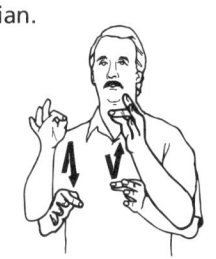

conservator or **conservatorship** A court-appointed guardian.

- **court** Move both *F hands,* palms facing each other, up and down in front of each side of the chest with a repeated alternating movement.

- **appoint** Beginning with the thumb side of the right *G hand,* palm facing down and fingers pointing forward, against the extended left index finger, palm facing forward and fingers pointing up, pull the right hand in toward the chest while pinching the index finger and thumb together.

- **take-care-of** With the little-finger side of the right *K hand* across the index-finger side of the left *K hand*, move the hands in a repeated flat circle in front of the body.

---- [sign continues] ---➤

87

conservator

- **person marker** Move both *open hands*, palms facing each other, downward along the sides of the body.

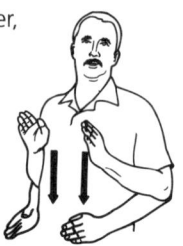

---

conservatorship See sign for CONSERVATOR.

---

consideration Something given or promised in a contract in exchange for the other's promise.

- **paper** Brush the heel of the right *open hand* with a double movement on the heel of the left *open hand*, palms facing each other.

- **sign** Place the extended fingers of the right *H hand*, palm down, firmly down on the upturned palm of the left *open hand* held in front of the chest.

- **itemize** Move the right extended index finger downward in a series of small arcs, pointing to each finger of the left *5 hand*, both palms in.

- **have** Bring the fingertips of both *bent hands*, palms facing in, in to touch each side of the chest.

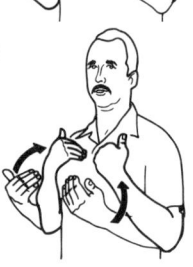

---

consign or **consignment** To place goods into the hands of a merchant for sale to others.

- **things** Beginning with both *open hands* in front of the body, palms facing up, move the hands to the sides away from each other in a double arc.

---- [sign continues] ---->

conspiracy

- **give-me**[1] Beginning with both *flattened O hands* in front of the body, palms up, bring the hands up to touch the fingertips on each side of the chest, palms in.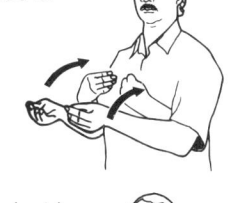

- **sell** Beginning with both *flattened O hands* held in front of each side of the chest, palms down and fingers pointing down, swing the fingertips forward and back by twisting the wrists upward with a double movement.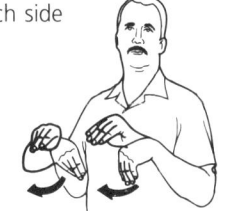

- **for** Beginning with the extended right index finger touching the right side of the forehead, twist the hand forward, ending with the index finger pointing forward.

- **you** Point the right extended index finger forward toward the referent.

consignment See sign for CONSIGN.

consolidate To combine two or more cases into one for administrative convenience.

- **inside** Move the fingers of the right *flattened O* hand downward with a short double movement in the palm side of the left *C hand* held in front of the chest.

conspiracy An agreement between two or more persons to do an unlawful act.

- **illegal** Hit the palm side of the right *L hand*, palm left, sharply on the palm of the left *open hand*, palm right, and off again.

---- [sign continues] ---->

conspiracy

- **do** Move both *C hands*, palms facing down, simultaneously back and forth in front of the body with a swinging movement.

- **agree-agree** Beginning with both extended index fingers pointing forward in front of each side of the body, both palms facing up, flip the hands toward each other, turning the palms down. Repeat sign in a different location.

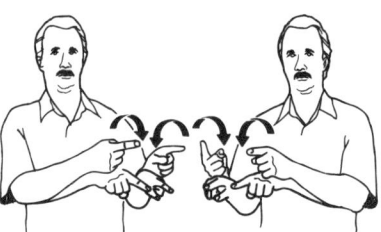

- **go-ahead** Beginning with both *bent hands* in front of the body, palms facing in and fingers pointing toward each other, simultaneously move the hands forward a short distance.

constitution The fundamental law of a nation, providing a framework against which the validity of all other laws is measured. Related forms: **constitutional, constitutionality**.

- Fingerspell abbreviation: U-S
- **constitution** Place the little-finger side of the right *C hand*, palm facing left, first on the fingers and then the heel of the left *open hand*, palm facing right and fingers pointing up.

constitutional right A right protected by the constitution of the United States.

- Fingerspell abbreviation: U-S
- **constitution** Place the little-finger side of the right *C hand*, palm facing left, first on the fingers and then the heel of the left *open hand*, palm facing right and fingers pointing up.

- **rights** Slide the little-finger side of the right *open hand*, palm facing left, in an upward arc across the upturned left palm held in front of the body.

---- [sign continues] ---➤

constructive

- **can** Move both *S hands*, palms facing down, downward simultaneously in front of each side of the body.

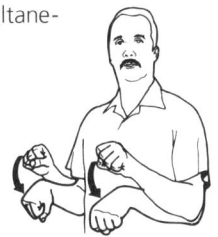

---

construction The process of determining the meaning of a law and its legal effect of a particular situation.

- **law** Place the palm side of the right *L hand*, palm facing left, first on the fingers and then on the heel of the left *open hand*, palm facing right and fingers pointing up.

- **mean** Touch the fingertips of the right *V hand*, palm facing down, in the palm of the left *open hand*, palm facing up and fingers pointing forward, and then twist the right wrist and touch the fingertips down again.

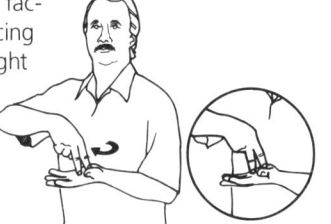

- **influence** Beginning with the fingertips of the right *flattened O hand* on the back of the left *open hand*, palm facing down, move the right hand forward while opening into a *5 hand*.

- **happen** Beginning with both extended index fingers in front of the body, palms facing up and fingers pointing forward, flip the hands over toward each other, ending with the palms facing down.

---

constructive Deemed by law to exist or to have occurred even though it is not actually true.

- **law** Place the palm side of the right *L hand*, palm facing left, first on the fingers and then on the heel of the left *open hand*, palm facing right and fingers pointing up.

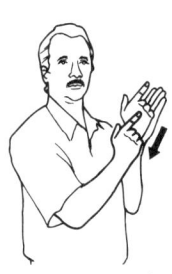

---- [sign continues] ---->

constructive

- **proof** Move the right *open hand* downward, ending with the back of the right hand on the palm of the left *open hand*, both palms facing up in front of the chest.

- **true** Beginning with the thumb side of the right *one hand* in front of the mouth, palm left, move the extended index finger forward.

consumer A person who purchases goods or services.

- **use** With the heel of the right *U hand* on the back of the left *S hand*, move the right hand in a small circle.

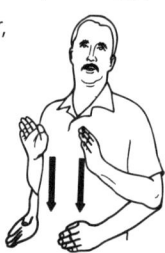

- **person marker** Move both *open hands*, palms facing each other, downward along the sides of the body.

contempt[1] or **contempt of court** Willful disobedience of an order or other willful conduct that disrupts the procedures of a court.

- **protest** Beginning with the right *S hand* in front of the right shoulder, palm facing back, twist the hand sharply forward.

- **court** Move both *F hands*, palms facing each other, up and down in front of each side of the chest with a repeated alternating movement.

---- [sign continues] ---→

contingent

- **order** Move the extended right index finger, palm forward and finger pointing up, from in front of the mouth forward and down, ending with the finger pointing forward and the palm down.

contempt[2] or **contempt of court** (alternate sign)

- **contempt** With the thumbs of both *10 hands* near each side of the forehead, palms facing each other, twist the hands forward turning the palms forward.

comtempt of court See signs for CONTEMPT[1,2].

contest To argue against or dispute the content or validity of a document or decision. Related form: **contested**.

- **person-person** Place the right extended index finger up in front of the body, and then place the left extended index finger up near the right finger, palms facing forward.

- **two-of-them** Swing the right *2 hand*, palm up, from side to side in front of the body.

- **disagree** Move the extended right index finger from touching the right side of the forehead downward to meet the extended left index finger held in front of the chest. Then, beginning with both index fingers pointing toward each other, palms facing in, bring the hands apart to each side of the chest.

contingent[1] Something will or will not occur depending on the occurrence of other circumstances. Related form: **contingency**.

- **something** Move the right *one hand* in a small circle in front of the right shoulder, palm facing back.

---- [sign continues] ---→

93

contingent

- **happen** Beginning with both extended index fingers in front of the body, palms facing up and fingers pointing forward, flip the hands over toward each other, ending with the palms facing down.

- **depend** With the extended right index finger across the extended left index finger, palms facing down, move both fingers down slightly with a double movement.

contingent[2] Related form: **contingency** (alternate sign).
- **depend** With the extended right index finger across the extended left index finger, palms facing down, move both fingers down.

continuance An order suspending or postponing a proceeding. Related form: **continue**.
- **postpone** Beginning with both *F hands* in front of the body, palms facing each other and the left hand nearer to the body than the right hand, move both hands forward in a small arc.

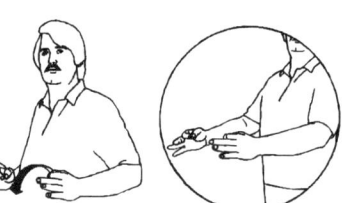

contract[1] A written agreement among two or more persons whereby at least one party promises to do something in exchange for something promised by others.
- **agree** Move the extended right index finger from touching the right side of the forehead downward to beside the extended left index finger, ending with both fingers pointing forward in front of the body, palms down.

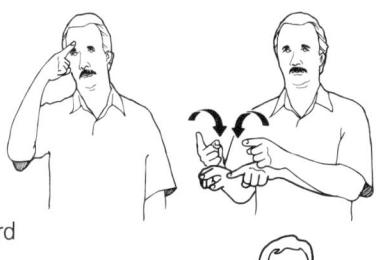

- **sign** Place the extended fingers of the right *H hand*, palm down, firmly down on the upturned palm of the left *open hand* held in front of the chest.

contract[2] See sign for AGREEMENT.

conviction

controlled substance[1] A drug that has addicting, intoxicating, or mood-altering qualities.

- **illegal** Hit the palm side of the right *L hand*, palm left, sharply on the palm of the left *open hand*, palm right, and off again.
- Fingerspell: D-R-U-G

controlled substance[2] (alternate sign)

- **drug** With a deliberate movement, hit the little-finger side of the *A hand* in the crook of the bent left arm held across the body.

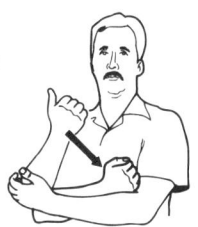

conveyance A transfer of interest in real estate by means of a deed.

- **paper** Brush the heel of the right *open hand* with a double movement on the heel of the left *open hand*, palms facing each other.

- **transfer** Move the right *bent V hand*, palm down, with a large movement from right to left in front of the body.

conviction Proving or officially declaring someone guilty of an offense as a result of a trial. Related form: **convict**.

- **decide** Move the extended right index finger from the right side of the forehead, palm left, down in front of the chest while changing into an *F hand*, ending with both *F hands* moving downward in front of the body, palms facing each other.

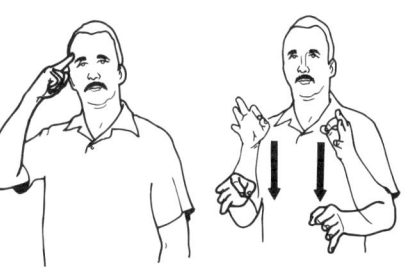

- **wrong** Bring the middle fingers of the right *Y hand*, palm in, back against the chin with a deliberate movement.

---- [sign continues] -->

conviction

- **you** Point the right extended index finger forward toward the referent.

---

cop *Slang.* See signs for POLICE[1,2].

---

copyright An exclusive right granted to the creator or owner of a written, musical, or artistic work that protects it for a specific time.

- **yourself** Push the thumb of the right *10 hand*, palm facing left, toward the person being talked to with a small double movement.

- **invent** Move the right *4 hand*, palm left, forward from the right side of the forehead.

- **other** Beginning with the right *10 hand* in front of the chest, palm down, flip the hand over, ending with palm up.

- **use** With the heel of the right *U hand* on the back of the left *S hand*, move the right hand in a small circle.

- **can't** Bring the extended index finger of the right *one hand* downward, hitting the extended index finger of the left *one hand* as it moves.

corroborate

corporate or **corporation** A legally recognized entity with ownership represented by shares of stock.
- Fingerspell: C-O-R-P

corporate charter See signs for CHARTER[1,2].

corporation See sign for CORPORATE.

corpus All the assets included in a trust.
- **business** Brush the base of the right *B hand*, palm forward, with a repeated movement on the back of the left *open hand*, palm down.

- **profit** Move the right *F hand*, palm facing down, downward with a double movement on the chest.

- **include** Swing the right *5 hand*, palm down, in a circular movement over the left *S hand*, palm in, while changing into a *flattened O hand*, ending with the fingertips of the right hand inserted in the center of the thumb side of the left hand.

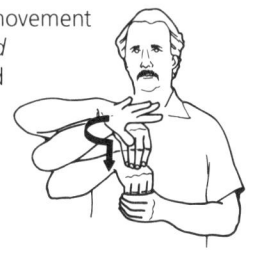

- **hold** Move the right *S hand*, palm facing up, in a circular movement in front of the right side of the chest.

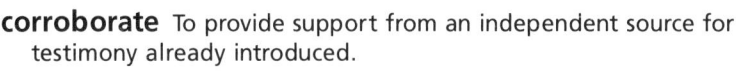

corroborate To provide support from an independent source for testimony already introduced.
- **your** Push the palm of the right *open hand*, palm forward and fingers pointing up, toward the person being talked to.

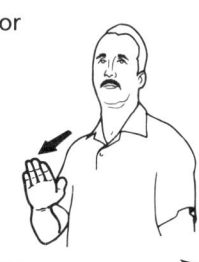

---- [sign continues] ---→

corroborate

- **vow** Bring the extended right index finger, palm facing left and finger pointing up, from in front of the lips downward, while changing into an *open hand*.

- **sentences** Beginning with the thumbs and index fingers of both *F hands* touching in front of the chest, palms facing each other, with a double movement pull the hands apart to in front of each side of the chest.

- **support** Push the knuckles of the right *S hand* upward under the little-finger side of the left *S hand*, both palms in, pushing the left hand upward a short distance in front of the chest.

costs or **court costs** Filing fees and other expenses related to trying a civil case, excluding attorney's fees.

- **court** Move both *F hands,* palms facing each other, up and down in front of each side of the chest with a repeated alternating movement.

- **connect** Beginning with both *curved 5 hands* in front of each side of the body, palms facing each other, bring the hands together while touching the thumb and index fingertips of each hand and intersecting with each other.

- **cost** Strike the knuckle of the right *X hand,* palm facing in, down on the palm of the left *open hand,* palm facing right and fingers pointing forward.

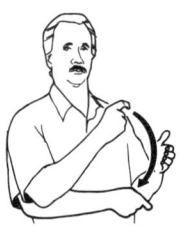

counsel See sign for ATTORNEY.

counteroffer

counselor See sign for ATTORNEY.

counselor at law See sign for ATTORNEY.

count Each distinct charge in a legal declaration or indictment.

- **complain** Tap the fingertips of the right *curved 5 hand* against the center of the chest.

- **file** Move the fingers of the right *V hand,* palm facing forward, downward on each side of the extended left index finger, which is pointing up in front of the chest.

- **different-different** Beginning with both extended index fingers crossed in front of the chest, palms forward, bring the hands apart from each other with a deliberate movement. Repeat sign in several locations.

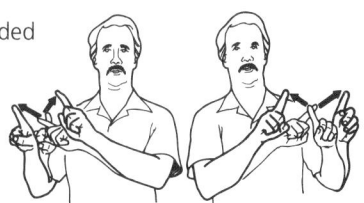

counterclaim A presentation of facts by the defendant against the plaintiff in a civil case.

- **file-against** (one side) Move the fingers of the right *V hand,* palm facing forward, downward on each side of the extended left index finger, pointing up in front of one side of the chest. Then hit the fingertips of the right *bent hand* into the left *open hand*, palm right and fingers pointing forward.

- **file-against** (other side) Move the fingers of the right *V hand,* palm facing forward, downward on each side of the extended left index finger, pointing up in front of the other side of the chest. Then hit the fingertips of the right *bent hand* into the left *open hand*, palm right and fingers pointing forward.

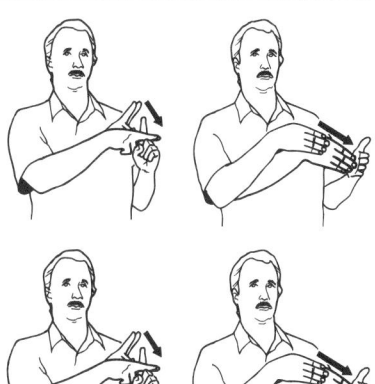

counteroffer A response to an offer that does not accept the offer as stated, but proposes different terms.

- **offer** Beginning with both *open hands* in front of the left side of the body, palms up, move the hands forward and to the right in simultaneous arcs.

---- [sign continues] ---→

counteroffer

- **you** Point the right extended index finger forward toward the referent.

- **other** Beginning with the right *10 hand* in front of the chest, palm down, flip the hand over, ending with palm up.

- **offer** Beginning with both *open hands* in front of left side of the body, palms up, move the hands forward and to the left in simultaneous arcs.

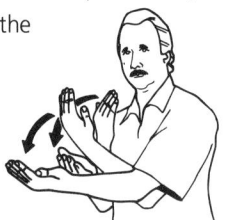

court[1] An institution of government whose function is to interpret and apply the law to specific cases. Same sign used for **forum, judge, trial**.
- **court** Move both *F hands,* palms facing each other, up and down in front of each side of the chest with a repeated alternating movement.

court[2] or **courtroom** The room in which court cases are tried. See sign for CHAMBERS.

court clerk See sign for CLERK.

court costs See sign for COSTS.

court of chancery See sign for CHANCERY.

court order See sign for ORDER.

court reporter A person who makes a word-for-word record of what is said during a trial.
- **court** Move both *F hands,* palms facing each other, up and down in front of each side of the chest with a repeated alternating movement.

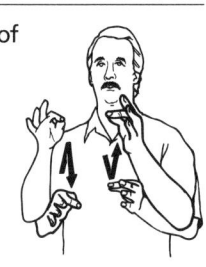

---- [sign continues] ---→

courtroom

- **type** While wiggling the fingers of both 5 hands, palms down, move the hands in an alternating up and down movement.

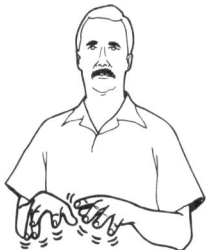

- **person** Move both *P hands*, palms facing each other, downward along the sides of the body.

court-martial A court of military personnel that tries a member of the military for an offense against military law.

- **army** Tap the palm side of both *A hands* against the right side of the chest, right hand above the left hand, with a repeated movement.

- **handcuffs** With the curved thumb and index finger of the left hand, palm facing down, grasp the wrist of the right *open hand*. Then repeat with the right hand on the wrist of the left hand. Then, beginning with the wrists of both *A hands* near each other in front of the chest, move the hands forward with a short deliberate movement.

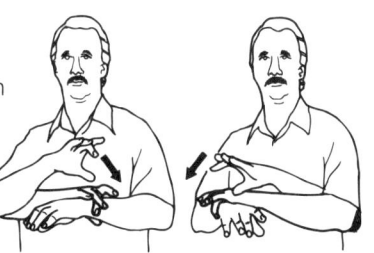

- **court** Move both *F hands,* palms facing each other, up and down in front of each side of the chest with a repeated alternating movement.

101

courtesy copy

courtesy copy An extra copy of a document being filed in a case, and delivered directly to the judge hearing the case.

- **copy**[1] Move the fingers of the right *curved hand*, palm facing up, downward from touching the downturned palm of the left *open hand* while closing the right fingers and thumb into a *flattened O hand*.

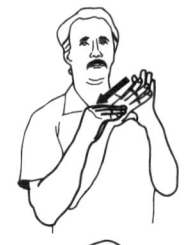

- **give**[1] Beginning with both *X hands* in front of the body, palms facing each other, move the hands forward in simultaneous arcs.

courtroom See sign for COURT[2].

cover To protect against a certain risk as listed in an insurance policy.

- **insurance** Move the right *I hand*, palm forward, from side to side with a repeated movement in front of the right shoulder.

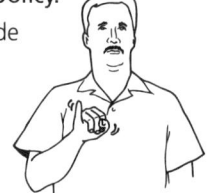

- **protect** With the wrists of both *S hands* crossed in front of the chest, palms facing in opposite directions, move the hands forward with a short double movement.

credible Worthy of belief.

- **believe** Move the extended right index finger from touching the right side of the forehead downward while opening the hand, ending with the right hand clasping the left *open hand*, palm facing up, in front of the body.

- **can** Move both *S hands*, palms facing down, downward simultaneously in front of each side of the body.

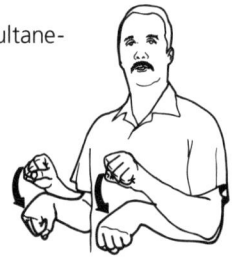

cross appeal

crime, infraction, offense, or **violation** An act that is contrary to laws established for the welfare of the public at large.

- **law** Place the palm side of the right *L hand*, palm facing left, first on the fingers and then on the heel of the left *open hand*, palm facing right and fingers pointing up.

- **break** Beginning with both *S hands* in front of the body, index fingers touching and palms down, move the hands away from each other while twisting the wrists with a deliberate movement, ending with the palms facing each other.

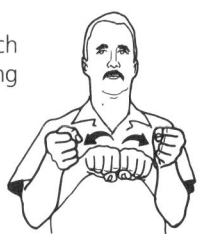

criminal or **offender** A person who commits a crime.

- **crime** Place the palm side of the right *L hand*, palm facing left, first on the fingers and then on the heel of the left *open hand*, palm facing right and fingers pointing up. Then beginning with both *S hands* in front of the body, index fingers touching and palms down, move the hands away from each other while twisting the wrists with a deliberate movement, ending with the palms facing each other.

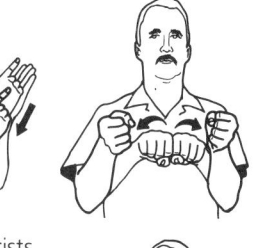

- **person marker** Move both *open hands*, palms facing each other, downward along the sides of the body.

cross appeal An appeal filed in a case where an appeal has already been filed but on different grounds.

- **file** Move the fingers of the right *V hand*, palm facing forward, downward on each side of the extended left index finger, which is pointing up in front of the chest.

- **higher** Move the right *10 hand*, thumb up and palm left, upward with a deliberate movement in front of the right side of the body.

[sign continues]

103

cross appeal

- **file** Move the fingers of the right *V hand*, palm facing forward, downward on each side of the extended left index finger, which is pointing up in front of the chest.

- **higher** Move the right *10 hand*, thumb up and palm left, upward with a deliberate movement in front of the left side of the body.

cross-examination The questioning of a witness called by the other side after the other side completes its questioning.

- **other** Beginning with the right *10 hand* in front of the chest, palm down, flip the hand over, ending with palm up.

- **lawyer** Place the palm side of the right *L hand*, palm facing left, first on the fingers and then on the heel of the left *open hand*, palm facing right and fingers pointing up. Move both *open hands*, palms facing each other, downward along the sides of the body.

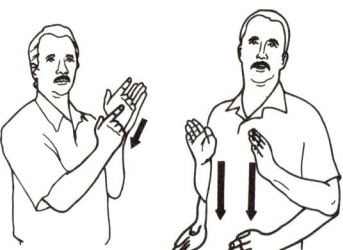

- **question**[2] Beginning with both extended index fingers pointing up in front of each side of the chest, palms facing forward, with an alternating movement move the right hand down while bending into an *X hand* and then the left hand down while bending into an *X hand*.

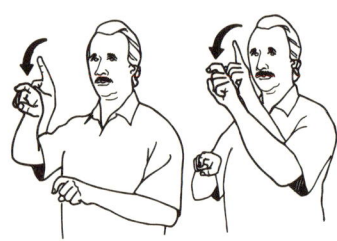

cruel and unusual punishment Punishment of a convicted person that is grossly disproportionate to the crime.

- **cruel** Beginning with the right *curved 5 hand* near the face and the left *curved 5 hand* in front of the body, close the right hand into an *A hand* while moving it quickly down and close the left hand into an *A hand* while moving it quickly up, brushing the knuckles of the hands together as they pass each other.

---- [sign continues] ---------------------------------→

customs

- **do** Move both *C hands*, palms facing down, simultaneously back and forth in front of the body with a swinging movement.

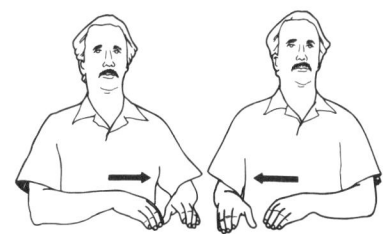

cruelty Physical or psychological abuse by one spouse causing married life to be intolerable by the other spouse.

- **cruel** Beginning with the right *curved 5 hand* near the face and the left *curved 5 hand* in front of the body, close the right hand into an *A hand* while moving it quickly down and close the left hand into an *A hand* while moving it quickly up, brushing the knuckles of the hands together as they pass each other.

culpable Blameworthy.

- **accuse** Push the little-finger side of the right *A hand*, palm facing left, forward across the back of the left *open hand*, palm facing down.

- **can** Move both *S hands*, palms facing down, downward simultaneously in front of each side of the body.

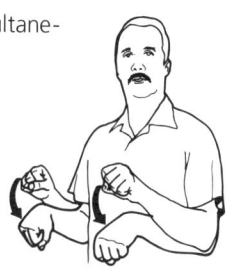

custody See signs for CHILD CUSTODY[1,2].

customs or **duties** Taxes imposed by the federal government on goods imported into or exported from the country.

- **government** Beginning with the extended right index finger pointing upward near the right side of the head, palm facing forward, twist the wrist to touch the finger to the right temple.
- Fingerspell: T-A-X

105

damages A sum of money awarded by a court in a civil case.
- **money** Tap the back of the right *flattened O hand*, palm facing up, with a double movement against the palm of the left *open hand*, palm facing up.

- **pay**[2] Beginning with the right *flattened O hand* in front of the right side of the body, palm facing up, move the hand forward while quickly sliding the thumb off each finger.

- **show** With the extended right index finger touching the palm of the left *open hand*, palm right and fingers pointing forward, move both hands forward a short distance.

- **hurt** Beginning with the extended index fingers of both *one hands* pointing toward each other, right palm down and left palm up, twist the wrists in opposite directions, ending with the right palm up and the left palm down.

- **suffer** Move the thumb of the right *10 hand*, palm left, in a wiggling movement down the chin.

dangerous weapon See sign for DEADLY WEAPON.

deadly weapon

date rape Rape by a person with whom the victim is on a date.
- **date** With the palm sides of both *A hands* together in front of the chest, shake the hands forward and back with a double movement.

- **force** Beginning with the right *C hand* in front of the right shoulder, palm forward, and the left arm bent across the body, move the right hand downward and forward, ending with the right wrist across the left wrist, both palms down.

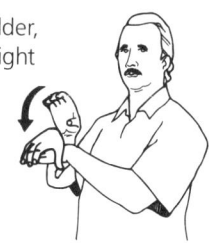

- **intercourse** Bring the right *V hand* downward in front of the chest to tap against the heel of the left *V hand* with a double movement, palms facing each other.

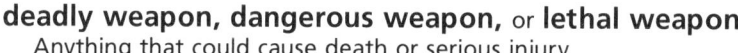

deadly weapon, dangerous weapon, or lethal weapon
Anything that could cause death or serious injury.
- Fingerspell: W-E-A-P-O-N
- **kill** Push the side of the extended right index finger, palm down, across the palm of the left *open hand*, palm right, with a deliberate movement.

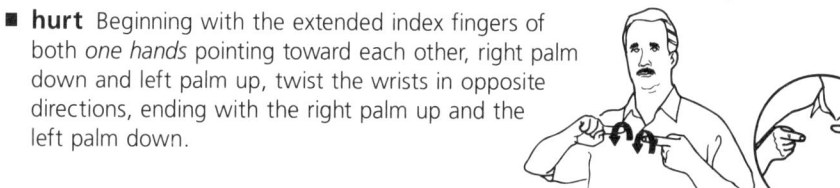

- **hurt** Beginning with the extended index fingers of both *one hands* pointing toward each other, right palm down and left palm up, twist the wrists in opposite directions, ending with the right palm up and the left palm down.

- **can** Move both *S hands*, palms facing down, downward simultaneously in front of each side of the body.

107

dealer

dealer A person who sells illegal drugs.

- **illegal** Hit the palm side of the right *L hand*, palm left, sharply on the palm of the left *open hand*, palm right, and off again.

- **drug** Pound the little-finger side of the right *S hand* with a double movement near the crook of the bent left arm.

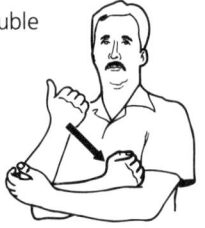

- **sell** Beginning with both *flattened O hands* held in front of each side of the chest, palms down and fingers pointing down, swing the fingertips forward and back by twisting the wrists upward with a double movement.

- **person marker** Move both *open hands*, palms facing each other, downward along the sides of the body.

death See sign for DEMISE.

death penalty See sign for CAPITAL PUNISHMENT.

debt or **payable** An obligation to pay a sum of money. Same sign used for **liability.**

- **owe** With a double movement, tap the extended right index finger against the palm of the left *open hand,* palm facing right.

deductible

decedent A person who has died.

- **die** Beginning with both *open hands* in front of the body, right palm up and left palm down, flip the hands to the right, turning the right palm down and the left palm up.

- **person marker** Move both *open hands*, palms facing each other, downward along the sides of the body.

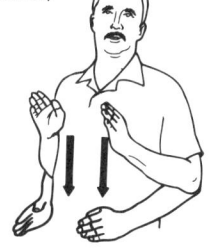

deceit See signs for FRAUD[1,2,3,4,5].

declaration or **statement** An oral or written statement.

- **sentences** Beginning with the thumbs and index fingers of both *F hands* touching in front of the chest, palms facing each other, with a double movement pull the hands apart to in front of each side of the chest.

declaration[2] See signs for STATEMENT[1,2,3,4].

decree A court's final decision in a case. See signs for DETERMINE, JUDGMENT[1], ORDER.

deductible The amount for which the insured is liable before the insurance company must begin paying under a policy.

- **pay**[2] Beginning with the right *flattened O hand* in front of the right side of the body, palm facing up, move the hand forward while quickly sliding the thumb off each finger.

- **only** Beginning with the extended right index finger pointing up in front of the right shoulder, palm facing forward, twist the wrist in, ending with the palm facing in near the right side of the chest.

---- [sign continues] -->

deductible

- **insurance** Move the right *I hand*, palm forward, from side to side with a repeated movement in front of the right shoulder.

- **pay**² Beginning with the right *flattened O hand* in front of the right side of the body, palm facing up, move the hand forward while quickly sliding the thumb off each finger.

deed¹ or title A formal document by which a living person can convey an interest in real estate.

- **document** Brush the heel of the right *open hand* with a double movement on the heel of the left *open hand*, palms facing each other. Then with both extended index fingers, palms down, trace a square in the air, beginning together in front of the chest, moving apart to each side, moving straight down, and then together again at the bottom.

- **proof** Move the right *open hand* downward, ending with the back of the right hand on the palm of the left *open hand*, both palms facing up in front of the chest.

- Fingerspell: O-W-N

deed² or title (alternate sign)

- **formal** Move the thumb of the right *5 hand*, palm facing left, upward and forward in a double circular movement in the center of the chest.

- **paper** Brush the heel of the right *open hand* with a double movement on the heel of the left *open hand*, palms facing each other.

---- [sign continues] -->

deed of trust

- **show** With the extended right index finger touching the palm of the left *open hand*, palm right and fingers pointing forward, move both hands forward a short distance.

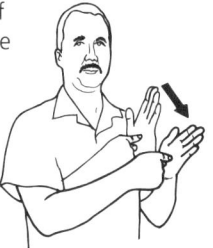

- **mine** Pat the palm of the right *open hand* on the chest with a double movement.

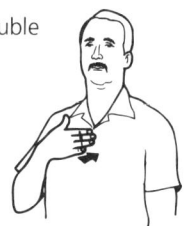

deed of trust A document by which property is conveyed to another to be held in trust.

- **paper** Brush the heel of the right *open hand* with a double movement on the heel of the left *open hand*, palms facing each other.

- **mine** Pat the palm of the right *open hand* on the chest with a double movement.

- **agree** Move the extended right index finger from touching the right side of the forehead downward to beside the extended left index finger, ending with both fingers pointing forward in front of the body, palms down.

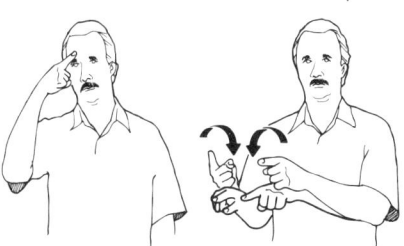

- **give**² Beginning with the fingers of both *flattened O hands* touching the chest, move the fingers forward in simultaneous arcs, ending with the palms up and fingers pointing forward.

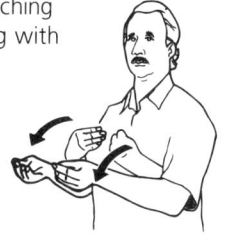

[sign continues]

111

deed of trust

- **hold** Move the right *S hand*, palm facing up, in a circular movement in front of the right side of the chest.

defalcation Misappropriation of funds held by a trustee.
- **cover-up** With the heel of the right *S hand* on the palm of the left *5 hand*, twist the right hand to the left.

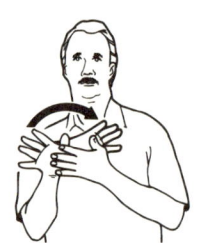

- **steal**[2] Beginning with the right *V hand*, palm facing up, in front of the chest, pull the hand deliberately back toward the chest while bending the fingers in tightly.

defamation The telling of a falsehood that is injurious to the reputation of a living individual.
- **lie** Move the index-finger side of the right *bent hand*, palm down and fingers pointing left, across the chin from right to left.

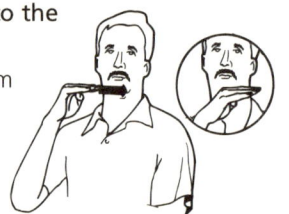

- **gossip** Move both *G hands*, palms facing each other, in a flat circular movement in front of the chest while pinching the index finger and thumb of each hand together with a repeated movement.

- **cruel** Beginning with the right *curved 5 hand* near the face and the left *curved 5 hand* in front of the body, close the right hand into an *A hand* while moving it quickly down and close the left hand into an *A hand* while moving it quickly up, brushing the knuckles of the hands together as they pass each other.

---- [sign continues] ---->

defect

- **name** Tap the middle-finger side of the right *H hand* across the index-finger side of the left *H hand* with a double movement.

default¹ Failure to fulfill a legal obligation.

- **fail** Beginning with the back of the right *V hand* on the heel of the left *open hand*, palm facing up, move the right hand across the left palm and off the fingers.

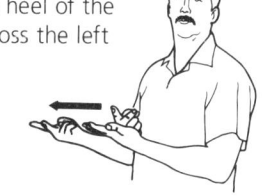

- **follow** With the knuckles of the right *10 hand*, palm facing left, near the wrist of the left *10 hand*, palm facing right, move both hands forward a short distance.

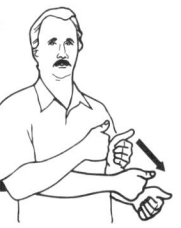

default² (alternate sign)

- **not-yet** Bend the wrist of the right *open hand*, palm back and fingers pointing down, back with a double movement near the right side of the waist.

- **do** Move both *C hands*, palms facing down, simultaneously back and forth in front of the body with a swinging movement.

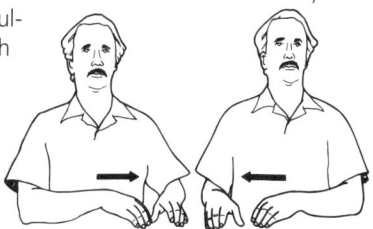

defect A flaw in design or manufacture that makes a product ineffective or dangerous.

- **accidental** With the middle fingers of the right *Y hand* against the chin, twist the hand with a deliberate movement.

113

defendant

defendant[1] The person against whom a lawsuit is brought. Same sign used for **guardian.**

- **protect** With the wrists of both *S hands* crossed in front of the chest, palms facing in opposite directions, move the hands forward with a short double movement.

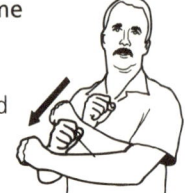

- **person marker** Move both *open hands*, palms facing each other, downward along the sides of the body.

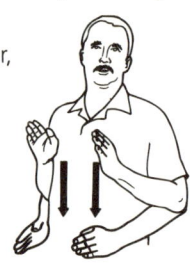

defendant[2] (alternate sign)

- **defend** With the wrists of both *D hands* crossed in front of the chest, palms facing in opposite directions, move the hands forward.

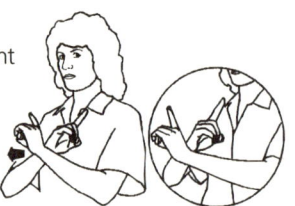

- **person marker** Move both *open hands*, palms facing each other, downward along the sides of the body.

defense The evidence and argument presented in opposition to a civil claim or criminal charge.

- **defend** With the wrists of both *D hands* crossed in front of the chest, palms facing in opposite directions, move the hands forward.

- Fingerspell: C-A-S-E

defraud See signs for FRAUD[1,2,3,4,5].

delinquent, juvenile delinquent, or youthful offender
A person who violates a criminal law, but is not yet old enough to be treated as an adult by the criminal justice system

- **young** Brush the little-finger sides of both *open hands*, palms up, upward with a small repeated movement on each side of the chest.

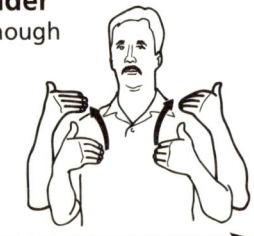

---- [sign continues] ---->

114

demand note

- **deviant** With the little-finger side of the right *open hand*, palm facing left, across the fingers of the left *open hand*, palm facing up, bend the right hand back toward the chest, ending with the palm facing in.

delivery The voluntary transfer of property or a piece of paper with the intent of completing a legal transaction.

- **don't-care** Beginning with the extended right index finger touching the nose, palm facing down, swing the hand forward by twisting the wrist.

- **give**[2] Beginning with the fingers of both *flattened O hands* touching the chest, move the fingers forward in simultaneous arcs, ending with the palms up and fingers pointing forward.

demand A call for someone to perform a legal obligation. See sign for MANDATORY. See sign for ORDER[1].

demand for relief See sign for PRAYER FOR RELIEF.

demand instrument See sign for DEMAND NOTE.

demand note, demand instrument, or **on demand** A negotiable instrument that does not specify a time for payment.

- **paper** Brush the heel of the right *open hand* with a double movement on the heel of the left *open hand*, palms facing each other.

- **order** Move the extended right index finger, palm forward and finger pointing up, from in front of the mouth forward and down, ending with the finger pointing forward and the palm down.

[sign continues]

115

demand note

- **pay**[2] Beginning with the right *flattened O hand* in front of the right side of the body, palm facing up, move the hand forward while quickly sliding the thumb off each finger.

demise or **death** The cessation of life when the brain, heart, and lungs stop functioning.

- **die** Beginning with both *open hands* in front of the body, right palm down and left palm up, flip the hands to the right, turning the right palm up and the left palm down.

demurer A motion or pleading in response to a complaint taking the position that the allegations contain no cause for legal action.

- **offer** Beginning with both *open hands* in front of each side of the body, palms up, move the hands upward and forward in simultaneous arcs.

- **pay**[2] Beginning with the right *flattened O hand* in front of the right side of the body, palm facing up, move the hand forward while quickly sliding the thumb off each finger.

- **not** Bring the thumb of the right *10 hand* forward from under the chin with a deliberate movement.

- **must** Move the bent index finger of the right *X hand* downward with a deliberate movement in front of the right side of the body by bending the wrist down.

depose

deny or **disclaim** To assert that a particular allegation is untrue.
- **deny** Beginning with the thumbs of both *A hands* under the chin, palms facing each other, move the hands forward with a deliberate movement.

dependent An individual who depends upon another for financial support.
- **depend** With the extended right index finger across the extended left index finger, palms facing down, move both fingers down slightly with a double movement.

- **person marker** Move both *open hands*, palms facing each other, downward along the sides of the body.

depose[1] To give a sworn statement or testimony. Related form: deposition.
- **testify** While holding the left *open hand* in front of the left side of the body, palm down and fingers pointing forward, move the right extended index finger from in front of the mouth, palm left, forward while opening to an *open hand*.

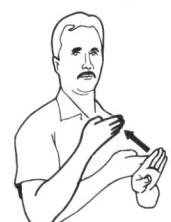

- **before** Beginning with the back of the right *open hand*, palm in and fingers pointing left, touching the back of the left *open hand*, palm forward, move the right hand in toward the chest.

- **court** Move both *F hands,* palms facing each other, up and down in front of each side of the chest with a repeated alternating movement.

117

depose

depose[2] (alternate sign)

- **sentences** Beginning with the thumbs and index fingers of both *F hands* touching in front of the chest, palms facing each other, with a double movement pull the hands apart to in front of each side of the chest.

- **before** Beginning with the back of the right *open hand*, palm in and fingers pointing left, touching the back of the left *open hand*, palm forward, move the right hand in toward the chest.

- **court** Move both *F hands*, palms facing each other, up and down in front of each side of the chest with a repeated alternating movement.

depreciation The gradual decrease in the value of tangible property that occurs because of wear and tear.

- **price** Tap the fingertips of both *F hands* together, palms facing each other, with a repeated movement.

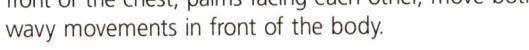

- **decline** Beginning with the thumbs of both *10 hands* pointing up in front of the chest, palms facing each other, move both hands down in wavy movements in front of the body.

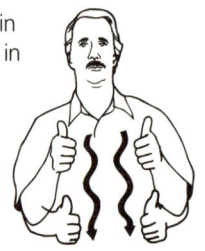

desertion The breaking off of living with one's spouse with the intent of not returning.

- **leave** Beginning with both *open hands* in front of the right side of the body, palms down, pull the hands upward toward the chest with a deliberate movement while closing into *10 hands*.

---- [sign continues] ---->

diligence

- **escape** Move the extended right index finger, palm left and finger pointing up, from between the index and middle fingers of the left *5 hand*, palm down in front of the chest, forward to the right with a deliberate movement.

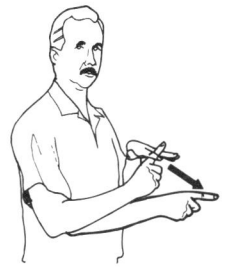

detain or **in custody** To keep a person in custody for a limited time for an official purpose.
- **jail**[3] Beginning with the right *curved 5 hand*, palm left, in front of the right side of the body, close the fingers into an *S hand*, and move it to the left under the downturned left *open hand*, held in front of the chest, fingers pointing right.

- **hold** Move the right *S hand,* palm facing up, in a circular movement in front of the right side of the chest.

determine, decree, disposition, or **judgment** To reach a decision on a matter.
- **decide** Move the extended right index finger from the right side of the forehead, palm left, down in front of the chest while changing into an *F hand*, ending with both *F hands* moving downward in front of the body, palms facing each other.

devise See signs for BEQUEATH[1,2].

diligence or **due diligence** Serious and persistent attention and effort. Same sign used for **hear ye.**
- **pay-attention** Move both *open hands* from near each cheek, palms facing each other, straight forward simultaneously.

119

diminished capacity

diminished capacity A mental condition that calls into question whether a defendant could have the necessary state of mind to commit a particular crime or is able to act on his or her own behalf.

- **mind** Tap the extended right index finger, palm facing in, against the right side of the forehead with a double movement.

- **decline** Beginning with both *10 hands* in front of each shoulder, palms facing in and thumbs pointing up, move both hands down in front of each side of the chest with wavy movements.

direct See sign for ORDER.

direct examination The questioning of a witness at a trial by the side that called the witness.

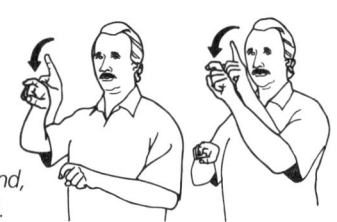

- **question**[2] Beginning with both extended index fingers pointing up in front of each side of the chest, palms facing forward, with an alternating movement move the right hand down while bending into an *X hand*, then the left hand down while bending into an *X hand*.

disability[1] or **handicap** A disease or injury that renders a person unable to do one's usual occupation, or a physical or mental condition making it impossible to hold gainful employment.

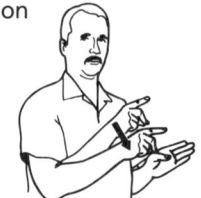

- **disability** Tap the fingertips of the right *D hand*, palm down, on the base of the thumb of the left *B hand*, palm right.

disability[2] (alternate sign)

- Fingerspell: D-A

disbar To take away an attorney's right to practice law because of unethical conduct.

- **law** Place the palm side of the right *L hand*, palm facing left, first on the fingers and then on the heel of the left *open hand*, palm facing right and fingers pointing up.

- **revoke-license** Beginning with the thumbs of both *L hands* touching in front of the chest, palms facing forward, twist the right hand down while keeping the thumb in place.

discovery

discharge To relieve one of an obligation. See signs for ACQUIT[1,2].

disclaim See sign for DENY.

disclosure[1] Documents and other information shared by either side as obtained during discovery.

- **list**[2] Touch the little-finger side of the right *bent hand* several times on the palm of the left *open hand*, palm right and fingers pointing up, as it moves from the fingers downward to the heel.

- **show** With the extended right index finger touching the palm of the left *open hand*, palm right and fingers pointing forward, move both hands forward a short distance.

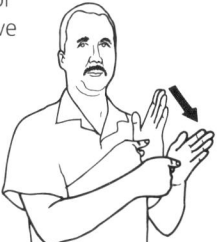

disclosure[2] (alternate sign)

- **put-down-put-down** Touch the fingertips of the right *flattened O hand*, palm down, to the palm of the left *open hand*, palm up. Then slap the palm of the right *open hand* against the left palm. Repeat.

discovery or **pretrial discovery** The set of procedures by which each side in a case may obtain pertinent information from the other.

- **information** Beginning with the fingertips of the right *flattened O hand* near the forehead and the left *flattened O hand* in front of the chest, move both hands forward while opening into *5 hands*, palms facing up.

- **exchange** Beginning with both *modified X hands* in front of the body, right hand somewhat forward of the left hand, move the right hand back toward the body in an upward arch while moving the left hand forward with a downward arc.

121

discredit

discredit To introduce evidence casting doubt upon the believability of a witness or authenticity of a document.

- **proof** Move the right *open hand* downward, ending with the back of the right hand on the palm of the left *open hand*, both palms facing up in front of the chest.

- **hold** Move the right *S hand*, palm facing up, in a circular movement in front of the right side of the chest.

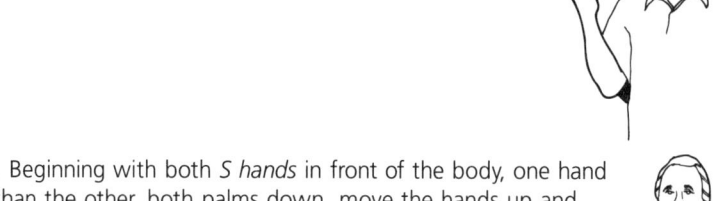

- **doubt** Beginning with both *S hands* in front of the body, one hand higher than the other, both palms down, move the hands up and down with a short alternating movement.

- **can** Simultaneously move both *S hands*, palms facing down, downward simultaneously movement in front of each side of the body.

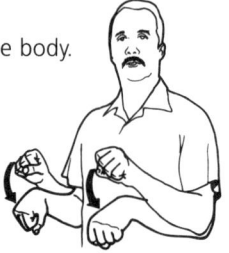

discretion The power to exercise one's own judgment in a matter and choose among various options in dealing with it.

- **think** Touch the right side of the forehead with the extended right index finger.

- **yourself** Push the thumb of the right *10 hand*, palm facing left, toward the person being talked to with a small double movement.

disorderly

discrimination Treating some people differently than others for reasons of group membership, such as race, sex, religion, or national origin.

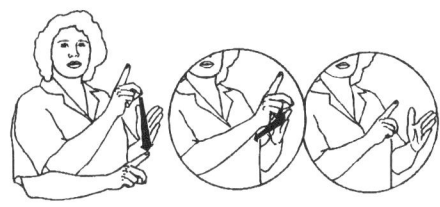

- **discriminate** With the extended index finger of the right *D hand*, draw a large X across the upturned left *open hand*.

disinterested Lacking in bias or interest in a case.

- **interest** Beginning with the right *modified C hand* in front of the nose, move the hand forward while pinching the thumb and index finger together.

- **none** Move both *O hands*, palms forward, from in front of the chest outward to each side.

dismissal An order or judgment in favor of a defendant throwing a case out of court without a trial or without completing a trial. See signs for ACQUIT[1,2]. Related form: **dismiss**.

disorderly[1], disorderly conduct, or disturbing the peace

A term used for such minor offenses such as public drunkenness, urinating in public, making too much noise, or other conduct that is disturbing to the public.

- **not** Bring the thumb of the right *10 hand* forward from under the chin with a deliberate movement.

- **right** With the index fingers of both hands extended forward at right angles, palms angled in and right hand above left, bring the little-finger side of the right hand sharply down across the thumb side of the left hand.

- **do** Move both *C hands*, palms facing down, simultaneously back and forth in front of the body with a swinging movement.

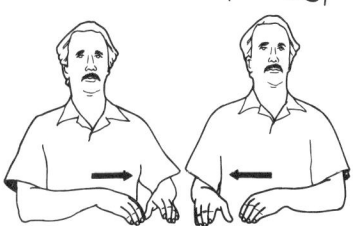

123

disorderly

disorderly[2], disorderly conduct, or disturbing the peace (alternate sign)

- **do** Move both *C hands*, palms facing down, simultaneously back and forth in front of the body with a swinging movement.

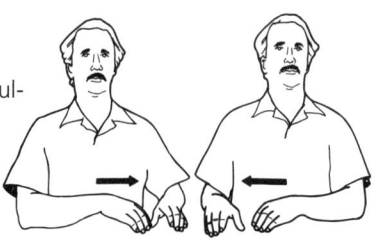

- **bother** Sharply tap the little-finger side of the right *open hand*, palm facing in at an angle, at the base of the thumb and index finger of the left *open hand*, with a double movement.

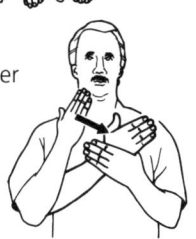

- **other** Beginning with the right *10 hand* in front of the chest, palm down, flip the hand over, ending with palm up.

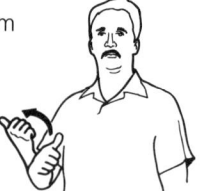

disorderly conduct See signs for DISORDERLY[1,2].

disposition[1] The final decisions as to the outcomes of a trial.

- **final** Bring the little finger of the right *I hand*, palm in, downward, striking the little finger of the left *I hand*, palm right, as it passes.

- **decide** Move the extended right index finger from the right side of the forehead, palm left, down in front of the chest while changing into an *F hand*, ending with both *F hands* moving downward in front of the body, palms facing each other.

disposition[2] See signs for DETERMINE, JUDGMENT.

dissent To declare formally that one disagrees with a course of action being taken by a body of which one is a member.

- **think** Touch the right side of the forehead with the extended right index finger.

---- [sign continues] ---------------------------→

distribution

- **opposite** Beginning with the fingertips of both extended index fingers touching in front of the chest, palms facing in, bring the hands straight apart to in front of each side of the chest.

dissolution The legal termination of a marriage whether by annulment or by divorce.

- **dissolve** Beginning with both *flattened O hands* in front of each side of the body, palms facing up, move the thumb of eacH hand smoothly across each fingertip, starting with the little fingers and ending as *10 hands* while moving the hands outward to each side.

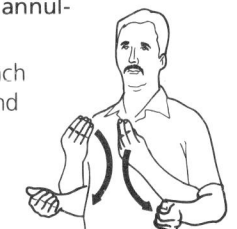

distinguish To recognize or point out differences between a previous case and a case currently under consideration that make it appropriate to reach a different result in the current case.

- **notice** Bring the curved index finger of the right *X hand* from touching the cheek near the right eye downward to touch the palm of the left *open hand*, palm right in front of the chest.

- **different** Beginning with both extended index fingers crossed in front of the chest, palms forward, bring the hands apart from each other with a deliberate movement.

distributee See sign for BENEFICIARY.

distribution The parceling out of the property in the estate of a person who died.

- **share-share** Move the little-finger side of the right *open hand*, palm facing in, back and forth with a double movement at the base of the index finger of the left *open hand*, palm facing in. Repeat sign in a different location.

125

district

district[1] Any geographic division established by a government for administrative convenience.

- **area**[1] Move the right 5 hand, palm facing down, in a flat circular movement near the right side of the body.

district[2] (alternate sign)

- **area**[2] Beginning with the thumbs of both A hands touching in front of the chest, palms facing down, move the hands apart in a backward circular movement until they touch again near the chest.

district attorney[1] The public official responsible for managing the prosecution of criminal offenses under state law in a particular locality.

- **government** Beginning with the extended right index finger pointing upward near the right side of the head, palm facing forward, twist the wrist to touch the finger to the right temple.

- **lawyer** Place the palm side of the right L hand, palm facing left, first on the fingers and then on the heel of the left open hand, palm facing right and fingers pointing up. Move both open hands, palms facing each other, downward along the sides of the body.

district attorney[2] (alternate sign)

- Fingerspell acronym: D-A

disturbing the peace See signs for DISORDERLY[1,2].

dividend A portion of the earnings and profits of a corporation distributed to the shareholders.

- **invest**[1] Beginning with the thumb of the right bent 3 hand on the palm of the left upturned open hand, move the right hand upward and forward in an arc.

---- [sign continues] ---->

docket

- **deposit** Beginning with the thumbs of both *10 hands* touching in front of the chest, both palms facing down, bring the hands downward and apart by twisting the wrists.

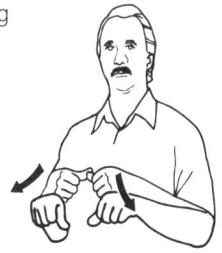

- **profit** Move the right *F hand*, palm facing down, downward with a double movement near the right side of the chest.

divorce[1] A legal declaration dissolving a marriage and releasing both spouses from all matrimonial obligations.

- **divorce**[1] Beginning with the fingertips of the both *D hands* touching in front of chest, palms facing each other and index fingers pointing up, swing the hands away from each other by twisting the wrists, ending with the hands in front of each side of the body, palms facing forward.

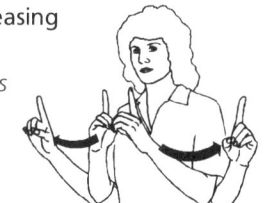

divorce[2] (alternate sign)

- **divorce**[2] Beginning with the right *curved hand*, palm facing down, clasping the left *curved hand*, palm facing up, bring the hands apart while opening into *5 hands*, fingers pointing up and palms forward.

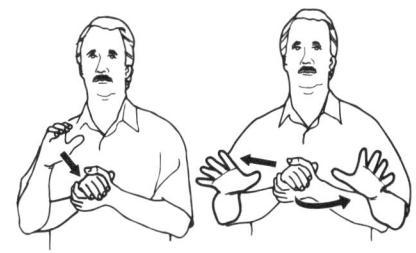

divorce[3] (alternate sign)

- **divorce**[3] With the fingertips of the right *flattened O hand*, pull upward from the base to the fingertip of the ring finger of the left *5 hand* and then move off to the right with a sudden movement while opening to a *5 hand*, palm down.

docket A court's calendar.

- **court** Move both *F hands*, palms facing each other, up and down in front of each side of the chest with a repeated alternating movement.

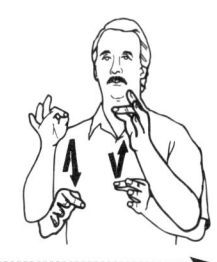

---- [sign continues] ---➤

127

docket

- **list**[2] Touch the little-finger side of the right *bent hand* several times on the palm of the left *open hand*, palm right and fingers pointing up, as it moves from the fingers downward to the heel.

- **name-name-name** As the hands move downward in front of the body, repeatedly tap the middle-finger side of the right *H hand* across the index-finger side of the left *H hand*.

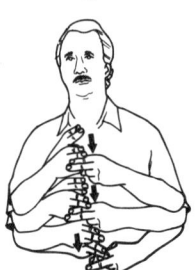

document[1] or **record** 1. A written piece of information in any form, including but not limited to a bill of sale, a deed, a passport, etc. 2. To record information. Same sign used for **for the record, of record.**

- **put-down-put-down** Touch the fingertips of the right *flattened O hand*, palm down, to the palm of the left *open hand*, palm up. Then slap the palm of the right *open hand* against the left palm. Repeat.

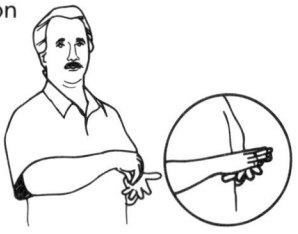

document[2] or **record** (alternate sign)

- **paper** Brush the heel of the right *open hand* with a double movement on the heel of the left *open hand*, palms facing each other.

- **put-down** Touch the fingertips of the right *flattened O hand*, palm down, to the palm of the left *open hand*, palm up. Then slap the palm of the right *open hand* against the left palm.

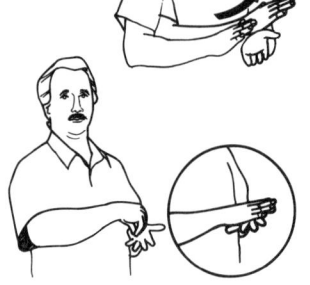

document[3] or **record** (alternate sign)

- **paper** Brush the heel of the right *open hand*, with a double movement on the heel of the left *open hand*, palms facing each other.

---- [sign continues] ---➤

domestic

- **rectangle** With both extended index fingers, palms down, trace a square in the air, beginning together in front of the chest, moving apart to each side, moving straight down, and then together again at the bottom.

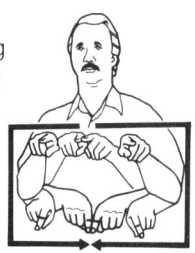

doing business Conducting the regular activities of a corporation within a particular state.

- **business** Brush the base of the right *B hand,* palm forward, with a repeated rocking movement on the back of the left *open hand,* palm down.

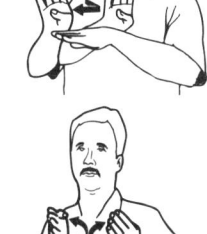

- **open** Beginning with the index-finger side of both *B hands* touching in front of the chest, palms facing forward and fingers angled up, twist both wrists while bringing the hands apart to in front of each side of the chest, ending with the palms facing in.

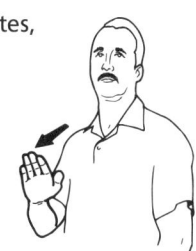

domestic[1] Pertaining to the internal workings of the United States, a particular state, or a family.

- Fingerspell acronym: U-S
- **your** Push the palm of the right *open hand,* palm forward and fingers pointing up, toward the person being talked to with a double movement.

domestic[2] (alternate sign)

- **state** Move the index-finger side of the right *S hand,* palm facing forward, down from the fingers to the heel of the left *open hand,* palm facing right and fingers pointing up, in front of the chest.

- **your** Push the palm of the right *open hand,* palm forward and fingers pointing up, toward the person being talked to with a double movement.

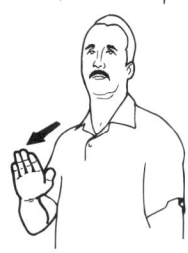

domestic

domestic[3] (alternate sign)

- **home** Touch the fingertips of the right *flattened O hand* first to the right side of the chin and then to the right cheek.

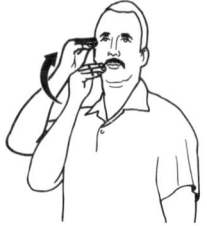

- **your** Push the palm of the right *open hand*, palm forward and fingers pointing up, toward the person being talked to with a double movement.

domestic partnership A committed relationship between two unmarried people. Same sign used for COHABIT, COMMON LAW MARRIAGE.

- **live** Move both *10 hands*, thumbs pointing up, upward on each side of the chest.

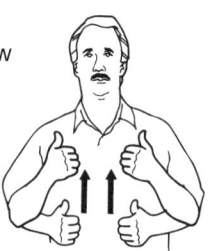

- **together** With the palm sides of both *A hands* together, move the hands forward with a short double movement.

- **marry** Bring the right *curved hand*, palm facing down, downward in front of the chest to clasp the left *curved hand*, palm facing up.

- **not** Bring the thumb of the right *10 hand* forward from under the chin with a deliberate movement. See signs for COHABIT[1,2].

double jeopardy

domestic relations See sign for FAMILY LAW.

domicile[1] **or residence** The place where one has one's permanent and primary home, or where a corporation has its headquarters.

- **home** Touch the fingertips of the right *flattened O hand* first to the right side of the chin and then to the right cheek.

domicile[2] **or residence** (alternate sign)

- **live** Move both *10 hands*, thumbs pointing up, upward on each side of the chest.

double jeopardy Being tried more than once for the same crime (prohibited by the Fifth Amendment).

- **court** Move both *F hands*, palms facing each other, up and down in front of each side of the chest with a repeated alternating movement.

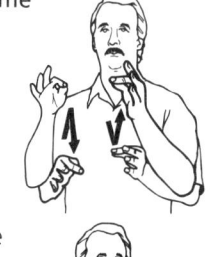

- **once** Beginning with the extended right index finger touching the palm of the left *open hand* held in front of the body, bring the right finger upward with a quick movement.

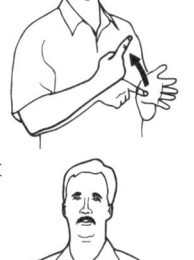

- **same** Move the right *Y hand*, palm down, from side to side in front of the body.

- **accuse** Push the little-finger side of the right *A hand*, palm facing left, forward across the back of the left *open hand*, palm facing down.

---- [sign continues] -->

131

double jeopardy

- **twice** Beginning with the middle finger of the right *2 hand* touching the left *open hand* held in front of the body, palm facing right and fingers pointing forward, bring the right hand upward with a quick movement while twisting the right wrist in, ending with the palm facing in.

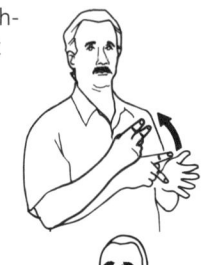

- **can't** Bring the extended index finger of the right *one hand* downward, hitting the extended index finger of the left *one hand* as it moves.

draft An instrument by which one person orders another to pay a specified sum of money to the order of someone else.
- **order** Move the extended right index finger, palm forward and finger pointing up, from in front of the mouth forward and down, ending with the finger pointing forward and the palm down.

- **pay**² Beginning with the right *flattened O hand* in front of the right side of the body, palm facing up, move the hand forward while quickly sliding the thumb off each finger.

draw up¹ To prepare a legal instrument.
- **type** While wiggling the fingers of both *5 hands*, palms down, move the hands in an alternating up and down movement.

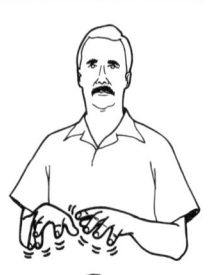

- **paper** Brush the heel of the right *open hand* with a double movement on the heel of the left *open hand*, palms facing each other.

draw up² See sign for MAKE.

due care

driving while intoxicated[1], DWI, or **drunk driving** The offense of driving a motor vehicle while intoxicated by alcohol or other drugs that impair driving ability.

- **drive** Beginning with both *S hands* in front of the chest, palms facing in, move the hands forward with a deliberate movement.

- **during** Extend both index fingers in front of each side of the body, palms down, then move them forward and upward in parallel arcs.

- **intoxicated** Move the thumb of the right *10 hand*, palm facing left, in an arc from right to left past the chin.

driving while intoxicated[2], DWI, or **drunk driving** (alternate sign)
- Fingerspell acronym: D-W-I

driving while intoxicated[3], DWI, or **drunk driving** (alternate sign)
- Fingerspell acronym for *driving under the influence*: D-U-I

drug[1] A substance intended to affect the function of the body for the purpose of diagnosis, treatment, or prevention of disease.
- Fingerspell: D-R-U-G

drug[2] (alternate sign)
- **medicine** With the bent middle finger of the right *5 hand*, palm facing down, in the palm of the left *open hand*, rock the right hand from side to side with a double movement while keeping the middle finger in place.

drunk driving See signs for DRIVING WHILE INTOXICATED[1,2,3].

due care See sign for CARE.

133

due demand

due demand A formal demand made before taking legal action.

- **order** Move the extended right index finger, palm forward and finger pointing up, from in front of the mouth forward and down, ending with the finger pointing forward and the palm down.

- **pay-me** Move the right *flattened O hand*, palm facing up, back toward the body while quickly sliding the thumb off each finger.

due diligence See sign for DILIGENCE.

due process Fair administration of law in accordance with established procedures and with due regard for fundamental rights.

- **law** Place the palm side of the right *L hand*, palm facing left, first on the fingers and then on the heel of the left *open hand*, palm facing right and fingers pointing up.

- **follow** With the knuckles of the right *10 hand*, palm facing left, near the wrist of the left *10 hand*, palm facing right, move both hands forward a short distance.

durable power of attorney An instrument by which an individual confers upon another the power to perform specific acts in his or her behalf even if the individual becomes competent.

- **give-power** Beginning with the fingertips of the right *bent 5 hand* touching the left upper arm, twist the wrist and move the right hand forward, ending with the palm forward.

- **continue** Beginning with the thumb of the right *10 hand* on the thumbnail of the left *10 hand*, both palms facing down in front of the chest, move the hands downward and forward in an arc.

134

DWI

duress The use of force to induce someone to do something that he or she otherwise would not do. See sign for UNDUE INFLUENCE.

duties See sign for CUSTOMS.

duty[1] or obligation Legal obligation.

- **law** Place the palm side of the right *L hand*, palm facing left, first on the fingers and then on the heel of the left *open hand*, palm facing right and fingers pointing up.

- **burden** With the fingertips of both bent hands on the right shoulder, push the shoulder down slightly.

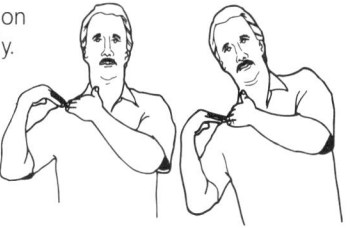

duty[2], import tax, or **export tax** A tax on imports or exports.
- Fingerspell: T-A-X

DWI See signs for DRIVING WHILE INTOXICATED[1,2,3].

135

earned income Income gained from working for another or in one's own business.
- **work** Tap the heel of the right *S hand*, palm forward, with a double movement on the back of the left *S hand* held in front of the body, palm down.

- **money** Tap the back of the right *flattened O hand*, palm facing up, with a double movement against the palm of the left *open hand*, palm facing up. Repeat sign in another location.

- **earn** Bring the little-finger side of the right *curved hand*, palm facing left, across the upturned left *open hand* from fingertips to heel while changing into an *S hand*.

easement An interest in land belonging to another, consisting of a right to use it or control its use for some purpose, but not to take anything from it or possess it.
- **land** Beginning with both *flattened O hands* in front of each side of the body, palms facing up, move the thumb of both hands smoothly with a double movement across each fingertip, starting with the little fingers and ending as *A hands* each time.

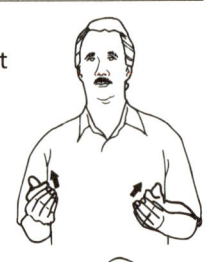

- **allow** Beginning with both *open hands* in front of the waist, palms facing each other and fingers pointing down, bring the fingers forward and upward by bending the wrists.

---- [sign continues] ---->

elective share

- **use** With the heel of the right *U hand* on the back of the left *S hand*, move the right hand in a small circle.

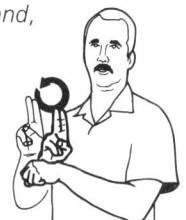

eavesdropping The act of listening in on conversations or activities of others without their knowledge.

- **quiet** Bring the thumb side of the right *one hand*, palm left, back firmly against the lips.

- **eavesdrop** Bring the thumb of the right *bent 3 hand* to the right ear, palm facing forward, bend the middle and index fingers up and down with a double movement.

elect[1] To make a choice in a situation where there are two permissible alternatives but only one is to be selected. Related form: **election**.

- **appoint**[1] Beginning with the thumb side of the right *G hand*, palm facing down and fingers pointing forward, near the extended left index finger, palm facing forward and fingers pointing up, pull the right hand in toward the chest while pinching the index finger and thumb together.

elect[2] (alternate sign)

- **appoint**[2] Beginning with the thumb side of the right *G hand*, palm facing down and fingers pointing forward, against the left *open hand*, palm facing right and fingers pointing up, pull the right hand in toward the chest while pinching the index finger and thumb together.

elective share The share of and the state that the surviving spouse is entitled to under state law when a married person dies and leaves a will.

- Fingerspell: W-I-L-L
- **give-me**[2] Beginning with both *X hands* in front of the body, palms facing each other, bring the hands back to touch on each side of the chest.

137

embezzlement

embezzlement The crime of converting to one's own use property of another that is unlawfully within one's possession.

- **steal¹-steal¹** Beginning with the index-finger side of the right *V hand*, palm facing down, on the elbow of the bent left arm, held at an upward angle across the chest, with a double movement pull the right hand upward toward the left wrist while bending the fingers in tightly each time.

encumbrance Any interest, right, or obligation with respect to property that reduces the value of the property owner's title.

- Fingerspell: T-I-T-L-E

- **only** Beginning with the extended right index finger pointing up in front of the right shoulder, palm facing forward, twist the wrist in, ending with the palm facing in near the right side of the chest.

- **name** Tap the middle-finger side of the right *H hand* across the index-finger side of the left *H hand* with a double movement.

- **not** Bring the thumb of the right *10 hand* forward from under the chin with a deliberate movement.

endorse¹ To express approval or support of a person or issue, especially in the political arena.

- **support** Push the knuckles of the right *S hand* upward under the little-finger side of the left *S hand*, both palms in, pushing the left hand upward a short distance in front of the chest.

endorse² To designate oneself as a payee by signing one's name, usually on the back.

- **endorse** Beginning with the left *open hand*, palm up, in front of the body, flip the left hand over, ending with the palm down.

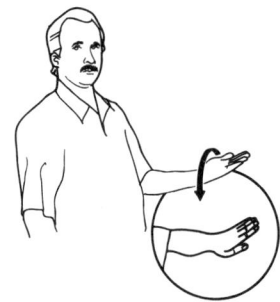

enticement

enjoin[1] To forbid by court order. Same sign used for **abate**.
- **stop** Hit the little-finger side of the right *open hand* on the palm of the left *open hand*.

enjoin[2] (alternate sign)
- **forbid** Hit the palm side of the right *L hand*, palm left, sharply on the palm of the left *open hand*, palm right.

enjoin[3] (alternate sign)
- **prevent** With the little-finger side of the right *B hand*, palm facing down, against the index-finger side of the left *B hand*, palm facing right, move the hands forward a short distance.

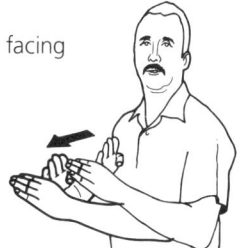

enjoy To possess or exercise a right or interest. See sign for POSSESSION.

enlarge To extend a procedural time limit.
- **extend** Beginning with the fingertips of both *F hands* together in front of the chest, palms facing each other, move the right hand forward.

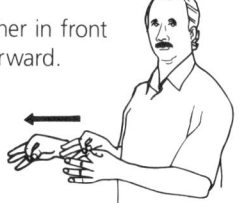

enter To place formally in the court record adding to the court file. See sign for FILE.

enticement **1.** The crime of luring a child into a secluded place without force for sexual purposes. **2.** The use of deceptive means to excite a desire in a person for a promised reward. Related form: **entice**.
- **entice** Beginning with both *modified X hands* in front of the chest, right hand more forward than the left, pull the hands back toward the chest with a circular movement over each other.

 [sign continues]

enticement

- **fool** Strike the knuckles of the right *A hand*, palm facing forward, against the extended left index finger with a double movement.

---

entitlement Legislatively created right or benefit that, once granted to a person, cannot be taken away without a fair hearing.

- **law** Place the palm side of the right *L hand*, palm facing left, first on the fingers and then on the heel of the left *open hand*, palm facing right and fingers pointing up.

- **give**² Beginning with both *flattened O hands* in front of the body, palms facing up, move the hands forward in simultaneous arcs.

---

entrapment¹ The planning of a crime by law officers and their procuring of its enactment by a person who would not have done it except for the trickery of the officers.

- **police** Tap the thumb side of the right *modified C hand*, palm facing left, against the left side of the chest with a double movement.

- **cover-up** With the heel of the right *S hand* on the palm of the left *5 hand*, twist the right hand to the left.

- **fool** Strike the knuckles of the right *A hand*, palm facing forward, against the extended left index finger with a deliberate movement.

---- [sign continues] ---------->

equal protection

- **arrest** Move the right *C hand* from in front of the right side of the chest, palm facing left, to the left to close around the extended left index finger held up in front of the chest, palm facing right.

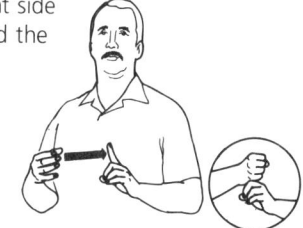

entrapment[2] (alternate sign)

- **police** Tap the thumb side of the right *modified C hand*, palm facing left, against the left side of the chest with a double movement.

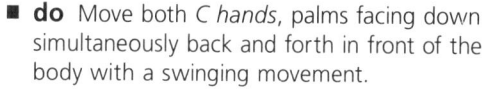

- **secret** Tap the thumb side of the right *A hand*, palm left, against the mouth with a repeated movement.

- **do** Move both *C hands*, palms facing down, simultaneously back and forth in front of the body with a swinging movement.

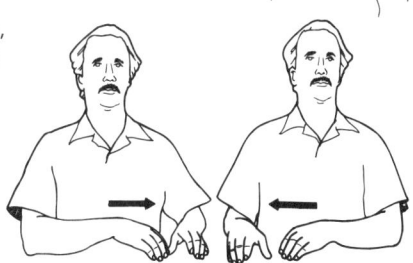

- **nab** Move the fingers of the right *V hand*, palm down, around the extended left index finger held up in front of the chest with a deliberate movement.

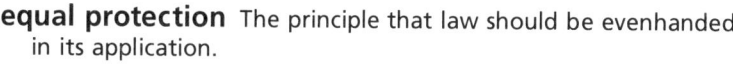

equal protection The principle that law should be evenhanded in its application.

- **protect** With the wrists of both *S hands* crossed in front of the chest, palms facing in opposite directions, move the hands forward with a short double movement.

---- [sign continues] ----

equal protection

- **fair-fair** Tap the fingertips of both *bent hands,* palms facing down, together with a repeated movement as the hands move in an arc in front of the chest.

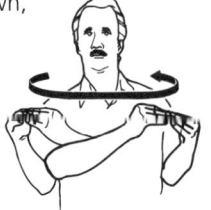

equitable Fair.

- **fair** Beginning with the fingertips of both *bent hands* together, palms facing down, bring the hands apart a short distance.

equitable distribution[1] A method in a divorce case of dividing the property acquired by the couple during their marriage.

- **fair** Beginning with the fingertips of both *bent hands* together, palms facing down, bring the hands apart a short distance.

- **share-share** Move the little-finger side of the right *open hand,* palm facing in, back and forth with a repeated movement at the base of the index finger of the left *open hand,* palm facing in, as the hands move in an arc in front of the body.

equitable distribution[2] (alternate sign)

- **fair** Beginning with the fingertips of both *bent hands* together, palms facing down, bring the hands apart a short distance.

- **donate** Beginning with the right *X hand* in front of the right shoulder and the left *X hand* in front of the left side of the body, palms facing in opposite directions, move the right hand downward in an arc and the left hand upward with a double alternating movement.

estate

equity The net value of an owner's interest in property.
- **myself** Bring the thumb side of the right *A hand*, palm left, against the chest with a double movement.
- **money** Tap the back of the right *flattened O hand*, palm facing up, with a double movement against the palm of the left *open hand*, palm facing up.
- **price** Tap the fingertips of both *F hands* together, palms facing each other, with a repeated movement.

escrow Money deposited with a third party for delivery upon the fulfillment of some condition.
- **money** Tap the back of the right *flattened O hand*, palm facing up, with a double movement against the palm of the left *open hand*, palm facing up.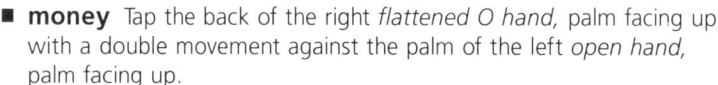
- **hold** Move the right *S hand*, palm facing up, in a circular movement in front of the right side of the chest.

estate[1] An aggregate of money and property administered as a unit.
- **money** Tap the back of the right *flattened O hand*, palm facing up, with a double movement against the palm of the left *open hand*, palm facing up.

---- [sign continues] ---→

estate

- **land** Beginning with both *flattened O hands* in front of each side of the body, palms facing up, move the thumb of both hands smoothly with a double movement across each fingertip, starting with the little fingers and ending as *A hands* each time.

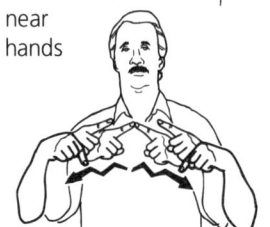

- **and-so-forth** Beginning with both extended index fingers near each other in front of the body, both palms down, bring the hands apart while bending the fingers up and down with a quick repeated movement.

estate[2] (alternate sign)
- Fingerspell: E-S-T-A-T-E

estate in fee See sign for FEE[2].

estate tax or inheritance tax
A tax imposed on large estates left by decedents, based on the value of the estate and required to be paid by estate funds before the estate is distributed to heirs.
- Fingerspell: E-S-T-A-T-E T-A-X

estimated tax
An advance on income taxes that must be paid quarterly by taxpayers whose withholding will not cover their tax liability for the year.
- Fingerspell: T-A-X
- **3-months** Bring the right *3 hand*, palm in, down in a repeated movement near the extended left index finger, palm right.

- **pay**[1] Beginning with the extended right index finger touching the palm of the left *open hand*, palms facing each other, move the right finger forward and off the left fingertips.

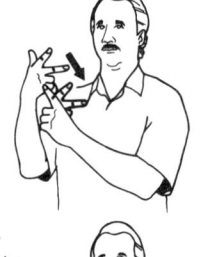

- **must** Move the bent index finger of the right *X hand* downward with a deliberate movement in front of the right side of the body by bending the wrist down.

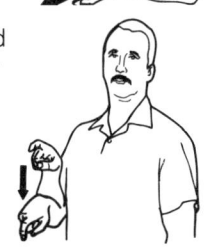

eviction

et al. *Latin.* Used primarily as a stand-in for the names of all parties except the first on each side of the case on court papers.

- **name-name-name** As the hands move downward in front of the body, repeatedly tap the middle-finger side of the right *H hand* across the index-finger side of the left *H hand*.

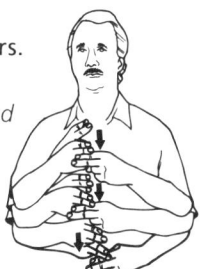

ethics¹ Standards of honesty and fairness in the conduct of a business or profession.
- Fingerspell: E-T-H-I-C-S

ethics² (*alternate sign*)

- **honest²** Slide the extended fingers of the right *H hand*, palm in and fingers pointing up, from the heel to the fingers of the upturned left *open hand*, palm right and fingers pointing up.

eviction¹ A landlord's exclusion of a tenant from possession of leased premises either by legal proceedings or by personal action.

- **kick-out** Bring the right *B hand* in front of the right side of the body, palm facing left and fingers angled down, upward to strike the index-finger side of the right hand against the little-finger side of the left *B hand* held in front of the body, palm facing in and fingers pointing right.

eviction² (*alternate sign*)

- **force** Beginning with the right *C hand* in front of the right shoulder, palm forward, and the left arm bent across the body, move the right hand downward and forward, ending with the right wrist across the left wrist, both palms down.

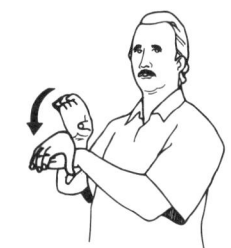

- **leave** Beginning with both *open hands* in front of the right side of the body, palms down, pull the hands upward toward the chest with a deliberate movement while closing into *10 hands*.

evidence

evidence[1] Information pertaining to a case, especially the testimony offered at trial for the judge or jury to consider. Same sign used for **authority, proof**.

- **proof** Move the right *open hand* downward, ending with the back of the right hand on the palm of the left *open hand*, both palms facing up in front of the chest.

evidence[2] (alternate sign)

- **evidence** Bring the right *E hand* from near the right eye downward to land in the left *open hand* held in front of the body, ending with both palms up.

ex officio *Latin*. Used to describe a position or power that comes automatically with a particular office.

- **include** Swing the right *5 hand*, palm down, in a circular movement over the left *S hand*, palm in, while changing into a *flattened O hand*, ending with the fingertips of the right hand inserted in the center of the thumb side of the left hand.

- **vote** Insert the fingertips of the right *F hand*, palm down, in the opening of the left *S hand*, palm right.

- **can't** Bring the extended index finger of the right *one hand* downward, hitting the extended index finger of the left *one hand* as it moves.

ex post facto *Latin*. After the fact.

- **happen** Beginning with both extended index fingers in front of the body, palms facing up and fingers pointing forward, flip the hands over toward each other, ending with the palms facing down.

---- [sign continues] -->

exclusion

- **after** Beginning with the palm of the right *bent hand* touching the back of the fingers of the left *open hand,* both palms facing in, slowly move the right hand forward a short distance.

exception A formal objection to a judge's overruling of an objection or denial of a motion at a trial.

- **formal** Move the thumb of the right *5 hand,* palm facing left, upward and forward in a double circular movement in the center of the chest.

- **complain** Tap the fingertips of the right *curved 5 hand* against the center of the chest.

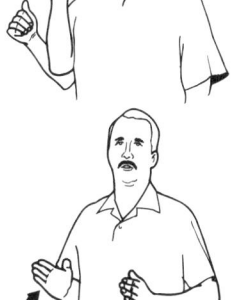

exclusion[1] A judge's refusal to allow evidence to be considered in a case.

- **refuse** Beginning with the right *10 hand* in front of the right shoulder, push the thumb back over the right shoulder.

- **allow** Beginning with both *open hands* in front of the waist, palms facing each other and fingers pointing down, bring the fingers forward and upward by bending the wrists.

exclusion[2] (alternate sign)

- **proof** Move the right *open hand* downward, ending with the back of the right hand on the palm of the left *open hand,* both palms facing up in front of the chest.

[sign continues]

147

exclusion

- **delete** Beginning with the index finger of the right *modified X hand*, palm in, touching the extended left index finger held up in front of the chest, palm right and finger pointing up, move the right hand upward to the right while flicking the thumb upward.

exculpatory statement A statement that, if true, tends to exonerate a suspect.

- **story** Bring the thumb and index finger of each *5 hand* to intersect with the other hand, palms facing each other, forming *F hands*. Then pull the hands apart to in front of each side of the chest. Repeat.

- **happen** Beginning with both extended index fingers in front of the body, palms facing up and fingers pointing forward, flip the hands over toward each other, ending with the palms facing down.

- **true** Beginning with the thumb side of the right *one hand* in front of the mouth, palm left, move the extended index finger forward.

- **person** Move both *P hands*, palms facing each other, downward along the sides of the body.

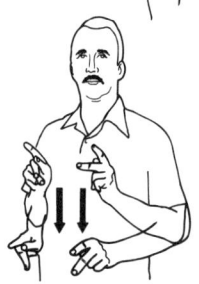

- **excuse** Wipe the fingertips of the right *open hand* across the upturned left *open hand* from the heel off the fingertips.

executive clemency

execute[1] To sign a legal instrument such as a deed, will, or contract.

- **sign** Place the extended fingers of the right *H hand*, palm down, firmly down on the upturned palm of the left *open hand* held in front of the chest.

- **do** Move both *C hands*, palms facing down, simultaneously back and forth in front of the body with a swinging movement. See signs for MAKE[1,2].

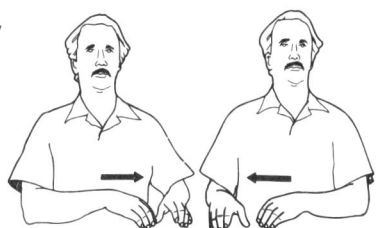

execute[2] (alternate sign)

- **sign** Place the extended fingers of the right *H hand*, palm down, firmly down on the upturned palm of the left *open hand* held in front of the chest.

- **start** Beginning with the extended right index finger, palm down, inserted between the index and middle fingers of the left *open hand*, palm right and fingers pointing forward, twist the right hand back, ending with palm in.

execute[3] To put a person to death pursuant to death sentence.

- **order** Move the extended right index finger, palm forward and finger pointing up, from in front of the mouth forward and down, ending with the finger pointing forward and the palm down.

- **kill** Push the side of the extended right index finger, palm down, across the palm of the left *open hand*, palm right, with a deliberate movement.

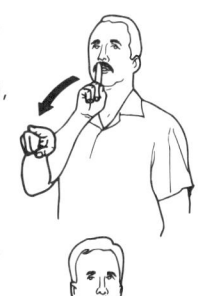

executive clemency See sign for CLEMENCY.

149

executive order

executive order An order issued by the president or a state governor on a matter having the force of law.

- **government** Beginning with the extended right index finger pointing upward near the right side of the head, palm facing forward, twist the wrist to touch the finger to the right temple.

- **order** Move the extended right index finger, palm forward and finger pointing up, from in front of the mouth forward and down, ending with the finger pointing forward and the palm down.

executive privilege The right of the president to refuse to disclose confidential communications within the executive branch.

- **president** Beginning with the index-finger sides of both C hands near each side of the forehead, palms facing forward, move the hands outward to above each shoulder while closing into S hands.

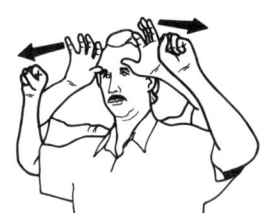

- **secret** Tap the thumb side of the right A hand, palm left, against the mouth with a repeated movement.

- **can** Move both S hands, palms facing down, downward simultaneously in front of each side of the body.

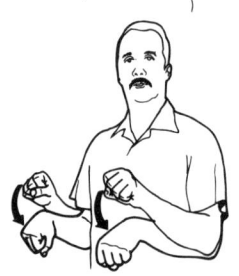

executor See sign for ADMINISTRATOR.

exhibit A document or object used as evidence at a trial.

- **proof** Move the right open hand downward, ending with the back of the right hand on the palm of the left open hand, both palms facing up in front of the chest.

---- [sign continues] -->

extradition

- **show** With the extended right index finger touching the palm of the left *open hand*, palm right and fingers pointing forward, move both hands forward a short distance.

expert witness A witness qualified by education or experience to testify about or to render opinions on specialized subjects.

- **specialty** Slide the little-finger side of the right *B hand*, palm left and fingers pointing forward, along the index-finger side of the left *B hand* held in front of the chest, palm right and fingers pointing forward.

- **skill** Grasp the little-finger side of the left *open hand* with the curved right fingers. Then pull the right hand forward and downward while closing the fingers into the palm.

- **testify** While holding the left *open hand* in front of the left side of the body, palm down and fingers pointing forward, move the right extended index finger from in front of the mouth, palm left, forward while opening to an *open hand*.

export tax See sign for DUTY².

extortion See sign for BLACKMAIL.

extradition The handing over by one state or country to another a suspect wanted for criminal prosecution in the second state.

- **police** Tap the thumb side of the right *modified C hand*, palm facing left, against the left side of the chest with a double movement.

- **other** Beginning with the right *10 hand* in front of the chest, palm down, flip the hand over, ending with palm up.

[sign continues]

151

extradition

- **grab** Beginning with the right *curved 5 hand* in front of the right shoulder, move the hand forward and down while closing into an *S hand*.

eyewitness A person who saw an event under discussion.

- **witness** With the index finger of the right *X hand* pull down slightly on the cheek near the outside corner of the right eye.

- **proof** Move the right *open hand* downward, ending with the back of the right hand on the palm of the left *open hand*, both palms facing up in front of the chest.

- **person** Move both *P hands*, palms facing each other, downward along the sides of the body.

face amount See sign for FACE VALUE.

face value or face amount The sum shown on the face of an instrument; the principal amount of an obligation.

- owe With a double movement, tap the extended right index finger against the palm of the left *open hand*, palm facing right.

- how-much Beginning with the right *S hand* in front of the right side of the chest, palm facing up, flick the fingers open quickly into a *5 hand*.

fact An event or circumstance. Same sign used for **real evidence**.

- true Beginning with the thumb side of the right *one hand* in front of the mouth, palm left, move the extended index finger forward.

- proof Move the right *open hand* downward, ending with the back of the right hand on the palm of the left *open hand*, both palms facing up in front of the chest.

factfinder The persons charged with deciding the factual issues in a proceeding. See signs for JUDGE[1,2].

153

failure to prosecute

failure to prosecute The failure of the plaintiff or prosecutor to pursue the case diligently once it has commenced.

- **accuse** Push the little-finger side of the right *A hand*, palm facing left, forward across the back of the left *open hand*, palm facing down.

- **person** Move both *P hands*, palms facing each other, downward along the sides of the body.

- **not** Bring the thumb of the right *10 hand* forward from under the chin with a deliberate movement.

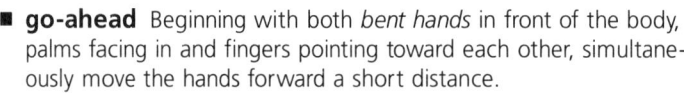

- **go-ahead** Beginning with both *bent hands* in front of the body, palms facing in and fingers pointing toward each other, simultaneously move the hands forward a short distance.

fair market value[1] or **market value** The price that a purchaser would pay and a seller would accept for a particular item in an open market.

- **value** Beginning with the index fingers of both *V hands* touching in front of the chest, palms facing each other, bring the hands outward in a circular movement, ending with the middle fingers of the *V hands* touching.

fair market value[2] or **market value** (alternate sign)

- **price** Tap the fingertips of both *F hands* together, palms facing each other, with a repeated movement.

false advertising

fair use Reasonable and limited use of a copyrighted work without permission of the owner.

- **rights** Slide the little-finger side of the right *open hand*, palm facing left, in an upward arc across the upturned left palm held in front of the body.

- **use** With the heel of the right *U hand* on the back of the left *S hand*, move the right hand in a small circle.

- **can** Move both *S hands*, palms facing down, downward simultaneously in front of each side of the body.

false advertising[1] or **bait and switch** Advertising that is materially misleading about the nature, quality, or price of a product.

- **advertise** Beginning with the thumb side of the right *S hand*, palm facing left, against the little-finger side of the left *S hand*, palm facing right, move the right hand forward and back with a double movement opening to a *5 hand* each time.

- **true** Beginning with the thumb side of the right *one hand* in front of the mouth, palm left, move the extended index finger forward.

- **not** Bring the thumb of the right *10 hand* forward from under the chin with a deliberate movement.

155

false advertising

false advertising[2] or bait and switch (alternate sign)

- **advertise** Beginning with the thumb side of the right *S hand*, palm facing left, against the little-finger side of the left *S hand*, palm facing right, move the right hand forward and back with a double movement.

- **lie** Move the index-finger side of the right *bent hand*, palm down and fingers pointing left, across the chin from right to left.

false arrest or false imprisonment Restricting a person to a particular area without legal justification.

- **jail**[3] Beginning with the right *curved 5 hand*, palm left, in front of the right side of the body, close the fingers into an *S hand*, and move it to the left under the downturned left *open hand*, held in front of the chest, fingers pointing right.

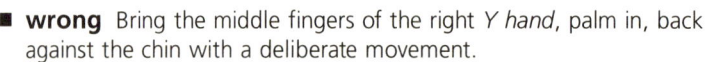

- **wrong** Bring the middle fingers of the right *Y hand*, palm in, back against the chin with a deliberate movement.

false imprisonment See sign for FALSE ARREST.

false pretenses The crime of obtaining personal property by means of false representations.

- **fool** Strike the knuckles of the right *A hand*, palm facing forward, against the extended left index finger with a double movement.

- **grab** Beginning with the right *curved 5 hand* in front of the right shoulder, palm facing left, move the hand forward and down while closing into an *S hand*.

fault

family law or **domestic relations** The area of law dealing with marriage, divorce, adoption, custody, and support of children.

- **law** Place the palm side of the right *L hand*, palm facing left, first on the fingers and then on the heel of the left *open hand*, palm facing right and fingers pointing up.

- **direct-to** Move the fingertips of the right *B hand*, palm left, against the extended left index finger, palm right.

- **family** Beginning with the fingertips of both *F hands* touching in front of the chest, palms facing forward, bring the hands away from each other in outward arcs while turning the palms in, ending with the little fingers touching.

fatal Describing an error that renders a legal activity invalid.

- **accidental** With the middle fingers of the right *Y hand* against the chin, twist the hand with a deliberate movement.

- **cruel** Beginning with the right *curved 5 hand* near the face and the left *curved 5 hand* in front of the body, close the right hand into an *A hand* while moving it quickly down and close the left hand into an *A hand* while moving it quickly up, brushing the knuckles of the hands together as they pass each other.

fault The doing of something that provides the basis for criminal action.

- **burden** With the fingertips of both *bent hands* on the right shoulder, push the shoulder down slightly.

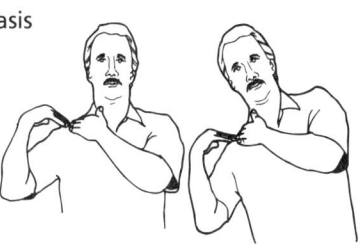

157

federal

federal Relating to the government of the United States.
- **federal** Beginning with the right *F hand* near the right side of the head, palm facing forward, twist the wrist forward and bring the fingertips against the right temple. See sign for GOVERNMENT.

federal law[1] A law adopted by the government that is uniformly applicable throughout the country.
- **federal** Beginning with the right *F hand* near the right side of the head, palm facing forward, twist the wrist forward and bring the fingertips against the right temple.

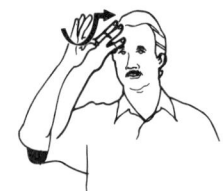

- **law** Place the palm side of the right *L hand*, palm facing left, first on the fingers and then on the heel of the left *open hand*, palm facing right and fingers pointing up.

fee[1] Compensation for services rendered.
- **cost** Strike the knuckle of the right *X hand*, palm facing in, down on the palm of the left *open hand*, palm facing right and fingers pointing forward.

- **how much** Beginning with the right *S hand* in front of the right side of the chest, palm facing up, flick the fingers open quickly into a *5 hand*.

fee[2]**, estate in fee,** or **fee estate** An interest in real estate for an indefinite duration.
- **land** Beginning with both *flattened O hands* in front of each side of the body, palms facing up, move the thumb of both hands smoothly with a double movement across each fingertip, starting with the little fingers and ending as *A hands* each time.

---- [sign continues] ---->

fee simple

- **include** Swing the right *5 hand*, palm down, in a circular movement over the left *S hand*, palm in, while changing into a *flattened O hand*, ending with the fingertips of the right hand inserted in the center of the thumb side of the left hand.

fee estate See sign for FEE².

fee simple An interest in real estate that is inheritable without limitation by any heir.

- **land** Beginning with both *flattened O hands* in front of each side of the body, palms facing up, move the thumb of both hands smoothly with a double movement across each fingertip, starting with the little fingers and ending as *A hands* each time.

- **pass-down** Beginning with both *flattened O hands* in front of the right shoulder, palms facing in and right hand above the left hand, roll the hands forward over each other with an alternating movement.

- **inherit** With the right *curved hand* over the left *curved hand*, palms facing each other, move the hands forward a short distance.

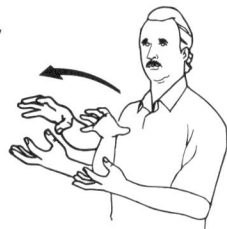

- **include** Swing the right *5 hand*, palm down, in a circular movement over the left *S hand*, palm in, while changing into a *flattened O hand*, ending with the fingertips of the right hand inserted in the center of the thumb side of the left hand.

- **can** Move both *S hands,* palms facing down, downward simultaneously in front of each side of the body.

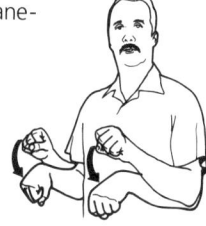

felon

felon or **prisoner** A person who commits a felony crime.

- **jail**[1] Bring the back of the right *4 hand* from near the chest forward with a double movement while bringing the left *4 hand* in to meet the right hand, ending with the fingers crossed at an angle, both palms facing in.

- **person marker** Move both *open hands*, palms facing each other, downward along the sides of the body.

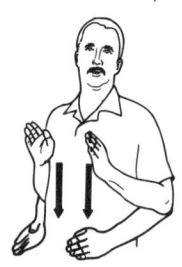

felony[1] A serious crime, defined as one punishable by death or imprisonment of more than one year.

- Fingerspell: F-E-L-O-N-Y
- **crime** Place the palm side of the right *L hand*, palm facing left, first on the fingers and then on the heel of the left *open hand*, palm facing right and fingers pointing up. Then beginning with both *S hands* in front of the body, index fingers touching and palms down, move the hands away from each other while twisting the wrists with a deliberate movement, ending with the palms facing each other.

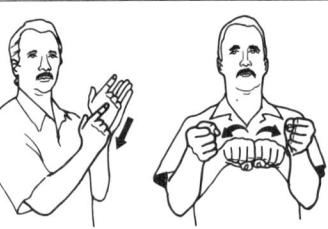

- **worse** Brush the back of the right *V hand* across the index-finger side of the left *V hand*, both palms facing in, as the hands cross with a double movement in front of the chest.

felony[2] (alternate sign)

- **crime** Place the palm side of the right *L hand*, palm facing left, first on the fingers and then on the heel of the left *open hand*, palm facing right and fingers pointing up. Then beginning with both *S hands* in front of the body, index fingers touching and palms down, move the hands away from each other while twisting the wrists with a deliberate movement, ending with the palms facing each other.

- **guilty** Tap the index-finger side of the right *one hand*, palm left, on the left side of the chest with a double movement.

---- [sign continues] ---->

fiduciary

- **punish** Strike the extended right index finger, palm facing left, downward across the elbow of the left bent arm.

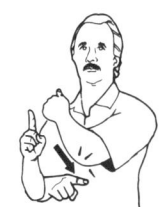

- **excess** Beginning with the right *bent hand* on the back of the left *bent hand*, both palms facing down, bring the right hand straight upward.

- **one-year** Hold up the extended right index finger. Then beginning with the little-finger side of the right *S hand*, palm left, on top of the index-finger side of the left *S hand*, palm right, move the right hand forward around the left hand, ending with the right *S hand* on the left *S hand*.

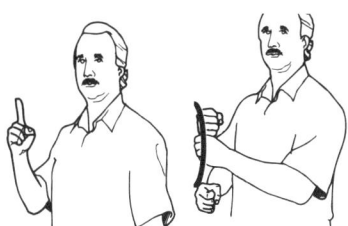

fiduciary A trustee upon whom another person or persons must rely to handle money or property.

- **money** Tap the back of the right *flattened O hand*, palm facing up, with a double movement against the palm of the left *open hand*, palm facing up.

- **manage** Beginning with both *modified X hands* in front of each side of the body, right hand forward of the left hand and palms facing each other, move the hands forward and back with a repeated movement.

- **person marker** Move both *open hands*, palms facing each other, downward along the sides of the body.

fiduciary duty

fiduciary duty The duty of utmost good faith, loyalty, and care the law imposes on every fiduciary.

- **money** Tap the back of the right *flattened O hand*, palm facing up, with a double movement against the palm of the left *open hand*, palm facing up.

- **manage** Beginning with both *modified X hands* in front of each side of the body, right hand forward of the left hand and palms facing each other, move the hands forward and back with a repeated movement.

- **responsible** With the fingertips of both *bent hands* on the right shoulder, push the shoulder down slightly.

file 1. To commence an action by depositing a copy of the complaint. 2. A folder, cabinet, or other container in which papers, letter, etc. are arranged in convenient order. Same sign used for **bring, enter.**

- **file** Move the fingers of the right *V hand*, palm facing forward, downward on each side of the extended left index finger, which is pointing up in front of the chest.

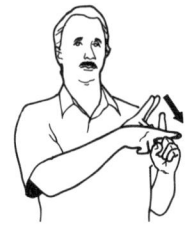

filing fee The fee that must be paid to the court to begin an action in that court.

- **file** Move the fingers of the right *V hand*, palm facing forward, downward on each side of the extended left index finger, which is pointing up in front of the chest.

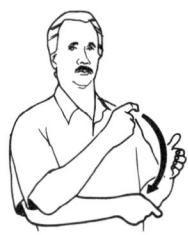

- **cost** Strike the knuckle of the right *X hand*, palm facing in, down on the palm of the left *open hand*, palm facing right and fingers pointing forward.

foreclosure

fine 1. A sum of money required to be paid as a penalty. 2. To impose a fee as a penalty.

- **cost** Strike the knuckle of the right *X hand*, palm facing in, down on the palm of the left *open hand*, palm facing right and fingers pointing forward.

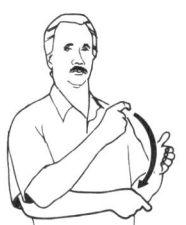

fishing expedition *Informal.* A term used to describe requests for a wide-ranging discovery. See sign for INQUEST[1].

follow or **precedent** To apply the principles used in another case to the case at hand.

- **past** Move the right *open hand*, palm back and fingers pointing up, back over the right shoulder by bending the fingers down.
- Fingerspell: C-A-S-E

- **decide** Move the extended right index finger from the right side of the forehead, palm left, down in front of the chest while changing into an *F hand*, ending with both *F hands* moving downward in front of the body, palms facing each other.

- **follow** With the knuckles of the right *10 hand*, palm facing left, near the wrist of the left *10 hand*, palm facing right, move both hands forward a short distance.

foreclosure The termination of a property owner's right when the owner has failed to pay the debt that secured the property.

- **pay**[1] Beginning with the extended right index finger touching the palm of the left *open hand*, palms facing each other, move the right finger forward and off the left fingertips.

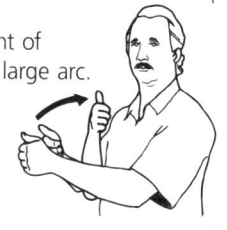

- **behind** Move the right *10 hand*, palm facing left, from in front of the left *10 hand*, palm facing right, back toward the chest in a large arc.

---- [sign continues] -->

163

foreclosure

- **seize** Beginning with both *curved 5 hands* in front of each shoulder, palms facing forward, move the hands downward while closing into *S hands*.

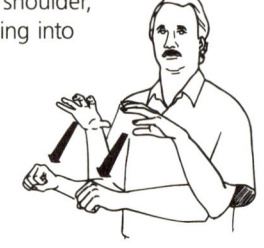

foreign commerce Trade, business, and travel between the United States and other countries.

- **country** Rub the palm of the right *open hand* in a circle near the elbow of the bent left arm with a repeated movement.

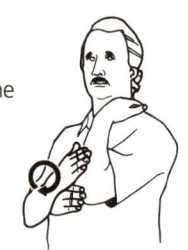

- **there** Point the extended right index finger in an arc from left to right in front of the body.

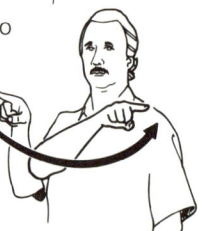

- **business** Brush the base of the right *B hand*, palm forward, with a repeated movement on the back of the left *open hand*, palm down.

- **connect** With the thumbs and index fingers of both *F hands* intersecting, move the hands in an arc in front of the body.

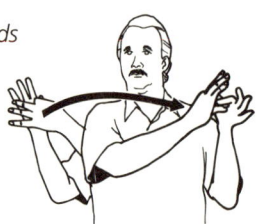

forensic The application of medical knowledge to questions of civil and criminal law.

- **science** Beginning with the right *10 hand* in front of the right shoulder and the left *10 hand* in front of the left side of the chest, both palms facing forward, move the hands in large alternating circles toward each other.

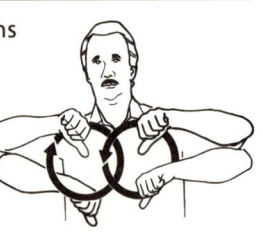

---- [sign continues] -->

fornication

- **investigate** Move the extended right index finger from near the right eye down to move from the heel to the fingers of the upturned palm of the left *open hand*.

forfeiture The loss of a right, license, or property as a civil or criminal penalty.

- **force** Beginning with the right *C hand* in front of the right shoulder, palm forward, and the left arm bent across the body, move the right hand downward and forward, ending with the right wrist across the left wrist, both palms down.

- **give-up** Beginning with both *open hands* in front of the body, palms facing down, flip the hands upward in large arcs while opening into *5 hands*, ending in front of each shoulder, palms facing forward.

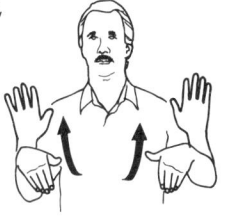

forgery The crime of making a writing, recording, coin, or other document and passing it off as genuine when it is not.

- **signature** Place the extended fingers of the right *H hand*, palm down, down on the upturned palm of the left *open hand* held in front of the chest with a double movement.

- **lie** Move the index-finger side of the right *bent hand*, palm down and fingers pointing left, across the chin from right to left.

form A preprinted document containing standard legal language for accomplishing a particular kind of transaction. See sign for INSTRUMENT.

fornication The crime of engaging in sexual intercourse while unmarried.

- **intercourse** Bring the right *V hand* downward in front of the chest to tap against the heel of the left *V hand* with a double movement, palms facing each other.

---- [sign continues] ---➤

fornication

- **two-of-them** Swing the right *2 hand*, palm up, from side to side in front of the body.

- **marry** Bring the right *curved hand*, palm facing down, downward in front of the chest to clasp the left *curved hand*, palm facing up.

- **not** Bring the thumb of the right *10 hand* forward from under the chin with a deliberate movement.

---

for the record or **of the record** Something said or done, not for immediate benefit, but to reserve a right or argument in the future. See sign for DOCUMENT.

forum The court in which an action is pending. See sign for COURT[1].

foundation Evidence establishing the admissibility of an exhibit or testimony.

- **base** Move the right *B hand*, palm facing forward, in a flat circle under the left *open hand*, palm facing down.

- **proof** Move the right *open hand* downward, ending with the back of the right hand on the palm of the left *open hand*, both palms facing up in front of the chest.

---

franchise A license granted by a company to market goods or services and use its trademark in a specific territory.

- **go-to** Move both extended index fingers from pointing up in front of the body, palms facing forward, then move the hands deliberately forward while bending the wrists so the fingers point forward.

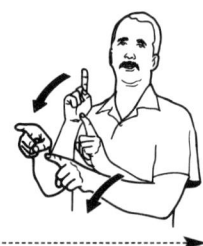

---- [sign continues] ---→

fraud

- **give**[1] Beginning with both *X hands* in front of the body, palms facing each other, move the hands forward in simultaneous arcs.

- **license** Tap the thumbs of both *L hands* with a double movement in front of the chest, palms facing forward.

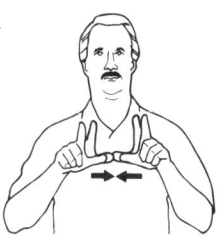

- **set-up**[2] Beginning with the fingertips of both *curved hands* touching in front of the chest, palms facing down, bend the fingers upward, ending with the fingers angled upward and touching each other.

- **business** Brush the base of the right *B hand*, palm forward, with a repeated movement on the back of the left *open hand*, palm down.

fraud[1]**, deceit,** or **defraud** Obtaining money or property by means of a false portrayal of facts. Related form: **fraudulent**.

- **false** Brush the extended right index finger, palm facing left, across the tip of the nose from right to left by bending the wrist.

fraud[2]**, deceit,** or **defraud** (alternate sign) Same sign used for **perjury**.

- **lie** move the index-finger side of the right *bent hand*, palm down and fingers pointing left, across the chin from right to left.

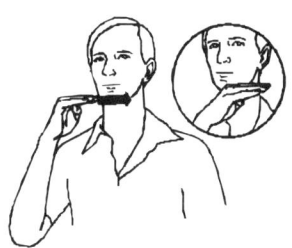

167

fraud

fraud³, deceit, or defraud (alternate sign)
- **fool** Strike the knuckles of the right *A hand*, palm facing forward, against the extended left index finger with a double movement.

fraud⁴, deceit, or defraud (alternate sign)
- **cover-up** With the heel of the right *5 hand* on the palm of the left *5 hand*, twist the right hand to the left.

fraud⁵, deceit, or defraud (alternate sign)
- **cheat** Slide the right *V hand* onto the index-finger side of the left *B hand* with a double movement.

freedom of assembly The right of people to gather peacefully for political or other purposes.
- **meeting** Beginning with both *open hands* in front of the chest, palms facing forward and fingers pointing up, close the fingers with a double movement into *flattened O hands* while moving the hands together.

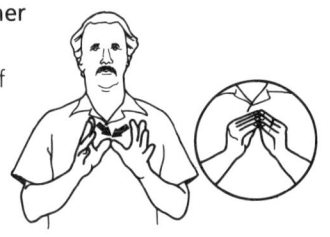

- **set-up**¹ Beginning with the right *10 hand* in front of the right shoulder, palm down, twist the wrist up with a circular movement and then move the right hand straight down to land on the little-finger side of the back of the left *open hand*, palm down.

- **can** Move both *S hands*, palms facing down, downward simultaneously in front of each side of the body.

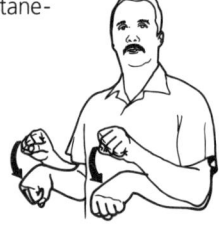

freedom of religion

Freedom of Information Act (FOIA)[1] The federal law that requires most government documents to be made available to the public upon request according to specified procedures.
- Fingerspell acronym: F-O-I-A

Freedom of Information Act (FOIA)[2] (alternate sign)
- **information** Beginning with the fingertips of the right *flattened O hand* near the forehead and the left *flattened O hand* in front of the chest, move both hands forward while opening into *5 hands*, palms facing up.

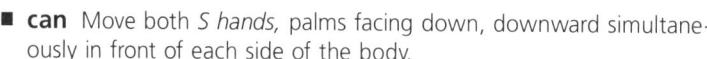

- **receive** Beginning with both *curved 5 hands* in front of the body, right hand higher than the left hand and both palms facing back, bring the hands back toward the chest while closing into *S hands*, ending with the right little finger on the index-finger side of the left hand.

- **can** Move both *S hands*, palms facing down, downward simultaneously in front of each side of the body.

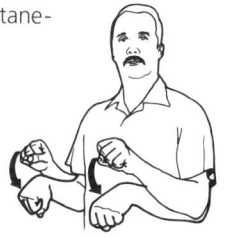

freedom of religion The freedom to practice one's religious beliefs and freedom from government involvement in religious matters.
- **worship** With the right *curved hand* cupped over the left *curved hand*, palms down, bring the hands downward in a short double movement.

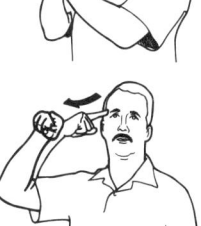

- **for** Beginning with the extended right index finger touching the right side of the forehead, twist the hand forward, ending with the index finger pointing forward.

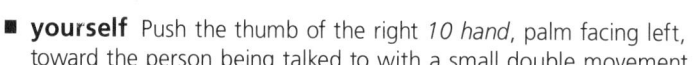

- **yourself** Push the thumb of the right *10 hand*, palm facing left, toward the person being talked to with a small double movement.

freedom of the press

freedom of the press The First Amendment right to publish books, newspapers, and magazines and distribute information largely free from government censorship.

- **print** Bring the thumb side of the right *G hand*, palm down, against the left *open hand*, palm up, and pinch the right thumb and index finger together with a double movement.

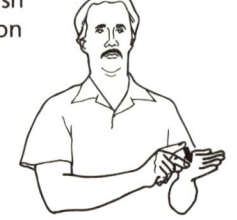

- **for** Beginning with the extended right index finger touching the right side of the forehead, twist the hand forward, ending with the index finger pointing forward.

- **yourself** Push the thumb of the right *10 hand*, palm facing left, toward the person being talked to with a small double movement.

fresh pursuit See sign for HOT PURSUIT.

friend of the court or **amicus curiae** A nonparty that volunteers or is invited by the court to submit views on the issues presented in a case.

- **court** Move both *F hands*, palms facing each other, up and down in front of each side of the chest with a repeated alternating movement.

- **volunteer** Pinch a piece of clothing on the right side of the chest with the bent index finger and thumb of the right *5 hand* and pull forward with a short double movement.

- **person marker** Move both *open hands*, palms facing each other, downward along the sides of the body.

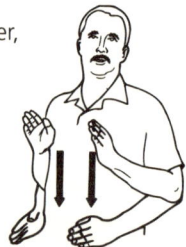

frisk

frisk[1] A brief detention accompanied by a pat-down for weapons.
- **frisk** Pat the palms of both *curved hands* downward on each side of an imaginary body beginning at the chest.

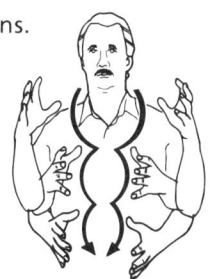

frisk[2] or **stop and frisk** (alternate sign)
- **police** Tap the thumb side of the right *modified C hand*, palm facing left, against the left side of the chest with a double movement.

- **stop** Hit the little-finger side of the right *open hand* on the palm of the left *open hand*.

- **frisk** Pat the palms of both *curved hands* downward on each side of an imaginary body beginning at the chest.

frisk[3] or **stop and frisk** (alternate sign)
- **stop** Hit the little-finger side of the right *open hand* on the palm of the left *open hand*.

- **investigate** Move the extended right index finger from near the right eye down to move from the heel to the fingers of the upturned palm of the left *open hand*.

---- [sign continues] -->

171

frisk

- **frisk** Pat the palms of both *curved hands* downward on each side of an imaginary body beginning at the chest.

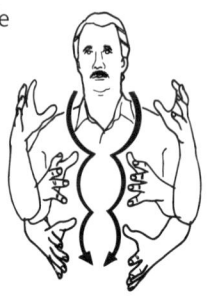

frivolous An action that clearly has no basis in law.

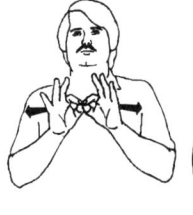

- **worthless** Beginning with the fingertips of both *F hands* touching in front of the chest, bring the hands quickly apart to each side while turning the palms forward and opening into *5 hands*.

fundamental right Any right guaranteed by the constitution.

- **constitution** Place the little-finger side of the right *C hand*, palm facing left, first on the fingers and then the heel of the left *open hand*, palm facing right and fingers pointing up.

- **allow** Beginning with both *open hands* in front of the waist, palms facing each other and fingers pointing down, bring the fingers forward and upward by bending the wrists.

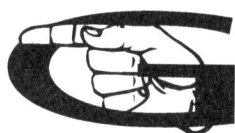

gag order A judge's order not to discuss the case publicly.

- **judge** Move the right *modified X hand*, palm left, with a double up and down movement.

- **order** Move the extended right index finger, palm forward and finger pointing up, from in front of the mouth forward and down, ending with the finger pointing forward and the palm down.

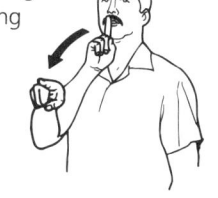

- **shut-up** Beginning with the thumb of the *flattened C hand* touching the chin, palm facing in, close the fingers to the thumb, forming a *flattened O hand*.

garnish The attachment of a debtor's wages so they can be used to satisfy the debtor's obligation. Related form: **garnishment**.

- **force** Beginning with the right *C hand* in front of the right shoulder, palm forward, and the left arm bent across the body, move the right hand downward and forward, ending with the right wrist across the left wrist, both palms down.

- **subtract** Beginning with the fingertips of the right *curved 5 hand* touching the palm of the left *open hand* held in front of the left side of the chest, palm facing right and fingers pointing up, bring the right hand down off the base of the left hand while changing into an *S hand*. Repeat.

general counsel

general counsel A company's chief legal officer.
- Fingerspell abbreviation for *company*: C-O
- **law** Place the palm side of the right *L hand*, palm facing left, first on the fingers and then on the heel of the left *open hand*, palm facing right and fingers pointing up.

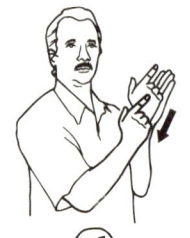

- **guide** With the fingers of the left *open hand*, palm facing right, being held by the fingers in the palm of the right hand, palm facing in, pull the left hand forward a short distance.

- **person marker** Move both *open hands*, palms facing each other, downward along the sides of the body.

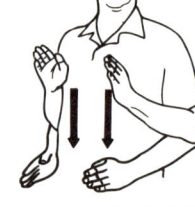

gentlemen's agreement, oral agreement, or **oral contract**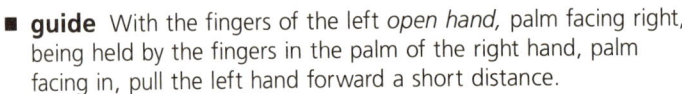
An agreement expected to be performed solely as a matter of personal friendship or honor.
- **voice** Move the fingers of the right *V hand*, palm down, upward with a double movement near the throat.
- **agree** Move the extended right index finger from touching the right side of the forehead downward to beside the extended left index finger, ending with both fingers pointing forward in front of the body, palms down.

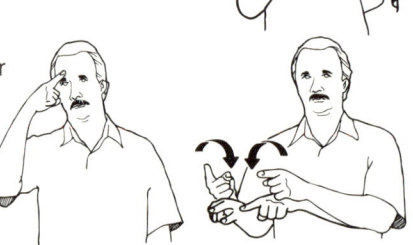

gift A voluntary transfer of money or property completed during one's lifetime. See signs for BEQUEATH[1,2].

gift tax A tax imposed by the federal government on very large gifts made during a person's lifetime.
- **give-me**[1] Beginning with both *flattened O hands* in front of the body, palms up, bring the hands up to touch the fingertips on each side of the chest, palms in.
- Fingerspell: T-A-X

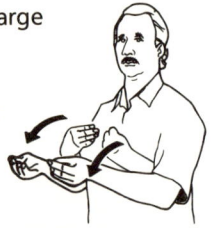

golden parachute

gloss An explanation or interpretation of a statute or traditional ruling.

- **interpret** With the fingertips of both *F hands* touching in front of the chest, palms facing each other, twist the hands in opposite directions to reverse positions.

go public To issue shares of a corporation to the general public for the first time.

- Fingerspell abbreviation for *company*: C-O
- **sale** Beginning with both *flattened O hands* held in front of each side of the chest, palms down and fingers pointing down, swing the fingertips forward and back by twisting the wrists upward.

- **invest**¹ Beginning with the thumb of the right *bent 3 hand* on the palm of the left upturned *open hand*, move the right hand upward and forward in an arc.

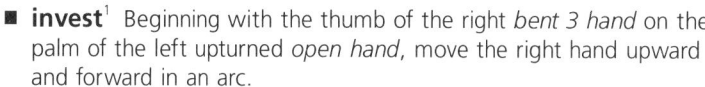

go to To be relevant to an issue.

- **connect** Beginning with both *curved 5 hands* in front of each side of the body, palms facing each other, bring the hands together while touching the thumb and index fingertips of each hand and intersecting with each other.

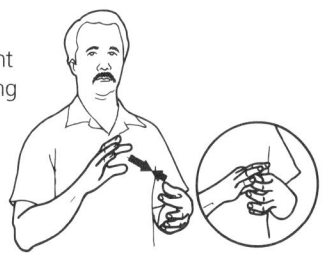

golden parachute A contract between a corporation and its high executive promising generous financial compensation in the event that he or she loses his or her job or resigns.

- Fingerspell abbreviation for *company*: C-O
- **promise** Bring the extended right index finger, palm facing left and finger pointing up, from in front of the lips downward, changing into an *open hand* and placing the palm of the right hand on the index-finger side of the left *S hand* held in front of the body, palm facing right.
- **work** Tap the heel of the right *S hand*, palm forward, with a double movement on the back of the left *S hand* held in front of the body, palm down.

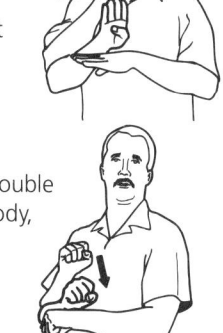

---- [sign continues] ---➤

175

golden parachute

- **quiet** Beginning with both *B hands* in front of the mouth, bring the hands downward and outward, ending with the hands in front of each side of the body, palms facing down.

- **more** Tap the fingertips of both *flattened O hands,* palms facing down, together in front of the chest with a double movement.

- **money** Tap the back of the right *flattened O hand,* palm facing up, with a double movement against the palm of the left *open hand,* palm facing up.

- **give-you** With the right *curved hand* over the left *curved hand,* palms facing each other, move the hands forward a short distance.

good cause A legally sufficient reason or excuse.

- **reason** Move the fingertips of the right *R hand,* palm facing in, in a circular movement in front of the right side of the forehead with a double movement.

- **have** Bring the fingertips of both *bent hands,* palms facing in, in to touch each side of the chest.

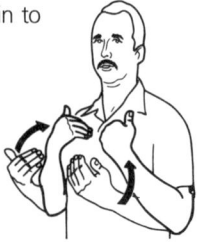

goods

good faith The state of mind processed by a person who is acting with sincerity and without intent to cheat another.

- **mean** Touch the fingertips of the right *V hand*, palm facing down, in the palm of the left *open hand*, palm facing up and fingers pointing forward, and then twist the right wrist and touch the fingertips down again.

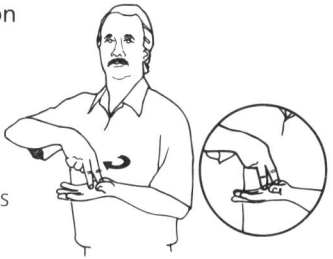

- **true** Beginning with the thumb side of the right *one hand* in front of the mouth, palm left, move the extended index finger forward with a double movement.

good will The benefit to a business of customer loyalty, brand name recognition, reputation for quality and honesty, and the like.

- **true** Beginning with the thumb side of the right *one hand* in front of the mouth, palm left, move the extended index finger forward.

- **sensitive** Beginning with the bent middle finger of the right *8 hand* touching the left side of the chest, twist the hand forward.

- **process** Beginning with both *open hands* in front of the body, palms facing in, left fingers pointing right and right fingers pointing left, and the left hand closer to the chest than the right hand, move the left hand over the right hand and then the right hand over the left hand in an alternating movement.

goods Any tangible personal property.

- **private** Tap the thumb side of the right *A hand*, palm left, against the mouth with a repeated movement.

---- [sign continues] --→

177

goods

- **things** Beginning with both *open hands* in front of the body, palms facing up, move the hands to the sides away from each other in a double arc.

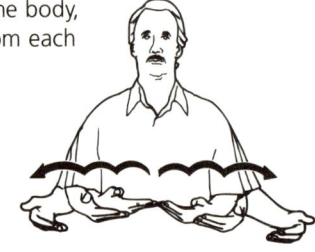

government or **federal** The ruling authorities of a city, state, nation, or other political unit.
- **government** Beginning with the extended right index finger pointing upward near the right side of the head, palm facing forward, twist the wrist to touch the finger to the right temple.

grandfather or **grandfather clause** To exempt a class of persons from a new law, permitting them to operate under a prior law.
- **excuse** Wipe the fingertips of the right *open hand* across the upturned left *open hand* from the heel off the fingertips.

- **for-for** With a questioning expression and beginning with the extended right finger touching the right side of the forehead, twist the hand forward with a double movement, turning the index finger forward each time.

- **before** Beginning with the back of the right *open hand*, palm in and fingers pointing left, touching the back of the left *open hand*, palm forward, move the right hand in toward the chest.

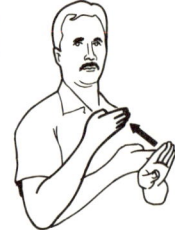

- **do** Move both *C hands*, palms facing down, simultaneously back and forth in front of the body with a swinging movement.

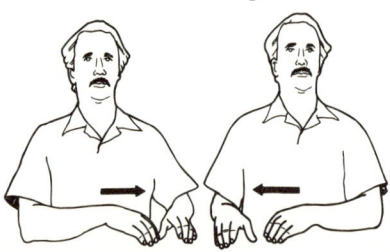

grant

grandfather clause See sign for GRANDFATHER.

grand jury[1] A group of citizens summoned to hear evidence presented by the prosecutor and to issue an indictment if they find sufficient evidence to warrant trying the case.

- **secret** Tap the thumb side of the right *A hand*, palm left, against the mouth with a repeated movement.
- Fingerspell: J-U-R-Y

grand jury[2] (alternate sign)

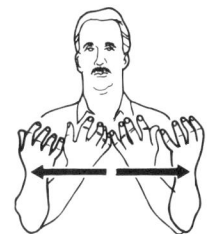

- Fingerspell: G-R-A-N-D
- **jury** Beginning with the little-finger sides of both *bent 4 hands*, palms in, together in front of the chest, move the hands apart to each side.

grand larceny The crime of wrongfully taking personal property that exceeds a certain amount from another.

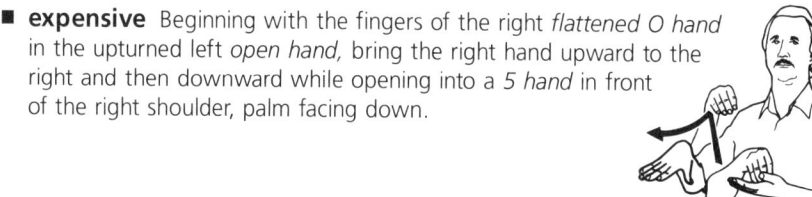

- **steal**[1] Beginning with the index-finger side of the right *V hand*, palm facing down, on the elbow of the bent left arm, held at an upward angle across the chest, pull the right hand upward toward the left wrist while bending the fingers in tightly.

- **expensive** Beginning with the fingers of the right *flattened O hand* in the upturned left *open hand,* bring the right hand upward to the right and then downward while opening into a *5 hand* in front of the right shoulder, palm facing down.

- **things** Beginning with both *open hands* in front of the body, palms facing up, move the hands to the sides away from each other in a double arc.

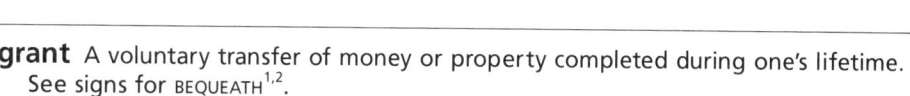

grant A voluntary transfer of money or property completed during one's lifetime. See signs for BEQUEATH[1,2].

green card

green card[1] An identification card issued to foreign nationals who have been granted permanent resident status in the United States.

- Fingerspell acronym for Immigration and Naturalization Service: I-N-S

- **card** Beginning with the fingertips of both *L hands* touching in front of the chest, palms facing forward, bring the hands apart to in front of each shoulder, and then pinch each thumb and index finger together.

green card[2] (alternate sign)

- **wave** Bring the right *4 hand*, palm in and fingers pointing left, with a wavy movement from left to right in front of the eyes.

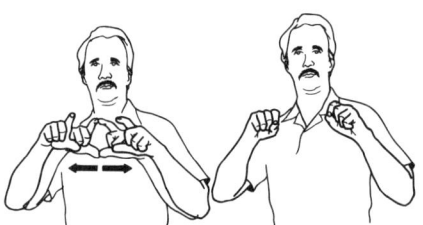

- **card** Beginning with the fingertips of both *L hands* touching in front of the chest, palms facing forward, bring the hands apart to in front of each shoulder, and then pinch each thumb and index finger together.

green card[3] (alternate sign)

- **green** Shake the right *G hand*, palm left, with a short repeated movement in front of the chest.

- **card** Beginning with the fingertips of both *L hands* touching in front of the chest, palms facing forward, bring the hands apart to in front of each shoulder, and then pinch each thumb and index finger together.

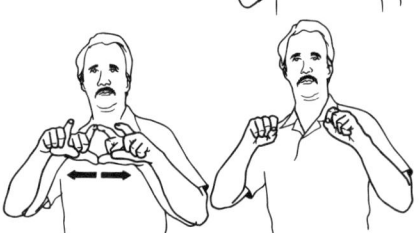

grievance In a unionized workplace, a formal complaint by an employee. Same sign used for **complaint, objection**.

- **complaint** With a double movement, tap the fingertips of the right *curved 5 hand* against the center of the chest.

guardian

gross income The total sum of money earned during a year before deductions and adjustment.

- **total** Beginning with both *curved 5 hands* in front of the body, right hand above the left hand and palms facing each other, move the hands toward each other while closing the fingers, ending with the fingertips of both *flattened O hands* touching in front of the chest.

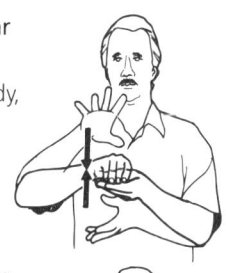

- **earn** Bring the little-finger side of the right *curved hand*, palm facing left, across the upturned left *open hand* from fingertips to heel while changing into an *S hand*.

grounds[1] The basic or governing principles in a case.

- **reason** Move the fingertips of the right *R hand*, palm facing in, in a circular movement in front of the right side of the forehead with a double movement.

grounds[2] See sign for IN THE MATTER OF.

guarantee or **guaranty** Any assurance. See sign for AFFIRM.

guardian[1] A person with responsibility for the care of a child or an incompetent adult and having control over their affairs.

- **take-care-of** With the little-finger side of the right *K hand* across the index-finger side of the left *K hand*, move the hands in a repeated flat circle in front of the body.

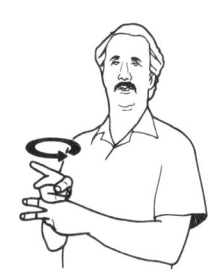

- **person** Move both *P hands*, palms facing each other, downward along the sides of the body.

181

guardian

guardian[2] See sign for DEFENDANT.

guilty[1] Adjudged by a court to have committed an offense.
- **guilty** Tap the index-finger side of the right *G hand*, palm left, on the left side of the chest with a double movement.

guilty[2] (alternate sign)
- **wrong** Bring the middle fingers of the right *Y hand*, palm in, back against the chin with a deliberate movement.

- **do** Move both *C hands*, palms facing down, simultaneously back and forth in front of the body with a swinging movement.

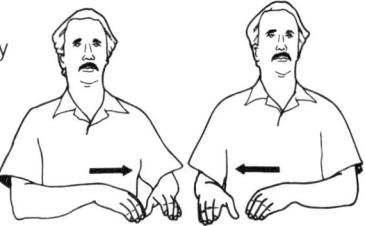

- **yes** Bend the wrist of the right *S hand* up and down with a short double movement.

guilty[3] (alternate sign)
- **crime** Place the palm side of the right *L hand*, palm facing left, first on the fingers and then on the heel of the left *open hand*, palm facing right and fingers pointing up. Then beginning with both *S hands* in front of the body, index fingers touching and palms down, move the hands away from each other while twisting the wrists with a deliberate movement, ending with the palms facing each other.

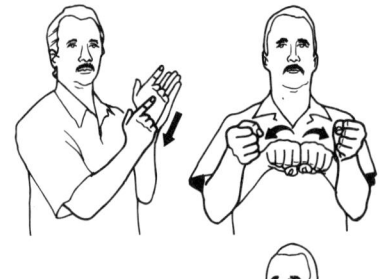

- **yes** Bend the wrist of the right *S hand* up and down with a short double movement.

gun control

gun control Legal restrictions on the manufacture, distribution, or possession of guns.

- Fingerspell: G-U-N
- **law** Place the palm side of the right *L hand*, palm facing left, first on the fingers and then on the heel of the left *open hand*, palm facing right and fingers pointing up.

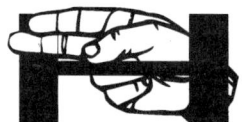

habeas corpus *Latin.* A procedure for testing custody to see if the person is being held legally.

- **police** Tap the thumb side of the right *modified C hand*, palm facing left, against the left side of the chest with a double movement.

- **order** Move the extended right index finger, palm forward and finger pointing up, from in front of the mouth forward and down, ending with the finger pointing forward and the palm down.

- **must** Move the bent index finger of the right *X hand* downward with a deliberate movement in front of the right side of the body by bending the wrist down.

- **hold** Move the right *S hand*, palm facing up, in a circular movement in front of the right side of the chest.

- **person** Move both *P hands*, palms facing each other, downward along the sides of the body.

- **why** Beginning with the right *5 hand* in front of the forehead, palm in and fingers pointing up, bend the middle and ring fingers with a repeated short movement.

harassment

habitual criminal See sign for REPEAT OFFENDER.

halfway house A residence for individuals who have been in prison, providing a supervised and structured environment.

- **short** Rub the middle-finger side of the right *H hand*, palm angled left, back and forth with a repeated movement on the index-finger side of the left *H hand*, palm angled right.

- **live** Move both *10 hands*, thumbs pointing up, upward on each side of the chest.

hand or **signature** The name or mark of a person placed on a document.

- **itself** Bring the knuckles of the right *10 hand*, palm facing left, firmly against the side of the extended left index finger, palm facing right and finger pointing up in front of the chest.

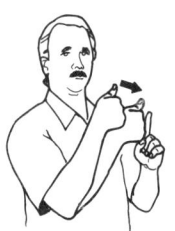

- **write** With the thumb and index finger of the right hand pinched together, move the right hand with a wiggling movement across the palm of the left *open hand* held in front of the body, palm up.
- Fingerspell: O-R
- **x** Place the extended right index finger across the extended left index finger to form an *X*.

handicap See sign for DISABILITY[1].

harassment[1] The crime of deliberately and repeatedly annoying a person.

- **pick-on** Tap the fingertips of the right *modified X hand*, palm facing left, against the extended left index finger, palm facing right and finger pointing up, in front of the chest with a double movement.

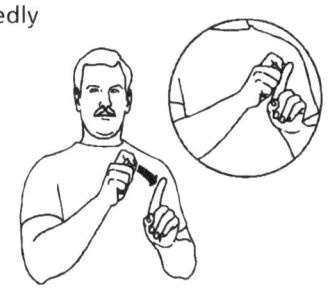

185

harassment

harassment[2] (alternate sign)

- **bother** Sharply tap the little-finger side of the right *open hand*, palm facing in at an angle, at the base of the thumb and index finger of the left *open hand*, with a double movement.

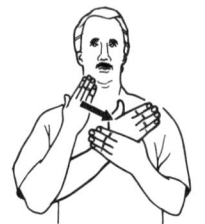

- **excess** Beginning with the right *bent hand* on the back of the left *bent hand*, both palms facing down, bring the right hand straight upward.

hate crime
A crime motivated by bias against a group identified by race, religion, other group characteristic.

- **crime** Place the palm side of the right *L hand*, palm facing left, first on the fingers and then on the heel of the left *open hand*, palm facing right and fingers pointing up. Then beginning with both *S hands* in front of the body, index fingers touching and palms down, move the hands away from each other while twisting the wrists with a deliberate movement, ending with the palms facing each other.

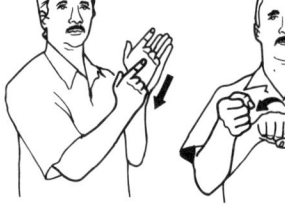

- **why** Beginning with the right *5 hand* in front of the forehead, palm in and fingers pointing up, bend the middle and ring fingers with a repeated short movement.

- **hate** Beginning with both *8 hands* in front of the chest, palms facing each other, flick the middle fingers forward, changing into *5 hands*.

head of household
An unmarried person or a person who is married but living separately who maintains a household for an unmarried child or a dependent relative.

- **family** Beginning with the fingertips of both *F hands* touching in front of the chest, palms facing forward, bring the hands away from each other in outward arcs while turning the palms in, ending with the little fingers touching.

---- [sign continues] ---->

hearsay

- **responsible** With the fingertips of both *bent hands* on the right shoulder, push the shoulder down slightly.

- **you** Point the right extended index finger forward toward the referent.

health care proxy See sign for LIVING WILL.

hear ye A phrase often called out at the opening of court proceedings to get everyone's attention. See sign for DILIGENCE.

hear A judge receiving evidence and argument orally, without a jury present. See sign for JUDGMENT.

hearing or **action** Any proceeding at which legal matters are presented for consideration. Same sign used for **appear**.

- **court** Move both *F hands,* palms facing each other, up and down in front of each side of the chest with a repeated alternating movement.

- **face-to-face** Beginning with both *open hands* in front of the chest, palms facing each other and fingers pointing up, move the right hand forward in a smooth movement toward the left hand.

hearsay[1] Any assertion made outside the courtroom and offered as evidence in a case.

- **story** Bring the thumb and index finger of each *5 hand* to intersect with the other hand, palms facing each other, forming *F hands.* Then pull the hands apart to in front of each side of the chest. Repeat.

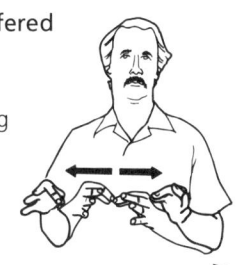

---- [sign continues] ---➤

187

hearsay

- **give-give-give** Move the right *flattened O hand*, palm facing up, from left to right in front of the body in a series of arcs.

- **give-me**² Beginning with one *X hand* in front of the body, bring the hand back to touch on the right side of the chest.

hearsay² (alternate sign)

- **other** Beginning with the right *10 hand* in front of the chest, palm down, flip the hand over, ending with palm up.

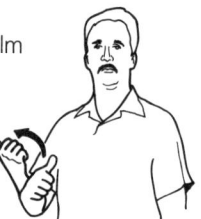

- **tell-you** Move the right extended index finger from touching the chin, palm down, in an arc forward by turning the palm up, ending with the index finger pointing forward.

- **yourself** Push the thumb of the right *10 hand*, palm facing left, toward the person being talked to with a small double movement.

- **witness** With the index finger of the right *X hand* pull down slightly on the cheek near the outside corner of the right eye.

---- [sign continues] -->

heir

- **not** Bring the thumb of the right *10 hand* forward from under the chin with a deliberate movement.

heat of passion Extreme anger or other emotions provoked by circumstances that the law regards as sufficient to make a reasonable person lose control.
- **blow-up** Beginning with the palm of the right *5 hand*, palm down, on the thumb side of the left *S hand*, palm right, bring the right hand upward and back down again.

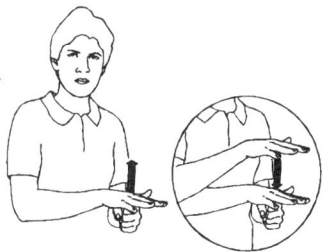

heir[1] The person to whom one's property passes by law if one dies without leaving a will or as specified in a will. Same sign used for **heirs and assigns**.
- **receive** Beginning with both *curved 5 hands* in front of the body, right hand higher than the left hand and both palms facing back, bring the hands back toward the chest while closing into *S hands*, ending with the right little finger on the index-finger side of the left hand.
- **from** Beginning with the knuckle of the right *X hand*, palm in, touching the extended left index finger pointing up in front of the body, pull the right hand back toward the chest.
- Fingerspell: W-I-L-L

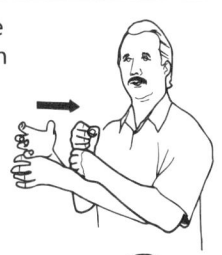

heir[2] (alternate sign) Same sign used for **heirs and assigns**.
- **inherit** With the right *curved hand* over the left *curved hand*, palms facing each other, move the hands forward a short distance.

heir[3] (alternate sign) Same sign used for **heirs and assigns**.
- **pass-down** Beginning with both *flattened O hands* in front of the right shoulder, palms facing in and right hand above the left hand, move the hands forward and down to the left in a series of arcs.

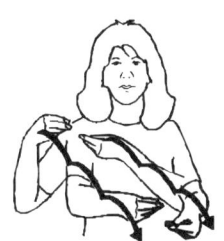

heirs and assigns

heirs and assigns Everyone who might have claim by succession to one's interest in property or other rights. See signs for HEIR[1,2].

high crimes and misdemeanors The phrase used in the Constitution to denote misconduct by the president of sufficient gravity to warrant impeachment and removal from office.

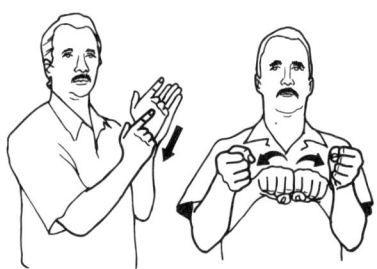

- **president** Beginning with the index-finger sides of both C hands near each side of the forehead, palms facing forward, move the hands outward to above each shoulder while closing into S hands.

- **crime** Place the palm side of the right L hand, palm facing left, first on the fingers and then on the heel of the left open hand, palm facing right and fingers pointing up. Then beginning with both S hands in front of the body, index fingers touching and palms down, move the hands away from each other while twisting the wrists with a deliberate movement, ending with the palms facing each other.

- **confess** Beginning with the palm sides of both 5 hands on the chest, move the hands forward in an arc.

- **punish** Strike the extended right index finger, palm facing left, downward across the elbow of the left bent arm.
- Fingerspell: O-R

- **delete** Beginning with the index finger of the right modified X hand, palm in, touching the extended left index finger held up in front of the chest, palm right and finger pointing up, move the right hand upward to the right while flicking the thumb upward.

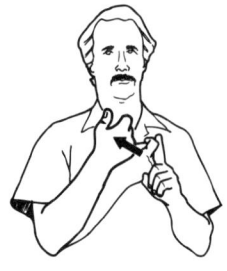

higher court See sign for APPELLATE COURT.

holding

hold To state the court's conclusion in a case.

- **court** Move both *F hands,* palms facing each other, up and down in front of each side of the chest with a repeated alternating movement.

- **decide** Move the extended right index finger from the right side of the forehead, palm left, down in front of the chest while changing into an *F hand*, ending with both *F hands* moving downward in front of the body, palms facing each other.

- **announce** Beginning with the extended index fingers of both hands pointing to each side of the mouth, palms facing in, twist the wrists and move the fingers forward and apart from each other, ending with the palms facing forward and the index fingers pointing outward in opposite directions.

hold up See sign for ROB.

holder The person in possession of an instrument endorsed to him or her.

- **hold** Move the right *S hand,* palm facing up, in a circular movement in front of the right side of the chest.

- **person marker** Move both *open hands*, palms facing each other, downward along the sides of the body.

holding The ruling of a court in a case.

- **court** Move both *F hands,* palms facing each other, up and down in front of each side of the chest with a repeated alternating movement.

---- [sign continues] --→

holding

- **decide** Move the extended right index finger from the right side of the forehead, palm left, in front of the chest while changing into an *F hand*, ending with both *F hands* moving downward in front of the body, palms facing each other.

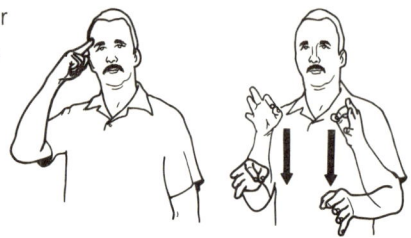

- **home rule** The right of a city, town, or local government to make its own laws.
  - **community** As the hands move from left to right in front of the body, with a repeated movement tap the fingertips of both *open hands*, palms angled toward each other.

  - **set-up**[1] Beginning with the right *10 hand* in front of the right shoulder, palm down, twist the wrist up with a circular movement, and then move the right hand straight down to land on the little-finger side of the back of the left *open hand*, palm down.

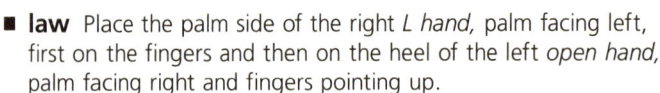

  - **law** Place the palm side of the right *L hand*, palm facing left, first on the fingers and then on the heel of the left *open hand*, palm facing right and fingers pointing up.

  - **can** Move both *S hands*, palms facing down, downward simultaneously in front of each side of the body.

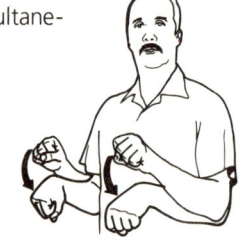

- **homicide**[1], **kill**, or **murder** The most serious form of unjustified conduct resulting in a person's death and undertaken with intent.
  - **kill** Push the side of the extended right index finger, palm down, across the palm of the left *open hand*, palm right, with a deliberate movement.

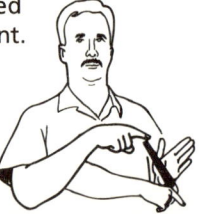

hot check

homicide[2]**, kill,** or **murder** (alternate sign)
- Modified Fingerspelling: K-I-L-L (forming the double L like a gun)

Honorable or **Your Honor** The title used to address a judge.
- **honor** Beginning with both *H hands* in front of the face, right hand higher than the left hand and palms facing in opposite directions, bring both hands downward and forward in a slight arc while bowing the head.

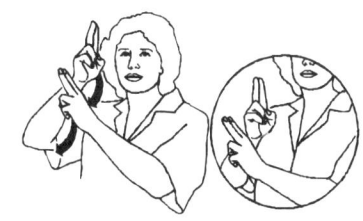

hostile witness See signs for ADVERSE WITNESS[1,2].

hostile working environment Working conditions in which an employee is subjected to harassment.
- **work** Tap the heel of the right *S hand*, palm forward, with a double movement on the back of the left *S hand* held in front of the body, palm down.

- **area**[3] Rub the palm of the right *open hand* on the index-finger side of the left *S hand* held in front of the body, palm right.

- **bother-me** With the fingers pointing back toward the chest, sharply tap the little-finger side of the right *open hand*, palm right, at the base of the thumb and index finger of the left *open hand*, with a double movement.

- **advance** Move both *bent hands*, palms facing each other, from near each side of the head upward a short distance in deliberate arcs while shaking the head negatively.

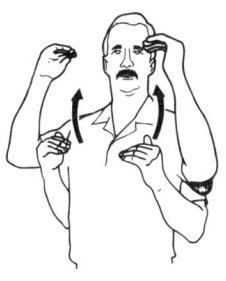

hot check See signs for KITE[1,2].

hot pursuit

hot pursuit or **fresh pursuit** Pursuit by a police officer of a felon who is fleeing and might escape.

- **police** Tap the thumb side of the right *modified C hand*, palm facing left, against the left side of the chest with a double movement.

- **chase** Move the right *A hand*, palm facing left, in a spiraling movement from in front of the chest forward, to behind the left *A hand* held somewhat forward of the body.

- **crime** Place the palm side of the right *L hand*, palm facing left, first on the fingers and then on the heel of the left *open hand*, palm facing right and fingers pointing up. Then beginning with both *S hands* in front of the body, index fingers touching and palms down, move the hands away from each other while twisting the wrists with a deliberate movement, ending with the palms facing each other.

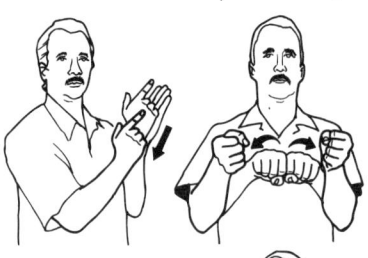

- **person marker** Move both *open hands*, palms facing each other, downward along the sides of the body.

---

hung jury A jury unable to reach a verdict.

- **jury** Beginning with the little-finger sides of both *bent 4 hands*, palms in, together in front of the chest, move the hands apart to each side.

- **decide** Move the extended right index finger from the right side of the forehead, palm left, down in front of the chest while changing into an *F hand*, ending with both *F hands* moving downward in front of the body, palms facing each other.

---- [sign continues] ---→

hypothetical

- **can't** Bring the extended index finger of the right *one hand* downward, hitting the extended index finger of the left *one hand* as it moves.

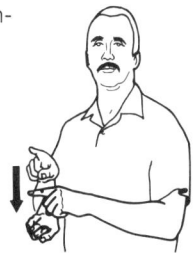

hypothetical[1] Assumed for purposes of discussion.

- **fake** Beginning with the index-finger side of the right *4 hand* touching the right side of the forehead, palm facing left, move the hand forward in an arc or a series of arcs.

hypothetical[2]

- **suppose** Tap the little finger of the right *I hand* near the right eye with a double movement, palm down.

195

illegal¹, against the law, or unlawful Contrary to law.
- **illegal** Hit the palm side of the right *L hand*, palm left, sharply on the palm of the left *open hand*, palm right, and off again.

illegal², against the law, or unlawful (alternate sign)
- **against** Hit the fingertips of the right *bent hand* into the left *open hand*, palm right and fingers pointing forward.

- **law** Place the palm side of the right *L hand*, palm facing left, first on the fingers and then on the heel of the left *open hand*, palm facing right and fingers pointing up.

illegal alien or undocumented alien An alien who has entered the U.S. without government authorization.
- **not** Bring the thumb of the right *10 hand* forward from under the chin with a deliberate movement.

- **American** With the fingers of both hands loosely entwined, palms facing in, move the hands in circle in front of the chest.

---- [sign continues] -->

immaterial

- **person marker** Move both *open hands*, palms facing each other, downward along the sides of the body.

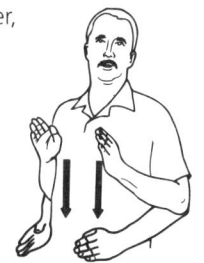

- **scurry** Move the right extended index finger, with a wiggly movement under the palm of the downturned left *open hand*.

immaterial[1] Not important.

- **not** Bring the thumb of the right *10 hand* forward from under the chin with a deliberate movement.

- **important** Beginning with the fingertips of both *F hands* touching, palms facing down, bring the hands upward in a circular movement, ending with the index-finger sides of the *F hands* touching in front of the chest.

immaterial[2] (alternate sign)

- **not** Bring the thumb of the right *10 hand* forward from under the chin with a deliberate movement.

- **connect** Beginning with both *curved 5 hands* in front of each side of the body, palms facing each other, with a double movement bring the hands together while touching the thumb and index fingertips of each hand and intersecting each with the other each time.

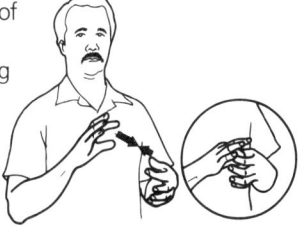

immigrant

immigrant A person who enters a country intending to live there permanently.

- **not** Bring the thumb of the right *10 hand* forward from under the chin with a deliberate movement.

- **American** With the fingers of both hands loosely entwined, palms facing in, move the hands in circle in front of the chest.

- **person marker** Move both *open hands*, palms facing each other, downward along the sides of the body.

- **move** Beginning with both *flattened O hands* in front of the body, palms facing down, move the hands forward in simultaneous arcs to the left.

- **settle** Beginning with both *5 hands* in front of each side of the chest, palms facing down, move the hands slowly down to in front of each side of the waist.

immunity Exemption from prosecution granted in particular cases.

- **person** Move both *P hands*, palms facing each other, downward along the sides of the body.

---- [sign continues] -->

impeachment

- **sentence** Beginning with the thumbs and index fingers of both *F hands* touching in front of the chest, palms facing each other, with a double movement pull the hands apart, ending in front of each side of the chest.

- **punish** Strike the extended right index finger, palm facing left, downward across the elbow of the left bent arm.

- **excuse** Wipe the fingertips of the right *open hand* across the upturned left *open hand* from the heel off the fingertips.

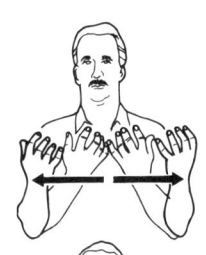

impanel To select and seat a jury for a case.

- **jury** Beginning with the little-finger sides of both *bent 4 hands*, palms in, together in front of the chest, move the hands apart to each side.

- **set-up**[1] Beginning with the right *10 hand* in front of the right shoulder, palm down, twist the wrist up with a circular movement and then move the right hand straight down to land on the little-finger side of the back of the left *open hand*, palm down.

impeachment The instituting of formal misconduct charges against a government official as a basis for removal from office. Related form: **impeach**.

- **government** Beginning with the extended right index finger pointing upward near the right side of the head, palm facing forward, twist the wrist to touch the finger to the right temple.

[sign continues]

impeachment

- **person** Move both *P hands*, palms facing each other, downward along the sides of the body.

- **wrong** Bring the middle fingers of the right *Y hand*, palm in, back against the chin with a deliberate movement.

- **do** Move both *C hands*, palms facing down, simultaneously back and forth in front of the body with a swinging movement.

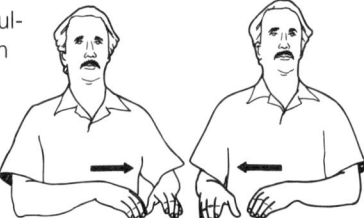

- **proof** Move the right *open hand* downward, ending with the back of the right hand on the palm of the left *open hand,* both palms facing up in front of the chest.

- **delete** Beginning with the index finger of the right *modified X hand*, palm in, touching the extended left index finger held up in front of the chest, palm right and finger pointing up, move the right hand upward to the right while flicking the thumb upward.

- **can** Move both *S hands,* palms facing down, downward simultaneously in front of each side of the body.

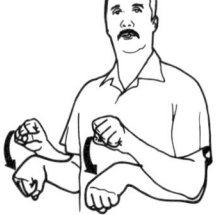

impound

implied Suggested by law, rather than explicitly stated. Same sign used for **apparent, quasi**.

- **seem** Beginning with the right *open hand* near the right shoulder, palm forward and fingers pointing up, turn the hand so the palm faces back.

import tax See sign for DUTY².

impossibility¹ The occurrence of an unforeseen circumstance rendering performance of a contract impossible.

- **can't** Bring the extended index finger of the right *one hand* downward with a double movement, hitting the extended index finger of the left *one hand* each time as it moves.

impossibility² (alternate sign)

- **impossible** Hit the palm of the right *Y hand* on the palm of the left *open hand*, which is held palm up in front of the chest.

impound To take property into the custody of a court.

- **pay**² Beginning with the right *flattened O hand* in front of the right side of the body, palm facing up, move the hand forward while quickly sliding the thumb off each finger.

- **behind** Move the right *10 hand*, palm facing left, from in front of the left *10 hand*, palm facing right, back toward the chest in a large arc.

- **other** Beginning with the right *10 hand* in front of the chest, palm down, flip the hand over, ending with palm up.

---- [sign continues] ---------→

impound

- **grab** Beginning with the right *curved 5 hand* in front of the right shoulder, move the hand forward and downward while closing into an *S hand*.

imprison See signs for JAIL[3,4,5].

in custody See sign for DETAIN.

in evidence Describing an exhibit that the judge has admitted into evidence.

- **proof** Move the right *open hand* downward, ending with the back of the right hand on the palm of the left *open hand*, both palms facing up in front of the chest.

- **accept** Beginning with both *5 hands* in front of the body, fingers pointing forward and palms down, pull both hands back to the chest while changing to *flattened O hands*.

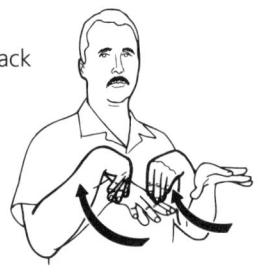

- **finish** With both *5 hands* apart in front of the body, palms up, quickly turn the hands over toward each other.

in house Describing a company's legal work being handled by lawyers who are salaried employees of that company.

- Fingerspell abbreviation for *company*: C-O
- **itself** Bring the knuckles of the right *10 hand*, palm facing left, firmly against the side of the extended left index finger, palm facing right and finger pointing up in front of the chest.

incest

in jeopardy See sign for JEOPARDY.

in kind Referring to payment made in goods or services rather than money. See sign for RECIPROCITY.

in the matter of An introductory phrase in certain case names. Same sign used for **grounds, proxy, represent**.

- **for** Beginning with the extended right index finger touching the right side of the forehead, twist the hand forward, ending with the index finger pointing forward.

in trust See sign for TRUST.

incapacity The absence of legal capacity to perform an act.

- **law** Place the palm side of the right *L hand*, palm facing left, first on the fingers and then on the heel of the left *open hand*, palm facing right and fingers pointing up.

- **allow** Beginning with both *open hands* in front of the waist, palms facing each other and fingers pointing down, bring the fingers forward and upward by bending the wrists.

- **not** Bring the thumb of the right *10 hand* forward from under the chin with a deliberate movement.

incest The crime of having sexual relations with a close relative.

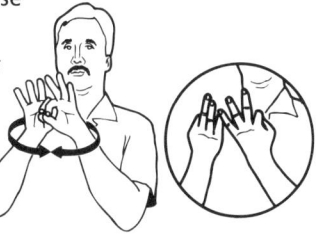

- **family** Beginning with the fingertips of both *F hands* touching in front of the chest, palms facing forward, bring the hands away from each other in outward arcs while turning the palms in, ending with the little fingers touching.

---- [sign continues] -->

203

incest

- **member** Move the fingertips of the right *M hand* from the left side of the chest in an arc around to touch again at the right side of the chest.

- **two-of-them** Swing the right *2 hand*, palm up, from side to side in front of the body.

- **include** Swing the right *5 hand*, palm down, in a circular movement over the left *S hand*, palm in, while changing into a *flattened O hand*, ending with the fingertips of the right hand inserted in the center of the thumb side of the left hand.

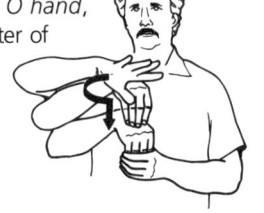

- **illegal** Hit the palm side of the right *L hand*, palm left, sharply on the palm of the left *open hand*, palm right, and off again.

- Fingerspell: S-E-X

income Money received for services rendered, gifts, investments, alimony, and the like.
- **money** Tap the back of the right *flattened O hand*, palm facing up, with a double movement against the palm of the left *open hand*, palm facing up.

- **earn** With a double movement, bring the little-finger side of the right *curved hand*, palm facing left, across the upturned left *open hand* from fingertips to heel while changing into an *S hand* each time.

inconsistent statement

income tax Federal, state, or local tax on a person's or married couple's annual income.

- **money** Tap the back of the right *flattened O hand,* palm facing up, with a double movement against the palm of the left *open hand,* palm facing up.

- **earn** Bring the little-finger side of the right *curved hand,* palm facing left, across the upturned left *open hand* from fingertips to heel while changing into an *S hand.*

- Fingerspell: T-A-X

---

incompetent An individual who does not possess sufficient mental capacity to make rational decisions about a legal matter.

- **think** Tap the right side of the forehead with the extended right index finger with a repeated movement.

- **not** Bring the thumb of the right *10 hand* forward from under the chin with a deliberate movement.

- **can** Move both *S hands,* palms facing down, downward simultaneously in front of each side of the body.

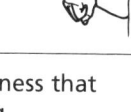

---

inconsistent statement[1] An earlier statement by a witness that is different from his or her testimony at a trial or hearing.

- **sentences** Beginning with the thumbs and index fingers of both *F hands* touching in front of the chest, palms facing each other, with a double movement pull the hands apart to in front of each side of the chest.

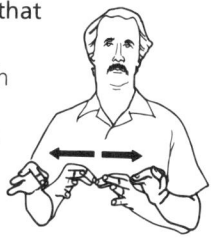

---- [sign continues] -->

205

inconsistent statement

- **standard** Beginning with both Y hands in front of the body, palms facing down, move the hands in a large flat circle.

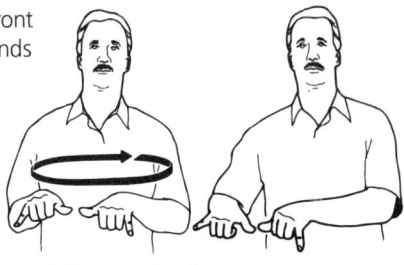

- **not** Bring the thumb of the right *10 hand* forward from under the chin with a deliberate movement.

inconsistent statement[2] (alternate sign)

- **sentences** Beginning with the thumbs and index fingers of both *F hands* touching in front of the chest, palms facing each other, with a double movement pull the hands apart to in front of each side of the chest.

- **not** Bring the thumb of the right *10 hand* forward from under the chin with a deliberate movement.

- **miss-the-point** Move the extended right index finger in a random pattern around the extended left index finger held up in front of the chest.

incorporated[1] The legal activity that causes a business to be recognized as an entity with ownership represented by shares of stock.
- Fingerspell: I-N-C

incorporated[2] (alternate sign)
- Fingerspell: I-N-C-O-R-P

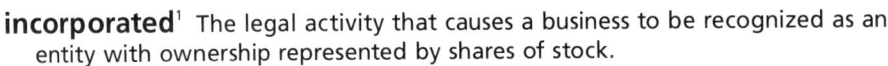

indictment

indemnify or **indemnity** To compensate a person for loss or liability.

- **pay**² Beginning with the right *flattened O hand* in front of the right side of the body, palm facing up, move the hand forward while quickly sliding the thumb off each finger.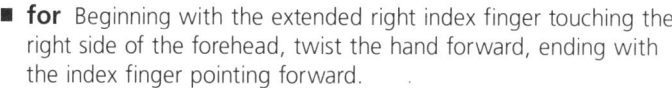

- **for** Beginning with the extended right index finger touching the right side of the forehead, twist the hand forward, ending with the index finger pointing forward.

- **you** Point the right extended index finger forward toward the referent.

indemnity See sign for INDEMNIFY.

independent counsel An attorney hired or appointed to handle a matter because the usual lawyers have a conflict of interest.

- **different** Beginning with both extended index fingers crossed in front of the chest, palms forward, bring the hands apart from each other with a deliberate movement.

- **lawyer** Place the palm side of the right *L hand*, palm facing left, first on the fingers and then on the heel of the left *open hand*, palm facing right and fingers pointing up. Move both *open hands*, palms facing each other, downward along the sides of the body.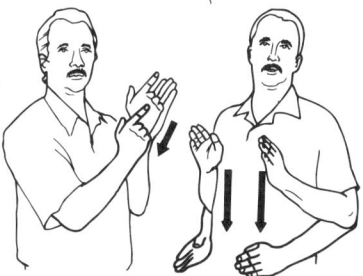

indictment Formally charging a person with a crime as determined by a grand jury, or the written instrument setting forth the charge.

- Fingerspell: G-R-A-N-D

- **jury** Beginning with the little-finger sides of both *bent 4 hands*, palms in, together in front of the chest, move the hands apart to each side.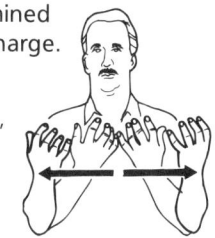

---- [sign continues] -->

207

indictment

- **decide** Move the extended right index finger from the right side of the forehead, palm left, down in front of the chest while changing into an *F hand*, ending with both *F hands* moving downward in front of the body, palms facing each other.

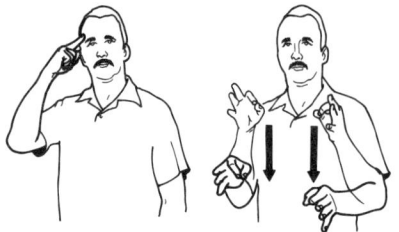

- **good** Beginning with the fingertips of the right *open hand* near the mouth, palm facing in and fingers pointing up, bring the hand downward, ending with the back of the right hand across the palm of the left *open hand*, both palms facing up.

- **reason** Move the fingertips of the right *R hand*, palm facing in, in a circular movement in front of the right side of the forehead with a double movement.

- **go-ahead** Beginning with both *bent hands* in front of the body, palms facing in and fingers pointing toward each other, simultaneously move the hands forward a short distance.

- **court** Move both *F hands*, palms facing each other, up and down in front of each side of the chest with a repeated alternating movement.

individual A human being as distinguished from an entity such as a corporation.

- **formal** Move the thumb of the right *5 hand*, palm facing left, upward and forward in a double circular movement in the center of the chest.

---- [sign continues] ---->

information and belief

- **accuse** Push the little-finger side of the right *A hand*, palm facing left, forward across the back of the left *open hand*, palm facing down.

information A formal instrument charging a person with a crime and filed by a prosecutor instead of a grand jury.

- **accuse** Push the little-finger side of the right *A hand*, palm facing left, forward across the back of the left *open hand*, palm facing down.

- **formal** Move the thumb of the right *5 hand*, palm facing left, upward and forward in a double circular movement in the center of the chest.

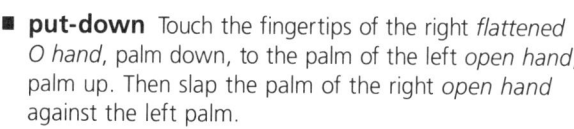

- **put-down** Touch the fingertips of the right *flattened O hand*, palm down, to the palm of the left *open hand*, palm up. Then slap the palm of the right *open hand* against the left palm.

- **offer** Beginning with both *open hands* in front of each side of the body, palms up, move the hands upward and forward in simultaneous arcs.

information and belief A basis for including facts in a pleading or other sworn statement even though one cannot claim personal knowledge.

- **add-to** Swing the right *5 hand* upward from the right side of the body while changing into a *flattened O hand*, ending with the right index finger touching the little-finger side of the left *flattened O hand* in front of the chest, both palms facing in.

---- [sign continues] ----

information and belief

- **sentences** Beginning with the thumbs and index fingers of both *F hands* touching in front of the chest, palms facing each other, with a double movement pull the hands apart to in front of each side of the chest.

informed consent See sign for CONSENT.

infraction[1] or **violation** A minor violation of a rule or law.

- **rule** Touch the fingertips of the right *R hand* first on the fingers and then on the heel of the left *open hand*, palms facing each other.

- **break** Place the palm side of the right *L hand*, palm facing left, first on the fingers and then on the heel of the left *open hand*, palm facing right and fingers pointing up. Then beginning with both *S hands* in front of the body, index fingers touching and palms down, move the hands away from each other while twisting the wrists with a deliberate movement, ending with the palms facing each other.

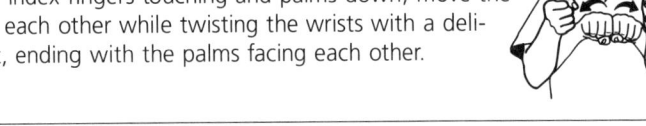

infraction[2] See sign for CRIME.

infringe To violate another's copyright, patent, or trademark by using the protected work without permission.

- **take-advantage** With a double movement flick the bent middle finger of the right *5 hand* upward off the heel of the upturned left *open hand*.

- **allow** Beginning with both *open hands* in front of the waist, palms facing each other and fingers pointing down, bring the fingers forward and upward by bending the wrists.

- **not** Bring the thumb of the right *10 hand* forward from under the chin with a deliberate movement.

innocent

inherit To receive property from the estate of a decedent. Related form: **inheritance**.

- **die** Beginning with both *open hands* in front of the body, right palm up and left palm down, flip the hands to the right, turning the right palm down and the left palm up.

- **inherit** With the right *curved hand* over the left *curved hand*, palms facing each other, move the hands forward a short distance.

inheritance tax See sign for ESTATE TAX.

initiative Lawmaking procedure that bypasses the state legislature but is voted on at a local general election.

- **start** Beginning with the extended right index finger, palm down, inserted between the index and middle fingers of the left *open hand*, palm right and fingers pointing forward, twist the right hand back, ending with palm in.

injunction See sign for CEASE AND DESIST ORDER.

injury Any harm to an individual through conduct regarded by law as wrongful, including bodily injury, mental suffering, harm to reputation, etc.

- **hurt** Beginning with the extended index fingers of both *one hands* pointing toward each other, right palm down and left palm up, twist the wrists in opposite directions, ending with the right palm up and the left palm down. See sign for CRUELTY.

innocent[1] Acting in good faith, or genuinely free from guilt.

- **not** Bring the thumb of the right *10 hand* forward from under the chin with a deliberate movement.

- **wrong** Bring the middle fingers of the right *Y hand*, palm in, back against the chin with a deliberate movement.

---- [sign continues] ---->

211

innocent

- **do** Move both *C hands*, palms facing down, simultaneously back and forth in front of the body with a swinging movement.

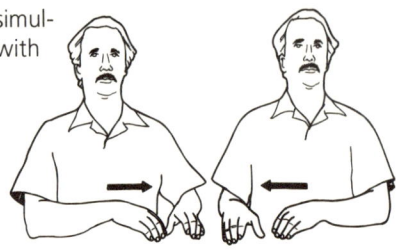

innocent² (alternate sign)

- **innocent** Beginning with the fingers of both *U hands* touching the mouth, palms facing in, move the hands forward and outward to in front of each shoulder.

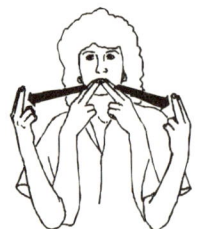

inquest¹ A name given certain kinds of fact-finding proceedings. Same sign used for **fishing expedition, search**.

- **investigate** Move the extended right index finger from near the right eye down to move from the heel to the fingers of the upturned palm of the left *open hand*.

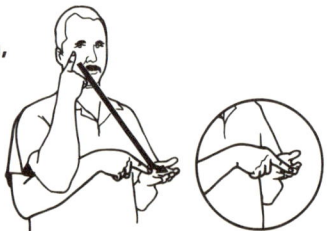

inquest² (alternate sign) Same sign used for **interrogation, interrogatory, question**.

- **question²** Beginning with both extended index fingers pointing up in front of each side of the chest, palms facing forward, with an alternating movement move the right hand down while bending into an *X hand* and then the left hand down while bending into an *X hand*.

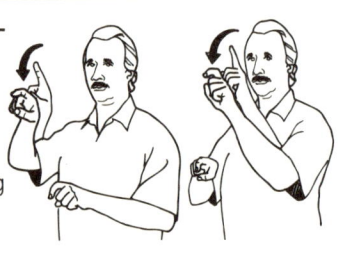

insanity defense¹ A defense to a criminal charge under which a defendant proves he was insane at the time of the crime, and thus, is not responsible.

- **mind** Tap the extended right index finger, palm facing in, against the right side of the forehead with a double movement.

- **not** Bring the thumb of the right *10 hand* forward from under the chin with a deliberate movement.

---- [sign continues] ----

insider trading

- **right** With the index fingers of both hands extended forward at right angles, palms angled in and right hand above left, bring the little-finger side of the right hand sharply down across the thumb side of the left hand.

insanity defense[2] (alternate sign)

- **insane** Touch the extended right index finger to the right side of the forehead. Then wave the fingers of the right *4 hand*, palm in and fingers pointing up, with a double movement in front of the face.

insanity defense[3] (alternate sign)

- **mind** Tap the bent extended right index finger, palm facing in, against the right side of the forehead with a double movement.

- **deviant** With the little-finger side of the right *open hand*, palm facing left, across the fingers of the left *open hand*, palm facing up, bend the right hand back toward the chest, ending with the palm facing in.

insider trading Buying or selling stock in a publicly held corporation on the basis of information known only to people inside the company.

- **business** Brush the base of the right *B hand*, palm forward, with a repeated movement on the back of the left *open hand*, palm down.

- **knowledge** Tap the fingertips of the right *bent hand*, palm down, with a double movement on the right side of the forehead.

---- [sign continues] ---->

insider trading

- **secret** Tap the thumb side of the right *A hand*, palm left, against the mouth with a repeated movement.

- **take-advantage** With a double movement flick the bent middle finger of the right *5 hand* upward off the heel of the upturned left *open hand*.

- **bribe** Move the right *B hand*, palm facing up and fingers pointing forward, forward under the downturned palm of the left *open hand*.

insolvent Unable to pay one's debts in the ordinary course of business as they become due.
- **penniless** Hit the little-finger side of the right *open hand*, palm down and fingers pointing back, against the right side of the neck with a deliberate movement.

- **still** Move both *Y hands*, palms facing down, from in front of the body forward and upward in simultaneous arcs.

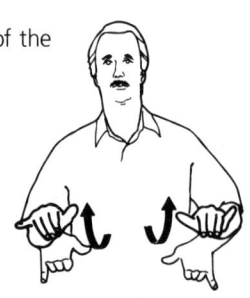

- **owe** With a double movement, tap the extended right index finger against the palm of the left *open hand*, palm facing right.

instruction

installment One of a series of payments required by a contract.

- **installment** Move the little-finger side of the right *open hand*, palm left, with repeated short movements across palm of the upturned left *open hand*.

instant or **at hand** Referring to that which is currently under consideration.

- **here**² Lay both *open hands* down with a deliberate movement in front of the body, palms facing up.

instruct See sign for ORDER.

instruction A judge's instruction to the jury on a particular point of law.

- **your** Push the palm of the right *open hand*, palm forward and fingers pointing up, toward the person being talked to.

- **responsible** With the fingertips of both *bent hands* on the right shoulder, push the shoulder down slightly.

- **judge** Move the right *modified X hand*, palm left, with a double up and down movement.

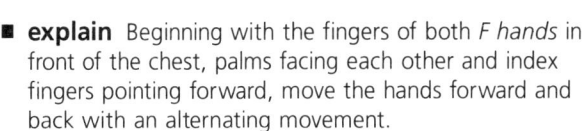

- **explain** Beginning with the fingers of both *F hands* in front of the chest, palms facing each other and index fingers pointing forward, move the hands forward and back with an alternating movement.

215

instrument

instrument A formal legal document, especially one that embodies legal rights (stocks) or operates to cause legal consequences (deed or will). Same sign used for **form, legal form, pleading**.

- **law** Place the palm side of the right *L hand,* palm facing left, first on the fingers and then on the heel of the left *open hand,* palm facing right and fingers pointing up.

- **paper** Brush the heel of the right *open hand* with a double movement on the heel of the left *open hand*, palms facing each other.

insufficient cause A legally insufficient reason for taking a particular action.

- **reason** Move the fingertips of the right *R hand,* palm facing in, in a circular movement in front of the right side of the forehead with a double movement.

- **not** Bring the thumb of the right *10 hand* forward from under the chin with a deliberate movement.

- **enough** Push the palm side of the right *open hand*, palm down, forward across the thumb side of the left *S hand*.

insurance A contractual arrangement whereby a company agrees to compensate its customer in the event of certain loss or injury.

- **insurance** Move the right *I hand*, palm forward, from side to side with a repeated movement in front of the right shoulder.

interest

intent[1] A state of mind in which one either desires to achieve a certain result by one's action, or one knows that such a result will happen.

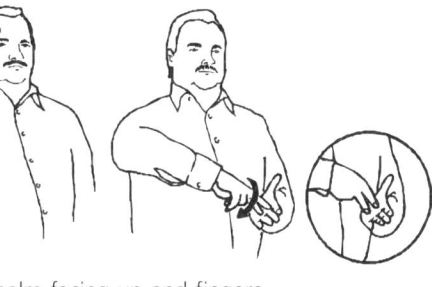

- **intend** Touch the right side of the forehead with the extended right index finger. Then touch the fingertips of the right *V hand*, palm facing down, in the palm of the left *open hand*, palm facing up and fingers pointing forward, and then twist the right wrist and touch the fingertips down again.

intent[2] (alternate sign)

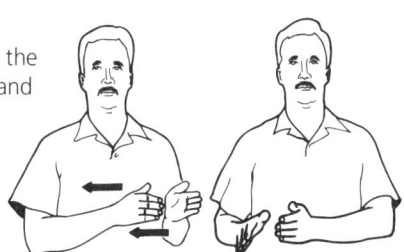

- **plan** Move both *open hands* from in front of the left side of the body, palms facing each other and fingers pointing forward, in a long smooth movement to in front of the right side of the body.

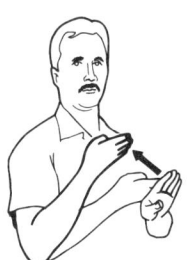

- **before** Beginning with the back of the right *open hand*, palm in and fingers pointing left, touching the back of the left *open hand*, palm forward, move the right hand in toward the chest.

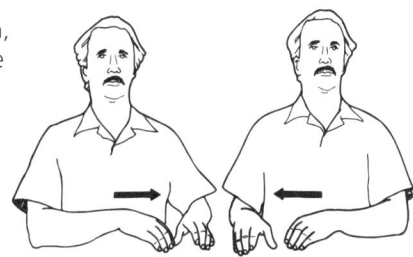

- **do** Move both *C hands*, palms facing down, simultaneously back and forth in front of the body with a swinging movement.

interest[1] A financial or other direct legal stake in a matter.

- **money** Tap the back of the right *flattened O hand*, palm facing up, with a double movement against the palm of the left *open hand*, palm facing up.

---- [sign continues] ---->

217

interest

- **include** Swing the right *5 hand*, palm down, in a circular movement over the left *S hand*, palm in, while changing into a *flattened O hand*, ending with the fingertips of the right hand inserted in the center of the thumb side of the left hand.

interest² (alternate sign)
- Fingerspell: O-W-N

interest³ or points
A sum of money paid or charged for the use of money or for the privilege of deferring payment.

- **interest** Rub the little-finger side of the right *I hand*, palm facing the chest, in a repeated circle on the back of left *open hand*, palm facing down.

international law
A body of principles generally accepted among the nations of the world and governing their dealings with each other and with their citizens.

- **international** Move both *I hands* in circles around each other, palms facing each other, ending with the little-finger side of the right hand on the index-finger side of the left hand in front of the chest.

- **law** Place the palm side of the right *L hand*, palm facing left, first on the fingers and then on the heel of the left *open hand*, palm facing right and fingers pointing up.

interrogation
The questioning of a criminal suspect by law enforcement authorities. See sign for INQUEST².

interrogatory
Pertaining to the questioning of a criminal suspect by law enforcement authorities. See sign for INQUEST².

interstate commerce
Trade, business, and travel across state lines.

- **business** Brush the base of the right *B hand*, palm forward, with a repeated movement on the back of the left *open hand*, palm down.

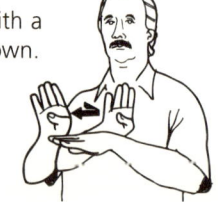

---- [sign continues] ---->

invasion of privacy

- **state** Move the index-finger side of the right *S hand*, palm facing forward, down from the fingers to the heel of the left *open hand*, palm facing right and fingers pointing up, in front of the chest.

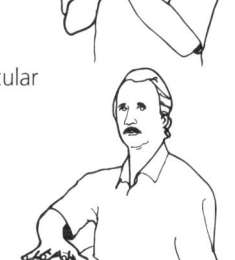

- **area**[1] Move the right *5 hand*, palm facing down, in a flat circular movement near the right side of the body.

intervene To insert oneself as a party in a lawsuit that is already pending between other parties in order to protect some interest.

- **interrupt** Sharply hit the little-finger side of the right *open hand*, palm facing in at an angle, at the base of the thumb and index finger of the left *open hand*.

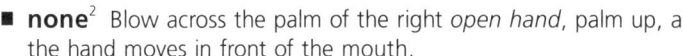

intestate Lacking a valid will at the time of one's death.

- **die** Beginning with both *open hands* in front of the body, right palm up and left palm down, flip the hands to the right, turning the right palm down and the left palm up.

- Fingerspell: W-I-L-L

- **none**[2] Blow across the palm of the right *open hand*, palm up, as the hand moves in front of the mouth.

invasion of privacy Intrusion into an individual's private and personal affairs, or disclosure of personal information about a private person without a legitimate new purpose.

- **secret** Tap the thumb side of the right *A hand*, palm left, against the mouth with a repeated movement.

[sign continues]

invasion of privacy

- **your** Push the palm of the right *open hand*, palm forward and fingers pointing up, toward the person being talked to.

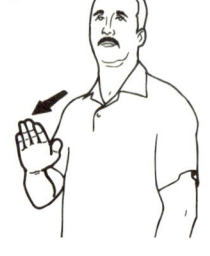

- **pry** Bring the index finger of the right *X hand*, palm facing forward, from in front of the face downward in a large arc, ending with the bent right index finger inserted into the index-finger side opening of the left *S hand* held in front of the body, palm facing right.

involuntary Not voluntary; independent of one's will. See signs for COERCE[1,2].

involuntary manslaughter[1] Causing death through recklessness or negligence.

- **kill** Push the side of the extended right index finger, palm down, across the palm of the left *open hand*, palm right, with a deliberate movement.

- **not** Bring the thumb of the right *10 hand* forward from under the chin with a deliberate movement.

- **intend** Touch the right side of the forehead with the extended right index finger. Then touch the fingertips of the right *V hand*, palm facing down, in the palm of the left *open hand*, palm facing up and fingers pointing forward, and then twist the right wrist and touch the fingertips down again.

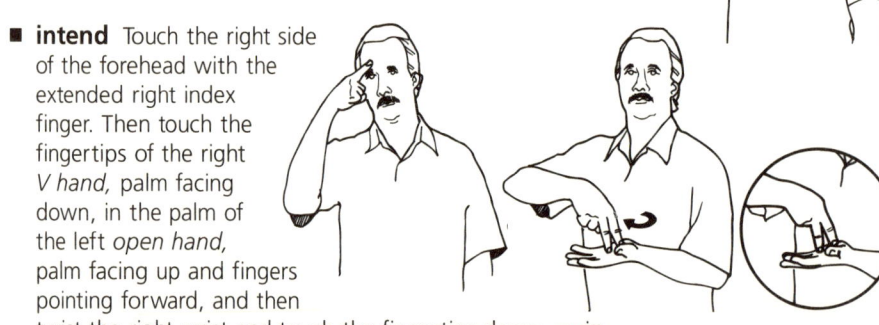

issue

involuntary manslaughter[2] (alternate sign)

- **accidental** With the middle fingers of the right *Y hand* against the chin, twist the hand with a deliberate movement.

- **kill** Push the side of the extended right index finger, palm down, across the palm of the left *open hand*, palm right, with a deliberate movement.

involuntary servitude See sign for SERVITUDE.

irreconcilable differences Issues that cannot be solved by arbitration or mediation and are used for grounds in divorce proceedings.

- **get-along** Beginning with both *open hands* in front of the body, palms facing in and fingers pointing toward each other, simultaneously move the hands forward a short distance.

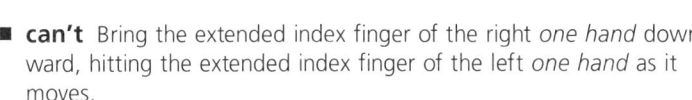

- **can't** Bring the extended index finger of the right *one hand* downward, hitting the extended index finger of the left *one hand* as it moves.

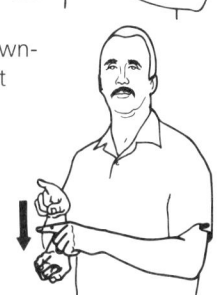

issue Any material fact or legal principle upon which the two sides in a case may disagree.

- **point** Bring the right extended index finger, palm left, with a deliberate movement to touch the left extended index finger held in front of the chest, palm facing right and finger pointing up.

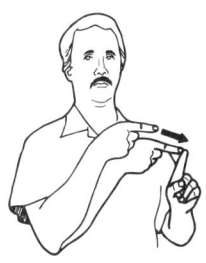

itemized deduction

itemized deduction Any of a number of specific types of expense that must be specifically listed on a tax return to be claimed as a deduction.

- **put-down** Touch the fingertips of the right *flattened O hand*, palm down, several places down the palm of the left *open hand*, palm up.

- **subtract** Beginning with the fingertips of the right *curved 5 hand* touching the palm of the left *open hand* held in front of the left side of the chest, palm facing right and fingers pointing up, bring the right hand down off the base of the left hand while changing into an S hand.

jail[1] An institution, usually run by a county or municipality, for locking up offenders serving short sentences and to hold people awaiting trial. Same sign used for **penitentiary, prison**.

- **jail**[1] Bring the back of the right *4 hand* from near the chest forward with a double movement while bringing the left *4 hand* in to meet the right hand, ending with the fingers crossed at an angle, both palms facing in.

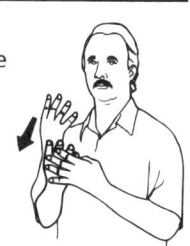

jail[2] (alternate sign) Same sign used for **penitentiary, prison**.

- **jail**[2] Bring the back of the fingers of the right *V hand* from near the chest forward to meet at an angle across the fingers of the left *V hand*, both palms facing in.

jail[3], **commit, imprison,** or **put in jail** To take into or hold in lawful custody.

- **jail**[3] Beginning with the right *curved 5 hand*, palm left, in front of the right side of the body, close the fingers into an *S hand*, and move it to the left under the downturned left *open hand*, held in front of the chest, fingers pointing right.

jail[4], **commit, imprison,** or **put in jail** (alternate sign)

- **jail**[4] Beginning with the right *4 hand*, palm forward, near the right side of the face, swing the hand around, ending with the right palm in front of the face.

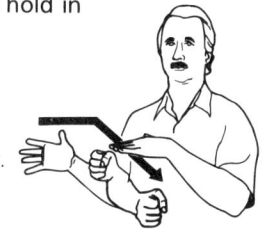

jail[5], **commit, imprison,** or **put in jail** (alternate sign)

- **jail**[5] Shove the right *S hand*, palm left, forward under the left *open hand*, palm down, with a deliberate movement.

Jane Doe

Jane Doe or **John Doe** A fictitious name used in legal documents either to conceal a person's identity or because the person's real name is not known.

- **don't know** Beginning with the fingers of the right *open hand* touching the right side of the forehead, swing the hand forward by twisting the wrist, ending with the fingers pointing forward in front of the right shoulder.

- **who** With the extended right index finger, palm down, draw a little circle around the mouth.

jeopardy or **in jeopardy** Risk of punishment for an offense.

- **danger** Move the thumb of the right *10 hand*, palm left, upward on the back of the left *A hand*, palm in, with a double movement.

John Doe See signs for JANE DOE.

join To bring an additional claim or party into the case. Same sign used for **vested**.

- **include** Swing the right *5 hand*, palm down, in a circular movement over the left *S hand*, palm in, while changing into a *flattened O hand*, ending with the fingertips of the right hand inserted in the center of the thumb side of the left hand.

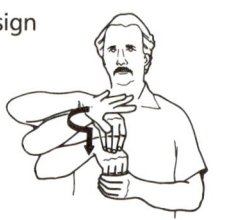

joint Involving two or more people or entities acting or being dealt with together.

- **with** Beginning with both *A hands* in front of the chest, palms facing each other, bring the hands together with a double movement.

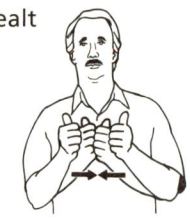

joint adventure See sign for JOINT VENTURE.

joint and several When multiple defendants are named in a lawsuit, the accusations can apply to each person named individually or to all defendants as a group at the option of the person initiating the action.

- **together** With the palm sides of both *A hands* together, move the hands forward in an arc in front of the body.

---- [sign continues] ---->

joint custody

- **only** Beginning with the extended right index finger pointing up in front of the right shoulder, palm facing forward, twist the wrist in, ending with the palm facing in near the right side of the chest.

joint custody An arrangement whereby divorced parents continue to share responsibility for raising their children.

- **divorce**[2] Beginning with the right *curved hand*, palm facing down, clasping the left *curved hand*, palm facing up, bring the hands apart while opening into *5 hands*, fingers pointing up and palms forward.

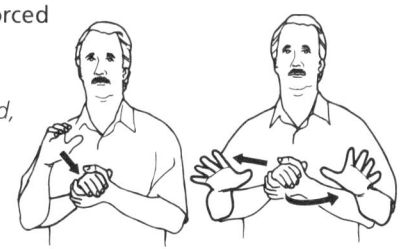

- **finish** With both *5 hands* apart in front of the body, palms up, quickly turn the hands over toward each other.

- **two-of-them** Swing the right *2 hand*, palm up, from side to side in front of the body.

- **children** Beginning with the index fingers of both *B hands* touching in front of the body, palms down and fingers pointing forward, move the hands outward to each side with a bouncing movement.

- **raise** Bring the right *open hand*, palm facing down and fingers pointing left, from in front of the chest upward.

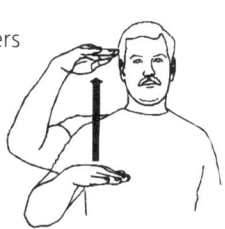

joint owner

joint owner See sign for JOINT TENANT.

joint tenant or **joint owner** Refers to concurrent ownership or interest in property by two or more people with equal interests.

- **s/he** Point the extended right index finger to the right, palm down.

- **s/he** Point the extended right index finger to the left, palm down.

- **two-of-them** Swing the right *2 hand*, palm up, from side to side in front of the body.

- Fingerspell: O-W-N

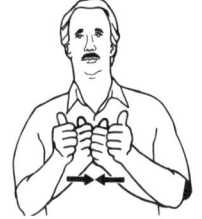

joint venture or **joint adventure** An arrangement between two or more people or entities to work together on a specific project.

- **with** Beginning with both *A hands* in front of the chest, palms facing each other, bring the hands together with a double movement.

- **work** Tap the heel of the right *S hand*, palm forward, with a double movement on the back of the left *S hand* held in front of the body, palm down.

judge¹, magistrate, justice, judicial, or **judiciary** A public official whose function is to hear and decide legal disputes, preside over trials, and move cases toward a final settlement or decision. Same sign used for **factfinder, trier of fact.**

- **judge** Move the right *modified X hand*, palm left, with a double up and down movement.

---- [sign continues] ---→

226

jump bail

- **person marker** Move both *open hands*, palms facing each other, downward along the sides of the body.

judge², magistrate, justice, judicial, or **judiciary** (alternate sign) Same sign used for **factfinder, trier of fact**.

- **court** Move both *F hands,* palms facing each other, up and down in front of each side of the chest with a repeated alternating movement.

- **person marker** Move both *open hands*, palms facing each other, downward along the sides of the body.

judgment¹, decree, or **disposition** A final decision in a case. Same sign used for **bench trial, hear, nonjury trial**.

- **judge** Move the right *modified X hand*, palm left, with a double up and down movement.

- **decide** Move the extended right index finger from the right side of the forehead, palm left, down in front of the chest while changing into an *F hand*, ending with both *F hands* moving downward in front of the body, palms facing each other.

judgement² See signs for DETERMINE, ORDER.

judicial See signs for JUDGE[1,2].

judiciary See signs for JUDGE[1,2].

jump bail To flee while free on bail.

- **money¹** Tap the back of the right *flattened O hand,* palm facing up, with a double movement against the palm of the left *open hand*, palm facing up.

---- [sign continues] ---->

jump bail

- **deposit** Beginning with the thumbs of both *10 hands* touching in front of the chest, both palms facing down, bring the hands downward and apart by twisting the wrists.

- **escape** Move the extended right index finger, palm left and finger pointing up, from between the index and middle fingers of the left *5 hand*, palm down in front of the chest, forward to the right with a deliberate movement.

jurisdiction The scope of power and authority of a court or administrative tribunal to decide legal issues and disputes.

- **authority** Beginning with the thumb of the right *A hand* touching the left upper arm, palm facing down, move the hand downward while turning the palm up, ending with the little-finger side touching the arm.

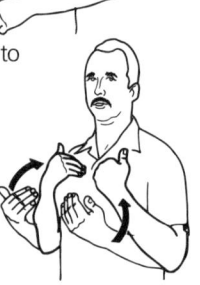

- **have** Bring the fingertips of both *bent hands*, palms facing in, in to touch each side of the chest.

jurisprudence The philosophy of law; the body of judicial opinions on record.

- **law** Place the palm side of the right *L hand*, palm facing left, first on the fingers and then on the heel of the left *open hand*, palm facing right and fingers pointing up.

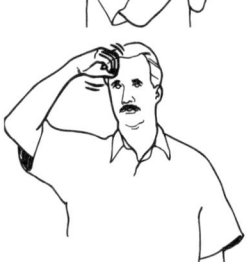

- **opinion** Move the right *O hand*, palm left in front of the forehead, downward in front of the head with a double movement.

---- [sign continues] -->

just compensation

- **put-down** Touch the fingertips of the right *flattened O hand*, palm down, to the palm of the left *open hand*, palm up. Then slap the palm of the right *open hand* against the left palm.

juror A member of the jury.

- **jury** Beginning with the little-finger sides of both *bent 4 hands*, palms in, together in front of the chest, move the hands apart to each side.

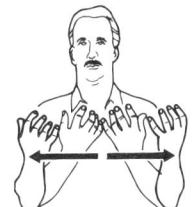

- **person marker** Move both *open hands*, palms facing each other, downward along the sides of the body.

jury or **petit jury** A group of citizens called upon to hear the evidence at a trial, decide the facts, and render a verdict.

- **jury** Beginning with the little-finger sides of both *bent 4 hands*, palms in, together in front of the chest, move the hands apart to each side.

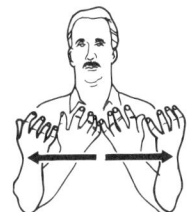

jury trial See sign for TRIAL BY JURY.

just compensation The compensation required by the Fifth Amendment that the state or federal government must pay to a property owner whose property is taken for public use.

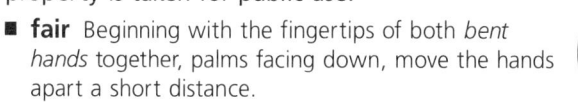

- **fair** Beginning with the fingertips of both *bent hands* together, palms facing down, move the hands apart a short distance.

- **pay**[2] Beginning with the right *flattened O hand* in front of the right side of the body, palm facing up, move the hand forward while quickly sliding the thumb off each finger. See sign for COMPENSATORY DAMAGES.

justice

justice[1] The ideal and fair treatment of all people by each other and their governments.

- **court** Move both *F hands,* palms facing each other, up and down in front of each side of the chest with a repeated alternating movement.

- **fair** Beginning with the fingertips of both *bent hands* together, palms facing down, move the hands apart a short distance.

justice[2] See signs for JUDGE[1,2].

justification A legally sufficient excuse (e.g., entrapment, duress, etc.) for having done something that otherwise would have been considered a crime.

- **law** Place the palm side of the right *L hand,* palm facing left, first on the fingers and then on the heel of the left *open hand,* palm facing right and fingers pointing up.

- **reason** Move the fingertips of the right *R hand,* palm facing in, in a circular movement in front of the right side of the forehead with a double movement.

juvenile delinquent See sign for DELINQUENT.

kangaroo court A mock court set up by criminals to reach a predetermined verdict of guilty.

- **court** Move both *F hands,* palms facing each other, up and down in front of each side of the chest with a repeated alternating movement.

- **false** Brush the extended right index finger, palm facing left, across the tip of the nose from right to left by bending the wrist.

kickback A form of bribery in which a company that is awarded a contract turns over a portion of the money received to an employee of the other party as a reward for helping it win the contract.

- **pay-me** Move the right *flattened O hand*, palm facing up, back under the downturned palm of the left *open hand* while quickly sliding the thumb off each finger.

- **give-underhanded** Move the right *flattened O hand*, palm facing up, forward under the downturned palm of the left *open hand*.

kidnapping or **abduction** The crime of carrying off a person for the purpose of demanding money for his or her release.

- **kidnap** Beginning with the right *V hand,* palm facing up, in front of the chest, pull the hand deliberately back toward the chest while bending the fingers in tightly.

kill

kill See signs for HOMICIDE[1,2,3].

kite[1], bad check, hot check, or **NSF check** 1. To write a check knowing that there are not yet sufficient funds in the account to cover it. 2. A worthless or fraudulently written check.

- **hot** Beginning with the right *curved 5 hand* in front of the mouth, palm facing in, with a double movement twist the wrist forward with a deliberate movement while moving the hand downward a short distance.

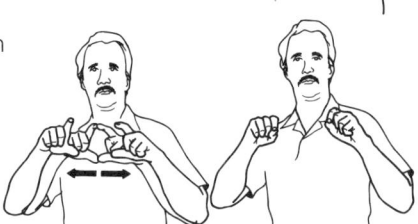

- **check** Beginning with the fingertips of both *L hands* touching in front of the chest, palms facing forward, take the hands apart to in front of each shoulder, and then pinch each thumb and index finger together.

kite[2], bad check, hot check, or **NSF check**
(alternate sign)

- **check** Beginning with the fingertips of both *L hands* touching in front of the chest, palms facing forward, take the hands apart to in front of each shoulder, and then pinch each thumb and index finger together.

- **no-good** With the right hand form an *N hand*; then quickly twist the wrist and form a *G hand*.

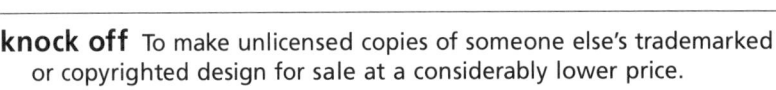

knock off To make unlicensed copies of someone else's trademarked or copyrighted design for sale at a considerably lower price.

- **go-to** Move both extended index fingers from pointing up in front of the body, palms facing forward, then move the hands deliberately forward while bending the wrists so the fingers point forward.

- **your** Push the palm of the right *open hand*, palm forward and fingers pointing up, toward the person being talked to.

---- [sign continues] -->

knowledge

- **name** Tap the middle-finger side of the right *H hand* across the index-finger side of the left *H hand* with a double movement.

- **take-advantage** With a double movement flick the bent middle finger of the right *5 hand* upward off the heel of the upturned left *open hand*.

- **sell** Beginning with both *flattened O hands* held in front of each side of the chest, palms down and fingers pointing down, swing the fingertips forward and back by twisting the wrists upward with a double movement.

- **cheap** Brush the index-finger side of the right *B hand* downward on the palm of the left *open hand*.

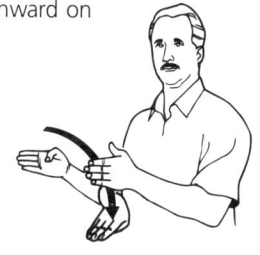

knowledge or **actual knowledge** Awareness of a fact.

- **knowledge** Tap the fingertips of the right *bent hand*, palm down, with a double movement on the right side of the forehead.

233

labor union See signs for UNION[1,2].

land, real property, real estate, or **realty** An interest in land or things attached to it, including buildings or structures.

- Fingerspell: R-E-A-L
- **land** Beginning with both *flattened O hands* in front of each side of the body, palms facing up, move the thumb of both hands smoothly with a double movement across each fingertip, starting with the little fingers and ending as *A hands* each time.

- **and** Move the right *5 hand,* palm facing left, to the right in front of the body while closing the fingers to the thumb, ending in a *flattened O hand.*

- **things** Beginning with both *open hands* in front of the body, palms facing up, move the hand to the sides away from each other in a double arc.

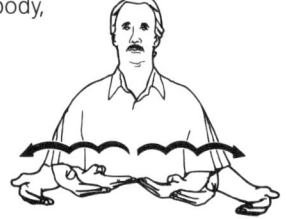

landlord[1] The person who grants a lease on real property to a tenant.

- **landlord** Move the right *L hand*, palm down, in an arc from left to right in front of the chest.

landlord[2] (alternate sign)

- Fingerspell: C-O-N
- **person marker** Move both *open hands*, palms facing each other, downward along the sides of the body.

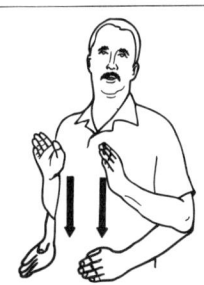

lapse

landmark case A case whose decision establishes a new legal principle of historic importance.

- **law** Place the palm side of the right *L hand*, palm facing left, first on the fingers and then on the heel of the left *open hand*, palm facing right and fingers pointing up.

- **decide** Move the extended right index finger from the right side of the forehead, palm left, down in front of the chest while changing into an *F hand*, ending with both *F hands* moving downward in front of the body, palms facing each other.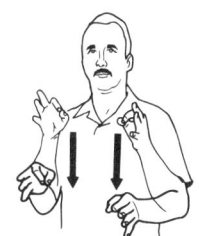

- **only** Beginning with the extended right index finger pointing up in front of the right shoulder, palm facing forward, twist the wrist in, ending with the palm facing in near the right side of the chest.

- **time** Tap the bent index finger of the right *X hand*, palm down, with a double movement on the wrist of the downturned left hand.

- **important** Beginning with the fingertips of both *F hands* touching, palms facing down, bring the hands upward in a circular movement, ending with the index-finger sides of the *F hands* touching in front of the chest.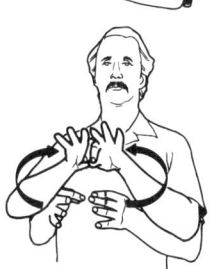

lapse To expire because of the passage of time.

- **time** Tap the bent index finger of the right *X hand*, palm down, with a double movement on the wrist of the downturned left hand.

---- [sign continues] ---→

lapse

- **used-up** Beginning with little-finger side of the right *5 hand*, palm left, on the back of the downturned left *open hand*, slide the right hand off to the right while closing into an *S hand*.

larceny The crime of wrongfully taking possession of personal property from another with intent to convert it to one's own use. Same sign used for **steal, theft**.

- **steal**[1] Beginning with the index-finger side of the right *V hand*, palm facing down, on the elbow of the bent left arm, held at an upward angle across the chest, pull the right hand upward toward the left wrist while bending the fingers in tightly.

last will and testament See sign for WILL.

latent Not obvious, but could be discovered with careful inspection.

- **vague** With the palms of both *5 hands*, move the right hand in a circular movement on the left palm.

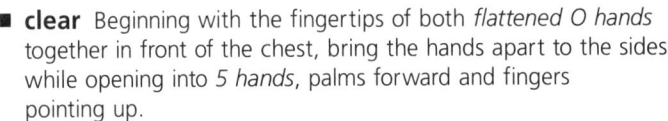

- **clear** Beginning with the fingertips of both *flattened O hands* together in front of the chest, bring the hands apart to the sides while opening into *5 hands*, palms forward and fingers pointing up.

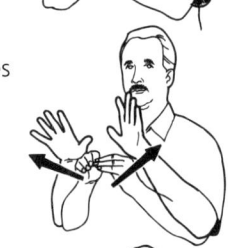

- **not** Bring the thumb of the right *10 hand* forward from under the chin with a deliberate movement.

law, act, legislation, legislative, or **statute** The body of rules and principles for human behavior and the conduct of government. Same sign used for **code, legal**.

- **law** Place the palm side of the right *L hand*, palm facing left, first on the fingers and then on the heel of the left *open hand*, palm facing right and fingers pointing up.

lease

law clerk A recent law graduate employed as an assistant to a judge for one or two years.

- **judge** Move the right *modified X hand*, palm left, with a double up and down movement.

- **assistant** Use the thumb of the right *L hand* under the little-finger side of the left *A hand* to push the left hand upward in front of the chest.

- **person marker** Move both *open hands*, palms facing each other, downward along the sides of the body.

lawyer See sign for ATTORNEY.

leading question A question phrased so as to suggest the desired answer.

- **question**¹ Move the extended right index finger from pointing forward in front of the right shoulder, palm facing down, downward with a curving movement while retracting the index finger.

- **entice** Beginning with both *modified X hands* in front of the chest, right hand more forward than the left, pull the hands back toward the chest with a circular movement over each other.

lease A contract temporarily conveying the right to exclusive possession and use of tangible personal property.

- **monthly** Move the extended right index finger, palm facing in and finger pointing left, downward with a double movement from the tip to the base of the extended left index finger, palm facing right and finger pointing up in front of the chest.

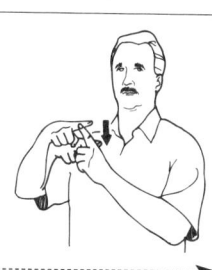

---- [sign continues] --→

237

lease

- **paper** Brush the heel of the right *open hand* with a double movement on the heel of the left *open hand*, palms facing each other.

- **sign** Place the extended fingers of the right *H hand*, palm down, firmly down on the upturned palm of the left *open hand* held in front of the chest.

leave or leave of court Permission from a court to take some action.

- **allow** Beginning with both *open hands* in front of the waist, palms facing each other and fingers pointing down, bring the fingers forward and upward by bending the wrists.

- **can** Move both *S hands,* palms facing down, downward simultaneously in front of each side of the body.

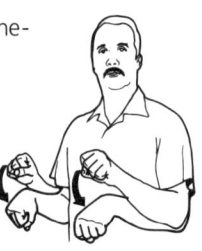

leave of court See sign for LEAVE.

legacy A gift of property as designated in a will. See sign for BEQUEATH. See sign for WILL.

legal Permitted by law or pertaining to law. See sign for LAW.

legal action, action, or proceeding Broadly, any matter handled by or filed with a court.

- **court** Move both *F hands,* palms facing each other, up and down in front of each side of the chest with a repeated alternating movement.
- Fingerspell: C-A-S-E

legal right

legal age The age at which a person becomes legally capable of exercising certain rights or assuming certain responsibilities.
- **law** Place the palm side of the right *L hand*, palm facing left, first on the fingers and then on the heel of the left *open hand*, palm facing right and fingers pointing up.

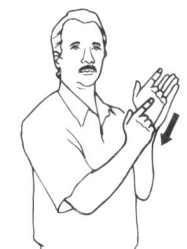

- **age** Beginning with the right *C hand* near the chin, palm left, pull the hand downward with a double movement changing into a *S hand* each time.

legal assistant See sign for PARALEGAL.

legal capacity See sign for CAPACITY.

legal form See sign for FORM.

legal right¹ Broadly, any right protected by law.
- **law** Place the palm side of the right *L hand*, palm facing left, first on the fingers and then on the heel of the left *open hand*, palm facing right and fingers pointing up.

- **allow** Beginning with both *open hands* in front of the waist, palms facing each other and fingers pointing down, bring the fingers forward and upward by bending the wrists.

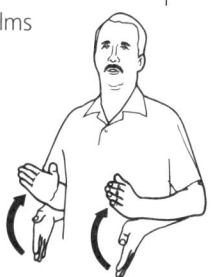

legal right² (alternate sign)
- **law** Place the palm side of the right *L hand*, palm facing left, first on the fingers and then on the heel of the left *open hand*, palm facing right and fingers pointing up.

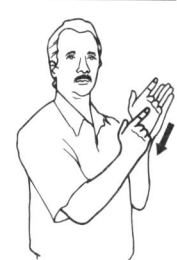

---- [sign continues] -->

legal right

- **rights** Slide the little-finger side of the right *open hand*, palm facing left, in an upward arc across the upturned left palm held in front of the body.

legal tender[1] or money Currency that may lawfully be used in payment of debts.

- **money** Tap the back of the right *flattened O hand*, palm facing up, with a double movement against the palm of the left *open hand*, palm facing up.

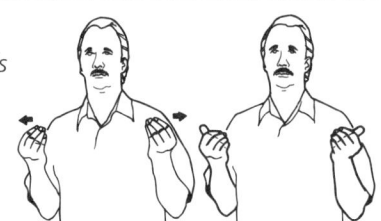

legal tender[2] or money (alternate sign)

- **money** Beginning with both *flattened O hands* in front of each side of the body, palms facing up, move the thumb of each hand smoothly across each fingertip, starting with the little fingers and ending as *10 hands*.

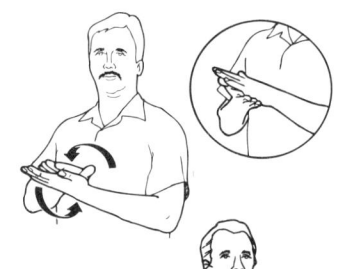

legalize To adopt legislation making conduct that formerly was unlawful lawful.

- **become** Beginning with the palm of the right *open hand* laying across the upturned palm of the left *open hand*, rotate the hands, exchanging positions while keeping the palms together.

- **law** Place the palm side of the right *L hand*, palm facing left, first on the fingers and then on the heel of the left *open hand*, palm facing right and fingers pointing up.

legislation Related form: **legislative**. See sign for LAW.

legislature The lawmaking branch of the government.

- **legislature** Move the index-finger side of the right *L hand* from the right side of the chest in an arc around to touch again at the left side of the chest.

lethal weapon See sign for DEADLY WEAPON.

levy

letter of credit A letter in which a bank or other person, at the request of a customer, promises a third person that it will honor demands for sums owed by the customer.

- **letter** Touch the extended thumb of the right *10 hand* to the lips, palm in, and then move the thumb downward to touch the palm of the left *open hand* held in front of the chest, palm up.

- **borrow** With the little-finger side of the right *V hand* across the index-finger side of the left *V hand,* bring the hands back, ending with the right index finger against the chest.

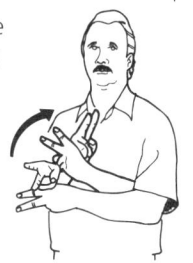

- **will** Move the right *open hand*, palm left and fingers pointing up, from the right side of the chin forward while tipping the fingers down.

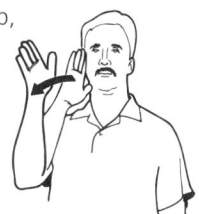

letter of intent A letter confirming an agreement to agree.

- **letter** Touch the extended thumb of the right *10 hand* to the lips, palm in, and then move the thumb downward to touch the palm of the left *open hand* held in front of the chest, palm up.

- **agree** Move the extended right index finger from touching the right side of the forehead downward to beside the extended left index finger, ending with both fingers pointing forward in front of the body, palms down.

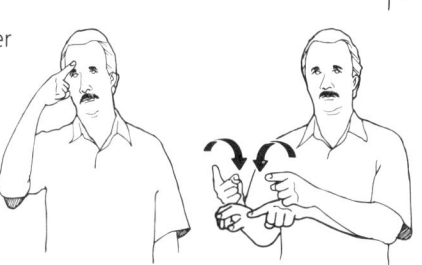

levy[1] To impose a tax or fine.

- **require** With the extended index finger of the right *X hand* touching the palm of the left *open hand,* bring both hands back toward the chest.
- Fingerspell: T-A-X

levy

levy[2] (alternate sign)

- **require** With the extended index finger of the right *X hand* touching the palm of the left *open hand*, bring both hands back toward the chest.

- **cost** Strike the knuckle of the right *X hand*, palm facing in, down on the palm of the left *open hand*, palm facing right and fingers pointing forward.

liability The sum that one is ordered to pay in damages or fines when found liable for a crime. See sign for DEBT.

liable Legally responsible.

- **law** Place the palm side of the right *L hand*, palm facing left, first on the fingers and then on the heel of the left *open hand*, palm facing right and fingers pointing up.

- **responsible** With the fingertips of both *bent hands* on the right shoulder, push the shoulder down slightly.

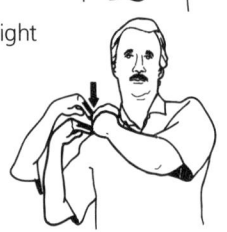

libel 1. A form of defamation in which a statement is communicated in writing, on film, or some other medium with a degree of permanence. 2. To misrepresent with damaging or defamatory information.

- **lie** Move the index-finger side of the right *bent hand*, palm down and fingers pointing left, across the chin from right to left.

- **ruin** Beginning with the right *curved 5 hand* near the face and the left *curved 5 hand* in front of the body, close the right hand into an *A hand* while moving it quickly down and close the left hand into an *A hand* while moving it quickly up, brushing the knuckles of the hands together as they pass each other.

---- [sign continues] ---->

liberty

- **name** Tap the middle-finger side of the right *H hand* across the index-finger side of the left *H hand* with a double movement.

- **your** Push the palm of the right *open hand*, palm forward and fingers pointing up, toward the person being talked to with a double movement.

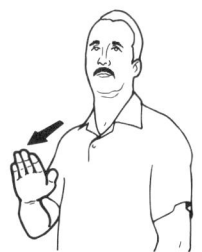

liberal construction or **broad construction** A broad interpretation of a statute that considers the overall purposes for which the statute was enacted.

- **law** Place the palm side of the right *L hand,* palm facing left, first on the fingers and then on the heel of the left *open hand,* palm facing right and fingers pointing up.

- **interpret** With the fingertips of both *F hands* touching in front of the chest, palms facing each other, twist the hands in opposite directions to reverse positions.

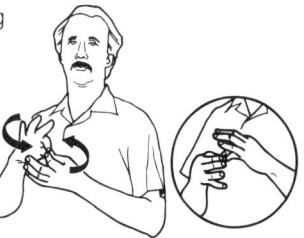

liberty[1] Freedom of action to control one's own life.
- **liberty** Beginning with both *L hands* crossed at the wrists in front of the chest, palms facing in opposite directions, twist the wrists and move the hands apart, ending with the hands in front of each shoulder, palms facing forward.

liberty[2] (alternate sign)
- **free** Beginning with both *S hands* crossed at the wrists in front of the chest, palms facing in opposite directions, twist the wrists and move the hands apart, ending with the hands in front of each shoulder, palms facing forward.

license

license Government permission for a person to do something otherwise forbidden; a certificate evidencing such permission (e.g., doctor's license). Same sign used for **certificate, certification.**
- **license** Tap the thumbs of both L hands with a double movement in front of the chest, palms facing forward.

lie detector See sign for POLYGRAPH.

lien¹ An attachment that a creditor may obtain on property so the property may be seized if the debtor fails to make payment.
- **file** Move the fingers of the right V hand, palm facing forward, downward on each side of the extended left index finger, which is pointing up in front of the chest.

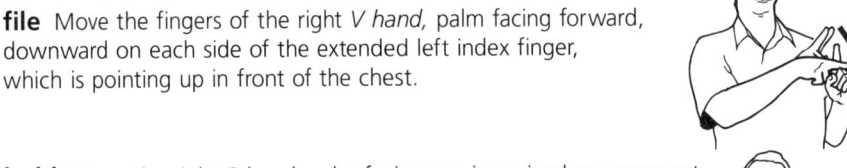

- **hold** Move the right S hand, palm facing up, in a circular movement in front of the right side of the chest.

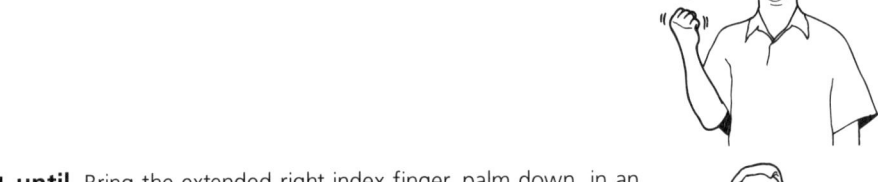

- **until** Bring the extended right index finger, palm down, in an upward arc to touch the extended left index finger.

- **catch-up** Move the right A hand, palm facing left, to behind the left A hand held somewhat forward of the body.

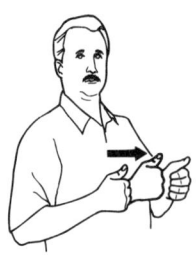

lien² (alternate sign)
- **file** Move the fingers of the right V hand, palm facing forward, downward on each side of the extended left index finger, which is pointing up in front of the chest.

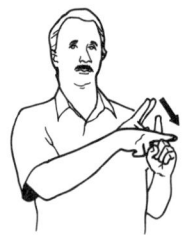

---- [sign continues] -->

life estate

- **land** Beginning with both *flattened O hands* in front of each side of the body, palms facing up, move the thumb of both hands smoothly with a double movement across each fingertip, starting with the little fingers and ending as *A hands* each time.

- **hold** Move the right *S hand*, palm facing up, in a circular movement in front of the right side of the chest.

life estate or **tenancy** An estate whose duration is measured by the life of some person or groups of people.

- **sign** Place the extended fingers of the right *H hand*, palm down, firmly down on the upturned palm of the left *open hand* held in front of the chest.

- **understand** Beginning with the right *modified X hand*, palm in, near the right side of the forehead, flick the index finger upward with a deliberate movement.

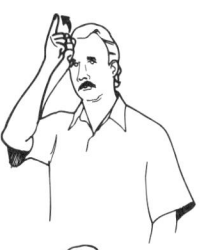

- **live** Move both *10 hands*, thumbs pointing up, upward on each side of the chest.

- **can** Move both *S hands*, palms facing down, downward simultaneously in front of each side of the body.

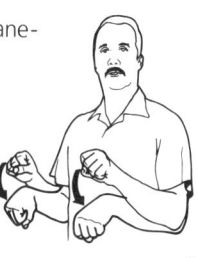

---- [sign continues] ---➤

life estate

- **happen** Beginning with both extended index fingers in front of the body, palms facing up and fingers pointing forward, flip the hands over toward each other, ending with the palms facing down.

- **die** Beginning with both *open hands* in front of the body, right palm down and left palm up, flip the hands to the right, turning the right palm up and the left palm down.

- **mean** Touch the fingertips of the right *V hand*, palm facing down, in the palm of the left *open hand*, palm facing up and fingers pointing forward, and then twist the right wrist and touch the fingertips down again.

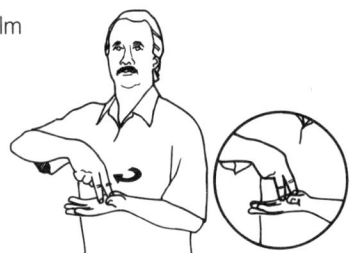

- **give-me**² Beginning with both *X hands* in front of the body, palms facing each other, bring the hands back to touch on each side of the chest.

life insurance Insurance under which the insurance company is to pay out a specified sum of money upon the death of the insured person.

- **live** Move both *10 hands*, thumbs pointing up, upward on each side of the chest.

- **insurance** Move the right *I hand*, palm forward, from side to side with a repeated movement in front of the right shoulder.

litigate

limitation period See sign for STATUE OF LIMITATIONS.

limited liability A contractual arrangement by which one party agrees to a ceiling on the other's liability in case something goes wrong.

- **responsible** With the fingertips of both *bent hands* on the right shoulder, push the shoulder down slightly.

- **limit** Beginning with both *bent hands* in front of the chest, right hand above the left hand and both palms facing down, move both hands forward simultaneously.

liquidate To sell assets for cash, especially other than in the ordinary course of business. Related form: **liquidation**.

- **sell** Beginning with both *flattened O hands* held in front of each side of the chest, palms down and fingers pointing down, swing the fingertips forward and back by twisting the wrists upward with a double movement.

- **everything** Bring the knuckle side of the right *10 hand* down the thumb side of the left *10 hand*. Then beginning with both *5 hands* together, throw the hands out to each side, palms up.

litigant See signs for PLAINTIFF[1,2].

litigate[1] To make something the subject of a lawsuit; to perform the tasks entailed in the pursuit of a court case. Related form: **litigation**. Same sign used for **charge**.

- **against** With a deliberate movement, hit the fingertips of the right *bent hand* into the left *open hand*, palm right and fingers pointing forward.

litigate[2] (alternate sign) Same sign used for **charge**. Related form: **litigation**.

- **file** Move the fingers of the right *V hand,* palm facing forward, downward on each side of the extended left index finger, which is pointing up in front of the chest.

---- [sign continues] ---→

247

litigate

- **court** Move both *F hands*, palms facing each other, up and down in front of each side of the chest with a repeated alternating movement.

- **go-ahead** Beginning with both *open hands* in front of the body, palms facing in and fingers pointing toward each other, simultaneously move the hands forward a short distance.

---

litigate[3] (alternate sign) Related form: **litigation**. Same sign used for **charge**.

- **litigate** Throw both *bent V hands* forward while opening into *V hands*, palms facing each other, and then pull the hands back while closing to *bent V hands* again near the chest.

---

living separate and apart The period of time designated by a state that a couple must not cohabit prior to a divorce.

- **two-of-them** Swing the right *2 hand*, palm up, from side to side in front of the body.

- **separate** Beginning with the knuckles of both *10 hands* touching in front of the chest, palms facing in, take the hands apart.

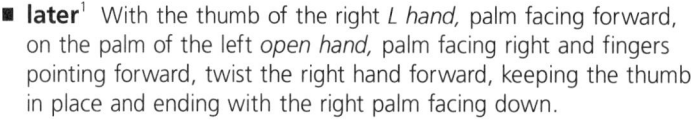

- **later**[1] With the thumb of the right *L hand*, palm facing forward, on the palm of the left *open hand*, palm facing right and fingers pointing forward, twist the right hand forward, keeping the thumb in place and ending with the right palm facing down.

- **divorce**[2] Beginning with the right *curved hand*, palm facing down, clasping the left *curved hand*, palm facing up, take the hands apart while opening into *5 hands*, fingers pointing up and palms forward.

248

living trust

living trust A trust established and effective during the grantor's lifetime.

- **money** Tap the back of the right *flattened O hand,* palm facing up, with a double movement against the palm of the left *open hand,* palm facing up.

- **inherit** With the right *curved hand* over the left *curved hand,* palms facing each other, move the hands forward a short distance.

- **other** Beginning with the right *10 hand* in front of the chest, palm down, flip the hand over, ending with palm up.

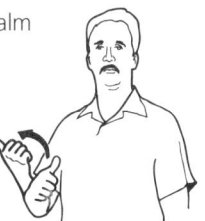

- **can** Move both *S hands,* palms facing down, downward simultaneously in front of each side of the body.

- **subscribe** With right *modified C hand* in front of the right shoulder, palm left, bring the hand downward with a double movement, closing the fingers to form an *A hand* each time.

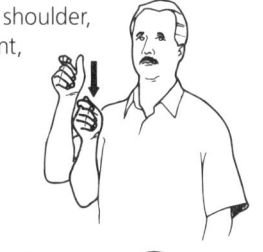

- **can** Move both *S hands,* palms facing down, downward simultaneously in front of each side of the body.

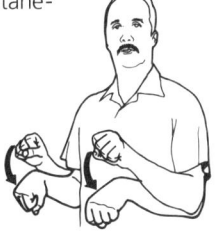

living will

living will, advance directive, or health-care proxy
A formal instrument in which an individual states what medical measures he or she wants taken or withheld in the event of terminal illness.

- **itself** Bring the knuckles of the right *10 hand*, palm facing left, firmly against the side of the extended left index finger, palm facing right and finger pointing up in front of the chest.

- **sick** Touch the bent middle finger of the right *5 hand* to the forehead while touching the bent middle finger of the left *5 hand* to the abdomen.

- **information** Beginning with the fingertips of the right *flattened O hand* near the forehead and the left *flattened O hand* in front of the chest, move both hands forward while opening into *5 hands*, palms facing up.

- **other** Beginning with the right *10 hand* in front of the chest, palm down, flip the hand over, ending with palm up.

- **how** Beginning with the knuckles of both *curved hands* touching in front of the chest, palms facing down, twist the hands upward and forward, ending with the fingers together pointing up and the palms facing up.

- **keep** Tap the little-finger side of the right *K hand* across the index-finger side of the left *K hand* palms facing in opposite directions.

lower court

local Referring to a jurisdiction smaller than a state.

- **area**[3] Rub the palm of the right *open hand* on the index-finger side of the left *S hand* held in front of the body, palm right.

loss In a sale of property, the amount by which the value received falls short of the owner's basis in the property.

- **lost** Beginning with the fingertips of both *flattened O hands* touching in front of the body, palms facing up, drop the fingers quickly downward and away from each other while opening into *5 hands,* ending with both palms angled down and fingers angled downward.

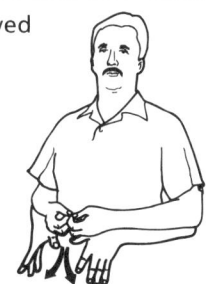

lower court The first-level court where trials are conducted, but whose decisions are subject to appeal in a higher court.

- **court** Move both *F hands,* palms facing each other, up and down in front of each side of the chest with a repeated alternating movement.

- **lower** Beginning with both *bent hands* in front of each shoulder, palms facing each other, move them downward in front of each side of the chest.

251

magistrate A judge in an inferior court (e.g., a police court, justice of the peace court) with limited jurisdiction to deal with minor offenses.
- **judge** Move the right *modified X hand*, palm left, with a double up and down movement.

- **person marker** Move both *open hands*, palms facing each other, downward along the sides of the body.

- **lower** Beginning with both *bent hands* in front of each shoulder, palms facing each other, move them downward in front of each side of the chest. See signs for JUDGE[1,2].

mail fraud The federal crime of using the mail in connection with a scheme to defraud.
- **fool** Strike the knuckles of the right *A hand*, palm facing forward, against the extended left index finger with a repeated movement as the hands move from left to right in front of the body.

- **letter** Touch the extended thumb of the right *10 hand* to the lips, palm in, and then move the thumb downward to touch the palm of the left *open hand* held in front of the chest, palm up.

---- [sign continues] -->

make whole

- **how** Beginning with the knuckles of both *curved hands* touching in front of the chest, palms facing down, twist the hands upward and forward, ending with the fingers together pointing up and the palms facing up.

- **distribute** Beginning with the back of both *flattened O hands* touching in front of the chest, palms facing up, move the hands forward and apart while opening into *curved 5 hands,* ending in front of each side of the body, palms facing up.

maintenance See signs for ALIMONY[1,2].

make, **draw up,** or **execute** To execute an instrument.

- **start** Beginning with the extended right index finger, palm down, inserted between the index and middle fingers of the left *open hand*, palm right and fingers pointing forward, twist the right hand back, ending with palm in.

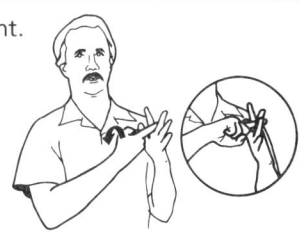

- **process** Beginning with both *open hands* in front of the body, palms facing in, left fingers pointing right and right fingers pointing left, and the left hand closer to the chest than the right hand, move the left hand over the right hand and then the right hand over the left hand in an alternating movement.

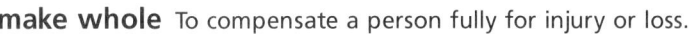

make whole To compensate a person fully for injury or loss.

- **pay**[2] Beginning with the right *flattened O hand* in front of the right side of the body, palm facing up, move the hand forward while quickly sliding the thumb off each finger.

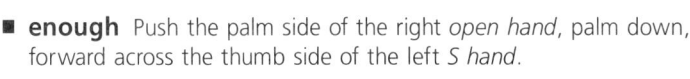

- **enough** Push the palm side of the right *open hand*, palm down, forward across the thumb side of the left *S hand*.

253

malice

malice Generally, criminal intent to do serious bodily injury.

- **intend** Touch the right side of the forehead with the extended right index finger. Then touch the fingertips of the right *V hand*, palm facing down, in the palm of the left *open hand*, palm facing up and fingers pointing forward, and then twist the right wrist and touch the fingertips down again.

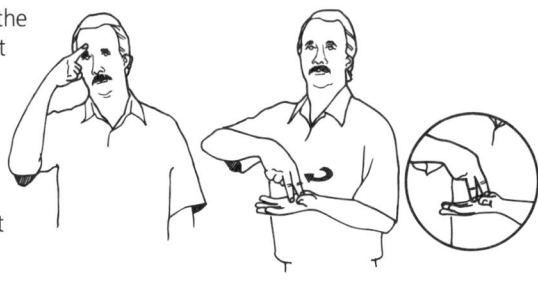

- **hurt** Beginning with the extended index fingers of both *one hands* pointing toward each other, right palm down and left palm up, twist the wrists in opposite directions, ending with the right palm up and the left palm down.

malpractice Negligence or other failure by a professional to live up to reasonable professional standards in the performance of client services.

- **specialty** Slide the little-finger side of the right *B hand*, palm left and fingers pointing forward, along the index-finger side of the left *B hand* held in front of the chest, palm right and fingers pointing forward.

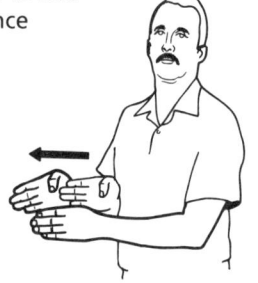

- **careless** Beginning with both *V hands* near each side of the head, palms facing each other, move the hands toward and past each other in front of the eyes with a short double movement.

mandate An order from an appellate court to the lower court communicating the higher court's decision as to how the case should be dealt with.

- **order** Move the extended right index finger, palm forward and finger pointing up, from in front of the mouth forward and down, ending with the finger pointing forward and the palm down.

---- [sign continues] -->

marshal

- **go-to** Move both extended index fingers from pointing up in front of the body forward with a deliberate movement to the right while turning the palms down.

mandatory Ordered by an authority. Same sign used for demand.

- **require** With the extended index finger of the right *X hand* touching the palm of the left *open hand*, bring both hands back toward the chest.

market value See signs for FAIR MARKET VALUE[1,2].

marketable title See signs for CLEAR TITLE[1,2].

marriage The legal relationship of husband and wife, carrying various rights and duties imposed by law.

- **marry** Bring the right *curved hand*, palm facing down, downward in front of the chest to clasp the left *curved hand*, palm facing up.

marshal[1] The federal officer who serves summonses, escorts criminal defendants, and otherwise assists in the functioning of a federal court.

- **government** Beginning with the extended right index finger pointing upward near the right side of the head, palm facing forward, twist the wrist to touch the finger to the right temple.

- **police** Tap the thumb side of the right *modified C hand*, palm facing left, against the left side of the chest with a double movement.

marshal[2] See signs for POLICE[1,2].

255

martial law

martial law or **military law** Government by the military, using military law and institutions in the place of civilian government.

- **army** Tap the palm side of both *A hands* against the right side of the chest, right hand above the left hand, with a repeated movement.

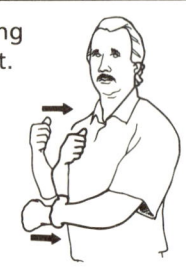

- **law** Place the palm side of the right *L hand*, palm facing left, first on the fingers and then on the heel of the left *open hand*, palm facing right and fingers pointing up.

material Important; of consequence.

- **important** Beginning with the fingertips of both *F hands* touching, palms facing down, bring the hands upward in a circular movement, ending with the index-finger sides of the *F hands* touching in front of the chest.

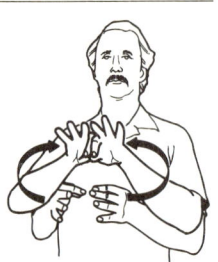

material witness A witness whose testimony is essential to one side or the other in a criminal case.

- **important** Beginning with the fingertips of both *F hands* touching, palms facing down, bring the hands upward in a circular movement, ending with the index-finger sides of the *F hands* touching in front of the chest.

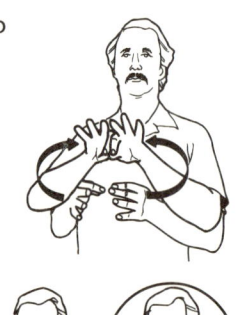

- **witness** With the index finger of the right *X hand* pull down slightly on the cheek near the outside corner of the right eye.

- **person marker** Move both *open hands*, palms facing each other, downward along the sides of the body.

Megan's Law

mediation A procedure in which a neutral outsider assists the parties to a dispute in reaching a settlement. Related form: **mediate**. See sign for NEGOTIATE[1].

meeting of the minds Derived from a view that there is no contract unless the parties share the same understanding of the deal. See sign for CONCUR.

Megan's Law A statute, originating in New Jersey, requiring registration by prior sex offenders whenever they take up residence in the state and prior to any subsequent change of address.

- **special** Grasp the left extended index finger, palm in and finger pointing up, with the fingers of the right *G hand* and pull upward in front of the chest.

- **law** Place the palm side of the right *L hand,* palm facing left, first on the fingers and then on the heel of the left *open hand,* palm facing right and fingers pointing up.

- **name** Tap the middle-finger side of the right *H hand* across the index-finger side of the left *H hand* with a double movement.
- Fingerspell: M-E-G-A-N

- **direct-to** Move the fingertips of the right *B hand,* palm left against the extended left index finger.

- **crime** Place the palm side of the right *L hand,* palm facing left, first on the fingers and then on the heel of the left *open hand,* palm facing right and fingers pointing up. Then beginning with both *S hands* in front of the body, index fingers touching and palms down, move the hands away from each other while twisting the wrists with a deliberate movement, ending with the palms facing each other.

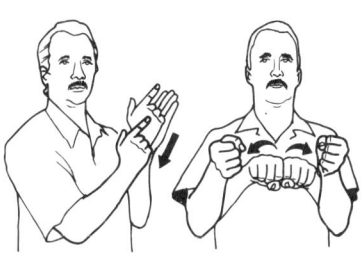

---- [sign continues] ---->

Megan's Law

- **person marker** Move both *open hands*, palms facing each other, downward along the sides of the body.

- **require** With the extended index finger of the right *X hand* touching the palm of the left *open hand,* bring both hands back toward the chest.

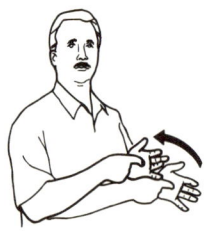

- **register** Tap the extended fingers of the right *R hand* on the palm of the left *open hand,* first to the heel and then to the fingertips.

- **name** Tap the middle-finger side of the right *H hand* across the index-finger side of the left *H hand* with a double movement.

- **must** Move the bent index finger of the right *X hand* downward with a deliberate movement in front of the right side of the body by bending the wrist down.

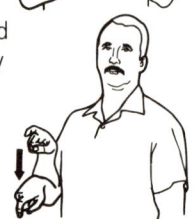

memorandum A brief written record or communication.
- Fingerspell: M-E-M-O

memory[1], recollection, or recovered memory
The ability to remember facts.

- **memory**[1] Beginning with the right extended index finger touching the forehead, palm down, pull the hand forward while closing to an *X hand*.

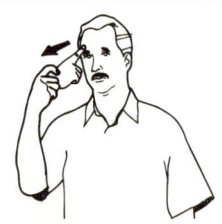

merits

memory², recollection, or recovered memory
(alternate sign)

- **remember** Move the thumb of the right *10 hand* from the right side of the forehead, palm facing left, smoothly down to touch the thumb of the left *10 hand* held in front of the body, palm facing down.

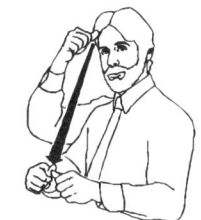

memory³, recollection, or recovered memory
(alternate sign)

- **memory²** With the thumb of the right *10 hand* on the forehead, palm up, twist the hand down.

mental cruelty
A traditional ground for divorce, consisting of a pattern of psychological abuse by one spouse rendering married life intolerable for the other.

- **mind** Tap the extended right index finger, palm facing in, against the right side of the forehead with a double movement.

- **cruel** Beginning with the right *curved 5 hand* near the face and the left *curved 5 hand* in front of the body, close the right hand into an *A hand* while moving it quickly down and close the left hand into an *A hand* while moving it quickly up, brushing the knuckles of the hands together as they pass each other.

merger
The absorption of one entity or other thing into another, so the first ceases to have independent existence and is superseded by the second.

- **merge** Beginning with both *5 hands* In front of each side of the chest, palms facing in, bring the hands together, ending with the bent fingers of both hands meshed together in front of the chest.

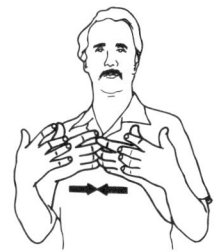

merits or on the merits
The substance of a case, claim, controversy, or the like, as distinguished from procedural or technical aspects.

- Fingerspell: C-A-S-E

- **points** With the extended right index finger, palm down, pointing at the left extended index finger, palm right and finger pointing up, push the right finger toward the left finger with a short repeated movement as both hands move downward in front of the body.

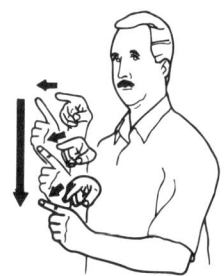

military law

military law See sign for MARTIAL LAW.

minor¹ or **underage** A person who has not yet reached the age deemed by law that a person is mature enough to enter into contracts.
- **below** Beginning with the left *open hand* on the back of the right *open hand,* both palms facing down, bring the right hand downward in an arc, ending several inches below the left hand.

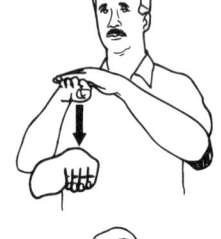

- **age** Beginning with the right *C hand* near the chin, palm left, pull the hand downward while changing into an *S hand*.

minor² or **underage** (alternate sign)
- Fingerspell: M-I-N-O-R

minor³ or **underage** (alternate sign)
- **below** Beginning with the left *open hand* on the back of the right *open hand,* both palms facing down, bring the right hand downward in an arc, ending several inches below the left hand.

- **age** Beginning with the right *C hand* near the chin, palm left, pull the hand downward while changing into an *S hand*.
- Fingerspell: 21
- Fingerspell: O-R
- Fingerspell: 18

Miranda rule¹ or **Miranda warning** The rule that criminal suspects must be informed of certain basic constitutional rights before being questioned.
- Fingerspell: M-I-R-A-N-D-A
- **warn** Pat the fingers of the right *open hand* on the back of the left *open hand,* palm facing down, with a repeated movement.

misdemeanor

Miranda rule[2] or Miranda warning (alternate sign)

- **your** Push the palm of the right *open hand*, palm forward and fingers pointing up, toward the person being talked to.

- **rights** Slide the little-finger side of the right *open hand*, palm facing left, in an upward arc across the upturned left palm held in front of the body.

- **explain** Beginning with the fingers of both *F hands* in front of the chest, palms facing each other and index fingers pointing forward, move the hands forward and back with an alternating movement.

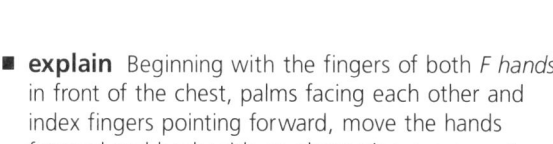

Miranda warning See signs for MIRANDA RULE[1,2].

misdemeanor A crime less serious than a felony, usually punishable by incarceration for up to one year.

- **crime** Place the palm side of the right *L hand*, palm facing left, first on the fingers and then on the heel of the left *open hand*, palm facing right and fingers pointing up. Then beginning with both *S hands* in front of the body, index fingers touching and palms down, move the hands away from each other while twisting the wrists with a deliberate movement, ending with the palms facing each other.

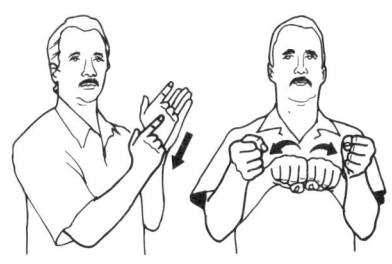

- **punish** Strike the extended right index finger, palm facing left, downward across the elbow of the left bent arm.

---- [sign continues] -->

261

misdemeanor

- **up-to** Bring the back of the right *open hand* up to touch the palm of the left *open hand*, both palms down.

- **one-year** Hold up the extended right index finger. Then beginning with the little-finger side of the right *S hand*, palm left, on top of the index-finger side of the left *S hand*, palm right, move the right hand forward around the left hand, ending with the right *S hand* on the left *S hand*.

misrepresentation A false or misleading statement of facts or conduct having the effect of preventing another's discovery of material facts.

- **sentences** Beginning with the thumbs and index fingers of both *F hands* touching in front of the chest, palms facing each other, with a double movement pull the hands apart to in front of each side of the chest.

- **lie** Move the index-finger side of the right *bent hand*, palm down and fingers pointing left, across the chin from right to left.

mistrial A trial that ends without a verdict, decision, or settlement.

- **court** Move both *F hands*, palms facing each other, up and down in front of each side of the chest with a repeated alternating movement.

- **mix-up** Beginning with the right *curved 5 hand* over the left *curved 5 hand*, palms facing each other in front of the chest, move the hands in circles moving in opposite directions.

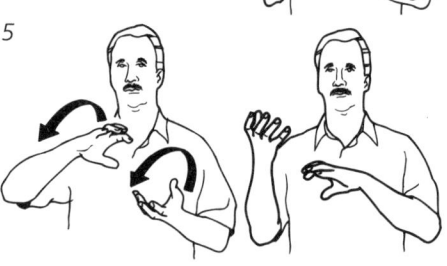

---- [sign continues] ---->

mitigating circumstances

- **start** Beginning with the extended right index finger, palm down, inserted between the index and middle fingers of the left *open hand*, palm right and fingers pointing forward, twist the right hand back, ending with palm in.

- **again** Beginning with the right *bent hand* beside the left *curved hand*, both palms up, bring the right hand up while turning it over, ending with the fingertips of the right hand touching the palm of the left hand.

- **must** Move the bent index finger of the right *X hand* downward with a deliberate movement in front of the right side of the body by bending the wrist down.

mitigate To make less serious.

- **accuse** Push the little-finger side of the right *A hand*, palm facing left, forward across the back of the left *open hand*, palm facing down.

- **less** Beginning with the fingers of the right *bent hand* above the left *bent hand*, both palms facing down and fingers pointing in opposite directions, move the right hand down a short distance in front of the chest.

mitigating circumstances or **special circumstances** Circumstances reducing the liability of a person for a crime.

- **happen** Beginning with both extended index fingers in front of the body, palms facing up and fingers pointing forward, flip the hands over toward each other, ending with the palms facing down. Repeat sign toward another direction.

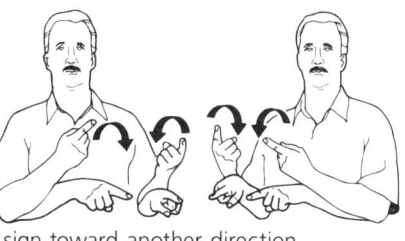

---- [sign continues] ---->

263

mitigating circumstances

- **cause** Beginning with both *S hands* near the body, palms facing up and left hand nearer the body than the right hand, move both hands forward in an arc while opening into *5 hands*.

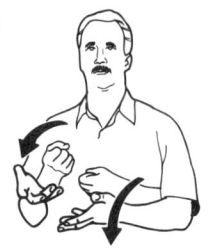

- **responsible** With the fingertips of both *bent hands* on the right shoulder, push the shoulder down slightly.

- **less** Beginning with the fingers of the right *bent hand* above the left *bent hand*, both palms facing down and fingers pointing in opposite directions, move the hands toward each other in front of the chest.

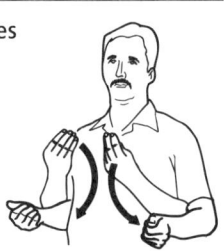

money See sign for LEGAL TENDER[1,2].

moot No longer a real controversy with practical consequences for the parties.

- **solve** Beginning with both *flattened O hands* in front of each side of the body, palms facing up, move the thumb of each hand smoothly across each fingertip, starting with the little fingers and ending as *10 hands* while moving the hands outward to each side.

mortgage A security interest in real property that secures the repayment of a loan borrowed to buy the property.

- **paper** Brush the heel of the right *open hand* with a double movement on the heel of the left *open hand*, palms facing each other.

- **signature** Place the extended fingers of the right *H hand*, palm down, down on the upturned palm of the left *open hand* held in front of the chest with a double movement.

[sign continues] ➝

municipal

- **promise** Bring the extended right index finger, palm facing left and finger pointing up, from in front of the lips downward, changing into an *open hand* and placing the palm of the right hand on the index-finger side of the left *S hand* held in front of the body, palm facing right.

- **pay**[1] Beginning with the extended right index finger touching the palm of the left *open hand,* palms facing each other, move the right finger forward and off the left fingertips.

motion An application, either orally or in writing, asking the court for an order and made while the case is pending. Same sign used for **move, offer, proffer, submit, tender.**

- **offer** Beginning with both *open hands* in front of each side of the body, palms up, move the hands upward and forward in simultaneous arcs.

move To make a motion. See sign for MOTION.

move to strike A request to the court to remove a witness's recent testimony from the court's record, and that the jury not consider the testimony as part of its deliberation.

- **ask** Bring the palms of both *open hands* together, fingers angled upward, while moving the hands down and in toward the chest.

- **delete** Beginning with the index finger of the right *modified X hand*, palm in, touching the extended left index finger held up in front of the chest, palm right and finger pointing up, move the right hand upward to the right while flicking the thumb upward.

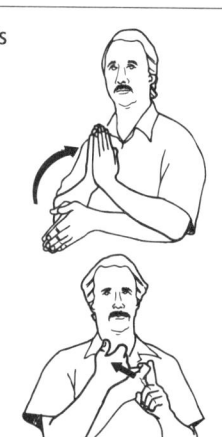

municipal A local governmental unit. Related form: **municipality.**

- **community** As the hands move from left to right in front of the body, with a double movement tap the fingertips of both *open hands,* palms angled toward each other.

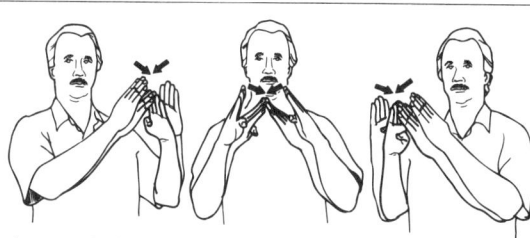

---- [sign continues] -->

265

municipal

- **government** Beginning with the extended right index finger pointing upward near the right side of the head, palm facing forward, twist the wrist to touch the finger to the right temple.

murder See signs for HOMICIDE[1,2].

mutiny A concerted refusal of the military or of a ship's crew to obey officers or perform duties.
- **army** Tap the palm side of both *A hands* against the right side of the chest, right hand above the left hand, with a repeated movement.

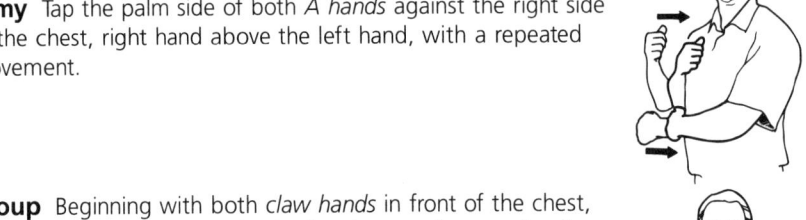

- **group** Beginning with both *claw hands* in front of the chest, palms facing each other, take the hands away from each other in outward arcs while turning the palms in, ending with the little fingers near each other.

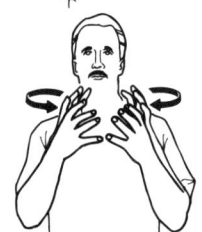

- **protest** Beginning with the right *S hand* in front of the right shoulder, palm facing back, twist the hand sharply forward.

mutual Held in common; shared.
- **two-of-them** Swing the right *2 hand*, palm up, from side to side in front of the body.

- **agree** Move the extended right index finger from touching the right side of the forehead downward to beside the extended left index finger, ending with both fingers pointing forward in front of the body, palms down.

narrow construction, narrow interpretation, or **strict construction** An interpretation of a statute that focuses on specific words used and tends to reject circumstances that do not fall within the ordinary meaning of those words.

- **strict** Bring the index-finger side of the right *bent V hand*, palm left, back to touch the nose with a deliberate movement.

- **interpret** With the fingertips of both *F hands* touching in front of the chest, palms facing each other, twist the hands in opposite directions to reverse positions.

narrow interpretation See sign for NARROW CONSTRUCTION.

national See sign for CITIZEN.

naturalize To confer citizenship upon an individual who was not a citizen.

- **government** Beginning with the extended right index finger pointing upward near the right side of the head, palm facing forward, twist the wrist to touch the finger to the right temple.

- **become** Beginning with the palm of the right *open hand* laying across the upturned palm of the left *open hand*, rotate the hands, exchanging positions while keeping the palms together.

- Fingerspell: U-S or the name of any other nation to which the alien is applying for citizenship.

- **person** Move both *P hands*, palms facing each other, downward along the sides of the body.

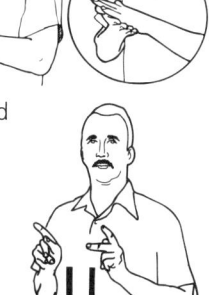

267

necessary party

necessary party A person whose rights are sufficiently involved in an action that he or she is required to join the action.

- **include** Swing the right *5 hand*, palm down, in a circular movement over the left *S hand*, palm in, while changing into a *flattened O hand*, ending with the fingertips of the right hand inserted in the center of the thumb side of the left hand.

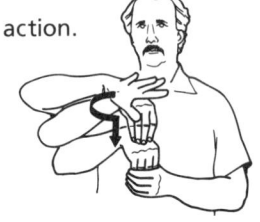

- **require** With the extended index finger of the right *X hand* touching the palm of the left *open hand* bring both hands back toward the chest.

necessity A circumstance leaving a person no reasonable choice but to do something that normally would be a crime in order to avoid a greater evil.

- **must** Move the bent index finger of the right *X hand* downward with a deliberate movement in front of the right side of the body by bending the wrist down.

negligence Conduct involving an unreasonable risk of injury or loss to others. Related form: **neglect**.

- **careless** Beginning with both *V hands* near each side of the head, palms facing each other, move the hands toward and past each other in front of the eyes with a short double movement.

- **do** Move both *C hands*, palms facing down, simultaneously back and forth in front of the body with a swinging movement.

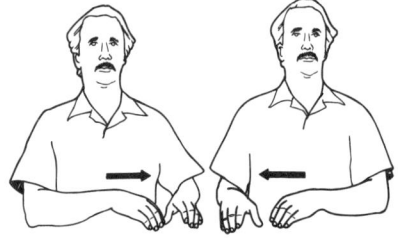

negotiable Describing an instrument having certain transferable rights upon endorsement by the recipient (e.g., bond, stock certificate, title).

- **can** Move both *S hands*, palms facing down, downward simultaneously in front of each side of the body.

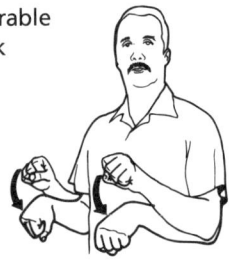

---- [sign continues] ---->

no-fault divorce

- **transfer** Move the right *bent V hand*, palm down, with a large movement from right to left in front of the body.

negotiate[1] To bargain or haggle. Same sign used for **mediate, mediation.**

- **discuss-discuss** Tap the side of the extended right index finger, palm facing in, on the upturned left *open hand* with a repeated movement while moving the hands to and from the body with a double movement.

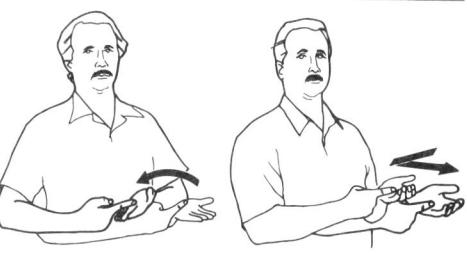

negotiate[2] (alternate sign) Same sign used for **bargain.**

- **negotiate** With the index-finger sides of both *flattened O hands* in front of the body, palms down, move the hands from side to side while each index finger flips up and down.

next friend A person who files a lawsuit on behalf of a minor or incompetent, and who stands in for that person as a party in the case.

- **file** Move the fingers of the right *V hand*, palm facing forward, downward on each side of the extended left index finger, which is pointing up in front of the chest.

- **for-you** Beginning with the extended right index finger touching the right side of the forehead, twist the hand forward, pushing the index finger pointing forward.

no-fault divorce A divorce obtained without assessing blame on either party for the breakdown of the marriage.

- **Divorce**[2] Beginning with the right *curved hand*, palm facing down, clasping the left *curved hand*, palm facing up, take the hands apart while opening into *5 hands*, fingers pointing up and palms forward.

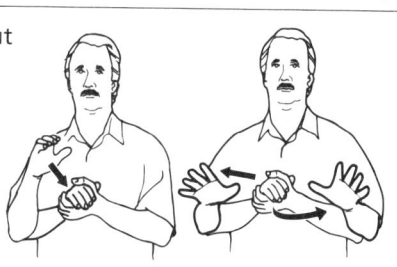

---- [sign continues]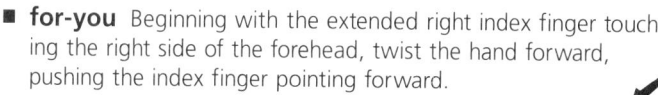

269

no-fault divorce

- **accuse** Push the little-finger side of the right *A hand*, palm facing left, to the left across the back of the left *open hand*, palm facing down.

- **accuse** Push the little-finger side of the left *A hand*, palm facing to the right, to the right across the back of the right *open hand*, palm facing down.

- **none** Move both *O hands*, palms forward, from in front of the chest outward to each side.

no-fault insurance A type of automobile insurance under which compensation is made regardless of which driver involved in the accident was more at fault.

- **insurance** Move the right *I hand*, palm forward, from side to side with a repeated movement in front of the right shoulder.

- **have** Bring the fingertips of both *bent hands*, palms facing in, in to touch each side of the chest.

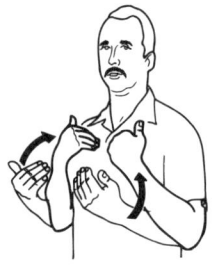

- **accident** Beginning with both *curved 5 hands* in front of each side of the chest, palms in, move the hands toward each other while changing to *A hands* and hit the knuckles of both *A hands* against each other in front of the chest.

---- [sign continues] ---------->

nominal damages

- **happen** Beginning with both extended index fingers in front of the body, palms facing up and fingers pointing forward, flip the hands over toward each other, ending with the palms facing down.

- **responsible** With the fingertips of both *bent hands* on the right shoulder, push the shoulder down slightly.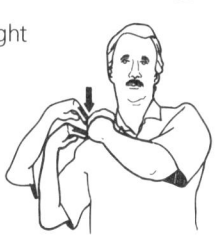

- **who** With the extended right index finger, palm down, draw a little circle around the mouth.

- **have** Bring the fingertips of both *bent hands*, palms facing in, in to touch each side of the chest.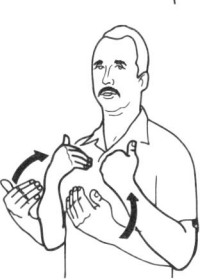

- **none** Move both *O hands*, palms forward, from in front of the chest outward to each side.

---

nominal damages An award of a token amount, indicating that the defendant did the alleged wrong but the plaintiff did not prove that significant damage was done.

- **money** Tap the back of the right *flattened O hand*, palm facing up, with a double movement against the palm of the left *open hand*, palm facing up.

---- [sign continues] -->

271

nominal damages

- **give-me**[3] Beginning with the right *X hand* in front of the body, palms facing left, bring the hand back toward the chest.

- **nothing**[1] Move both *F hands,* palms facing forward, from side to side with a small repeated movement in front of each side of the chest.

noncontested Having no dispute as to the validity of a contract, will, etc.

- **person-person** Place the right extended index finger up in front of the body, and then place the left extended index finger up near the right finger, palms facing forward.

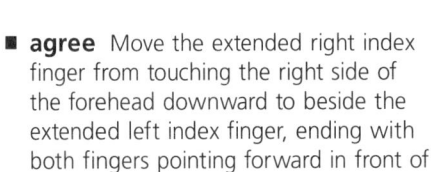

- **two-of-them** Swing the right *2 hand*, palm up, from side to side in front of the body.

- **agree** Move the extended right index finger from touching the right side of the forehead downward to beside the extended left index finger, ending with both fingers pointing forward in front of the body, palms down.

nonjury trial A trial in which no jury is present and all factual issues are decided by the judge. See sign for JUDGMENT.

nonprofit or **not-for-profit** Describing a organization or institution organized for purposes other than to make a profit (e.g., educational, charitable, etc.).

- **not** Bring the thumb of the right *10 hand* forward from under the chin with a deliberate movement.

---- [sign continues] ---->

nonresident alien

- **for** Beginning with the extended right index finger touching the right side of the forehead, twist the hand forward, ending with the index finger pointing forward.

- **profit** Move the right *F hand*, palm facing down, downward with a double movement near the right side of the chest.

nonrecourse Lacking the right to proceed personally against an obligor in the event of nonpayment or default.

- **owe** With a double movement, tap the extended right index finger against the palm of the left *open hand*, palm facing right.

- **can't** Bring the extended index finger of the right *one hand* downward, hitting the extended index finger of the left *one hand* as it moves.

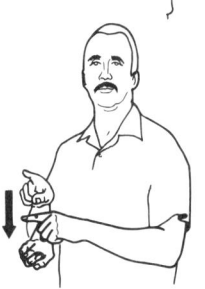

- **receive** Beginning with both *curved 5 hands* in front of the body, right hand higher than the left hand and both palms facing back, bring the hands back toward the chest while closing into *S hands*, ending with the right little finger on the index-finger side of the left hand.

nonresident alien An alien whose permanent residence is in another country.

- **not** Bring the thumb of the right *10 hand* forward from under the chin with a deliberate movement.
- Fingerspell: U-S or the name of any other nation to which the alien is applying for citizenship.

[sign continues]

273

nonresident alien

- **person** Move both *P hands*, palms facing each other, downward along the sides of the body.

- **short** Rub the middle-finger side of the right *H hand*, palm angled left, back and forth with a repeated movement on the index-finger side of the left *H hand*, palm angled right.

- **live** Move both *10 hands*, thumbs pointing up, upward on each side of the chest.

- **here**[1] Beginning with both *curved hands* in front of each side of the body, palms facing up, move the hands toward each other with short repeated movements.

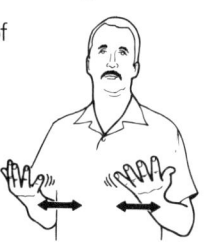

nonresponsive Describing a witness whose answers avoid the question.

- **answer** Beginning with both extended index fingers pointing up in front of the mouth, right hand nearer the mouth than the left and palms forward, bend the wrists down simultaneously, ending with the fingers pointing forward and the palms down.

- **point** Bring the right extended index finger, palm left, to touch the left extended index finger held in front of the chest, palm facing right and finger pointing up.

---- [sign continues] ---->

not-for-profit

- **not** Bring the thumb of the right *10 hand* forward from under the chin with a deliberate movement.

- **miss-the-point** Move the extended right index finger in a random pattern around extended left index finger held up in front of the chest.

nonsupport The crime of failing to provide needed financial support to one's spouse, child, or other dependent.
- **child** Move the right *open hand* downward in front of the right side of the body, palm facing down.

- **support** Push the knuckles of the right *S hand* upward under the little-finger side of the left *S hand*, both palms in, pushing the left hand upward a short distance in front of the chest.

- **pay**[2] Beginning with the right *flattened O hand* in front of the right side of the body, palm facing up, move the hand forward while quickly sliding the thumb off each finger.

- **behind** Move the right *10 hand*, palm facing left, from in front of the left *10 hand*, palm facing right, back toward the chest in a large arc.

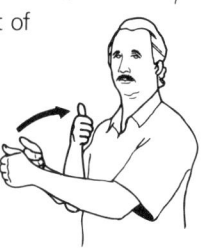

not-for-profit See sign for NONPROFIT.

not guilty

not guilty Acquitted of a criminal charge.
- **not** Bring the thumb of the right *10 hand* forward from under the chin with a deliberate movement.

- **wrong** Bring the middle fingers of the right *Y hand*, palm in, back against the chin with a deliberate movement.

not guilty by reason of insanity Deemed not legally responsible for a criminal act on the ground that the defendant was insane at the time.
- **not** Bring the thumb of the right *10 hand* forward from under the chin with a deliberate movement.

- **wrong** Bring the middle fingers of the right *Y hand*, palm in, back against the chin with a deliberate movement.

- **why** Beginning with the right *5 hand* in front of the forehead, palm in and fingers pointing up, bend the middle and ring fingers with a repeated short movement.

- **insane** Touch the extended right index finger to the right side of the forehead, palm facing down. Then, with the little-finger side of the right *open hand*, palm facing left, across the fingers of the left *open hand*, palm facing up, bend the right hand back toward the chest, ending with the palm facing in.

note

notarize To authenticate a document by affixing the signature and seal of a notary public.

- **sign** Place the extended fingers of the right *H hand*, palm down, firmly down on the upturned palm of the left *open hand* held in front of the chest.

- **punch** Bring the index-finger side of the right *modified C hand*, up to clasp little-finger side of left *open hand*, palm up.

notary See sign for NOTARY PUBLIC.

notary public or **notary** A person authorized by the government to administer oaths and affirmations related to legal documents and transactions.

- **attach**[2] Bring the palm side of the right *curved hand*, up to clasp little-finger side of left *open hand*.

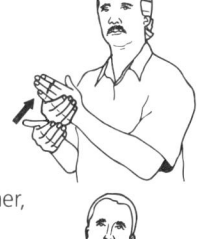

- **person marker** Move both *open hands*, palms facing each other, downward along the sides of the body.

note See sign for BOND.

note or **promissory note** An instrument representing a promise to pay a sum of money.

- **sign** Place the extended fingers of the right *H hand*, palm down, firmly down on the upturned palm of the left *open hand* held in front of the chest.

- **promise** Bring the extended right index finger, palm facing left and finger pointing up, from in front of the lips downward, changing into an *open hand* and placing the palm of the right hand on the index-finger side of the left *S hand* held in front of the body, palm facing right.

---- [sign continues] ---→

277

note

- **pay**[2] Beginning with the right *flattened O hand* in front of the right side of the body, palm facing up, move the hand forward while quickly sliding the thumb off each finger.

- **will** Move the right *open hand*, palm left and fingers pointing up, from the right side of the chin forward while tipping the fingers down.

notice or **service** The act of conveying information of legal significance to a person.
- **law** Place the palm side of the right *L hand*, palm facing left, first on the fingers and then on the heel of the left *open hand*, palm facing right and fingers pointing up.

- **information** Beginning with the fingertips of the right *flattened O hand* near the forehead and the left *flattened O hand* in front of the chest, move both hands forward while opening into *5 hands*, palms facing up.

notorious Open; well known.
- **famous** Beginning with both extended index fingers pointing to each side of the mouth, palms facing in, move the hands forward and outward in double arcs, ending with the index fingers pointing upward in front of each shoulder.

NSF check See signs for KITE[1,2].

nuisance Conduct that unreasonably interferes with either another's use and enjoyment of his or her own property or with the welfare of the public at large.
- **bother** Sharply tap the little-finger side of the right *open hand*, palm facing in at an angle, at the base of the thumb and index finger of the left *open hand*, with a double movement.

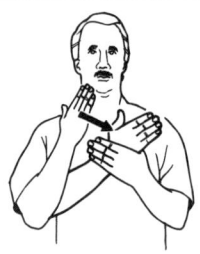

null and void

null[1], **null and void,** or **void** Having no legal force or effect; not enforceable. Same sign used for **petty, petit**.

- **nothing**[1] Move both *F hands,* palms facing down, from side to side with a small repeated movement in front of each side of the chest.

null[2] See sign for SET ASIDE.

null and void Having no legal force or effect; not enforceable. See sign for SET ASIDE.

279

oath A solemn declaration that certain facts are true or that one will speak the truth. See sign for TESTIFY. See sign for AFFIRM.

objection A formal statement or notice that one regards a procedural step invalid; a request that a particular course of action not be permitted or pursued. See sign for GRIEVANCE.

obligation[1] A legal requirement that one perform or refrain from performing some act.
- **responsible** With the fingertips of both *bent hands* on the right shoulder, push the shoulder down slightly.

obligation[2] See sign for DUTY[1].

obscenity Any form of expression that deals with sex in a way that is regarded so offensive or repulsive as to be beyond the protection of freedom of speech.
- **obscene** Beginning with the right *Y hand* under the chin, palm down, wiggle the hand as it moves forward.

obstruction of justice The crime of attempting to impede the administration of justice, as by concealing evidence, influencing witnesses, etc.
- **court** Move both *F hands,* palms facing each other, up and down in front of each side of the chest with a repeated alternating movement.
- **process** Beginning with both *open hands* in front of the body, palms facing in, left fingers pointing right and right fingers pointing left, and the left hand closer to the chest than the right hand, move the left hand over the right hand and then the right hand over the left hand in an alternating movement.
- **interrupt** Sharply hit the little-finger side of the right *open hand,* palm facing in at an angle, at the base of the thumb and index finger of the left *open hand*.

off the record

occupancy[1] Actual possession of real property.
- **live** Move both *10 hands*, thumbs pointing up, upward on each side of the chest.

occupancy[2] See sign for POSSESSION[1].

of age Having reached the legal age for entering into contracts as designated by law.
- **age** Beginning with the right *C hand* near the chin, palm left, pull the hand downward while changing into an *S hand*.

- **enough** Push the palm side of the right *open hand*, palm down, back across the thumb side of the left *S hand* with a double movement.

of record Contained in a record. See sign for FOR THE RECORD.

of the essence See sign for TIME IS OF THE ESSENCE.

off the record Describing informal discussion that the court reporter in a proceeding is requested not to take down.
- **sentences** Beginning with the thumbs and index fingers of both *F hands* touching in front of the chest, palms facing each other, with a double movement pull the hands apart to in front of each side of the chest.

- **put-down** Touch the fingertips of the right *flattened O hand*, palm down, to the palm of the left *open hand*, palm up. Then slap the palm of the right *open hand* against the left palm.

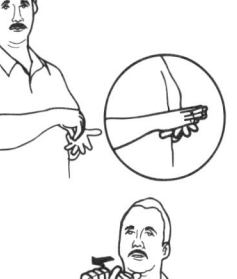

- **not** Bring the thumb of the right *10 hand* forward from under the chin with a deliberate movement.

offender

offender See sign for CRIMINAL.

offense See sign for CRIME.

offer A proposal to enter into a contract upon specified terms. See sign for MOTION.

officer[1] or **official** A person appointed or elected to a position of responsibility in government or private organization.

- **boss** Tap the fingertips of the right *curved 5 hand* on the right shoulder with a repeated movement.

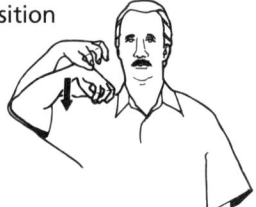

officer[2] See signs for POLICE[1,2].

officer of the court An employee of the court or any lawyer involved in a matter before the court.

- **court** Move both *F hands,* palms facing each other, up and down in front of each side of the chest with a repeated alternating movement.

- **work** Tap the heel of the right *S hand*, palm forward, with a double movement on the back of the left *S hand* held in front of the body, palm down.

- **person marker** Move both *open hands*, palms facing each other, downward along the sides of the body.

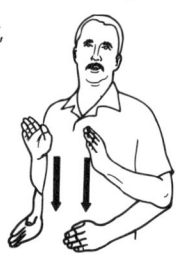

official See sign for OFFICER[1].

omission A failure to do something that one should have done.

- **missing** Pull the right *flattened C hand,* palm facing in, downward through the left *C hand,* palm facing right, while closing the fingers and thumb of the right hand together.

on the merits

on demand Whenever requested.

- **require** With the extended index finger of the right *X hand* touching the palm of the left *open hand* bring both hands back toward the chest.

- **must** Move the bent index finger of the right *X hand* downward with a deliberate movement in front of the right side of the body by bending the wrist down. See sign for DEMAND NOTE.

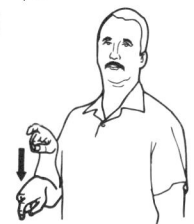

on notice Describing a procedural step taken after all concerned parties have been given notice.

- **inform** Beginning with the fingertips of the right *flattened O hand* near the forehead and the left *flattened O hand* in front of the chest, move both hands forward while opening into *5 hands*, palms facing up.

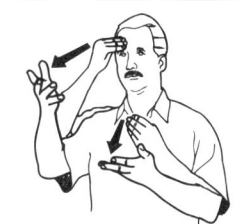

- **finish** With both *5 hands* apart in front of the body, palms up, quickly turn the hands over toward each other.

on or about On approximately the date specified.

- **approximately** Move the right *5 hand,* palm angled facing forward, in a circle in front of the right shoulder with a double movement.

on the lam *Slang*. Hiding or running away from the police to avoid arrest.

- **scurry** Move the right extended index finger with a wiggly movement under the palm of the downturned left *open hand*.

on the merits See sign for MERITS.

283

on the record

on the record Describing anything said in a proceeding that is taken down by the court reporter.

- **sentences** Beginning with the thumbs and index fingers of both *F hands* touching in front of the chest, palms facing each other, with a double movement pull the hands apart to in front of each side of the chest.

- **put-down** Touch the fingertips of the right *flattened O hand*, palm down, to the palm of the left *open hand*, palm up. Then slap the palm of the right *open hand* against the left palm.

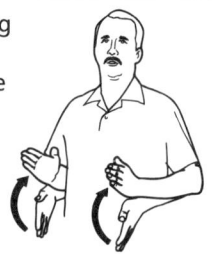

open To reconsider a matter that once was regarded as closed. See sign for PUBLIC[1].

open the door To raise an issue at a trial or hearing by asking questions or submitting evidence about it, thus entitling the other side to introduce evidence that otherwise wouldn't have been allowed.

- **allow** Beginning with both *open hands* in front of the waist, palms facing each other and fingers pointing down, bring the fingers forward and upward by bending the wrists.

opening statement A lawyer's address to the judge or jury in advance of presenting evidence, to outline the case.

- **start** Beginning with the extended right index finger, palm down, inserted between the index and middle fingers of the left *open hand*, palm right and fingers pointing forward, twist the right hand back, ending with palm in.
- **sentences** Beginning with the thumbs and index fingers of both *F hands* touching in front of the chest, palms facing each other, with a double movement pull the hands apart to in front of each side of the chest.

opinion The conclusions one draws from observation of an incident, as distinguished from a mere description of what one has observed.

- **opinion** Move the right *O hand*, palm left in front of the forehead, downward in front of the head with a double movement.

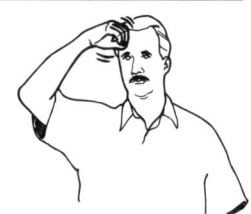

oral agreement

opportunity to be heard The right to present evidence and argument to a neutral decision maker in a fair proceeding in an action affecting one's rights.

- **turn** Beginning with the right *L hand* in front of the right side of the chest, palm facing down and index finger pointing forward, move the hand to the right, ending with the palm facing up.

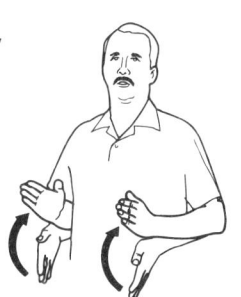

- **allow** Beginning with both *open hands* in front of the waist, palms facing each other and fingers pointing down, bring the fingers forward and upward by bending the wrists.

- **will** Move the right *open hand*, palm left and fingers pointing up, from the right side of the chin forward while tipping the fingers down.

option[1] A contractual right, good for a specified length of time, to go through with a certain transaction on specified terms or to cancel it.

- **choose**[2] Beginning with the bent thumb and index finger of the right *5 hand* touching the index finger of the left *5 hand*, palms facing each other, pull the right hand back toward the right shoulder while pinching the thumb and index finger together. Repeat from each finger of the left *5 hand*.

option[2] (alternate sign)

- **choose**[1] Bring the back of the right *5 hand*, palm forward, back against the palm of the left *open hand*, palm forward, while pinching the thumb and index finger together.

oral agreement See sign for GENTLEMEN'S AGREEMENT.

285

oral argument

oral argument An oral presentation to a court of the reasons why a party contends that the court should reach a particular conclusion.

- **say²** Move the extended right index finger in a repeated upward circular movement in front of the chin, palm facing in and finger pointing left.

- **discuss** Tap the side of the extended right index finger, palm facing in, on the upturned left *open hand* with a double movement.

oral contract See sign for GENTLEMEN'S AGREEMENT.

order, court order, direct, or **instruct** A ruling or direction of a court. Same sign used for **decree, demand, judgment.**

- **order** Beginning with the extended right index finger pointing up in front of the mouth, palm facing left, and the extended left index finger pointing up somewhat forward of the chest, palm facing right, move both hands forward simultaneously, ending with the fingers pointing forward and the palms facing down.

ordinance A municipal law.

- **community** As the hands move from left to right in front of the body, with a double movement tap the fingertips of both *open hands*, palms angled toward each other.

- **law** Place the palm side of the right *L hand*, palm facing left, first on the fingers and then on the heel of the left *open hand*, palm facing right and fingers pointing up.

overrule

out on bail Free from custody because bail has been posted. Same sign used for **post bail**.

- **money**[1] Tap the back of the right *flattened O hand*, palm facing up, with a double movement against the palm of the left *open hand*, palm facing up.

- **deposit** Beginning with the thumbs of both *10 hands* touching in front of the chest, both palms facing down, bring the hands downward and apart by twisting the wrists.

- **allow** Beginning with both *open hands* in front of the waist, palms facing each other and fingers pointing down, bring the fingers forward and upward by bending the wrists.

- **leave** Beginning with both *open hands* in front of the right side of the body, palms down, pull the hands upward toward the chest with a deliberate movement while closing into *10 hands*.

overrule To nullify a legal principle relied upon in a previous case by reaching a result inconsistent with it in a subsequent trial.

- **decide** Move the extended right index finger from the right side of the forehead, palm left, down in front of the chest while changing into an *F hand*, ending with both *F hands* moving downward in front of the body, palms facing each other.

- **reject** Beginning with the right *10 hand* in front of the right shoulder, elbow extended and palm facing down, twist the wrist downward, ending with the thumb pointing down and the palm facing right.

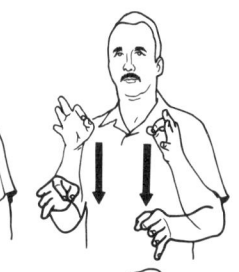

overt act

overt act An act that of itself may not be illegal, but furthers the execution of a criminal act.

- **do** Move both *C hands*, palms facing down, simultaneously back and forth in front of the body with a swinging movement.

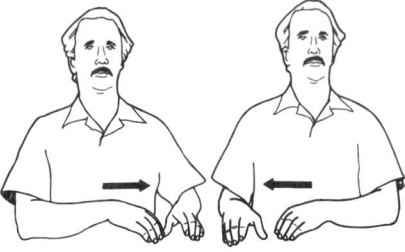

- **show** With the extended right index finger touching the palm of the left *open hand*, palm right and fingers pointing forward, move both hands forward a short distance.

owner[1] A person with a right to control and dispose of real or personal property.

- Fingerspell: O-W-N
- **person marker** Move both *open hands*, palms facing each other, downward along the sides of the body.

owner[2] (alternate sign)

- **have** Bring the fingertips of both *bent hands*, palms facing in, in to touch each side of the chest.

- **person marker** Move both *open hands*, palms facing each other, downward along the sides of the body.

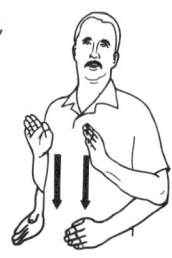

palimony A financial provision awarded upon the breakup of an unmarried couple who lived together.

- **live** Move both *10 hands*, thumbs pointing up, upward on each side of the chest.

- **together** With the palm sides of both *A hands* together, move the hands forward with a short double movement.

- **separate** Beginning with the knuckles of both *10 hands* touching in front of the chest, palms facing in, bring the hands apart.

- **pay**[2] Beginning with the right *flattened O hand* in front of the right side of the body, palm facing up, move the hand forward while quickly sliding the thumb off each finger.

- **must** Move the bent index finger of the right *X hand* downward with a deliberate movement in front of the right side of the body by bending the wrist down. See signs for COHABIT[1,2].

palming off See sign for PASSING OFF.

panel

panel The set of judges hearing a case.
- **court** Move both *F hands*, palms facing each other, up and down in front of each side of the chest with a repeated alternating movement.

- **jury** Beginning with the little-finger sides of both *bent 4 hands*, palms in, together in front of the chest, move the hands apart to each side.

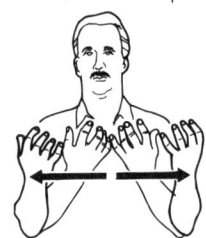

papers The documents generated by lawyers in a case.
- **paper** Brush the heel of the right *open hand* with a double movement on the heel of the left *open hand*, palms facing each other.

par value The face value of a share of stock or bond.
- **invest**[2] Move the curved middle fingers, index fingers, and thumbs of both hands from in front of each side of the chest, palms forward, upward and forward in alternating arcs.

- **price** Tap the fingertips of both *F hands* together, palms facing each other, with a repeated movement.

paralegal or **legal assistant** A nonlawyer employed to assist a lawyer by performing a variety of legal tasks.
- **law** Place the palm side of the right *L hand*, palm facing left, first on the fingers and then on the heel of the left *open hand*, palm facing right and fingers pointing up.

---- [sign continues] ---→

parental neglect

- **assistant** Use the thumb of the right *L hand* under the little-finger side of the left *A hand* to push the left hand upward in front of the chest.

pardon[1] The release of a person from penalties for a past offense.

- **excuse** Wipe the fingertips of the right *open hand* across the upturned left *open hand* from the heel off the fingertips.

- **out** Beginning with the right *5 hand,* palm facing down, in front of the right shoulder, bring the hand outward to the right, closing the fingers and thumb together into a *flattened O hand.*

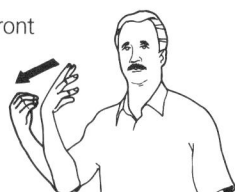

pardon[2] See sign for CLEMENCY.

parent company A corporation that owns more than 50% of the voting stock of another corporation.

- Fingerspell abbreviation for *company*: C-O
- **higher** Move the right *10 hand*, thumb up and palm left, upward with a deliberate movement.

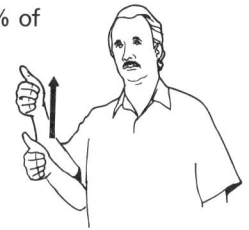

parental liability Liability of parents for damages caused by criminal conduct of their children.

- **parents** Touch the thumb of the right *5 hand,* palm facing left, first to the chin, then to the forehead.

- **responsible** With the fingertips of both *bent hands* on the right shoulder, push the shoulder down slightly.

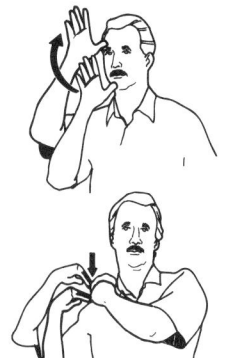

parental neglect See sign for CHILD NEGLECT.

291

parliamentary law

parliamentary law Rules of procedure for meetings of organizations.

- **parliamentary** Touch the middle finger of the right *P hand*, palm facing left, first to the bottom of the wrist and then near the elbow of the left arm held in front of the chest, palm facing down.

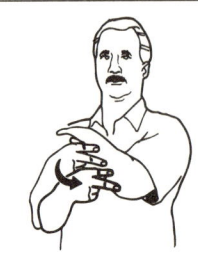

- **law** Place the palm side of the right *L hand*, palm facing left, first on the fingers and then on the heel of the left *open hand*, palm facing right and fingers pointing up.

parole[1] To release a convicted criminal from jail or prison after he or she has served part of a sentence.

- Fingerspell: E-A-R-L-Y

- **excuse** Wipe the fingertips of the right *open hand* across the upturned left *open hand* from the heel off the fingertips.

parole[2] (alternate sign)

- **excuse** Wipe the fingertips of the right *open hand* across the upturned left *open hand* from the heel off the fingertips.

- **before** Beginning with the back of the right *open hand*, palm in and fingers pointing left, touching the back of the left *open hand*, palm forward, move the right hand in toward the chest.

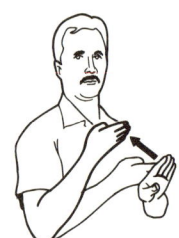

partition To divide property among its co-owners by selling it and dividing the proceeds.

- **divide** Beginning with the little-finger side of the right *B hand* at an angle across the index-finger side of the left *B hand*, palms angled in opposite directions, with a large movement bring the hands downward and apart, ending with the hands in front of each side of the body, palms facing down.

passing off

partner See sign for PARTNERSHIP.

partnership or **partner** An association of two or more people to conduct a business for profit.

- **merge** Beginning with both *5 hands* in front of each side of the chest, palms facing in, bring the hands together, ending with the bent fingers of both hands meshed together in front of the chest.

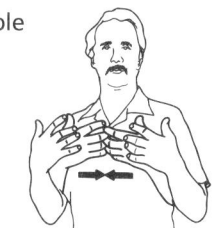

- **person marker** Move both *open hands*, palms facing each other, downward along the sides of the body.

party A person or entity directly and officially involved in a transaction. Same sign used for **person**.

- **person** Move both *P hands*, palms facing each other, downward along the sides of the body.

passing off or **palming off** Marketing one thing as if it were another, as in a counterfeit.

- **sell** Beginning with both *flattened O hands* held in front of each side of the chest, palms down and fingers pointing down, swing the fingertips forward and back by twisting the wrists upward with a double movement.

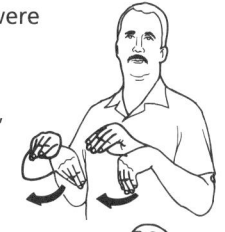

- **false** Brush the extended right index finger, palm facing left, across the tip of the nose from right to left by bending the wrist.

- **true** Move the side of the extended right index finger from in front of the mouth, palm facing left and finger pointing up, upward and forward in an arc.

[sign continues]

passing off

- **not** Bring the thumb of the right *10 hand* forward from under the chin with a deliberate movement.

patent The exclusive right to exploit an invention for a number of years.

- **invent** Move the right *4 hand*, palm left, forward from the right side of the forehead.

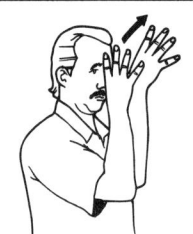

- **name** Tap the middle-finger side of the right *H hand* across the index-finger side of the left *H hand*.

paternity suit An action to establish that a particular man is the father of a child born out of wedlock.

- **decide** Move the extended right index finger from the right side of the forehead, palm left, down in front of the chest while changing into an *F hand*, ending with both *F hands* moving downward in front of the body, palms facing each other.

- **father** Tap the thumb of the right *5 hand*, palm facing left and fingers pointing up, against the middle of the forehead with a repeated movement.

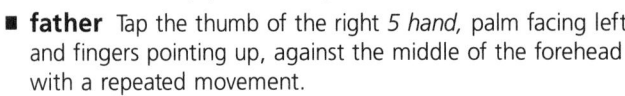

- **who** With the extended right index finger, palm down, draw a little circle around the mouth.

294

pawnbroker

pawn The deposit of goods as security for a loan.
- **sell** Beginning with both *flattened O hands* held in front of each side of the chest, palms down and fingers pointing down, swing the fingertips forward and back by twisting the wrists upward with a double movement.

pawnbroker A person in the business of making loans secured by personal property.
- **business** Brush the base of the right *B hand*, palm forward, with a repeated rocking movement on the back of the left *open hand*, palm down.

- **money** Tap the back of the right *flattened O hand*, palm facing up, with a double movement against the palm of the left *open hand*, palm facing up.

- **lend** With the little-finger side of the right *V hand* across the index-finger side of the left *V hand*, move the hands from near the chest forward and down a short distance.

- **things** Beginning with both *open hands* in front of the body, palms facing up, move the hand to the sides away from each other in a double arc.

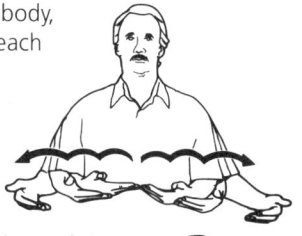

- **give-me**[4] Beginning with the right *flattened O hand* in front of the body, palms facing up, swing the fingertips back toward the chest in a series of arcs.

- **hold** Move the right *S hand*, palm facing up, in a circular movement in front of the right side of the chest.

payroll tax

payroll tax Any of several kinds of tax paid by employers on the basis of employee count or employee salaries.
- **work** Tap the heel of the right *S hand*, palm forward, with a double movement on the back of the left *S hand* held in front of the body, palm down.

- **earn** With a double movement, bring the little-finger side of the right *curved hand*, palm facing left, across the upturned left *open hand* from fingertips to heel while changing into an *S hand* each time.
- Fingerspell: T-A-X

penal or **penal law** Pertaining to a crime and punishment.
- Fingerspell: P-E-N-A-L
- **law** Place the palm side of the right *L hand*, palm facing left, first on the fingers and then on the heel of the left *open hand*, palm facing right and fingers pointing up.

penal law See sign for PENAL.

penalty clause A contract clause requiring payment of a specific sum of money as a penalty in the event of breach of contract.
- **punish** Strike the extended right index finger, palm facing left, with a double movement downward across the elbow of the left bent arm.

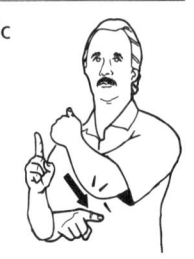

- **sentences** Beginning with the thumbs and index fingers of both *F hands* touching in front of the chest, palms facing each other, with a double movement pull the hands apart to in front of each side of the chest.

penitentiary See signs for JAIL[1,2].

pension Regular payments to a retired employee from a fund. See sign for RETIREMENT PLAN.

perjury

pension plan See sign for RETIREMENT PLAN.

per capita Per person; divided equally among all the people.

- **person-person** Move both *P hands*, palms facing each other, downward along the sides of the body. Repeat by shifting the body to the side.

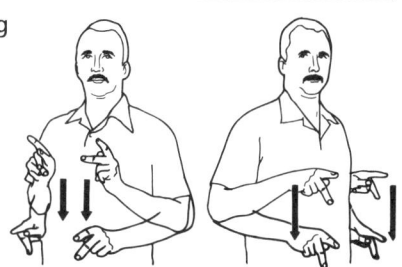

perjury The crime of making a false statement under oath on a material issue in a judicial proceeding, other than in the belief that what is being said is true.

- **promise** Bring the extended right index finger, palm facing left and finger pointing up, from in front of the lips downward, changing into an *open hand* and placing the palm of the right hand on the index-finger side of the left *S hand* held in front of the body, palm facing right.

- **honest**[1] Slide the extended fingers of the right *H hand*, palm facing left, forward from the heel to the fingers of the upturned left *open hand*.

- **off-point** Move the extended right index finger toward the extended left index finger held up in front of the chest and then move quickly off to the right.

- **lie** Move the index-finger side of the right *bent hand*, palm down and fingers pointing left, across the chin from right to left.

perjury[2] See sign for fraud[2].

297

perpetuate

perpetuate To obtain and preserve testimony in a form suitable for later use at a trial, in case the witness is unavailable.

- **receive** Beginning with both *curved 5 hands* in front of the body, right hand higher than the left hand and both palms facing back, bring the hands back toward the chest while closing into *S hands*, ending with the right little finger on the index-finger side of the left hand.

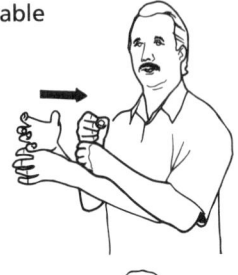

- **keep** Tap the little-finger side of the right *K hand* across the index-finger side of the left *K hand*, palms facing in opposite directions.

person A human being, organization, or entity, such as a corporation, recognized by the law as capable of performing legal acts. See sign for PARTY.

petit *French.* See sign for PETTY.

petit jury See sign for JURY.

petit larceny The theft of lesser items of a certain value and contrasted with grand larceny.

- **steal**[1] Beginning with the index-finger side of the right *V hand*, palm facing down, on the elbow of the bent left arm, held at an upward angle across the chest, pull the right hand upward toward the left wrist while bending the fingers in tightly.

- **not** Bring the thumb of the right *10 hand* forward from under the chin with a deliberate movement.

- **expensive** Beginning with the fingers of the right *flattened O hand* in the upturned left *open hand*, bring the right hand upward to the right and then downward while opening into a *5 hand* in front of the right shoulder, palm facing down.

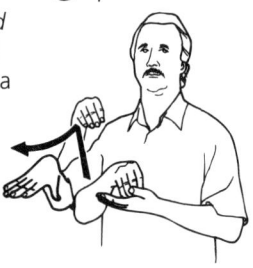

---- [sign continues]

physician-assisted suicide

- **things** Beginning with both *open hands* in front of the body, palms facing up, move the hands to the sides away from each other in a double arc.

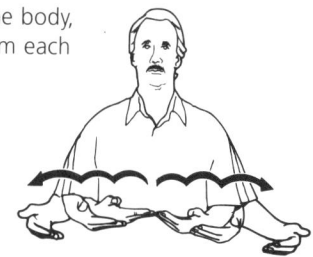

petition A formal request soliciting some benevolent exercise of power.

- **offer** Beginning with both *open hands* in front of each side of the body, palms up, move the hands upward and forward in simultaneous arcs.

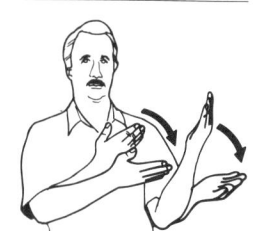

- **file** Move the fingers of the right *V hand*, palm facing forward, downward on each side of the extended left index finger, which is pointing up in front of the chest.

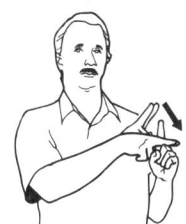

petty or **petit** Small, minor, or lesser.

- **small** Beginning with both *open hands* near each other in front of the chest, palms facing each other and fingers pointing forward, bring the palms close to each other in front of the chest with a short double movement while pursing the lips.

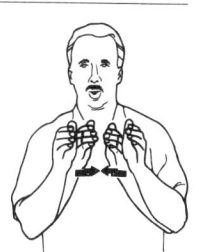

physician-assisted suicide Killing oneself with a physician rendering assistance.

- **doctor** Tap the fingertips of the right *M hand* on the wrist of the upturned left *open hand* with a double movement.

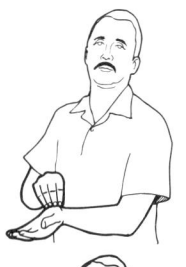

- **help** With the little-finger side of the right *A hand* in the upturned left *open hand*, move both hands upward in front of the chest.

---- [sign continues] ---------------------->

physician-assisted suicide

- **kill** Push the side of the extended right index finger, palm down, across the palm of the left *open hand*, palm right, with a deliberate movement.

physician-patient privilege The privilege of a patient to prevent his or her doctor from disclosing medical records and information obtained in connection with or during medical services.

- **doctor** Tap the fingertips of the right *M hand* on the wrist of the upturned left *open hand* with a double movement.

- **patient**[2] Move the extended middle finger of the right *P hand* first down and then forward on the left upper arm.

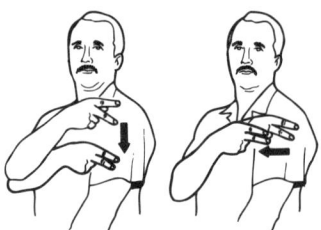

- **two-of-them** Swing the right *2 hand*, palm up, from side to side in front of the body.

- **discuss-discuss** Tap the side of the extended right index finger, palm facing in, on the upturned left *open hand* with a repeated movement while moving the hands to and from the body with a double movement.

- **quiet** Bring the thumb side of the right *one hand*, palm left, back firmly against the lips.

plagiarize

picket To stand or parade in front of a place of employment, carrying signs to publicize a labor grievance and to discourage customers from patronizing the establishment until the dispute is resolved.

- **picket** With the little-finger side of the right *S hand*, palm left, on the index-finger side of the left *S hand*, palm right, move the hands forward.

piracy The unauthorized reproduction of copyrighted work, patented invention, or trademarked product.

- **steal**[1] Beginning with the index-finger side of the right *V hand*, palm facing down, on the elbow of the bent left arm, held at an upward angle across the chest, pull the right hand upward toward the left wrist while bending the fingers in tightly.

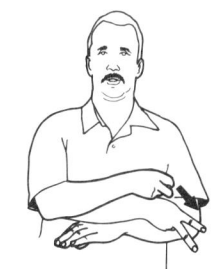

- **other** Beginning with the right *10 hand* in front of the chest, palm down, flip the hand over, ending with palm up.

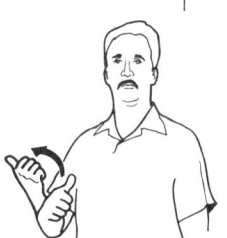

- **work** Tap the heel of the right *S hand*, palm forward, with a double movement on the back of the left *S hand* held in front of the body, palm down.

plagiarize To present another's ideas, words, or other form of expression as one's own.

- **copy**[2] Move the back of the right *5 hand* back to touch the palm of the left *open hand*, both palms forward, while closing the right fingers and thumb into a *flattened O hand*.

- **other** Beginning with the right *10 hand* in front of the chest, palm down, flip the hand over, ending with palm up.

---- [sign continues] ---→

301

plagiarize

- **say**[1] Tap the extended right index finger, palm facing in, on the chin with a double movement.

- **mine** Pat the palm of the right *open hand* on the chest with a double movement.

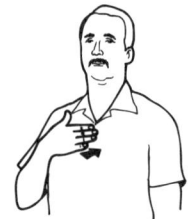

---

plaintiff[1] or **litigant** The person who starts a lawsuit by serving or filing a complaint.

- **file** Move the fingers of the right *V hand*, palm facing forward, downward on each side of the extended left index finger, which is pointing up in front of the chest.

- **person** Move both *P hands*, palms facing each other, downward along the sides of the body.

---

plaintiff[2] or **litigant** (alternate sign)

- **complain** Tap the fingertips of the right *curved 5 hand* against the center of the chest.

- **person** Move both *P hands*, palms facing each other, downward along the sides of the body.

plea bargain

plea[1] A criminal defendant's formal response to charges. Same sign used for **plead**.

- **say**[2] Move the extended right index finger in a repeated upward circular movement in front of the chin, palm facing in and finger pointing left.

plea[2] See sign for ANSWER[1].

plea bargain[1] A negotiated agreement between the prosecution and a criminal defendant whereby the prosecution grants some concessions in exchange for the defendant's plea of guilty.

- **discuss** Tap the side of the extended right index finger, palm facing in, on the upturned left *open hand* with a double movement.

- **for** Beginning with the extended right finger touching the right side of the forehead, twist the hand forward, ending with the index finger pointing forward.

- **less** Beginning with the fingers of the right *bent hand* above the left *bent hand*, both palms facing down and fingers pointing in opposite directions, move the hands toward each other in front of the chest.

- **what** Beginning with the right *5 hand* in front of the right side of the body, palm up, shake the hand loosely from side to side from the wrist with a double movement.

- **cost** Strike the knuckle of the right *X hand*, palm facing in, down on the palm of the left *open hand*, palm facing right and fingers pointing forward.

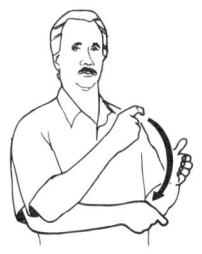

---- [sign continues] -->

303

plea bargain

- **punish** Strike the extended right index finger, palm facing left, downward across the elbow of the left bent arm.

- **and-so-forth** Beginning with both extended index fingers near each other in front of the body, both palms down, take the hands apart while bending the fingers up and down with a quick repeated movement.

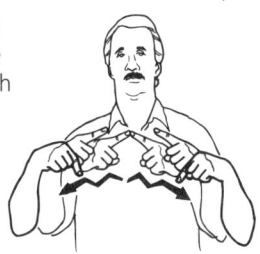

plea bargain (alternate sign)

- **accept** Beginning with both 5 hands in front of the body, fingers pointing forward and palms down, pull both hands back to the chest while changing to flattened O hands.

- **burden** With the fingertips of both bent hands on the right shoulder, push the shoulder down slightly.

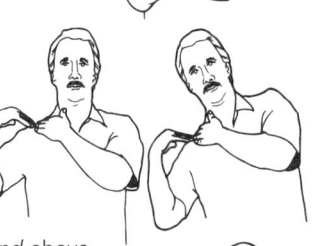

- **less** Beginning with the fingers of the right bent hand above the left bent hand, both palms facing down and fingers pointing in opposite directions, move the hands toward each other in front of the chest.

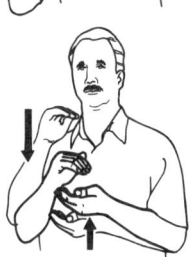

plead To assert an answer to charges. See sign for PLEA¹.

pleading¹ The formal document that sets forth the cause of action or defense of a case.

- **file** Move the fingers of the right V hand, palm facing forward, downward on each side of the extended left index finger, which is pointing up in front of the chest.

---- [sign continues] ---->

point

- **person** Move both *P hands*, palms facing each other, downward along the sides of the body.

- **write** With the thumb and index finger of the right hand pinched together, move the right hand across the palm of the left *open hand* held in front of the body, palm up. Repeat continuously as the hands move downward.

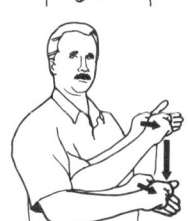

- **itemize** Move the right extended index finger, palm left, downward in a series of small arcs pointing to each finger of the left *5 hand,* palm right. See sign for INSTRUMENT.

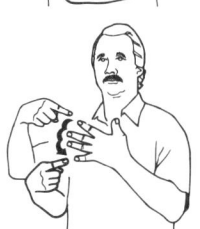

pleading[2] See sign for INSTRUMENT.

pledge A deposit of personal property with a lender as security for a loan or other obligation. See sign for RETAINER.

point A proposition of fact or law.

- **proof** Move the right *open hand* downward, ending with the back of the right hand on the palm of the left *open hand,* both palms facing up in front of the chest.
- Fingerspell: O-R

- **law** Place the palm side of the right *L hand,* palm facing left, first on the fingers and then on the heel of the left *open hand,* palm facing right and fingers pointing up.

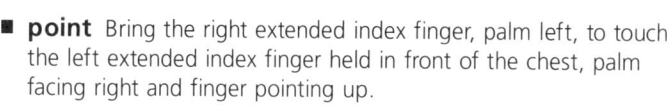

- **point** Bring the right extended index finger, palm left, to touch the left extended index finger held in front of the chest, palm facing right and finger pointing up.

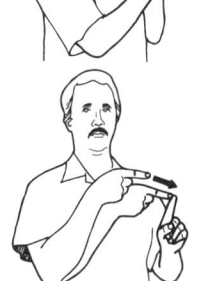

305

points

points See sign for INTEREST[3].

police[1], cop, marshal, officer, police officer, or sheriff

An organized civil force for maintaining order and enforcing laws or a person serving within that force. Same sign used for **badge**.

- **police**[1] Tap the thumb side of the right *modified C hand*, palm facing left, against the left side of the chest with a double movement.

police[2], cop, marshal, officer, police officer, or sheriff

(alternate sign) Same sign used for **badge**.

- **police**[2] Tap the thumb side of the right *C hand*, palm facing left, against the left side of the chest with a double movement.

police officer See signs for POLICE[1,2].

poll tax A fixed tax imposed on everyone regardless of income.

- Fingerspell: T-A-X
- **standard** Beginning with both *Y hands* in front of the body, palms facing down, move the hands in a large flat circle.

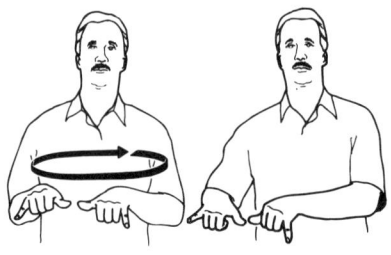

poll the jury To require the jurors in a case in which a verdict has just been announced to declare in open court, one by one, whether that is, in fact, their verdict.

- **jury** Beginning with the little-finger sides of both *bent V hands* together in front of the chest, palms facing up, move the hands apart to each side.

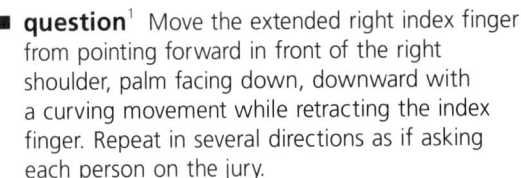

- **question**[1] Move the extended right index finger from pointing forward in front of the right shoulder, palm facing down, downward with a curving movement while retracting the index finger. Repeat in several directions as if asking each person on the jury.

- **vote** Insert the fingertips of the right *F hand*, palm down, with a double movement in the opening of the left *S hand*, palm right.

---- [sign continues] ---->

pornography

- **how** Beginning with the knuckles of both *curved hands* touching in front of the chest, palms facing down, twist the hands upward and forward, ending with the fingers together pointing up and the palms facing up.

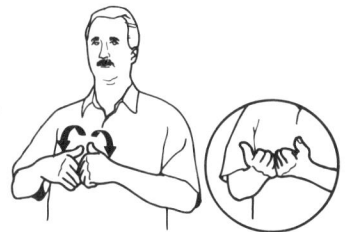

polygraph or **lie detector** A device for measuring certain involuntary bodily responses, such as blood pressure and perspiration, from which an opinion is drawn as to whether or not the person being tested is telling the truth.

- **lie** Move the index-finger side of the right *bent hand*, palm down and fingers pointing left, across the chin from right to left.

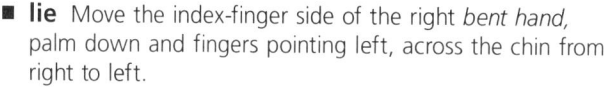

- **test** Beginning with both extended index fingers pointing forward in front of the chest, palms down, bring the hands downward while bending the index fingers into *X hands* and continuing down while extending the index fingers again.

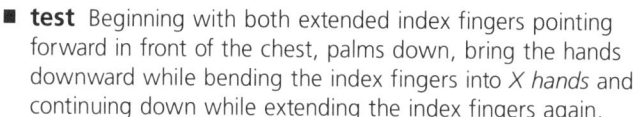

- **machine** With the fingers of both *curved 5 hands* loosely meshed together, palms facing in, move the hands up and down in front of the chest with a repeated movement.

pornography[1] Any sexually explicit material intended primarily to provide sexual entertainment and arousal. Same sign used for **X-rated**.

- **dirty** With the back of the right *open hand* under the chin, palm facing down, wiggle the fingers.

- **picture** Move the right *C hand*, palm facing forward, from near the right side of the face, downward, ending with the index-finger side of the right *C hand* against the palm of the left *open hand*, palm facing right.

pornography[2] (alternate sign) Same sign used for **X-rated**.

- Fingerspell: P-O-R-N-O

307

possession

possession or **occupancy** Occupation or control of real property, or knowing dominion and control over personal property. Same sign used for **enjoy**.
- **have** Bring the fingertips of both *bent hands*, palms facing in, in to touch each side of the chest.

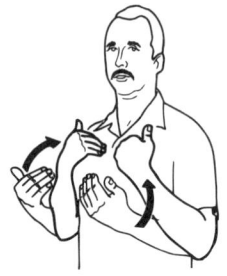

possession of a controlled substance Having illegal drugs.
- **have** Bring the fingertips of both *bent hands*, palms facing in, in to touch each side of the chest.

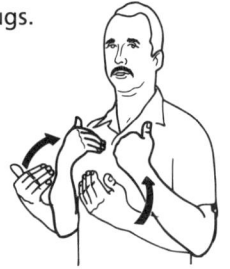

- **things** Beginning with both *open hands* in front of the body, palms facing up, move the hand to the sides away from each other in a double arc.

- **illegal** Hit the palm side of the right *L hand*, palm left, sharply on the palm of the left *open hand*, palm right, and off again.

- **show** With the extended right index finger touching the palm of the left *open hand*, palm right and fingers pointing forward, move both hands forward a short distance.
- Fingerspell: D-R-U-G-S

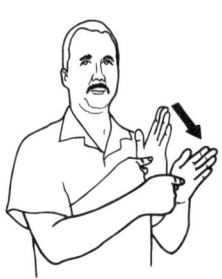

post bail To provide the required cash or bond for bail. See sign for OUT ON BAIL.

power of attorney

power[1] Legal authority to perform acts, especially the authority of a legislative body to make laws.

- **authority** Beginning with the thumb of the right *A hand* touching the left upper arm, palm facing down, move the hand downward while turning the palm up, ending with the little-finger side touching the arm.

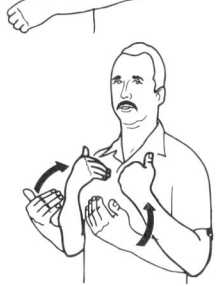

- **have** Bring the fingertips of both *bent hands*, palms facing in, in to touch each side of the chest.

power[2] (alternate sign)

- **power** Place the fingertips of the right *claw hand* on the left upper arm.

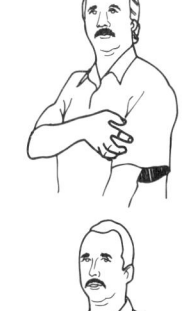

- **have** Bring the fingertips of both *bent hands*, palms facing in, in to touch each side of the chest.

power of attorney An instrument by which one individual confers upon another the power to perform specified acts on his or her behalf.

- **paper** Brush the heel of the right *open hand* with a double movement on the heel of the left *open hand*, palms facing each other.

- **say**[1] Tap the extended right index finger, palm facing in, on the chin with a double movement.

---- [sign continues] ---->

power of attorney

- **give-me**[2] Beginning with both *X hands* in front of the body, palms facing each other, bring the hands back to touch on each side of the chest.

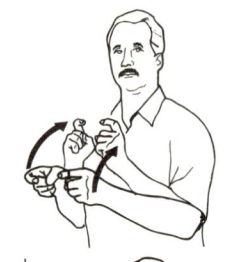

- **manage** Beginning with both *modified X hands* in front of each side of the body, right hand forward of the left hand and palms facing each other, move the hands forward and back with a repeated movement.

practice The presentation of matters to courts and the manner in which cases are handled (e.g., civil practice).

- **law** Place the palm side of the right *L hand*, palm facing left, first on the fingers and then on the heel of the left *open hand*, palm facing right and fingers pointing up.

- **process** Beginning with both *open hands* in front of the body, palms facing in, left fingers pointing right and right fingers pointing left, and the left hand closer to the chest than the right hand, move the left hand over the right hand and then the right hand over the left hand in an alternating movement.

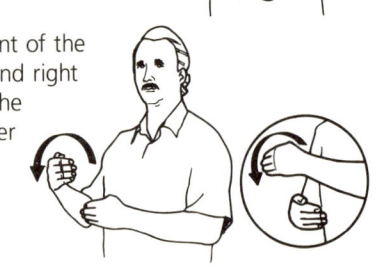

prayer for relief or **demand for relief** The portion at the end of a complaint in which the plaintiff states the damages or other remedy being sought for the action.

- **ask** Bring the palms of both *open hands* together, fingers angled upward, while moving the hands down and in toward the chest.

- **pay-me** Move the right *flattened O hand*, palm facing up, back under the downturned palm of the left *open hand* while quickly sliding the thumb off each finger.

predecessor

precedent[1] A judicial decision cited as authority in a subsequent case involving similar facts and issues.

- **past** Move the fingertips of the right *open hand*, palm facing back, from near the right cheek back and down to touch the right shoulder.

- **law** Place the palm side of the right *L hand*, palm facing left, first on the fingers and then on the heel of the left *open hand*, palm facing right and fingers pointing up.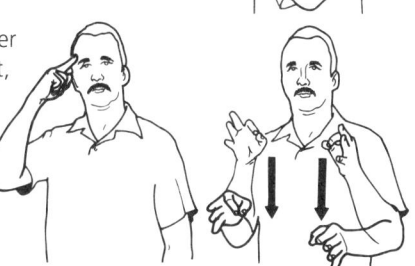

- **decide** Move the extended right index finger from the right side of the forehead, palm left, down in front of the chest while changing into an *F hand*, ending with both *F hands* moving downward in front of the body, palms facing each other.

- **follow** With the knuckles of the right *10 hand*, palm facing left, near the wrist of the left *10 hand*, palm facing right, move both hands forward a short distance. See sign for FOLLOW.

precedent[2] See sign for FOLLOW.

predecessor One who previously possessed a right, interest, or duty now belonging to another.

- **past** Move the fingertips of the right *open hand*, palm facing back, from near the right cheek back and down to touch the right shoulder.
- Fingerspell: O-W-N

- **now** Bring both *Y hands*, palms facing up, downward in front of each side of the body.

---- [sign continues]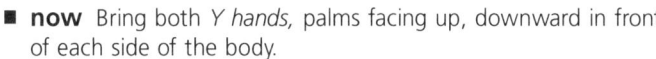

311

predecessor

- **not** Bring the thumb of the right *10 hand* forward from under the chin with a deliberate movement.

---

prejudice Bias or prejudgment in a case.
- **mind** Tap the extended right index finger, palm facing in, against the right side of the forehead with a double movement.

- **against** Hit the fingertips of the right *bent hand* into the left *open hand*, palm right and fingers pointing forward.

---

preliminary hearing An early stage in a felony prosecution, in which the prosecutor must show a court that there is sufficient evidence to justify a trial.
- **first** Touch the extended right index finger, palm facing in, against the extended thumb of the left *10 hand*, palm facing right.

- **time** Tap the bent index finger of the right *X hand*, palm down, with a double movement on the wrist of the downturned left hand.

- **face-to-face** Beginning with both *open hands* in front of the chest, palms facing each other and fingers pointing up, move the right hand forward in a smooth movement toward the left hand.

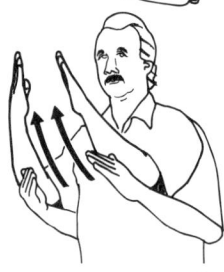

---- [sign continues] ---→

premeditated murder

- **court** Move both *F hands,* palms facing each other, up and down in front of each side of the chest with a repeated alternating movement.

premarital agreement See sign for PRENUPTIAL AGREEMENT.

premeditation Acting with willful deliberation and planning in advance.

- **prepare** Move both *open hands* from in front of the left side of the body, palms facing each other and fingers pointing forward, in a series of small upward arcs to in front of the right side of the body.

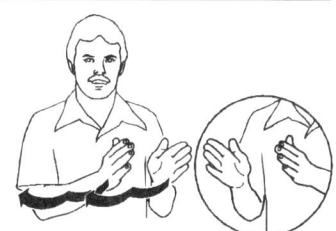

premeditated murder[1] A murder that was contemplated, even if for a brief time, before it was committed.

- **plan** Move both *open hands* from in front of the left side of the body, palms facing each other and fingers pointing forward, in a long smooth movement to in front of the right side of the body.

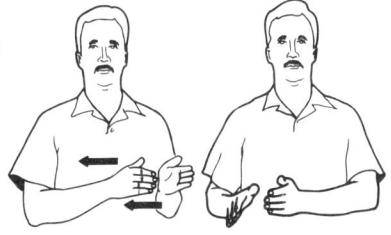

- **kill** Push the side of the extended right index finger, palm down, across the palm of the left *open hand*, palm right, with a deliberate movement.

premeditated murder[2] (alternate sign)

- **think** Touch the right side of the forehead with the extended right index finger.

- **kill** Push the side of the extended right index finger, palm down, across the palm of the left *open hand*, palm right, with a deliberate movement.

313

prenuptial agreement

prenuptial agreement or premarital agreement
A contract between two people who are about to marry regarding their respective property and support rights upon termination.

- **before** Beginning with the back of the right *open hand*, palm in and fingers pointing left, touching the back of the left *open hand*, palm forward, move the right hand in toward the chest.

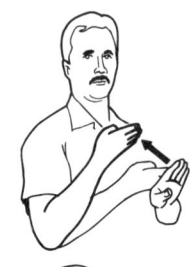

- **marry** Bring the right *curved hand*, palm facing down, downward in front of the chest to clasp the left *curved hand*, palm facing up.

- **agree-agree** Beginning with both extended index fingers pointing forward in front of each side of the body, both palms facing up, flip the hands toward each other, turning the palms down. Repeat sign in a different location.

- **sign** Place the extended fingers of the right *H hand*, palm down, firmly down on the upturned palm of the left *open hand* held in front of the chest.

prepayment penalty
A monetary penalty that a debtor must pay if the debt, usually a mortgage or other loan agreement, is repaid early.

- **add-to** Swing the right *5 hand* upward from the right side of the body while changing into a *flattened O hand*, ending with the right index finger touching the little-finger side of the left *flattened O hand* in front of the chest, both palms facing in.

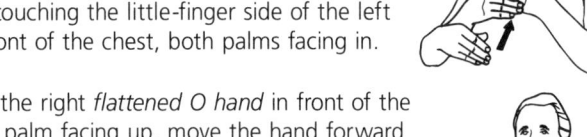

- **pay²** Beginning with the right *flattened O hand* in front of the right side of the body, palm facing up, move the hand forward while quickly sliding the thumb off each finger.

---- [sign continues] ---➤

314

preponderance of the evidence

- **must** Move the bent index finger of the right *X hand* downward with a deliberate movement in front of the right side of the body by bending the wrist down.

preponderance of the evidence The minimum amount of evidence needed to persuade the jury in a civil case that a fact is more likely true than not true and, thus, find for the plaintiff.

- **base** Move the right *B hand*, palm facing forward, in a flat circle under the left *open hand*, palm facing down.

- **proof** Move of the right *open hand*, from in front of the mouth downward, ending with the back of the right hand on the palm of the left *open hand*, both palms facing up in front of the chest.

- **support** Push the knuckles of the right *S hand* upward under the little-finger side of the left *S hand*, both palms in, pushing the left hand upward a short distance in front of the chest.

- **file** Move the fingers of the right *V hand*, palm facing forward, downward on each side of the extended left index finger, which is pointing up in front of the chest.

- **person marker** Move both *open hands*, palms facing each other, downward along the sides of the body.

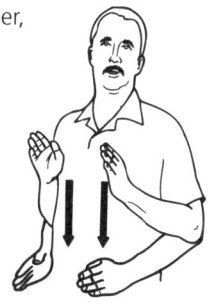

presumption

presumption A legal assumption that if one fact exists, then another fact must also exist, so only the first fact has to be proved.

- **proof** Move the right *open hand* downward, ending with the back of the right hand on the palm of the left *open hand*, both palms facing up in front of the chest.

- **have** Bring the fingertips of both *bent hands*, palms facing in, in to touch each side of the chest.

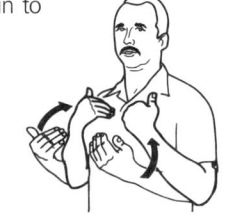

- **assume** Move the right *C hand*, palm facing left, from near the right side of the forehead in a quick downward arc in front of the face while closing into an *S hand*, ending with the palm facing down.

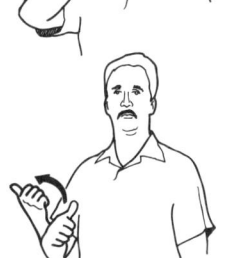

- **other** Beginning with the right *10 hand* in front of the chest, palm down, flip the hand over, ending with palm up.

- **have** Bring the fingertips of both *bent hands*, palms facing in, in to touch each side of the chest.

presumption of innocence The principle that a criminal defendant need not introduce evidence of innocence to be found not guilty, but rather the prosecution must prove the crime to convict.

- **protect** With the wrists of both *S hands* crossed in front of the chest, palms facing in opposite directions, move the hands forward with a short double movement.
- **wrong** Bring the middle fingers of the right *Y hand*, palm in, back against the chin with a deliberate movement.

---- [sign continues] ---->

price fixing

- **not** Bring the thumb of the right *10 hand* forward from under the chin with a deliberate movement.

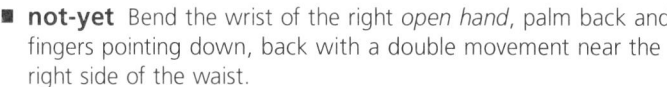

- **not-yet** Bend the wrist of the right *open hand*, palm back and fingers pointing down, back with a double movement near the right side of the waist.

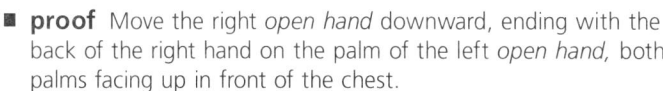

- **proof** Move the right *open hand* downward, ending with the back of the right hand on the palm of the left *open hand*, both palms facing up in front of the chest.

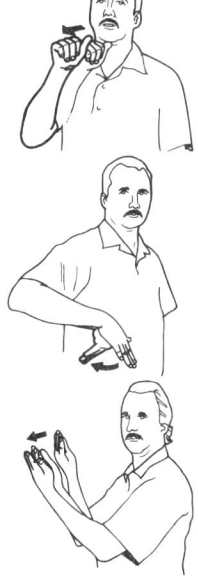

pretrial discovery See sign for DISCOVERY.

price fixing The setting of prices at which goods or services are to be sold by means of an agreement or arrangement.

- **secret** Tap the thumb side of the right *A hand*, palm left, against the mouth with a repeated movement.

- **decide** Move the extended right index finger from the right side of the forehead, palm left, down in front of the chest while changing into an *F hand*, ending with both *F hands* moving downward in front of the body, palms facing each other.

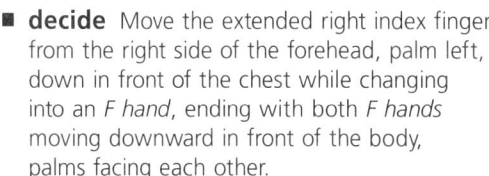

- **standard** Beginning with both *Y hands* in front of the body, palms facing down, move the hands in a large flat circle.

- **cost** Strike the knuckle of the right *X hand*, palm facing in, down on the palm of the left *open hand*, palm facing right and fingers pointing forward.

317

principal

principal A person who authorizes another to act as his or her agent.

- **person** Move both *P hands*, palms facing each other, downward along the sides of the body.

- **manage** Beginning with both *modified X hands* in front of each side of the body, right hand forward of the left hand and palms facing each other, move the hands forward and back with a repeated movement.

- **gift** Move both *X hands* from in front of the body, palms facing each other, forward in simultaneous arcs.

prison A state or federal facility in which people convicted of serious crimes and given long sentences are incarcerated. See sign for JAIL.

prisoner See sign for FELON.

privacy Freedom from unwarranted intrusion into one's personal life and unwanted publicity about oneself. Related form: **private**.

- **private** Tap the thumb side of the right *A hand*, palm left, against the mouth with a repeated movement.

privilege A special right or exemption that the law allows to a person or class of persons.

- **special** Grasp the left extended index finger, palm in and finger pointing up, with the fingers of the right *G hand* and pull upward in front of the chest.

---- [sign continues] -->

probable cause

- **allow** Beginning with both *open hands* in front of the waist, palms facing each other and fingers pointing down, bring the fingers forward and upward by bending the wrists.

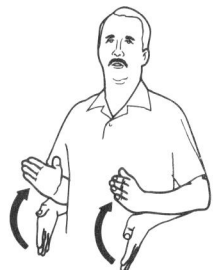

privileged communication A communication that may be withheld from evidence because it was made within an approved confidential relationship.

- **secret** Tap the thumb side of the right *A hand*, palm left, against the mouth with a repeated movement.

- **communication** Move both *C hands*, palms facing each other, forward and back from the mouth with an alternating movement.

probable cause[1] Reasonable grounds for believing a fact is true.

- **enough** Push the palm side of the right *open hand*, palm down, forward across the thumb side of the left *S hand*.

- **reason** Move the fingertips of the right *R hand*, palm facing in, in a circular movement in front of the right side of the forehead with a double movement.

- **true** Beginning with the thumb side of the right *one hand* in front of the mouth, palm left, move the extended index finger forward.

319

probable cause

probable cause[2] (alternate sign)

- **enough** Push the palm side of the right *open hand*, palm down, back across the thumb side of the left *S hand*.

- **proof** Move the right *open hand* downward, ending with the back of the right hand on the palm of the left *open hand*, both palms facing up in front of the chest.

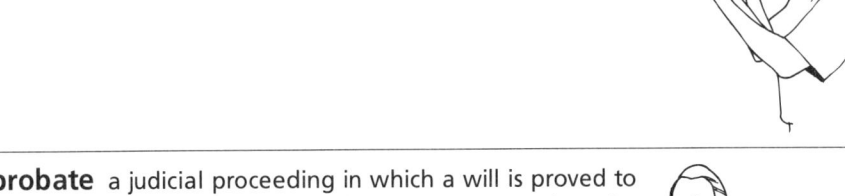

probate a judicial proceeding in which a will is proved to be genuine and distribution of the estate is monitored.

- Fingerspell: W-I-L-L
- **process** Beginning with both *open hands* in front of the body, palms facing in, left fingers pointing right and right fingers pointing left, and the left hand closer to the chest than the right hand, move the left hand over the right hand and then the right hand over the left hand in an alternating movement.
- **look-at** Move the right *V hand*, palm facing down and extended fingers pointing forward, forward with a short double movement in the direction of the referent.

probate[2] (alternate sign)

- **court** Move both *F hands*, palms facing each other, up and down in front of each side of the chest with a repeated alternating movement.

- **proof** Move the right *open hand* downward, ending with the back of the right hand on the palm of the left *open hand*, both palms facing up in front of the chest.
- Fingerspell: W-I-L-L

320

probation officer

probation The conditional release of a prisoner under the supervision of a probation officer.

- **understand** Beginning with the right *modified X hand*, palm in, near the right side of the forehead, flick the index finger upward with a deliberate movement.

- **under** Move the right *A hand* from in front of the chest downward and forward under the left *open hand* held in front of the chest, palm down and fingers pointing right.

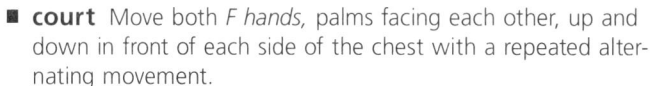

- **court** Move both *F hands*, palms facing each other, up and down in front of each side of the chest with a repeated alternating movement.

- **watch** Beginning with both *V hands* in front of the left side of the body, palms down and fingers pointing forward, swing the hands in large simultaneous arcs to the right.

probation officer An officer who monitors and reports on the conduct of offenders who are free on probation.

- **watch** Beginning with both *V hands* in front of the left side of the body, palms down and fingers pointing forward, swing the hands in large simultaneous arcs to the right.

- **police** Tap the thumb side of the right *modified C hand*, palm facing left, against the left side of the chest with a double movement.

- **boss** Tap the fingertips of the right *curved 5 hand* on the right shoulder with a repeated movement.

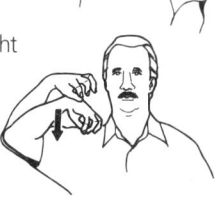

321

procedure

procedure¹ The methods used in investigating, presenting, managing, and deciding legal cases.

- **process** Beginning with both *open hands* in front of the body, palms facing in, left fingers pointing right and right fingers pointing left, and the left hand closer to the chest than the right hand, move the left hand over the right hand and then the right hand over the left hand in an alternating movement.

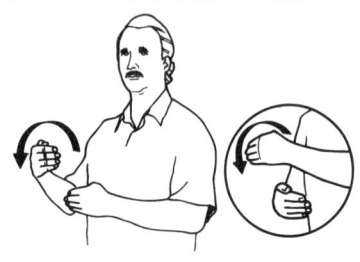

procedure² (alternate sign)

- **plan** Move both *open hands* from in front of the left side of the body, palms facing each other and fingers pointing forward, in a long smooth movement to in front of the right side of the body.

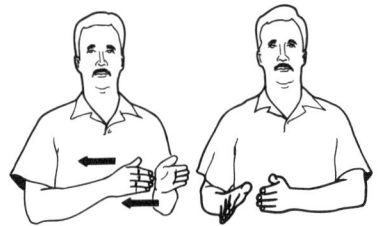

proceeding See sign for LEGAL ACTION.

process A formal document through which a court obtains jurisdiction over a person or property, or compels a person to appear in court.

- **court** Move both *F hands*, palms facing each other, up and down in front of each side of the chest with a repeated alternating movement.

- **paper** Brush the heel of the right *open hand* with a double movement on the heel of the left *open hand*, palms facing each other.

- **order** Move the extended right index finger, palm forward and finger pointing up, from in front of the mouth forward and down, ending with the finger pointing forward and the palm down.

- **face-to-face** Beginning with both *open hands* in front of the chest, palms facing each other and fingers pointing up, move the right hand forward in a smooth movement toward the left hand.

property

proffer See sign for MOTION.

profit Financial gain from an investment, enterprise, or transaction.
- **profit** Move the right *F hand,* palm facing down, downward with a double movement on the chest.

promise A commitment to perform, or refrain from performing, some act in the future.
- **promise** Bring the extended right index finger, palm facing left and finger pointing up, from in front of the lips downward, changing into an *open hand* and placing the palm of the right hand on the index-finger side of the left *S hand* held in front of the body, palm facing right.

- **will** Move the right *open hand*, palm left and fingers pointing up, from the right side of the chin forward while tipping the fingers down.

- **do** Move both *C hands*, palms facing down, simultaneously back and forth in front of the body with a swinging movement.

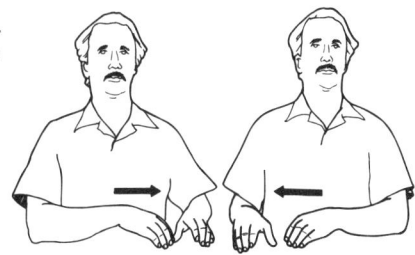

promissory note See sign for NOTE.

proof The persuasive effect of evidence in the mind of a factfinder. See sign for EVIDENCE[1].

property A thing, interest, or right that is capable of being owned and transferred.
- **land** Beginning with both *flattened O hands* in front of each side of the body, palms facing up, move the thumb of both hands smoothly with a double movement across each fingertip, starting with the little fingers and ending as *A hands* each time.

323

property tax

property tax A state or local tax imposed annually on owners of real or personal property and based on value of the property.

- **land** Beginning with both *flattened O hands* in front of each side of the body, palms facing up, move the thumb of both hands smoothly with a double movement across each fingertip, starting with the little fingers and ending as *A hands* each time.
- Fingerspell: T-A-X

proponent One who presents evidence in a case or offers a will for probate.

- **proof** Move the right *open hand* downward, ending with the back of the right hand on the palm of the left *open hand*, both palms facing up in front of the chest.

- **offer** Beginning with both *open hands* in front of each side of the body, palms up, move the hands upward and forward in simultaneous arcs.

- **person marker** Move both *open hands*, palms facing each other, downward along the sides of the body.

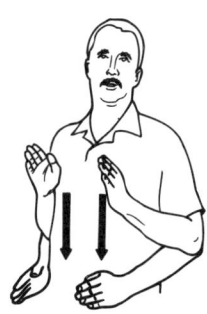

proprietary Pertaining to ownership.

- Fingerspell: O-W-N
- **person marker** Move both *open hands*, palms facing each other, downward along the sides of the body.

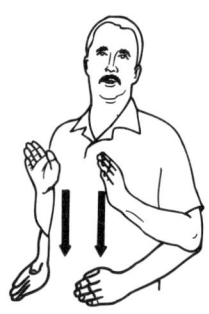

protective order

prosecute or **sue** To pursue a civil or criminal action against someone. Related form: **prosecution.** Same sign used for **suit.**

- **file** Move the fingers of the right *V hand,* palm facing forward, downward on each side of the extended left index finger, which is pointing up in front of the chest.

- **against** Hit the fingertips of the right *bent hand* into the left *open hand,* palm right and fingers pointing forward.

prostitution The crime of engaging in sexual intercourse or other sexual activity for hire.

- **prostitution** Twist the back of the fingers of the right *bent hand,* palm back, forward on the right side of the chin with a double movement, changing into an *open hand* each time.

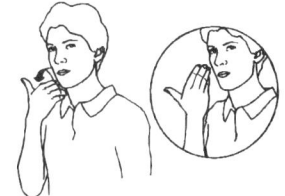

protective order A court order prohibiting a party to a case from doing any activity that unnecessarily annoys, burdens, or embarrasses the adversary.

- **court** Move both *F hands,* palms facing each other, up and down in front of each side of the chest with a repeated alternating movement.

- **order** Move the extended right index finger, palm forward and finger pointing up, from in front of the mouth forward and down, ending with the finger pointing forward and the palm down.

- **protect** With the wrists of both *S hands* crossed in front of the chest, palms facing in opposite directions, move the hands forward with a short double movement.

325

protest

protest A formal written statement objecting to some action of another.

- **complaint** With a double movement, tap the fingertips of the right *curved 5 hand* against the center of the chest.

- **write** With the thumb and index finger of the right hand pinched together, move the right hand with a wiggling movement across the palm of the left *open hand* held in front of the body, palm up.

- **points** Move the right extended index finger, palm left, downward in a series of small arcs pointing to each finger of the left *5 hand,* palm in and fingers pointing right.

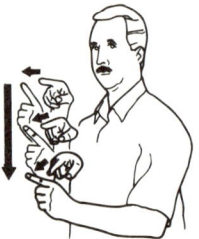

proxy An instrument authorizing one person to act on behalf of another, especially by voting or otherwise participating in a meeting. See sign for IN THE MATTER OF.

public[1] Pertaining, belonging, or available generally to the people of a municipality, a state, or a country. Same sign used for **open**.

- **open** Beginning with the index-finger side of both *B hands* touching in front of the chest, palms facing forward and fingers angled up, twist both wrists while bringing the hands apart to in front of each side of the chest, ending with the palms facing in.

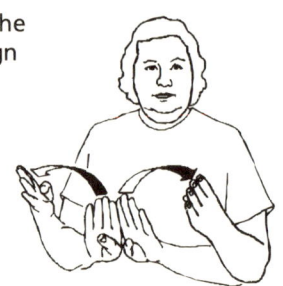

public[2] (alternate sign)

- **hearing** Move the side of the extended right index finger, pointing left, in a small double circular movement upward and forward in front of the lips.

public defender

public accommodation A place offering services to the general public, such as a hotel, gas station, etc.

- **open** Beginning with the index-finger side of both *B hands* touching in front of the chest, palms facing forward and fingers angled up, twist both wrists while bringing the hands apart to in front of each side of the chest, ending with the palms facing in.

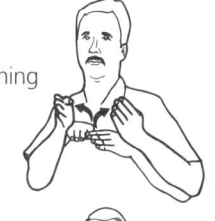

- **business** Brush the base of the right *B hand,* palm forward, with a repeated rocking movement on the back of the left *open hand,* palm down.

public defender[1] A lawyer who represents indigent defendants in criminal cases.

- **government** Beginning with the extended right index finger pointing upward near the right side of the head, palm facing forward, twist the wrist to touch the finger to the right temple.

- **give**[1] Beginning with both *X hands* in front of the body, palm facing each other, move the hands forward in simultaneous arcs.

- **lawyer** Place the palm side of the right *L hand,* palm facing left, first on the fingers and then on the heel of the left *open hand,* palm facing right and fingers pointing up. Move both *open hands,* palms facing each other, downward along the sides of the body.

public defender[2] (alternate sign)

- Fingerspell acronym: P-D

public defender[3] (alternate sign)

- **court** Move both *F hands,* palms facing each other, up and down in front of each side of the chest with a repeated alternating movement.

---- [sign continues] ---->

327

public defender

- **order** Move the extended right index finger, palm forward and finger pointing up, from in front of the mouth forward and down, ending with the finger pointing forward and the palm down.

- **lawyer** Place the palm side of the right *L hand*, palm facing left, first on the fingers and then on the heel of the left *open hand*, palm facing right and fingers pointing up. Move both *open hands*, palms facing each other, downward along the sides of the body.

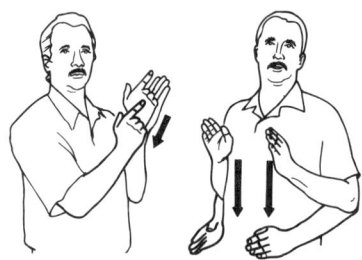

public domain The status of a work or invention upon which the copyright or patent has expired or was never held, making the work available for copy or use by anyone.

- **for** Beginning with the extended right finger touching the right side of the forehead, twist the hand forward, ending with the index finger pointing forward.

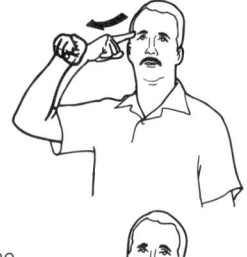

- **any** Beginning with the right *10 hand* in front of the chest, palm left, twist the wrist and move the hand down and to the right, ending with the palm facing down.

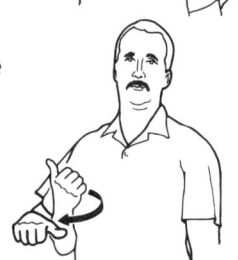

public figure A public official who has intentionally assumed a prominent role in matters of public importance.

- **person** Move both *P hands*, palms facing each other, downward along the sides of the body.

- **open** Beginning with the index-finger side of both *B hands* touching in front of the chest, palms facing forward and fingers angled up, twist both wrists while bringing the hands apart to in front of each side of the chest, ending with the palms facing in.

put in jail

public policy A general concept of public good that affects judicial decisions in every field.
- **people** Move both *P hands*, palms facing down, in alternating forward circles in front of each side of the body.

- **policy** Touch the palm of the right *P hand* first against the fingers and then against the heel of the left *open hand*, palm facing forward and fingers pointing up.

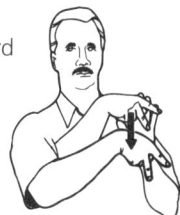

punitive damages[1] Payment awarded by the court in excess of actual damages in cases where the crime is deemed especially egregious.
- **punish** Strike the extended right index finger, palm facing left, downward across the elbow of the left bent arm.

- **pay**[2] Beginning with the right *flattened O hand* in front of the right side of the body, palm facing up, move the hand forward while quickly sliding the thumb off each finger.

punitive damages[2] (alternate sign)
- **punish** Strike the extended right index finger, palm facing left, downward across the elbow of the left bent arm.

- **cost** Strike the knuckle of the right *X hand*, palm facing in, down on the palm of the left *open hand*, palm facing right and fingers pointing forward.

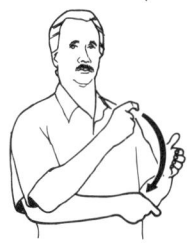

put in jail See signs for JAIL[3,4,5].

qualified Limited or conditional, such as qualified immunity.
- **limit** Beginning with both *bent hands* in front of the chest, right hand above the let hand and both palms facing down, move both hands forward simultaneously.

quasi *Latin.* A prefix placed in front of a legal term to mean "resembling, but different in some legally insignificant aspect." See sign for IMPLIED.

query A question, or to raise a question.
- **question**[1] Move the extended right index finger from pointing forward in front of the right shoulder, palm facing down, downward with a curving movement while retracting the index finger.

question Something asked at a trial, hearing, or deposition. See sign for INQUEST[2].

quid pro quo *Latin.* Something given or expected, legally or illegally, in exchange for something else.
- **cost** Strike the knuckle of the right *X hand*, palm facing in, down on the palm of the left *open hand*, palm facing right and fingers pointing forward.

- **not** Bring the thumb of the right *10 hand* forward from under the chin with a deliberate movement.

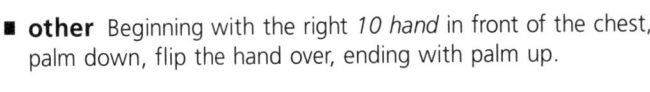

- **other** Beginning with the right *10 hand* in front of the chest, palm down, flip the hand over, ending with palm up.

---- [sign continues] ----

quitclaim

- **exchange** Beginning with both *modified X hands* in front of the body, right hand somewhat forward of the left hand, move the right hand back toward the body in an upward arc while moving the left hand forward with a downward arc.

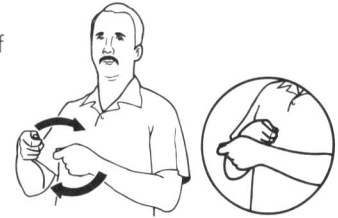

quiet enjoyment The use and possession of real property free from interference by someone with a superior right to the property.

- **secret** Tap the thumb side of the right *A hand*, palm left, against the mouth with a repeated movement.

- **pleasure** Rub the palms of both *open hands* on the chest, right hand above the left hand and fingers pointing in opposite directions, in repeated circles moving in opposite directions.

quit To vacate the premises.

- **quit** Beginning with both *flattened O hands* in and fingers pointing down, move the hands forward while opening to *5 hands*, palms down and fingers pointing forward.

quitclaim Abandonment of a claim, or a document given as evidence of such abandonment.

- **no-no** In quick succession, snap the extended right index and middle fingers closed to the extended right thumb, palm down, while moving the hand down slightly each time.

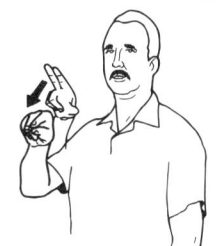

- **give-up** Beginning with both *open hands* in front of the body, palms facing down, flip the hands upward in large arcs while opening into *5 hands,* ending in front of each shoulder, palms facing forward.

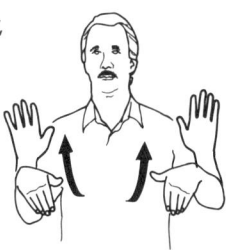

331

race[1] As used in the Constitution and civil rights, a term applicable to any grouping on the basis of race, ancestry, or ethnicity.
- Fingerspell: R-A-C-E

race[2] or color (alternate sign)

- **skin** Pinch the skin of the right cheek with the index finger and thumb of the right hand, palm facing left.

- **color** Wiggle the fingers of the right *5 hand* in front of the mouth, fingers pointing up and palm facing in.

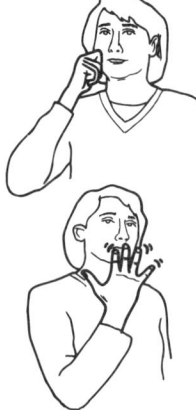

raise To invoke or bring into being.
- **offer** Beginning with both *open hands* in front of each side of the body, palms up, move the hands upward and forward in simultaneous arcs.

ransom Money paid to secure the release of a kidnapped person.
- **person** Move both *P hands*, palms facing each other, downward along the sides of the body.

- **steal**[1] Beginning with the index-finger side of the right *V hand*, palm facing down, on the elbow of the bent left arm, held at an upward angle across the chest, pull the right hand upward toward the left wrist while bending the fingers in tightly.

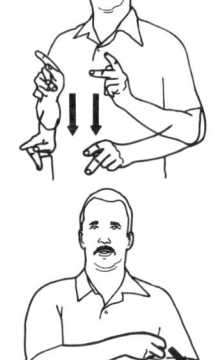

---- [sign continues] -->

real property

- **pay**[2] Beginning with the right *flattened O hand* in front of the right side of the body, palm facing up, move the hand forward while quickly sliding the thumb off each finger.

- **give-me**[2] Beginning with both *X hands* in front of the body, palms facing each other, bring the hands back to touch on each side of the chest.

rape[1] The crime of forcing a person to submit to sexual intercourse against his or her will.

- **force** Beginning with the right *C hand* in front of the right shoulder, palm forward, and the left arm bent across the body, move the right hand downward and forward, ending with the right wrist across the left wrist, both palms down.

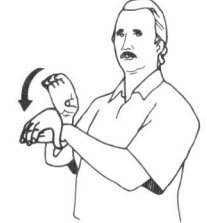

- **intercourse** Bring the right *V hand* downward in front of the chest to tap against the heel of the left *V hand* with a double movement, palms facing each other.

rape[2] (alternate sign)

- **rape** Beginning with both *curved 5 hands* in front of the chest, the right hand higher than the left, move the right hand down and the left hand up while changing to *S hands*.

ratify To manifest approval of a previous action to make it legally binding. See signs for ADOPTION[1,2].

real evidence Any document or other object that is offered as having been involved in the events that are the subject of the case. See sign for FACT.

real estate See sign for LAND.

real property See sign for LAND.

333

realize

realize See sign for RECOGNIZE.

realty See signs for LAND.

reasonable Appropriate in view of the circumstances; legally sufficient.

- **law** Place the palm side of the right *L hand*, palm facing left, first on the fingers and then on the heel of the left *open hand*, palm facing right and fingers pointing up.

- **enough** Push the palm side of the right *open hand*, palm down, back across the thumb side of the left *S hand*.

reasonable care See sign for CARE.

rebut To present evidence or argument to overcome the evidence or argument just presented by an adversary. Related form: **rebuttal**.

- **answer** Beginning with both extended index fingers pointing up in front of the mouth, right hand nearer the mouth than the left and palms forward, bend the wrists down simultaneously, ending with the fingers pointing forward and the palms down.
- Fingerspell: B-A-C-K

recall[1] To call back to the stand a witness who previously testified in a case for further testimony.

- **testify** While holding the left *open hand* in front of the left side of the body, palm down and fingers pointing forward, move the right extended index finger from in front of the mouth, palm left, forward while opening to an *open hand*.

- **call** Slap the fingers of the right *open hand* on the back of the left *open hand*, palm facing down, dragging the right fingers upward and closing them into an *A hand* in front of the right shoulder.

---- [sign continues] ----

recess

■ **again** Beginning with the right *bent hand* beside the left *curved hand*, both palms up, bring the right hand up while turning it over, ending with the fingertips of the right hand touching the palm of the left hand.

recall[2] or **remove** To remove an elected official from office before expiration of his or her term by special vote of the people. Same sign used for **challenge, waive**.

- **delete** Beginning with the index finger of the right *modified X hand*, palm in, touching the extended left index finger held up in front of the chest, palm right and finger pointing up, move the right hand upward to the right while flicking the thumb upward.

recall[3] To vacate a previous order or judgment of the same court because of a factual error. See sign for SET ASIDE.

receive To admit into evidence.

- **court** Move both *F hands*, palms facing each other, up and down in front of each side of the chest with a repeated alternating movement.

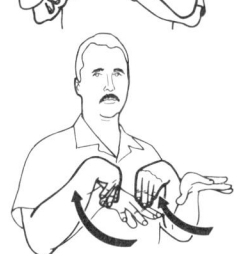

- **accept** Beginning with both *5 hands* in front of the body, fingers pointing forward and palms down, pull both hands back to the chest while changing to *flattened O hands*.

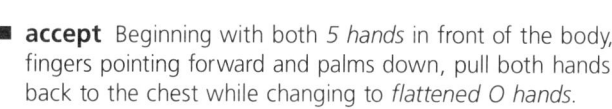

recess A brief break in a trial or hearing.

- **court** Move both *F hands*, palms facing each other, up and down in front of each side of the chest with a repeated alternating movement.

- **suspend** With the index fingers of both *X hands* hooked around each other, move both hands upward in front of the chest.

335

reciprocity

reciprocity A relationship between two states in which each grants certain rights to the other and its people in exchange for equivalent rights for itself. Same sign used for **in kind**.

- **exchange** Beginning with both *modified X hands* in front of the body, right hand somewhat forward of the left hand, move the right hand back toward the body in an upward arc while moving the left hand forward with a downward arc.

recklessness Conscious disregard of the safety or rights of others.

- **careless** Beginning with both *V hands* near each side of the head, palms facing each other, move the hands toward and past each other in front of the eyes with a short double movement.

recognize or **realize** To include a gain or loss in one's income tax calculations, usually in the year that the gain or loss is realized. Same sign used for **recover**.

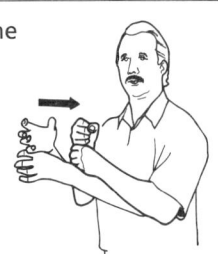

- **receive** Beginning with both *curved 5 hands* in front of the body, right hand higher than the left hand and both palms facing back, bring the hands back toward the chest while closing into *S hands*, ending with the right little finger on the index-finger side of the left hand.

recollection See signs for MEMORY[1,2,3].

record To document findings, testimony, and other information pertinent to a case. See sign for FOR THE RECORD. See signs for DOCUMENT[1,2,3].

recovered memory See signs for MEMORY[1,2,3].

recover To obtain money or property by means of litigation, either by judgment or settlement. See sign for RECOGNIZE.

recuse To remove oneself from participation in a matter because of a conflict of interest. Related form: **recusal**.

- **resign** Beginning with the fingers of the right *bent U hand*, palm facing down, in the opening of the left *O hand*, palm facing right, pull the right fingers out to the right.

referendum A procedure by which certain proposed state statutes must be put to a vote by the people before becoming effective.

- **offer** Beginning with both *open hands* in front of each side of the body, palms up, move the hands upward and forward in simultaneous arcs.

---- [sign continues] ---→

regular

- **people** Move both *P hands*, palms facing down, in alternating forward circles in front of each side of the body.

- **vote** Insert the fingertips of the right *F hand*, palm down, with a double movement in the opening of the left *S hand*, palm right.

refresh To jog memory.

- **step-back** Beginning with both extended index fingers pointing down in front of the chest, palms back, move the hands back toward the chest in alternating arcs.

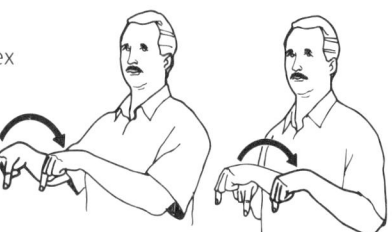

- **consider** Beginning with both extended index fingers in front of each side of the forehead, palms facing in and fingers angled up, move the fingers in repeated alternating circular movements toward each other in front of the face.

regular Conforming with legal requirements as to form.

- **require** With the extended index finger of the right *X hand* touching the palm of the left *open hand* bring both hands back toward the chest.

- **follow** With the knuckles of the right *10 hand*, palm facing left, near the wrist of the left *10 hand*, palm facing right, move both hands forward a short distance.

regulation

regulation A directive adopted by an administrative agency for its own internal procedures or to govern public behavior in matters over which it has authority. Same sign used for **code, rule.**

- **rule** Touch the fingertips of the right *R hand* first on the fingers and then on the heel of the left *open hand*, palms facing each other.

regulatory agency An agency having powers delegated by congress to adopt regulations governing public conduct.

- **agency** Beginning with the thumbs of both *A hands* touching in front of the chest, palms down, move the hands apart and forward in a circular movement by twisting the wrists until the little fingers touch and the palms face in.

- **manage** Beginning with both *modified X hands* in front of each side of the body, right hand forward of the left hand and palms facing each other, move the hands forward and back with a repeated movement.

rehabilitation Questioning of a witness or introduction of evidence designed to restore the credibility of a witness.

- **again** Beginning with the right *bent hand* beside the left *curved hand*, both palms up, bring the right hand up while turning it over, ending with the fingertips of the right hand touching the palm of the left hand.

- **set-up** Beginning with the right *10 hand* in front of the right shoulder, palm down, twist the wrist up with a circular movement and then move the right hand straight down to land on the little-finger side of the back of the left *open hand*, palm down.

- **honest**[1] Slide the extended fingers of the right *H hand*, palm left, forward from the heel to the fingers of the upturned left *open hand*.

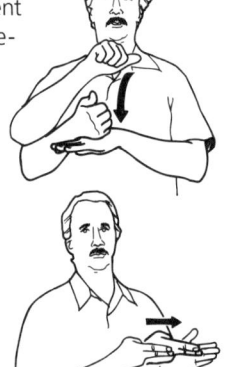

338

relevant

release A formal document relieving another person from an obligation or liability. See signs for ACQUIT[1,2].

release on own recognizance (ROR)[1] or release on personal recognizance Pretrial release of a criminal defendant upon his promise to appear in court as needed, without requirement of bail.
- Fingerspell acronym: R-O-R

release on own recognizance (ROR)[2] or release on personal recognizance
- **sign** Place the extended fingers of the right *H hand*, palm down, firmly down on the upturned palm of the left *open hand* held in front of the chest.

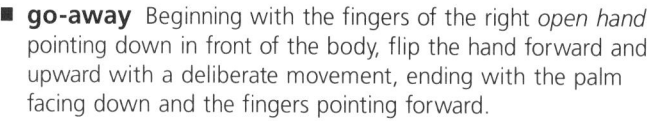

- **go-away** Beginning with the fingers of the right *open hand* pointing down in front of the body, flip the hand forward and upward with a deliberate movement, ending with the palm facing down and the fingers pointing forward.

- **trust** Beginning with both *curved hands* in front of the chest, right hand above the left and palms facing in, move both hands downward a short distance with a deliberate movement while closing into *S hands*.

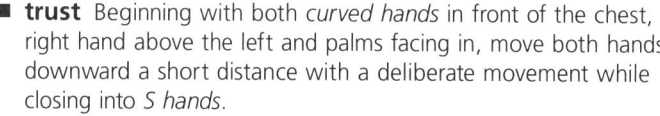

- **come** Beginning with both extended index fingers pointing up in front of the body, palms facing in, bring the fingers back toward the chest.

release on personal recognizance See signs for RELEASE ON OWN RECOGNIZANCE[1,2].

relevant Describing evidence that has direct consequence in a case.
- **relate** With the thumbs and index fingers of both *F hands* intersecting, move the hands forward and back toward the chest with a double movement.

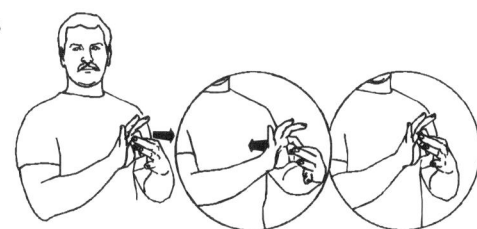

339

reliance

reliance The taking of or failure to take some action because of trust in what someone else has said or done.

- **trust** Beginning with both *curved hands* in front of the chest, right hand above the left and palms facing in, move both hands downward a short distance with a deliberate movement while closing into *S hands*.

remand To send a case back from an appellate court to the lower court from which it was appealed.

- **court** Move both *F hands*, palms facing each other, up and down in front of each side of the chest with a repeated alternating movement.

- **advance** Move both *bent hands*, palms facing each other, from near each side of the head upward a short distance in deliberate arcs.

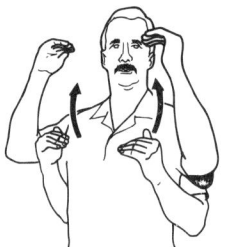

- **order** Move the extended right index finger, palm forward and finger pointing up, from in front of the mouth forward and down, ending with the finger pointing forward and the palm down.

- **lower** Beginning with both *bent hands* in front of each shoulder, palms facing each other, move them downward in front of each side of the chest.

remedy Any type of judgment that can be issued by a court in a civil action.

- **court** Move both *F hands*, palms facing each other, up and down in front of each side of the chest with a repeated alternating movement.

---- [sign continues] ---->

repeal

- **solve** Beginning with both *flattened O hands* in front of each side of the body, palms facing up, move the thumb of each hand smoothly across each fingertip, starting with the little fingers and ending as *10 hands* while moving the hands outward to each side.

remove See sign for RECALL².

render To issue or announce, such as render a verdict.

- **announce** Beginning with the extended index fingers of both hands pointing to each side of the mouth, palms facing in, twist the wrists and move the fingers forward and apart from each other, ending with the palms facing forward and the index fingers pointing outward in opposite directions.

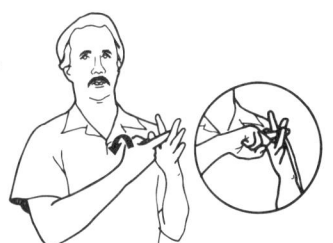

renew To begin again, such as renew a lease.

- **start** Beginning with the extended right index finger, palm down, inserted between the index and middle fingers of the left *open hand*, palm right and fingers pointing forward, twist the right hand back, ending with palm in.

- **again** Beginning with the right *bent hand* beside the left *curved hand*, both palms up, bring the right hand up while turning it over, ending with the fingertips of the right hand touching the palm of the left hand.

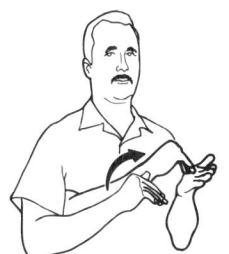

renounce To give up a right, interest, or claim.

- **give-up** Beginning with both *open hands* in front of the body, palms facing down, flip the hands upward in large arcs while opening into *5 hands,* ending in front of each shoulder, palms facing forward.

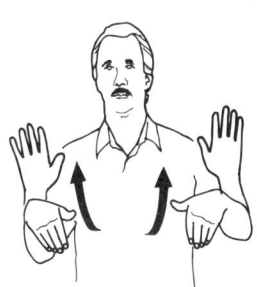

repeal The nullification of a statue. See sign for SET ASIDE.

341

repeat offender

repeat offender or habitual criminal
A person convicted more than once of the same kind or different kinds of crime.

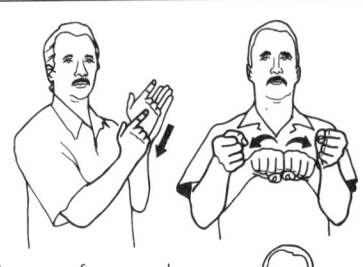

- **crime** Place the palm side of the right *L hand*, palm facing left, first on the fingers and then on the heel of the left *open hand*, palm facing right and fingers pointing up. Then beginning with both *S hands* in front of the body, index fingers touching and palms down, move the hands away from each other while twisting the wrists with a deliberate movement, ending with the palms facing each other.

- **person marker** Move both *open hands*, palms facing each other, downward along the sides of the body.

- **again** Beginning with the right *bent hand* beside the left *curved hand*, both palms up, with a double movement bring the right hand up while turning it over, ending with the fingertips of the right hand touching the palm of the left hand each time.

reply See signs for ANSWER[1,2].

report A written account of something based on the writer's observation, investigation, or analysis.

- **write** With the thumb and index finger of the right hand pinched together, move the right hand with a wiggling movement across the palm of the left *open hand* held in front of the body, palm up.

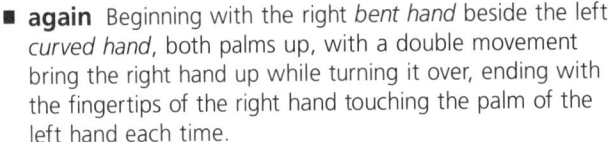

- **points** Move the right extended index finger, palm left, downward in a series of small arcs pointing to each finger of the left *5 hand*, palm in and fingers pointing right.

- **answer** Beginning with both extended index fingers pointing up in front of the mouth, right hand nearer the mouth than the left and palms forward, bend the wrists down simultaneously, ending with the fingers pointing forward and the palms down.

residence

repossess To take back property in which one has retained a security interest upon the failure of the buyer to keep up with payments. Related form: **repossession**.

- **grab** Beginning with the right *curved 5 hand* in front of the right shoulder, palm facing left, move the hand forward and downward while closing into an *S hand*.

represent To act on behalf of another. Related form: **representation**. See sign for IN THE MATTER OF.

reprieve The postponement of execution by executive order. Same sign used for **rescind**.

- **postpone** Beginning with both *F hands* in front of the body, palms facing each other and the left hand nearer to the body than the right hand, move both hands forward in a small arc.

- **die** Beginning with both *open hands* in front of the body, right palm down and left palm up, flip the hands to the right, turning the right palm up and the left palm down. See sign for CLEMENCY.

repudiation Refusal to carry out a duty.

- **refuse** Beginning with the right *10 hand* in front of the right shoulder, elbow extended and palm facing down, push the thumb back over the right shoulder.

- **do** Move both *C hands*, palms facing down, simultaneously back and forth in front of the body with a swinging movement.

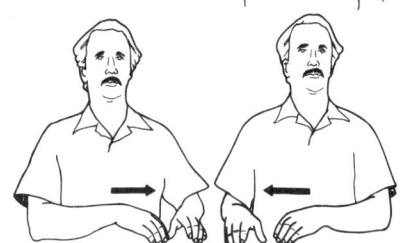

rescind To nullify a previous decision. See signs for REPRIEVE, SET ASIDE.

residence See signs for DOMICILE[1,2].

343

resident alien

resident alien An alien who has lawfully established a permanent residence in the United States or other country.

- **not** Bring the thumb of the right *10 hand* forward from under the chin with a deliberate movement.
- Fingerspell: U-S or other country, as appropriate.

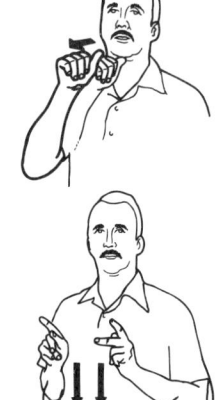

- **person** Move both *P hands*, palms facing each other, downward along the sides of the body.

- **allow** Beginning with both *open hands* in front of the waist, palms facing each other and fingers pointing down, bring the fingers forward and upward by bending the wrists.

- **settle** Beginning with both *5 hands* in front of each side of the chest, palms facing down, move the hands slowly down to in front of each side of the waist.

respondent The name given to the party who must respond to a procedural step in a case, such as a petition, motion, etc.

- **answer** Beginning with both extended index fingers pointing up in front of the mouth, right hand nearer the mouth than the left and palms forward, bend the wrists down simultaneously, ending with the fingers pointing forward and the palms down.
- **person** Move both *P hands*, palms facing each other, downward along the sides of the body.

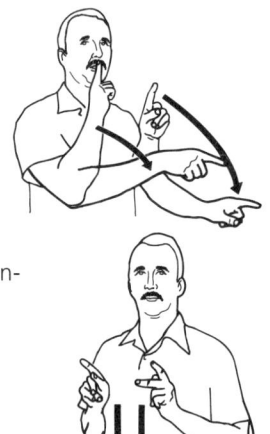

restraining order

restitution In criminal law, giving back ill-gotten gains or paying for property damage as part of one's sentence.

- **court** Move both *F hands,* palms facing each other, up and down in front of each side of the chest with a repeated alternating movement.

- **order** Move the extended right index finger, palm forward and finger pointing up, from in front of the mouth forward and down, ending with the finger pointing forward and the palm down.

- **money** Tap the back of the right *flattened O hand,* palm facing up, with a double movement against the palm of the left *open hand,* palm facing up.

- **pay**[1] Beginning with the extended right index finger touching the palm of the left *open hand,* palms facing each other, move the right finger forward and off the left fingertips.

restraining order or temporary restraining order (TRO)
An injunction that prohibits someone from taking some action.

- **court** Move both *F hands,* palms facing each other, up and down in front of each side of the chest with a repeated alternating movement.

- **order** Move the extended right index finger, palm forward and finger pointing up, from in front of the mouth forward and down, ending with the finger pointing forward and the palm down.

---- [sign continues] ---------→

345

restraining order

- **stay-away** Beginning with the thumbs of both *Y hands* together in front of the chest, palms down, move the hands apart in deliberate arcs to the sides.

retainer An initial fee paid to a lawyer upon being retained by a new client. Same sign used for **pledge, security, security deposit**.

- **deposit** Beginning with the thumbs of both *10 hands* touching in front of the chest, both palms facing down, take the hands downward and apart by twisting the wrists.

- **hold** Move the right *S hand*, palm facing up, in a circular movement in front of the right side of the chest.

retirement plan or **pension plan** An arrangement by which money is set aside during an individual's working years for use after retirement. Same sign used for **pension**.

- **subscribe** With right *modified C hand* in front of the right shoulder, palm left, bring the hand downward with a double movement, closing the fingers to form an *A hand* each time.

retrial A new trial granted because of some error or injustice in the first trial.

- **court** Move both *F hands*, palms facing each other, up and down in front of each side of the chest with a repeated alternating movement.

- **again** Beginning with the right *bent hand* beside the left *curved hand*, both palms up, bring the right hand up while turning it over, ending with the fingertips of the right hand touching the palm of the left hand.

right to counsel

return To submit to a court an account of action taken in a judicial matter: *The jury returned its verdict.*

- **decide** Move the extended right index finger from the right side of the forehead, palm left, down in front of the chest while changing into an *F hand*, ending with both *F hands* moving downward in front of the body, palms facing each other.

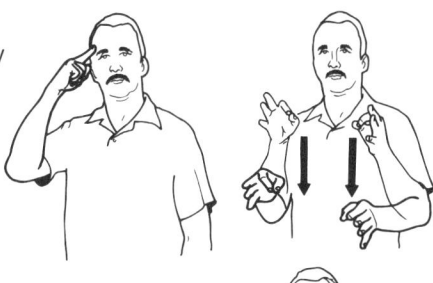

- **give-up** Beginning with both *open hands* in front of the body, palms facing down, flip the hands upward in large arcs while opening into *5 hands,* ending in front of each shoulder, palms facing forward.

return See sign for TAX RETURN.

review See signs for APPEAL[1,2].

revoke See sign for SET ASIDE.

rider A separate sheet of paper containing one or more additions or amendments to a legal document such as a contract or insurance policy. Same sign used for **amend, amendment**.

- **attach** Bring the palm side of the right *curved hand* up to clasp little-finger side of left *open hand*.

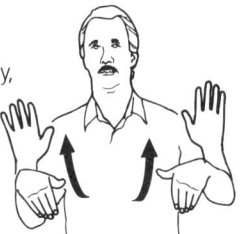

right of survivorship See sign for SURVIVORSHIP.

right to counsel The right of a criminal defendant to have a lawyer present at any significant step of a criminal prosecution, as guaranteed by the Sixth Amendment.

- **able** Move both *S hands,* palms facing down, downward simultaneously in front of each side of the body.

- **have** Bring the fingertips of both *bent hands*, palms facing in, in to touch each side of the chest.

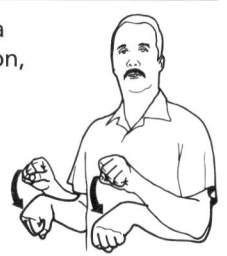

---- [sign continues] ---->

right to counsel

- **lawyer** Place the palm side of the right *L hand*, palm facing left, first on the fingers and then on the heel of the left *open hand*, palm facing right and fingers pointing up. Move both *open hands*, palms facing each other, downward along the sides of the body.

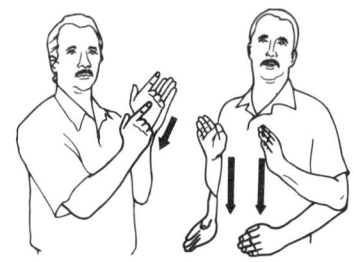

right to die Refers to the right of a competent adult to refuse medical care that would prolong life.

- **decide** Move the extended right index finger from the right side of the forehead, palm left, down in front of the chest while changing into an *f hand*, ending with both *F hands* moving downward in front of the body, palms facing each other.

- **die** Beginning with both *open hands* in front of the body, right palm down and left palm up, flip the hands to the right, turning the right palm up and the left palm down.

- **can** Move both *S hands*, palms facing down, downward simultaneously in front of each side of the body.

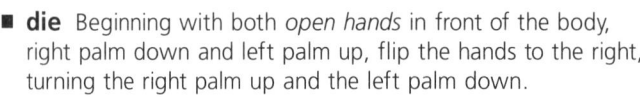

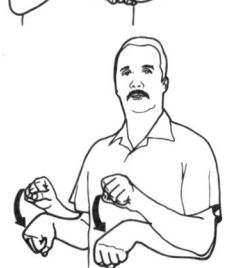

right to work laws Legislation passed in many states protecting the right of workers to gain and keep employment without joining or contributing to a union.

- **work** Tap the heel of the right *S hand*, palm forward, with a double movement on the back of the left *S hand* held in front of the body, palm down.

- **can** Move both *S hands*, palms facing down, downward simultaneously in front of each side of the body.
- Fingerspell: U-N-I-O-N

---- [sign continues] ---->

348

royalty

- **think-for-yourself** Touch the right side of the forehead with the extended right index finger. Then quickly move the right hand forward while changing into a *10 hand*, palm facing left.

ripe Ready for the next procedural step in a case.

- **process** Beginning with both *open hands* in front of the body, palms facing in, left fingers pointing right and right fingers pointing left, and the left hand closer to the chest than the right hand, move the left hand over the right hand and then the right hand over the left hand in an alternating movement.

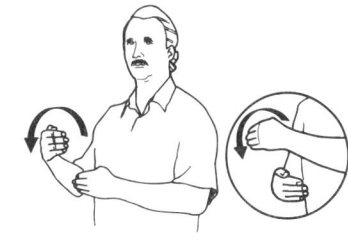

- **ready** Move both *R hands* from in front of the left side of the body, palms facing each other and fingers pointing forward, in a smooth movement to in front of the right side of the body.

risk The potential injury or loss covered by an insurance policy.

- **risk** Move the thumb of the right *10 hand*, palm left, upward on the back of the left *A hand*, palm in, with a double movement.

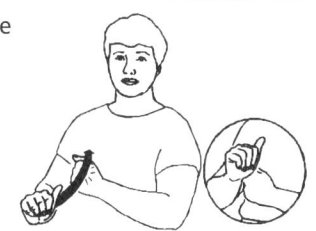

robbery or **hold up** The crime of taking someone's money or other personal property by force or threat of imminent harm. Related form: **rob**.

- **rob** Beginning with both *H hands* in front of each side of the waist, palms facing each other and fingers pointing down, twist the wrists upward, bringing the hands up in front of each side of the body, palms facing each other and fingers pointing forward.

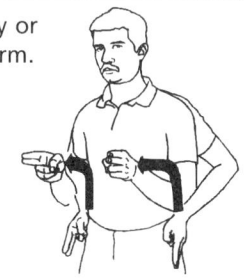

royalty A sum paid to the creator of copyrighted work for the right to exploit the creation, usually based on copies or units sold.

- **invent** Move the index-finger side of the right *4 hand*, palm left, from the forehead upward in an outward arc.

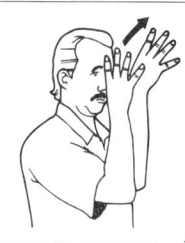

---- [sign continues] ---→

349

royalty

- **your** Push the palm of the right *open hand*, palm forward and fingers pointing up, toward the person being talked to.

- **pay**² Beginning with the right *flattened O hand* in front of the right side of the body, palm facing up, with a double movement, move the hand forward while quickly sliding the thumb off each finger.

rule Any of a set of principles and directives formally adopted by or imposed upon a body for its own administration. Related form: **ruling.** See sign for REGULATION.

said Previously referred to.
- say² Move the extended right index finger in a repeated upward circular movement in front of the chin, palm facing in and finger pointing left.

- finish With both *5 hands* apart in front of the body, palms up, quickly turn the hands over toward each other.

sale A transfer of title to property for money, or a contract for its transfer.
- sell Beginning with both *flattened O hands* held in front of each side of the chest, palms down and fingers pointing down, swing the fingertips forward and back by twisting the wrists upward.

sales tax A tax imposed by many states on purchases of goods and services, consisting of a fixed percentage added to the selling price.
- sell Beginning with both *flattened O hands* held in front of each side of the chest, palms down and fingers pointing down, swing the fingertips forward and back by twisting the wrists upward with a double movement.
- Fingerspell: T-A-X

satisfaction Full performance of an obligation, especially payment of a debt in full.
- pay-off Move the bent middle finger of the right *5 hand* across the palm of the left *open hand*. Then slap the palm of the right *open hand* on the palm of the left *open hand*.

351

scrutiny

scrutiny Judicial consideration of the purposes and effects of an administrative, state, or federal regulation to determine if it is valid.

- **court** Move both *F hands,* palms facing each other, up and down in front of each side of the chest with a repeated alternating movement.

- **analyze** With both *bent V hands* near each other in front of the chest, palms down, move the fingers apart from each other with a repeated movement as the hands move down in front of the body.

seal To place or keep items or records relating to a case shielded from public access.

- **save-me** With the fingers of the right *V hand* on the back of the left *S hand,* both palms facing in, move both hands back toward the chest.

- **take-advantage** With a double movement flick the bent middle finger of the right *5 hand* upward off the heel of the upturned left *open hand.*

- **can't** Bring the extended index finger of the right *one hand* downward, hitting the extended index finger of the left *one hand* as it moves.

search[1] Inspection by law enforcement officials of a person's body or home for any evidence of criminal activity.

- **search** Move the right *C hand,* palm facing left, with a double circular movement in front of the face.

search[2] See sign for INQUEST[1].

search warrant

search and seizure A search leading to seizure of property.
- **search** Move the right *C hand*, palm facing left, with a double circular movement in front of the face.

- **grab** Beginning with the right *curved 5 hand* in front of the right shoulder, palm facing left, move the hand forward and downward while closing into an *S hand*.

search warrant A warrant, issued upon showing probable cause, authorizing law enforcement to search for items connected in a crime believed to be found in a particular place.
- **court** Move both *F hands*, palms facing each other, up and down in front of each side of the chest with a repeated alternating movement.

- **paper** Brush the heel of the right *open hand* with a double movement on the heel of the left *open hand*, palms facing each other.

- **allow** Beginning with both *open hands* in front of the waist, palms facing each other and fingers pointing down, bring the fingers forward and upward by bending the wrists.

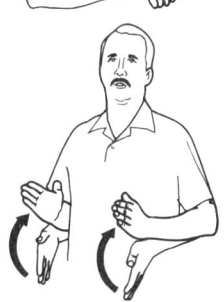

- **search** Move the right *C hand*, palm facing left, with a double circular movement in front of the face.

353

second mortgage

second mortgage An additional mortgage on property that is already subject to a mortgage.

- **house** Beginning with the fingertips of both *open hands* touching in front of the neck, palms angled toward each other, move the hands at a downward angle outward to in front of each shoulder and then straight down, ending with the fingers pointing up and the palms facing each other.

- **second** With the middle fingers of both *V hands* touching in front of the chest, twist the right hand back, ending with both palms facing in.

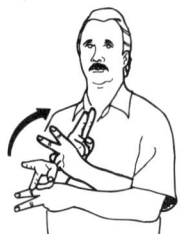

- **borrow** With the little-finger side of the right *V hand* across the index-finger side of the left *V hand*, bring the hands back, ending with the right index finger against the chest.

---

section[1] A subdivision of a statute or document, represented by the symbol §.

- **paragraph** Tap the fingertips of the right *C hand*, palm facing left, against the palm of the left *open hand*, palm facing right and fingers pointing up, with a double movement.

---

section[2] (alternate sign)

- **part** Slide the little-finger side of the right *open hand*, palm facing left, across the palm of left *open hand*, palm facing up, with a curved movement.

---

security or **security deposit** Money that is set aside and held to provide assurance of payment of a debt. See sign for RETAINER.

---

security interest See sign for COLLATERAL.

---

seizure In criminal matters, the taking of a weapon, contraband or evidence of a crime by law enforcement officials.

- **seize** Beginning with both *curved 5 hands* in front of each shoulder, palms facing forward, move the hands downward while closing into *S hands*.

354

self-incrimination

self-employment tax A tax on self-employed individuals requiring them to make a double contribution to the social security system, paying both the employer's share and the employee's share.

- **yourself** Push the thumb of the right *10 hand*, palm facing left, toward the person being talked to with a small double movement.

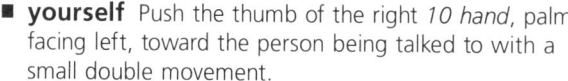

- **work** Tap the heel of the right *S hand*, palm forward, with a double movement on the back of the left *S hand* held in front of the body, palm down.

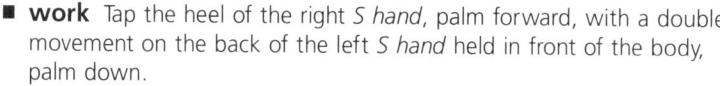

- Fingerspell: T-A-X

- **itself** Bring the knuckles of the right *10 hand*, palm facing left, firmly against the side of the extended left index finger, palm facing right and finger pointing up in front of the chest.

- **pay**[2] Beginning with the right *flattened O hand* in front of the right side of the body, palm facing up, move the hand forward while quickly sliding the thumb off each finger.

self-incrimination The making of a statement that exposes the speaker to criminal penalties.

- **yourself** Push the thumb of the right *10 hand*, palm facing left, toward the person being talked to with a small double movement.

- **confess** Beginning with the palm sides of both *flattened O hands* on the chest, move the hands forward in an arc while opening into *5 hands*.

sentence

sentence A court's judgment imposing a penalty upon a person convicted of an offense, or the penalty imposed, such as imprisonment, a fine, or community service.

- **court** Move both *F hands,* palms facing each other, up and down in front of each side of the chest with a repeated alternating movement.

- **order** Move the extended right index finger, palm forward and finger pointing up, from in front of the mouth forward and down, ending with the finger pointing forward and the palm down.

- **punish** Strike the extended right index finger, palm facing left, downward across the elbow of the left bent arm.

separation of church and state A phrase commonly used to summarize the purpose of the First Amendment's guarantee of freedom of religion without involvement of government in religious matters and that religion has no effect on governmental functions.

- **religion** Beginning with the fingertips of the right *R hand* touching the right side of the chest, palm facing down, twist the wrist outward, ending with the fingers pointing forward.
- **government** Beginning with the extended right index finger pointing upward near the right side of the head, palm facing forward, twist the wrist to touch the finger to the right temple.
- **separate** Beginning with the knuckles of both *10 hands* touching in front of the chest, palms facing in, take the hands apart.

---- [sign continues] -->

separation of powers

- **must** Move the bent index finger of the right *X hand* downward with a deliberate movement in front of the right side of the body by bending the wrist down.

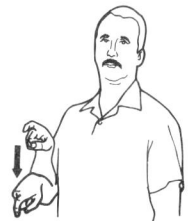

separation of powers The theory that government should have three separate branches: a legislative branch to make laws, an executive branch to administer them, and a judicial branch to interpret them and resolve disputes arising under them.

- **law** Place the palm side of the right *L hand*, palm facing left, first on the fingers and then on the heel of the left *open hand*, palm facing right and fingers pointing up.

- **group** Beginning with the body turned left and both *claw hands* in front of the chest, palms facing each other, take the hands away from each other in outward arcs while turning the palms in, ending with the little fingers near each other.

- **government** Beginning with the extended right index finger pointing upward near the right side of the head, palm facing forward, twist the wrist to touch the finger to the right temple.

- **group** Beginning with the body facing forward and both *claw hands* in front of the chest, palms facing each other, take the hands away from each other in outward arcs while turning the palms in, ending with the little fingers near each other.

- **court** Move both *F hands*, palms facing each other, up and down in front of each side of the chest with a repeated alternating movement.

---- [sign continues] ---->

357

separation of powers

- **group** Beginning with the body turned right and both *claw hands* in front of the chest, palms facing each other, take the hands away from each other in outward arcs while turning the palms in, ending with the little fingers near each other.

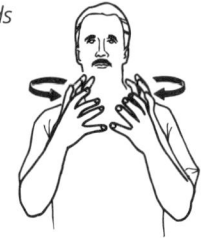

- **there-there-there** Point the extended right index finger to three different locations.

- **manage** Beginning with both *modified X hands* in front of each side of the body, right hand forward of the left hand and palms facing each other, move the hands forward and back with a repeated movement.

- **different-different-different** Beginning with both extended index fingers crossed in front of the chest, palms forward, take the hands apart from each other with a deliberate movement. Repeat sign in two other locations.

sequester To isolate witnesses or a jury to shield them from outside influences.

- **court** Move both *F hands*, palms facing each other, up and down in front of each side of the chest with a repeated alternating movement.

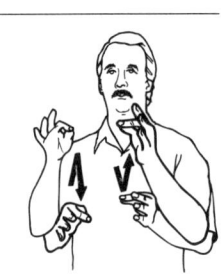

- **include** Swing the right *5 hand*, palm down, in a circular movement over the left *S hand*, palm in, while changing into a *flattened O hand*, ending with the fingertips of the right hand inserted in the center of the thumb side of the left hand.

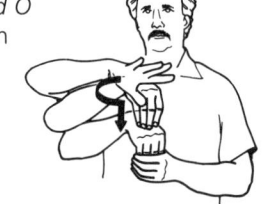

---- [sign continues] ---->

servitude

- **group** Beginning with the body turned left and both *claw hands* in front of the chest, palms facing each other, take the hands away from each other in outward arcs while turning the palms in, ending with the little fingers near each other.

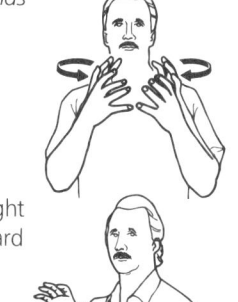

- **grab** Beginning with the right *curved 5 hand* in front of the right shoulder, palm facing left, move the hand forward and downward while closing into an *S hand*.

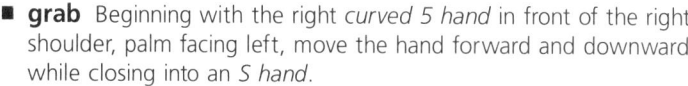

service¹ or **service of process** The giving of formal notice to a person involved, by delivery of any paper filed with the court.

- **court** Move both *F hands,* palms facing each other, up and down in front of each side of the chest with a repeated alternating movement.

- **paper** Brush the heel of the right *open hand* with a double movement on the heel of the left *open hand*, palms facing each other.

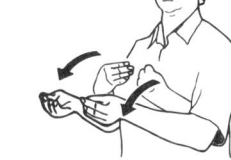

- **give²** Beginning with the fingers of both *flattened O hands* touching the chest, move the fingers forward in simultaneous arcs, ending with the palms up and fingers pointing forward.

service² See sign for NOTICE.

service of process See sign for SERVICE¹.

servitude, involuntary servitude, or **slavery** Working for another against one's will, whether for pay or not.

- **slavery** With the wrists of both *S hands* crossed in front of the body, palms down, move the arms in a large, flat circle in front of the body.

359

set aside

set aside, rescind, revoke, or vacate
To nullify a judgment, verdict, or court order. Same sign used for **null, null and void, recall, repeal, void.**

- **cancel** With the extended right index finger, draw a large X across the upturned left *open hand*.

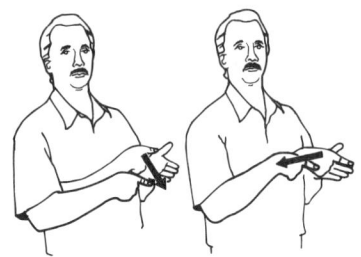

---

settle To reach agreement resolving a dispute. Related form: **settlement.**

- **two** Hold up the right *2 hand*, palm facing back, in front of the chest.

- **people** Move both *P hands*, palms facing down, in alternating forward circles in front of each side of the body.

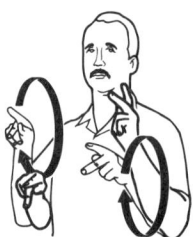

- **agree** Move the extended right index finger from touching the right side of the forehead downward to beside the extended left index finger, ending with both fingers pointing forward in front of the body, palms down.

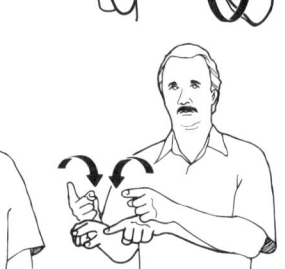

- **accept** Beginning with both *5 hands* in front of the body, fingers pointing forward and palms down, pull both hands back to the chest while changing to *flattened O hands*.

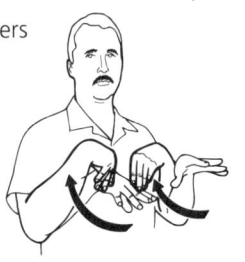

---

sex discrimination Treating men and women differently for reasons of their gender rather than the matter at hand.

- **sex** Touch the index-finger side of the right *X hand*, first near the right eye and then to the right side of the chin.

---- [sign continues] -->

sexual assault

- **discriminate** With the extended index finger of the right *D hand*, draw a large X across the upturned left *open hand*.

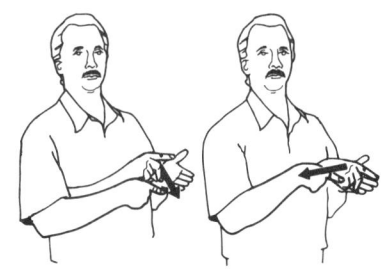

sexual assault The crime of intentionally touching or harming another person in a sexual way without that person's consent.
- **wrong** Bring the middle fingers of the right *Y hand*, palm in, back against the chin with a deliberate movement.

- **use** With the heel of the right *U hand* on the back of the left *S hand*, move the right hand in a small circle.
- Fingerspell: S-E-X

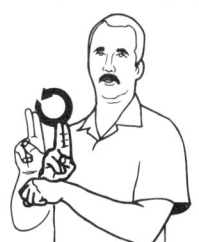

- **suppose** Move the extended little finger of the right *I hand*, palm in, forward from the right side of the forehead with a short double movement.

- **touch** Bring the bent middle finger of the right hand, palm down, downward to touch the back of the left *open hand* held in front of the body, palm down.

- **cruel** Beginning with the right *curved 5 hand* near the face and the left *curved 5 hand* in front of the body, close the right hand into an *A hand* while moving it quickly down and close the left hand into an *A hand* while moving it quickly up, brushing the knuckles of the hands together as they pass each other.

---- [sign continues] ----

361

sexual assault

- **take-advantage** With a double movement flick the bent middle finger of the right 5 hand upward off the heel of the upturned left open hand.

- **force** Beginning with the right C hand in front of the right shoulder, palm forward, and the left arm bent across the body, move the right hand downward and forward, ending with the right wrist across the left wrist, both palms down.

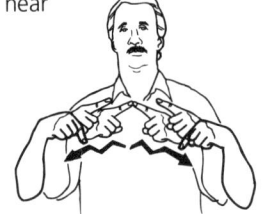

- **and-so-forth** Beginning with both extended index fingers near each other in front of the body, both palms down, bring the hands apart while bending the fingers up and down with a quick repeated movement.

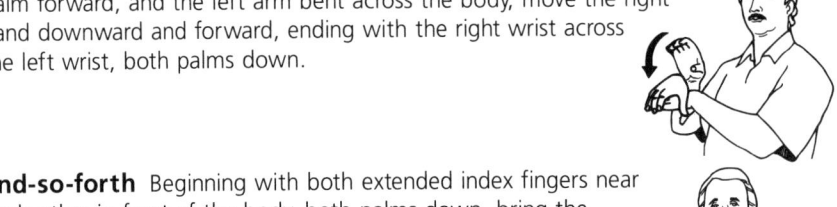

sexual harassment A form of unlawful employment discrimination consisting of harassment of an employee usually because of their sex.

- **illegal** Hit the palm side of the right L hand, palm left, sharply on the palm of the left open hand, palm right, and off again.
- Fingerspell: S-E-X

- **bother** Sharply tap the little-finger side of the right open hand, palm facing in at an angle, at the base of the thumb and index finger of the left open hand, with a double movement.

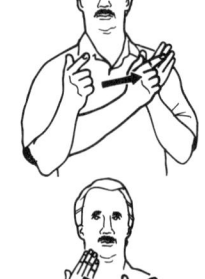

sexual predator A person with a history of sexual offenses against others, who is unlikely to be able to control the impulse to commit more such crimes in the future.

- Fingerspell: S-E-X
- **crime** Place the palm side of the right L hand, palm facing left, first on the fingers and then on the heel of the left open hand, palm facing right and fingers pointing up. Then beginning with both S hands in front of the body, index fingers touching and palms down, move the hands away from each other while twisting the wrists with a deliberate movement, ending with the palms facing each other.

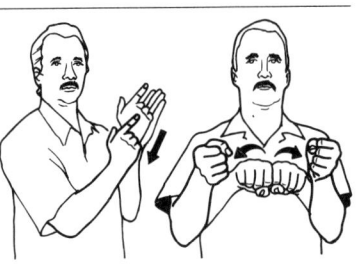

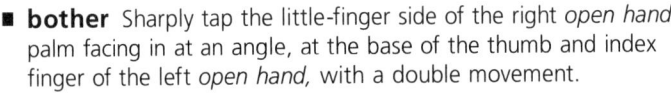

---- [sign continues] ----

show

- **person marker** Move both *open hands*, palms facing each other, downward along the sides of the body.

share A partial right or interest allotted to one of several people who together have the whole right or interest, such as ownership of a corporation.

- **share** Move the little-finger side of the right *open hand*, palm facing in, back and forth with a double movement at the base of the index finger of the left *open hand*, palm facing in.

sheriff See signs for POLICE[1,2].

shoplifting The crime of taking possession of merchandise in a store with the intention of keeping it without paying for it.

- **sell** Beginning with both *flattened O hands* held in front of each side of the chest, palms down and fingers pointing down, swing the fingertips forward and back by twisting the wrists upward with a double movement.

- **steal**[2]**-steal**[2]**-steal**[2] Beginning with the right *V hand*, palm facing left, in front of the left side of the chest, pull the hand upward toward the chest while bending the fingers in tightly. Repeat sign in two more locations.

show[1] or **show cause** To try to convince a court of something by evidence or legal argument.

- **show** With the extended right index finger touching the palm of the left *open hand*, palm right and fingers pointing forward, move both hands forward a short distance.

- **reason** Move the fingertips of the right *R hand*, palm facing in, in a circular movement in front of the right side of the forehead with a double movement.

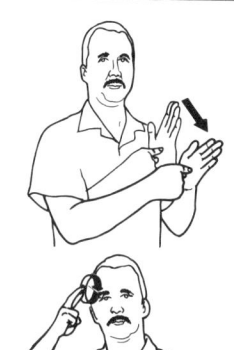

363

show

show[2] or show cause (alternate sign)

- **connect** Beginning with both *curved 5 hands* in front of each side of the body, palms facing each other, bring the hands together while touching the thumb and index fingertips of each hand and intersecting with each other.

- **for-for** With a questioning expression and beginning with the extended right finger touching the right side of the forehead, twist the hand forward with a double movement, turning the index finger forward each time.

show cause See signs for SHOW[1,2].

sidebar or bench conference In a jury trial, a brief courtroom conference among the judge and lawyers conducted at the bench so the jury cannot hear it.

- **judge** Move the right *modified X hand*, palm left, with a double up and down movement.

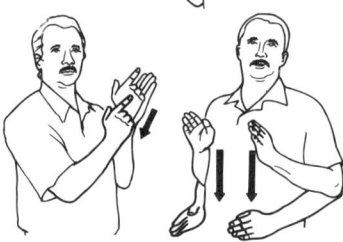

- **lawyer** Place the palm side of the right *L hand*, palm facing left, first on the fingers and then on the heel of the left *open hand*, palm facing right and fingers pointing up. Move both *open hands*, palms facing each other, downward along the sides of the body.

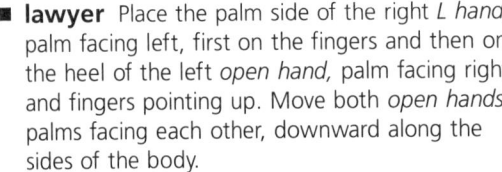

- **come-together** Beginning with both *curved 5 hands* in front of each side of the body, palms facing each other, bring the fingers together in front of the body.

- **discuss-discuss** Tap the side of the extended right index finger, palm facing in, on the upturned left *open hand* with a repeated movement while moving the hands to and from the body with a double movement.

- **secret** Tap the thumb side of the right *A hand*, palm left, against the mouth with a repeated movement.

simple

sign or **subscribe** To affix one's name or mark on a document to authenticate it.

- **sign** Place the extended fingers of the right *H hand*, palm down, firmly down on the upturned palm of the left *open hand* held in front of the chest.

subscribe See sign for SIGN.

signature[1] The name or mark of a person or entity placed on a document to authenticate it. Related form: **sign**.

- **signature** Place the extended fingers of the right *H hand*, palm down, down on the upturned palm of the left *open hand* held in front of the chest with a double movement.

signature[2] See sign for HAND.

silent partner A partner whose involvement in the partnership is not generally known.

- **merge** Beginning with both *5 hands* in front of each side of the chest, palms facing in, with a double movement bring the hands together, ending with the bent fingers of both hands meshed together in front of the chest each time.

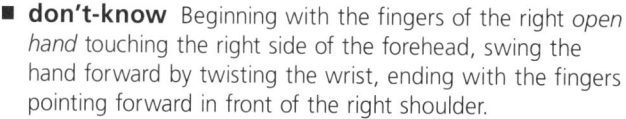

- **person marker** Move both *open hands*, palms facing each other, downward along the sides of the body.

- **don't-know** Beginning with the fingers of the right *open hand* touching the right side of the forehead, swing the hand forward by twisting the wrist, ending with the fingers pointing forward in front of the right shoulder.

simple Describing the basic form of something; lacking complicated features.

- **easy** Brush the fingertips of the right *curved hand* upward on the back of the fingertips of the left *curved hand* with a double movement, both palms up.

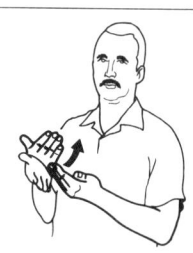

sit

sit To hold a formal session for the conduct of business: The supreme court sits from October to June.

- **court** Move both *F hands,* palms facing each other, up and down in front of each side of the chest with a repeated alternating movement.

- **go-ahead** Beginning with both *open hands* in front of the body, palms facing in and fingers pointing toward each other, simultaneously move the hands forward a short distance.

slander Defamation which is communicated orally.

- **say**[1] Tap the extended right index finger, palm facing in, on the chin with a double movement.

- **gossip** Move both *G hands,* palms facing each other, in a flat circular movement in front of the chest while pinching the index finger and thumb of each hand together with a repeated movement.

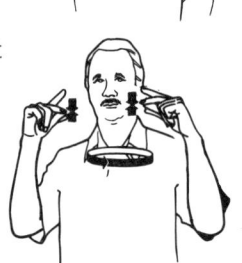

- **cruel** Beginning with the right *curved 5 hand* near the face and the left *curved 5 hand* in front of the body, close the right hand into an *A hand* while moving it quickly down and close the left hand into an *A hand* while moving it quickly up, brushing the knuckles of the hands together as they pass each other.

- **name** Tap the middle-finger side of the right *H hand* across the index-finger side of the left *H hand* with a double movement.

sodomy

slavery See sign for SERVITUDE.

small claims court A state court established to handle certain civil cases involving very small sums of money, using informal procedures without lawyers.

- Fingerspell: C-I-V-I-L
- **court** Move both *F hands,* palms facing each other, up and down in front of each side of the chest with a repeated alternating movement.
- **file** Move the fingers of the right *V hand,* palm facing forward, downward on each side of the extended left index finger, which is pointing up in front of the chest.

so ordered A formal expression often used by judges to make it clear that a pronouncement is an official order of the court.

- **court** Move both *F hands,* palms facing each other, up and down in front of each side of the chest with a repeated alternating movement.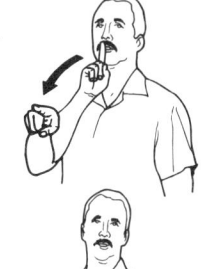
- **order** Move the extended right index finger, palm forward and finger pointing up, from in front of the mouth forward and down, ending with the finger pointing forward and the palm down.
- **finish** With both *5 hands* apart in front of the body, palms up, quickly turn the hands over toward each other.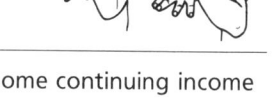

social security A federal program designed to provide some continuing income to most workers after they retire.

- Fingerspell acronym: S-S-I

sodomy[1] A term referring to any type of sex act disapproved by the legislature.

- **sodomy** Insert the little finger of the right *I hand,* palm back, into the index-finger side opening of the left *S hand* held in front of the chest, palm down.

367

sodomy

sodomy[2] (alternate sign)
- Fingerspell: S-O-D-O-M-Y

sole custody Custody of a child by one adult only, as often determined by the court after a divorce.
- **child** Move the right *open hand* downward in front of the right side of the body, palm facing down.

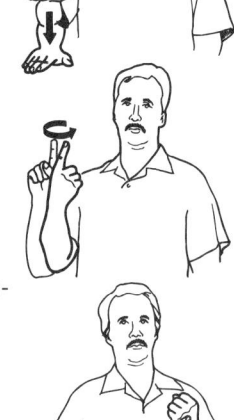

- **only** Beginning with the extended right index finger pointing up in front of the right shoulder, palm facing forward, twist the wrist in, ending with the palm facing in near the right side of the chest.

- **save** Tap the fingers of the right *V hand* with a double movement on the back of the left *V hand*, palms in.

sole proprietorship Ownership of an unincorporated business by one individual.
- Fingerspell: O-W-N
- **only** Beginning with the extended right index finger pointing up in front of the right shoulder, palm facing forward, twist the wrist in, ending with the palm facing in near the right side of the chest.

solicitation The crime of asking, advising, encouraging, or ordering another person to commit a crime.
- **urge** With both *modified X hands* in front of each side of the chest, palms facing in opposite directions and right hand closer to the chest than the left hand, move the hands forward with a short double movement.

- **solicit** Move the bent index and middle fingers of the right *bent V hand*, palm down, forward on each side of the extended left index finger held up in front of one side of the body. Repeat in front of the other side of the body.

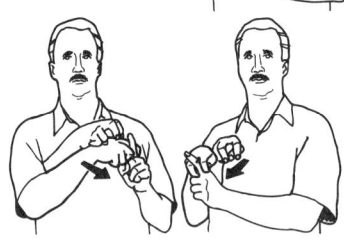

---- [sign continues] ----

special counsel

- **include** Swing the right 5 hand, palm down, in a circular movement over the left S hand, palm in, while changing into a *flattened O hand*, ending with the fingertips of the right hand inserted in the center of the thumb side of the left hand.

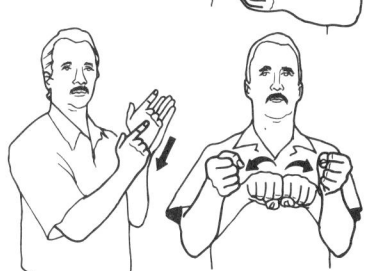

- **crime** Place the palm side of the right *L hand*, palm facing left, first on the fingers and then on the heel of the left *open hand*, palm facing right and fingers pointing up. Then beginning with both *S hands* in front of the body, index fingers touching and palms down, move the hands away from each other while twisting the wrists with a deliberate movement, ending with the palms facing each other.

sound or sound of body and mind Healthy, fit, normal.

- **mind** Tap the extended right index finger, palm facing in, against the right side of the forehead with a double movement.

- **body** Touch the fingers of both *open hands*, palms facing in and fingers pointing toward each other, first on each side of the chest and then on each side of the waist.

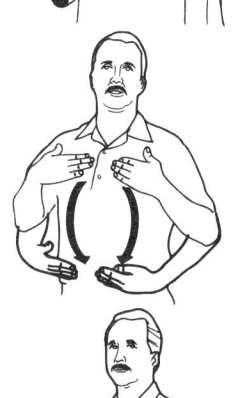

- **okay** Push the thumbs of both *10 hands*, palms facing each other, forward a short distance with a deliberate movement.

special circumstances See sign for MITIGATING CIRCUMSTANCES.

special counsel Counsel hired or appointed to assist in a matter because of special expertise.

- **special** Grasp the left extended index finger, palm in and finger pointing up, with the fingers of the right *G hand* and pull upward in front of the chest.

[sign continues]

369

special counsel

- **lawyer** Place the palm side of the right *L hand*, palm facing left, first on the fingers and then on the heel of the left *open hand*, palm facing right and fingers pointing up. Move both *open hands*, palms facing each other, downward along the sides of the body.

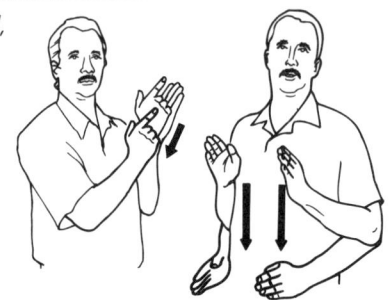

speech Within the meaning of the First Amendment, any form of expression, including words, pictures, or other visual devices, and expressive conduct.

- **confess-confess** Beginning with the fingers of both *5 hands* on the chest, move the hands forward in an arc. Repeat sign.

- **myself** Bring the thumb side of the right *A hand*, palm left, against the chest with a double movement.

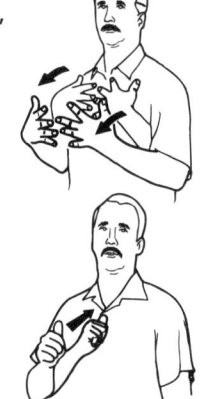

speedy trial A criminal trial commencing without unreasonable delay after arrest or indictment.

- **fast** Beginning with the extended index fingers of both *one hands* pointing forward in front of the chest, pull the hands back toward the chest while changing to *S hands*.

- **court** Move both *F hands*, palms facing each other, up and down in front of each side of the chest with a repeated alternating movement.

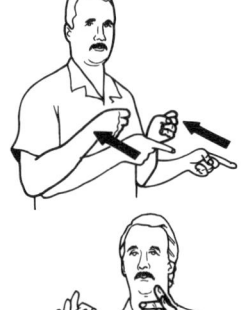

spousal abuse Physical or psychological abuse of one spouse by the other.

- **husband** Move the right *C hand* from the right side of the forehead, palm facing left, down to clasp the left *curved hand* held in front of the chest, palm facing up.

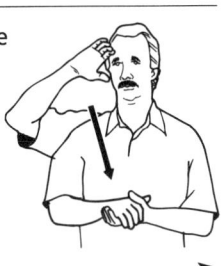

---- [sign continues] -->

spousal privilege

- **wife** Move the right *C hand* from near the right side of the chin, palm left, down to clasp the left *curved hand* held in front of the chest, palm up.

- **wrong** Bring the middle fingers of the right *Y hand*, palm in, back against the chin with a deliberate movement.

- **use** With the heel of the right *U hand* on the back of the left *S hand*, move the right hand in a repeated small circle.

spousal privilege The privilege to prevent disclosure of confidential communication to one's spouse.

- **husband** Move the right *C hand* from the right side of the forehead, palm facing left, down to clasp the left *curved hand* held in front of the chest, palm facing up.

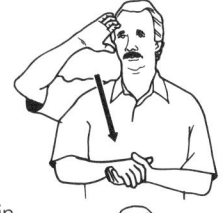

- **wife** Move the right *C hand* from near the right side of the chin, palm left, down to clasp the left *curved hand* held in front of the chest, palm up.

- **say**¹ Tap the extended right index finger, palm facing in, on the chin with a double movement.

- **not** Bring the thumb of the right *10 hand* forward from under the chin with a deliberate movement.

---- [sign continues] ---->

371

spousal privilege

- **must** Move the bent index finger of the right *X hand* downward with a deliberate movement in front of the right side of the body by bending the wrist down.

spousal support see sign for ALIMONY.

stalking The crime of following a person about in such a way as to instill fear of bodily harm. Related form: **stalk.**

- **stalk** With the palm side of the right *one hand* on the index-finger side of the left *one hand*, both palms facing forward, move both hands forward in a random movement.

stand See sign for WITNESS STAND.

standard of proof[1] The degree to which the court must be persuaded of a fact to find in favor of a party in a trial.

- **standard** Beginning with both *Y hands* in front of the body, palms facing down, move the hands in a large flat circle.

- **law** Place the palm side of the right *L hand*, palm facing left, first on the fingers and then on the heel of the left *open hand*, palm facing right and fingers pointing up.

standard of proof[2] See sign for BEYOND A REASONABLE DOUBT.

state of mind The condition of mind that accompanies an act, used to determine blameworthiness.

- **mind** Tap the extended right index finger, palm facing in, against the right side of the forehead with a double movement.

---- [sign continues] ---->

state's evidence

- **how** Beginning with the knuckles of both *curved hands* touching in front of the chest, palms facing down, twist the hands upward and forward, ending with the fingers together pointing up and the palms facing up.

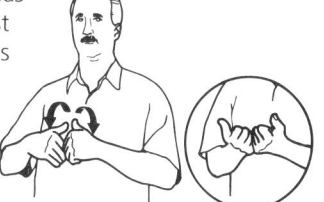

- **connect** Beginning with both *curved 5 hands* in front of each side of the body, palms facing each other, bring the hands together while touching the thumb and index fingertips of each hand and intersecting with each other.

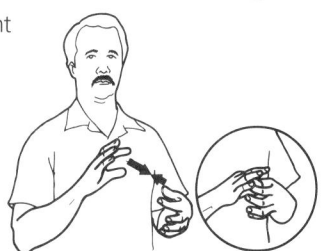

- **do** Move both *C hands*, palms facing down, simultaneously back and forth in front of the body with a swinging movement.

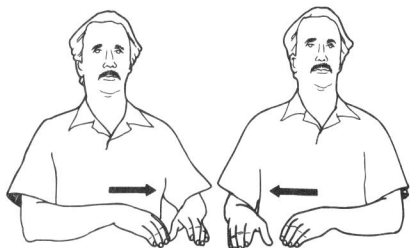

state's evidence or turn state's evidence
Evidence voluntarily given by an accomplice in a crime against others involved, usually in exchange for immunity or leniency.

- **crime** Place the palm side of the right *L hand*, palm facing left, first on the fingers and then on the heel of the left *open hand*, palm facing right and fingers pointing up. Then beginning with both *S hands* in front of the body, index fingers touching and palms down, move the hands away from each other while twisting the wrists with a deliberate movement, ending with the palms facing each other.

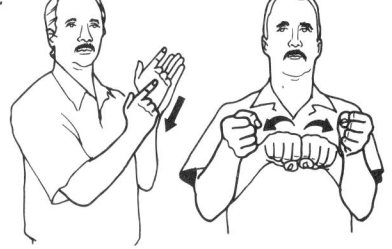

- **together** With the palm sides of both *A hands* together, move the hands forward with a short double movement.

- **solicit** Move the bent index and middle fingers of the right *bent V hand*, palm down, forward on each side of the extended left index finger held up in front of one side of the body. Repeat in front of the other side of the body.

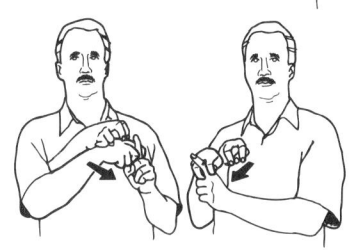

[sign continues]

state's evidence

- **promise** Bring the extended right index finger, palm facing left and finger pointing up, from in front of the lips downward, changing into an *open hand* and placing the palm of the right hand on the index-finger side of the left *S hand* held in front of the body, palm facing right.

- **again** Beginning with the right *bent hand* beside the left *curved hand*, both palms up, bring the right hand up while turning it over, ending with the fingertips of the right hand touching the palm of the left hand.

- **accuse** Push the little-finger side of the right *A hand*, palm facing left, forward across the back of the left *open hand*, palm facing down.

statement See sign for DECLARATION.

status quo *Latin*. The way things are at the time of speaking.
- **same-same** Beginning with both *Y hands* in front of the body, palms facing down, move the hands in large circles going in opposite directions away from each other.

statute See sign for LAW.

statute of limitations, limitation period, or **statutory period** A statute setting the length of time after an event within which a civil or criminal action must be brought.
- **time** Tap the bent index finger of the right *X hand*, palm down, with a double movement on the wrist of the downturned left hand.

---- [sign continues]

stay

- **limit** Beginning with both *bent hands* in front of the chest, right hand above the left hand and both palms facing down, move both hands forward simultaneously.

statutory period See sign for STATUTE OF LIMITATIONS.

statutory rape The crime of having sexual intercourse with a person below the age of consent.

- Fingerspell: S-E-X
- **have** Bring the fingertips of both *bent hands*, palms facing in, in to touch each side of the chest.

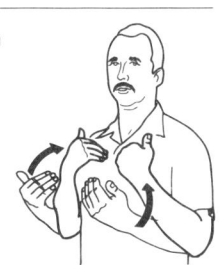

- **other** Beginning with the right *10 hand* in front of the chest, palm down, flip the hand over, ending with palm up.

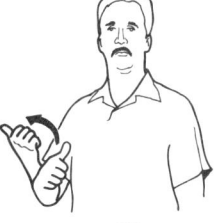

- **below** Beginning with the left *open hand* on the back of the right *open hand,* both palms facing down, bring the right hand downward in an arc, ending several inches below the left hand.

- **age** Beginning with the right *C hand* near the chin, palm left, pull the hand downward while changing into a *S hand*.

stay or **stay of execution** The postponement of a proceeding, such as an execution.

- **kill** Push the side of the extended right index finger, palm down, across the palm of the left *open hand*, palm right, with a deliberate movement.

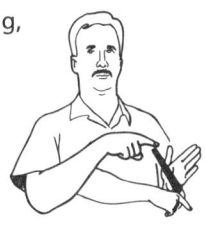

[sign continues]

stay

- **time** Tap the bent index finger of the right *X hand*, palm down, with a double movement on the wrist of the downturned left hand.

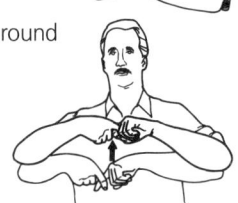

- **suspend** With the index fingers of both *X hands* hooked around each other, move both hands upward in front of the chest.

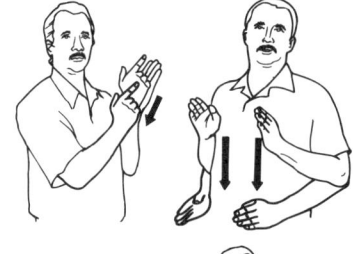

stay of execution See sign for STAY.

steal To obtain money or property by larceny or criminal means, such as robbery, embezzlement, or false pretenses. See sign for LARCENY.

stipulation[1] An agreement between opposing lawyers with respect to some procedural step in a case.

- **lawyer** Place the palm side of the right *L hand*, palm facing left, first on the fingers and then on the heel of the left *open hand*, palm facing right and fingers pointing up. Move both *open hands*, palms facing each other, downward along the sides of the body.
- **two-of-them** Swing the right *2 hand*, palm up, from side to side in front of the body.

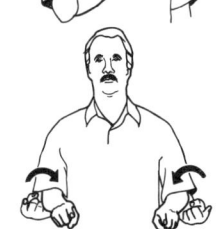

- **agree** Beginning with both extended index fingers pointing forward in front of each side of the body, both palms facing up, flip the hands toward each other, turning the palms down.

stipulation[2] See sign for CONCUR.

stock A security issued by a corporation, representing an ownership interest.

- **invest**[2] Move the curved middle fingers, index fingers, and thumbs of both hands from in front of each side of the chest, palms forward, upward and forward in alternating arcs.

strike

stock option A right to purchase or sell a specified number of shares of a particular stock at a specified price some time in the future.

- **invest**[2] Move the curved middle fingers, index fingers, and thumbs of both hands from in front of each side of the chest, palms forward, upward and forward in alternating arcs.

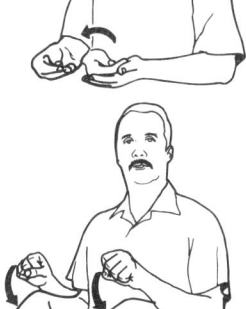

- **buy** Beginning with the back of the right *flattened O hand*, palm facing up, in the upturned palm of left *open hand*, move the right hand forward in an arc.

- **can** Move both *S hands*, palms facing down, downward simultaneously in front of each side of the body.

stop Momentary detention of a person by law enforcement officials, such as at a checkpoint for drunk drivers, etc.

- Fingerspell: C-A-R-S
- **pull-aside** Beginning with both *3 hands* near each other in front of the body, palms facing each other and right hand closer to the body than the left, move the right hand forward to the left, ending with the right hand near the heel of the left hand.

stop and frisk See signs for FRISK[2,3].

straight life insurance See sign for WHOLE LIFE INSURANCE.

strict construction See sign for NARROW CONSTRUCTION.

strike A concerted stopping of work by employees of a company in support of a demand for higher wages, better working conditions, or protest of some action of the employer.

- **work** Tap the heel of the right *S hand*, palm forward, with a double movement on the back of the left *S hand* held in front of the body, palm down.

---- [sign continues] ---->

377

strike

- **group** Beginning with both *claw hands* in front of the chest, palms facing each other, bring the hands away from each other in outward arcs while turning the palms in, ending with the little fingers near each other.

- **protest** Beginning with the right *S hand* in front of the right shoulder, palm facing back, twist the hand sharply forward.

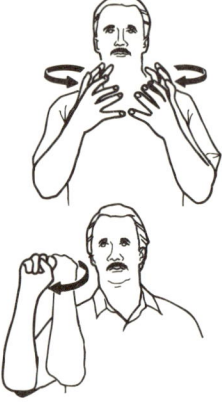

submit To place a matter formally into the hands of the proper body for decision. See sign for MOTION.

subpoena A process directing a witness to appear and give evidence in a court proceeding. See sign for SUMMONS.

subrogate[1] To substitute a new person for the original claimant with regard to a right or claim.
- **substitute** Beginning with both *F hands* in front of the body, one hand somewhat forward of the other hand, move the right hand back toward the body in an upward arc while moving the left hand forward with a downward arc to exchange places.

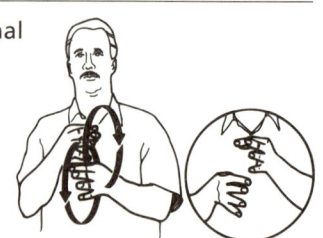

subrogate[2] (alternate sign)
- **exchange** Beginning with both *modified X hands* in front of the body, right hand somewhat forward of the left hand, move the right hand back toward the body in an upward arc while moving the left hand forward with a downward arc.

- **file** Move the fingers of the right *V hand*, palm facing forward, downward on each side of the extended left index finger, which is pointing up in front of the chest.

- **person marker** Move both *open hands*, palms facing each other, downward along the sides of the body.

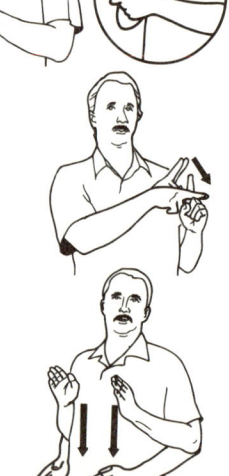

378

succeed

subsidiary A corporation more than 50% of whose voting stock is owned by the corporation.

- Fingerspell abbreviation for *company*: C-O

- **business** Brush the base of the right *B hand*, palm forward, with a repeated rocking movement on the back of the left *open hand*, palm down.

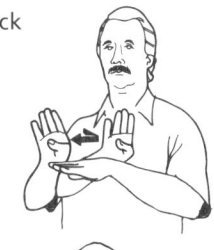

- **under** Move the right *A hand* from in front of the chest downward and forward under the left *open hand* held in front of the chest, palm down and fingers pointing right.

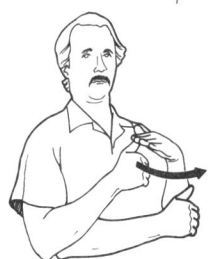

substance The real or underlying nature of a transaction, claim, law, or other matter, as distinguished from its form.

- **base** Move the right *B hand*, palm facing forward, in a flat circle under the left *open hand*, palm facing down.

- **things** Beginning with both *open hands* in front of the body, palms facing up, move the hands to the sides away from each other in a double arc.

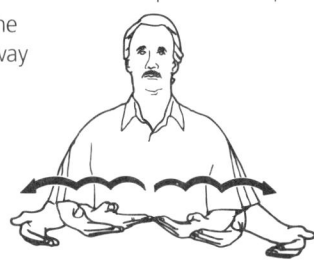

succeed To take over a right, interest, or duty of another.

- **manage** Beginning with both *modified X hands* in front of each side of the body, right hand forward of the left hand and palms facing each other, move the hands forward and back with a repeated movement.

- **turn** Beginning with the right *L hand* in front of the right side of the chest, palm facing down and index finger pointing forward, move the hand to the right, ending with the palm facing up.

379

sue

sue See sign for PROSECUTE.

suicide Killing oneself.
- **kill** Push the side of the extended right index finger, palm down, across the palm of the left *open hand*, palm right, with a deliberate movement.

- **myself** Bring the thumb side of the right *A hand*, palm left, against the chest with a double movement.

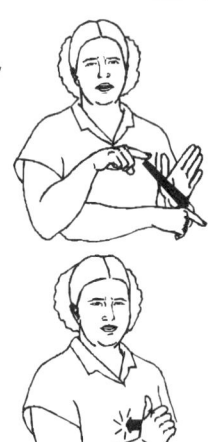

suit A civil action brought by one person against another. See sign for PROSECUTE.

summary Describing proceedings conducted in a simplified manner because the circumstances do not require more elaborate treatment.
- **summary** Beginning with both *5 hands* in front of the chest, right hand above the left hand and fingers pointing in opposite directions, bring the hands toward each other while squeezing the fingers together, ending with the little-finger side of the right *S hand* on top of the thumb side of the left *S hand*.

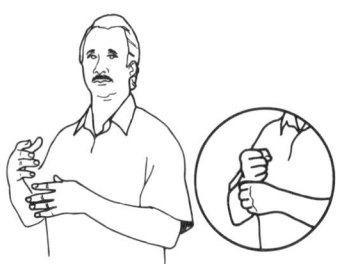

summation See signs for CLOSING[1,2].

summons A process directing a defendant to appear in court to answer a civil or criminal complaint. Same sign used for **subpoena**.
- **paper** Brush the heel of the right *open hand* with a double movement on the heel of the left *open hand*, palms facing each other.

- **order** Move the extended right index finger, palm forward and finger pointing up, from in front of the mouth forward and down, ending with the finger pointing forward and the palm down.

---- [sign continues] -->

sunset law

- **go-to** Move both extended right index fingers from pointing up in front of the body, palms facing forward, then move the hands deliberately forward while bending the wrists so the fingers point forward.

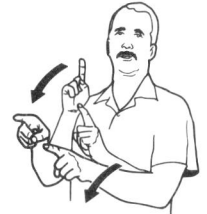

- **court** Move both *F hands,* palms facing each other, up and down in front of each side of the chest with a repeated alternating movement.

Sunday closing law See signs for BLUE LAW[1,2].

sunset law A statute that expires automatically after a certain amount of time.

- **law** Place the palm side of the right *L hand,* palm facing left, first on the fingers and then on the heel of the left *open hand,* palm facing right and fingers pointing up.

- **set-up** Beginning with the right *10 hand* in front of the right shoulder, palm down, twist the wrist up with a circular movement and then move the right hand straight down to land on the little-finger side on the back of the left *open hand*, palm down.

- **time** Tap the bent index finger of the right *X hand*, palm down, with a double movement on the wrist of the downturned left hand.

- **limit** Beginning with both *bent hands* in front of the chest, right hand above the left hand and both palms facing down, move both hands forward simultaneously.

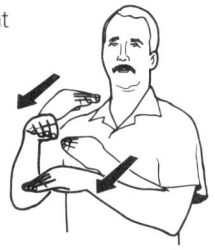

sunshine law

sunshine law A statute requiring that official meetings of governmental agencies be open to the public.

- **government** Beginning with the extended right index finger pointing upward near the right side of the head, palm facing forward, twist the wrist to touch the finger to the right temple.

- **business** Brush the base of the right *B hand*, palm forward, with a repeated rocking movement on the back of the left *open hand*, palm down.

- **open** Beginning with the index-finger side of both *B hands* touching in front of the chest, palms facing forward and fingers angled up, twist both wrists while bringing the hands apart to in front of each side of the chest, ending with the palms facing in.

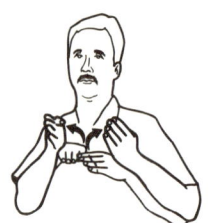

- **must** Move the bent index finger of the right *X hand* downward with a deliberate movement in front of the right side of the body by bending the wrist down.

superior court The name given in some states to the lowest court of general jurisdiction.

- **court** Move both *F hands*, palms facing each other, up and down in front of each side of the chest with a repeated alternating movement.

- **general** Beginning with both *open hands* in front of the chest, fingers angled toward each other, swing the fingers away from each other, ending with the fingers angled outward in front of each side of the body.

---- [sign continues] -->

surrogate mother

- **manage** Beginning with both *modified X hands* in front of each side of the body, right hand forward of the left hand and palms facing each other, move the hands forward and back with a repeated movement.

suppress To prohibit the prosecution from introducing evidence obtained in violation of the constitution, such as evidence derived from an unlawful search and seizure.

- **proof** Move the right *open hand* downward, ending with the back of the right hand on the palm of the left *open hand*, both palms facing up in front of the chest.

- **refuse** Beginning with the right *10 hand* in front of the right shoulder, elbow extended and palm facing down, push the thumb back over the right shoulder.

- **allow** Beginning with both *open hands* in front of the waist, palms facing each other and fingers pointing down, bring the fingers forward and upward by bending the wrists.

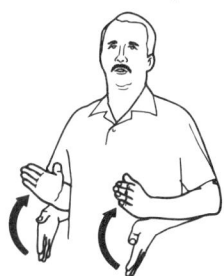

supra See sign for ABOVE.

supreme court The highest court of the federal judicial system, with final say in interpretation of federal law. See sign for APPELLATE COURT.

surety See sign for ACCOMMODATION.

surrogate mother A woman who bears a child for a couple when the wife is unable to do so, having agreed to give up parental rights when the baby is born.

- **woman** Beginning with the thumb of the right *open hand* touching the right side of the chin, palm left, bring the hand downward to touch the thumb on the chest.

---- [sign continues] ---------→

surrogate mother

- **pregnant** Beginning with both *5 hands* entwined in front of the abdomen, bring the hands forward.

- **inside** Move the fingers of the right *flattened O hand* downward with a short double movement in the palm side of the left *C hand* held in front of the chest.

- **for** Beginning with the extended right finger touching the right side of the forehead, twist the hand forward, ending with the index finger pointing forward.

- **other** Beginning with the right *10 hand* in front of the chest, palm down, flip the hand over, ending with palm up.

surveillance Covert monitoring of a person's movements and activities, especially by law enforcement authorities.

- **police**[1] Tap the thumb side of the right *modified C hand*, palm facing left, against the left side of the chest with a double movement.

- **watch** Beginning with both *V hands* in front of the left side of the body, both palms down and fingers pointing forward, swing the hands in large simultaneous arcs to the right.

suspect

survivorship or **right of survivorship** The characteristic of joint ownership of property whereby, upon the death of the co-owner, that owner's interest passes automatically to the surviving owners.

- **two-of-them** Swing the right *2 hand*, palm up, from side to side in front of the body.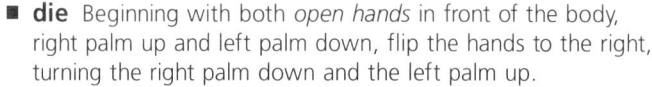
- Fingerspell: O-W-N
- **one** Hold up the right *one hand*, palm facing back, in front of the chest.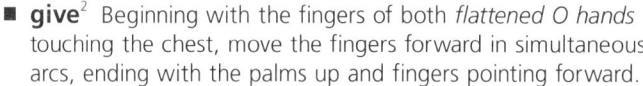

- **die** Beginning with both *open hands* in front of the body, right palm up and left palm down, flip the hands to the right, turning the right palm down and the left palm up.

- **give**² Beginning with the fingers of both *flattened O hands* touching the chest, move the fingers forward in simultaneous arcs, ending with the palms up and fingers pointing forward.

- **other** Beginning with the right *10 hand* in front of the chest, palm down, flip the hand over, ending with palm up.

suspect A person who is under suspicion of having committed a crime or other offense.

- **suspect** Beginning with the extended right index finger touching the right side of the forehead, palm facing down, bring the hand forward a short distance with a double movement, bending the index finger into an *X hand* each time.
- **person marker** Move both *open hands*, palms facing each other, downward along the sides of the body.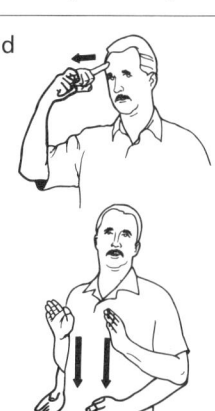

385

sustain

sustain¹ To rule favorably upon an objection: Sustain a motion.
- **judge** Move the right *modified X hand*, palm left, with a double up and down movement.

- **accept** Beginning with both *5 hands* in front of the body, fingers pointing forward and palms down, pull both hands back to the chest while changing to *flattened O hands*.

sustain² (alternate sign)
- **judge** Move the right *modified X hand*, palm left, with a double up and down movement.

- **support** Push the knuckles of the right *S hand* upward under the little-finger side of the left *S hand*, both palms in, pushing the left hand upward a short distance in front of the chest.

swear¹ To take an oath or to state under oath.
- **swear** Beginning with the fingers of the right *5 hand* pointing toward the chin, palm angled in, bring the hand downward with a deliberate movement while closing into an *S hand*.

swear² See sign for AFFIRM.

swear or affirm See sign for AFFIRM.

take the stand To go to the stand to testify. See sign for TESTIFY.

tangible property Physical property; property you can touch.
- **land** Beginning with both *flattened O hands* in front of each side of the body, palms facing up, move the thumb of both hands smoothly with a double movement across each fingertip, starting with the little fingers and ending as *A hands* each time.

- **touch** Bring the bent middle finger of the right hand, palm down, downward to touch the back of the left *open hand* held in front of the body, palm down.

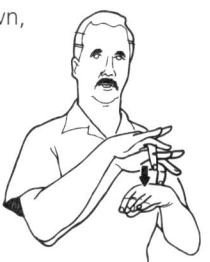

- **can** Move both *S hands,* palms facing down, downward simultaneously in front of each side of the body.

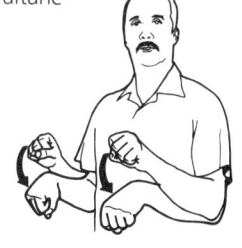

tax[1] A sum of money required to be paid to the federal, state, or local government for the support of government activities and services to the public at large.
- **tax** Strike the knuckle of the right *X hand,* palm facing in, down the palm of the left *open hand,* palm facing right and fingers pointing forward.

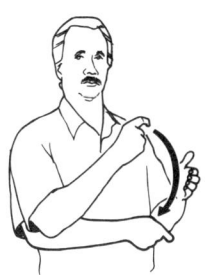

tax[2] (alternate sign)
- Fingerspell: T-A-X

387

tax bracket

taxable income Any kind of income subject to income tax.
- **income** Bring the little-finger side of the right *curved hand*, palm facing left, across the upturned left *open hand* from fingertips to heel while changing into an *S hand*. Repeat sign several times as the hands move in an arc in front of the body.
- Fingerspell: T-A-X
- **able** Move both *S hands*, palms facing down, downward simultaneously with a double movement in front of each side of the body.

tax bracket An income range to which a specific tax rate is applied for income tax purposes.
- Fingerspell: T-A-X
- **group** Beginning with both *C hands* in front of the chest, palms facing each other, take the hands away from each other in outward arcs while turning the palms in, ending with the little fingers near each other. Repeat sign two more times while moving the hands downward.

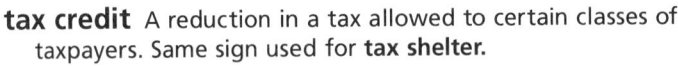

tax credit A reduction in a tax allowed to certain classes of taxpayers. Same sign used for **tax shelter**.
- Fingerspell: T-A-X
- **profit** Move the right *F hand*, palm facing down, downward with a double movement near the right side of the chest.

tax evasion The crime of contriving in any way not to pay the amount that one is legally obligated to pay in taxes.
- Fingerspell: T-A-X
- **avoid** Beginning with the knuckles of the right *A hand*, left, the base heel of the left *A hand*, palm right, bring the right hand back toward the body with a wavy movement.

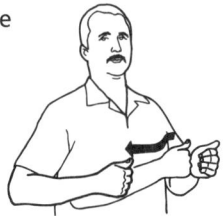

tax exempt or **tax free** Not required to pay taxes.
- Fingerspell: T-A-X
- **excuse** Wipe the fingertips of the right *open hand* across the upturned left *open hand* from the heel off the fingertips.

tenant

tax fraud The crime of intentionally filing a false tax return or making other false statements to taxing authorities.

- Fingerspell: T-A-X

- **lie** Move the index-finger side of the right *bent hand*, palm down and fingers pointing left, across the chin from right to left.

- **cover-up** With the heel of the right *S hand* on the palm of the left *5 hand*, twist the right hand to the left.

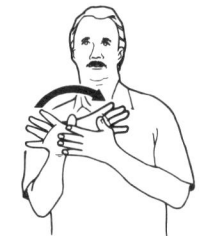

tax free See sign for TAX EXEMPT.

tax rate The percentage of taxable income or the value of taxable property that must be paid as tax.

- Fingerspell: T-A-X

- **how-much** Beginning with both *S hands* in front of the each side of the chest, palms facing up, flick the fingers open quickly into *5 hands*.

tax return or **return** The document in which a taxpayer reports to the government on matters having tax consequences.

- Fingerspell: T-A-X

- **file** Move the fingers of the right *V hand*, palm facing forward, downward on each side of the extended left index finger, which is pointing up in front of the chest.

tax shelter An investment that serves to reduce taxes or to generate income, offsetting deductions, and credits so as to minimize tax on all the income. See sign for TAX CREDIT.

temporary restraining order (TRO) See sign for RESTRAINING ORDER.

tenancy See sign for LIFE ESTATE.

tenant A person with a present right to possession of real property, especially the holder of a lease.

- **person-person** Move both *P hands*, palms facing each other, downward along the sides of the body. Repeat by shifting the body to the side.

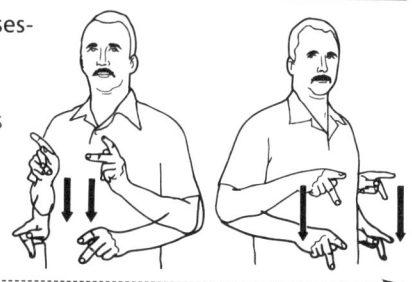

---- [sign continues] ---->

389

tenant

- **monthly** Move the extended right index finger, palm facing in and finger pointing left, downward with a double movement from the tip to the base of the extended left index finger, palm facing right and finger pointing up in front of the chest.

tender To offer something formally, in a way that makes it clear that the thing offered will be given, done, or effective immediately upon acceptance. See sign for MOTION.

term A specific, finite period of time during which an agreement is operative or an interest remains good, or at the end of which an obligation matures.

- **time** Tap the bent index finger of the right *X hand*, palm down, with a double movement on the wrist of the downturned left hand.

- **limit** Beginning with both *bent hands* in front of the chest, right hand above the left hand and both palms facing down, move both hands forward simultaneously.

term life insurance Life insurance which remains in effect only for a specified period of time, after which the policy usually may be renewed for another term, but at a higher premium.

- **live** Move both *10 hands*, thumbs pointing up, upward on each side of the chest.

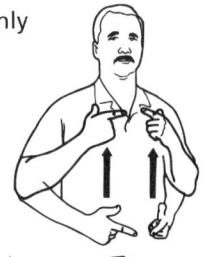

- **insurance** Move the right *I hand*, palm forward, from side to side with a repeated movement in front of the right shoulder.

- **limit** Beginning with both *bent hands* in front of the chest, right hand above the left hand and both palms facing down, move both hands forward simultaneously.

theft

terms and conditions[1] All the provisions of a contract.

- **sign** Place the extended fingers of the right *H hand*, palm down, firmly down on the upturned palm of the left *open hand* held in front of the chest.
- Fingerspell abbreviation: C-T

- **rule** Touch the fingertips of the right *R hand* first on the fingers and then on the heel of the left *open hand*, palms facing each other.

terms and conditions[2] (alternate sign)
- Fingerspell abbreviation: C-T

testament See sign for WILL.

testify To give evidence under oath at a trial, hearing, or deposition. Same sign used for **oath, take the stand**.

- **testify** While holding the left *open hand* in front of the left side of the body, palm down and fingers pointing forward, move the right extended index finger from in front of the mouth, palm left, forward while opening to an *open hand*.

testimony Statements made under oath by a witness at a trial, hearing, or deposition.

- **testify** While holding the left *open hand* in front of the left side of the body, palm down and fingers pointing forward, move the right extended index finger from in front of the mouth, palm left, forward while opening to an *open hand*.

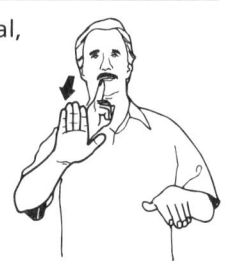

- **sentences** Beginning with the thumbs and index fingers of both *F hands* touching in front of the chest, palms facing each other, with a double movement pull the hands apart to in front of each side of the chest.

theft See sign for STEAL.

third party

third party A person who is not a party to a transaction, proceeding, or other matter under discussion, but who may be affected by it.

- **other** Beginning with the right *10 hand* in front of the chest, palm down, flip the hand over, ending with palm up.

- **person** Move both *P hands*, palms facing each other, downward along the sides of the body.

three strikes law A law specifying life imprisonment for anyone convicted of a particular type of crime for a third time.

- **crime** Place the palm side of the right *L hand*, palm facing left, first on the fingers and then on the heel of the left *open hand*, palm facing right and fingers pointing up. Then beginning with both *S hands* in front of the body, index fingers touching and palms down, move the hands away from each other while twisting the wrists with a deliberate movement, ending with the palms facing each other.

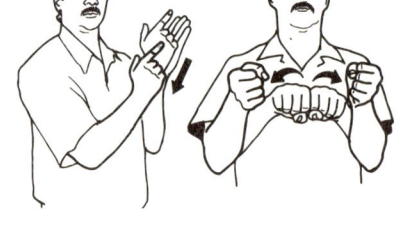

- **third** Flick the extended right index finger, palm left, upward on the back of the left *open hand* held in front of the body, palm right.

- **jail**[4] Shove the right *S hand*, palm left, forward under the left *open hand*, palm down, with a deliberate movement.

title insurance

ticket A piece of paper evidencing a contractual right to goods or services.

- **paper** Brush the heel of the right *open hand* with a double movement on the heel of the left *open hand*, palms facing each other.

- **allow** Beginning with both *open hands* in front of the waist, palms facing each other and fingers pointing down, bring the fingers forward and upward by bending the wrists.

time is of the essence or **of the essence** A phrase signifying that any failure to perform within the time specified in the contract will constitute a material breach.

- **time** Tap the bent index finger of the right *X hand*, palm down, with a double movement on the wrist of the downturned left hand.

- **limit** Beginning with both *bent hands* in front of the chest, right hand above the let hand and both palms facing down, move both hands forward simultaneously.

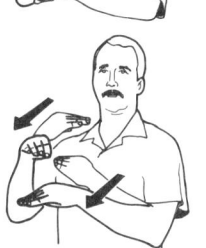

- **important** Beginning with the fingertips of both *F hands* touching, palms facing down, bring the hands upward in a circular movement, ending with the index-finger sides of the *F hands* touching in front of the chest.

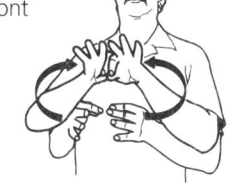

title See signs for DEED[1,2].

title insurance Insurance purchased by a buyer of real estate to protect himself, herself, or the bank holding the mortgage on the property from loss due to previous unrecognized claims to title.

- Fingerspell: T-I-T-L-E

- **insurance** Move the right *I hand*, palm forward, from side to side with a repeated movement in front of the right shoulder.

393

title search

title search The process of searching through public records by tracing the chain of title.

- **paper** Brush the heel of the right *open hand* with a double movement on the heel of the left *open hand*, palms facing each other.
- Fingerspell: O-W-N

- **before** Beginning with the back of the right *open hand*, palm in and fingers pointing left, touching the back of the left *open hand*, palm forward, move the right hand in toward the chest.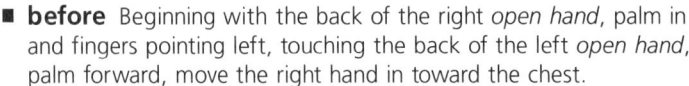

- **investigate** Move the extended right index finger from near the right eye down to move from the heel to the fingers of the upturned palm of the left *open hand*.

toll To suspend the statute of limitations under circumstances where the law recognizes that a plaintiff was prevented from commencing action through no fault of his or her own.

- **limit** Beginning with both *bent hands* in front of the chest, right hand above the left hand and both palms facing down, move both hands forward simultaneously.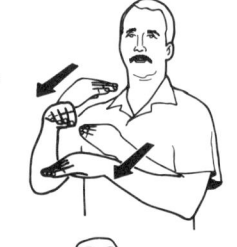

- **suspend** With the index fingers of both *X hands* hooked around each other, move both hands upward in front of the chest.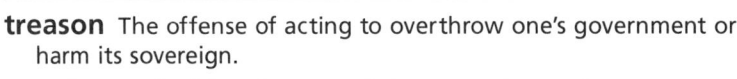

treason The offense of acting to overthrow one's government or harm its sovereign.

- Fingerspell: U-S or the name of the country in question.
- **person** Move both *P hands*, palms facing each other, downward along the sides of the body.

---- [sign continues] -->

trespassing

- **fight** Beginning with both *S hands* in front of each shoulder, palms facing each other, move the hands deliberately toward each other, ending with the wrists crossed in front of the chest.

- **against** Hit the fingertips of the right *bent hand* into the left *open hand*, palm right and fingers pointing forward.
- Fingerspell: U-S or the name of any other country in question.

treaty A formal agreement between two or more nations on matters of international concern.

- **country-country** Rub the palm of the right *open hand* in a circle near the elbow of the bent left arm with a repeated movement. Repeat sign in a different location.

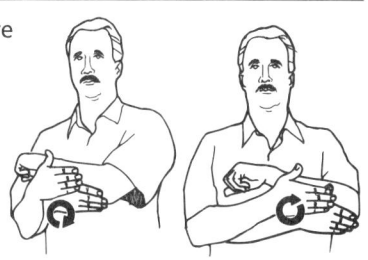

- **agree** Beginning with both extended index fingers pointing forward in front of each side of the body, both palms facing up, flip the hands toward each other, turning the palms down.

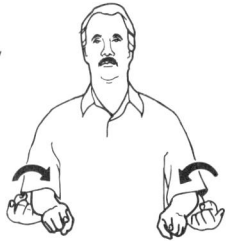

trespassing Intentional conduct that directly results in invasion of land possessed by another.

- **enter** Move the back of the right *open hand* forward in a downward arc under the palm of the left *open hand*, both palms down.

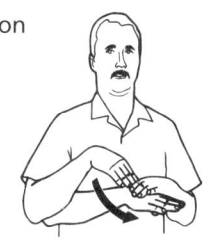

- **allow** Beginning with both *open hands* in front of the waist, palms facing each other and fingers pointing down, bring the fingers forward and upward by bending the wrists.

---- [sign continues] ----

trespassing

- **none** Move both *O hands*, palms forward, from in front of the chest outward to each side.

trial[1] The procedure by which evidence is presented in court under the supervision of a judge and the ultimate factual issues in a case are decided.

- **court** Move both *F hands*, palms facing each other, up and down in front of each side of the chest with a repeated alternating movement.

- **process** Beginning with both *open hands* in front of the body, palms facing in, left fingers pointing right and right fingers pointing left, and the left hand closer to the chest than the right hand, move the left hand over the right hand and then the right hand over the left hand in an alternating movement. See sign for COURT[1].

trial[2] See sign for COURT[1].

trial by jury or **jury trial** A trial in which the validity of the facts are determined by a jury.

- **court** Move both *F hands*, palms facing each other, up and down in front of each side of the chest with a repeated alternating movement.

- **with** Beginning with both *A hands* in front of the chest, palms facing each other, bring the hands together.

- **jury**[1] Beginning with the little-finger sides of both *bent 4 hands*, palms in, together in front of the chest, move the hands apart to each side.

trier of fact The persons charged with deciding the factual issues in a proceeding. See sign for FACTFINDER.

turn state's evidence

trust or **in trust** An arrangement in which one person holds property for the benefit of another and performs a fiduciary duty of safeguarding, managing, and disposing of the property and income. Same sign used for **abate**.

- **hold** Move the right *S hand*, palm facing up, in a circular movement in front of the right side of the chest.

trustee The person who holds the property in trust and administers it for the benefit of the beneficiaries.

- **hold** Move the right *S hand*, palm facing up, in a circular movement in front of the right side of the chest.

- **manage** Beginning with both *modified X hands* in front of each side of the body, right hand forward of the left hand and palms facing each other, move the hands forward and back with a repeated movement.

- **person marker** Move both *open hands*, palms facing each other, downward along the sides of the body.

try To conduct the trial of a case, either with or without a jury.

- **try** Beginning with both *T hands* in front of the chest, palms in, simultaneously twist the wrists forward, ending with the palms facing forward.

- **court** Move both *F hands*, palms facing each other, up and down in front of each side of the chest with a repeated alternating movement.
- Fingerspell: C-A-S-E

turn state's evidence See sign for STATE'S EVIDENCE.

397

unconstitutional In conflict with some provision of a constitution.
- Fingerspell: U-S or other country.
- **constitution** Place the little-finger side of the right *C hand*, palm facing left, first on the fingers and then the heel of the left *open hand*, palm facing right and fingers pointing up.

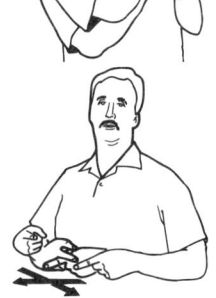

- **conflict** Beginning with both extended index fingers in front of each side of the body, palms facing in and fingers angled toward each other, move the hands toward each other, ending with the fingers crossed.

under arrest See signs for ARREST[1,2,3].

under protest An expression signifying that in complying with some demand, one is not conceding that the action is legally required and reserves the right to contest the issue in court.
- **complain** With a deliberate movement, hit the fingertips of the right *curved 5 hand* against the center of the chest.
- Fingerspell: W-I-L-L

underage See signs for MINOR[1,2,3].

undersigned A term used in the body of a document to designate the person whose signature appears at the end.
- **sign** Place the extended fingers of the right *H hand*, palm down, firmly down on the upturned palm of the left *open hand* held in front of the chest.
- **person** Move both *P hands*, palms facing each other, downward along the sides of the body.

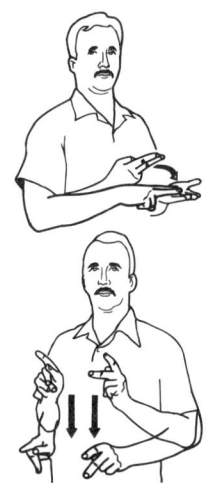

undue influence

understanding An informal agreement.
- **understand** Beginning with the right *modified X hand*, palm in, near the right side of the forehead, flick the index finger upward with a deliberate movement.

underwrite To provide insurance; to guarantee payment under an insurance policy.
- **insurance** Move the right *I hand*, palm forward, from side to side with a repeated movement in front of the right shoulder.

- **support** Push the knuckles of the right *S hand* upward under the little-finger side of the left *S hand*, both palms in, pushing the left hand upward a short distance in front of the chest.

- **will** Move the right *open hand*, palm left and fingers pointing up, from the right side of the chin forward while tipping the fingers down.

undocumented alien See sign for ILLEGAL ALIEN.

undue influence The use of a position of power to induce a person to enter into a transaction that does not reflect his or her true wishes. Same sign used for **duress**.
- **force** Beginning with the right *C hand* in front of the right shoulder, palm forward, and the left arm bent across the body, move the right hand downward and forward, ending with the right wrist across the left wrist, both palms down.

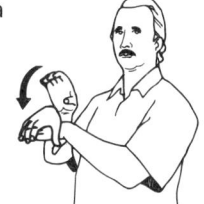

- **do** Move both *C hands*, palms facing down, simultaneously back and forth in front of the body with a swinging movement.

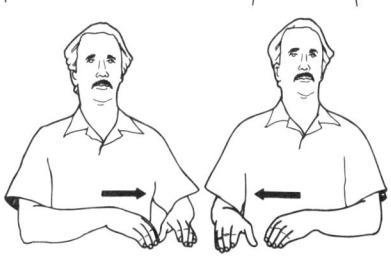

unearned income

unearned income Income derived from investments and other sources other than employment.

- **money** Tap the back of the right *flattened O hand*, palm facing up, with a double movement against the palm of the left *open hand*, palm facing up.

- **not** Bring the thumb of the right *10 hand* forward from under the chin with a deliberate movement.

- **earn** Bring the little-finger side of the right *curved hand*, palm facing left, across the upturned left *open hand* from fingertips to heel while changing into an *S hand*.

unemployment compensation Weekly payments made for a limited period of time to workers who lose their jobs through no fault of their own.

- Fingerspell: U-C
- **subscribe** With right *curved hand* in front of the right shoulder, palm facing back, bring the hand downward and inward toward the right side of the chest with a double movement, closing the fingers to form an *A hand* each time.

unethical Contrary to the generally accepted standards of honesty and fairness in the conduct of one's business.

- **not** Bring the thumb of the right *10 hand* forward from under the chin with a deliberate movement.

- **honest**[1] Slide the extended fingers of the right *H hand*, palm facing left, forward from the heel to the fingers of the upturned left *open hand*.

United States court of appeals

unfair competition The use of product names, packaging, or other devices similar to those of a competitor so as to confuse the public about whose product they are buying.

- **compete** With an alternating movement, move both *A hands* forward and back past each other quickly, palms facing each other in front of the body.

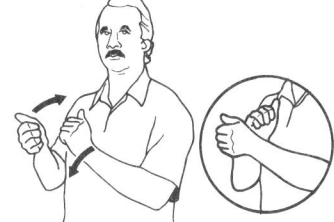

- **unfair** Bring the fingertips of the right *F hand*, palm left, downward, striking the fingertips of the left *F hand*, palm right, as it passes.

union[1] or **labor union** An organization of workers formed for the purpose of bargaining collectively with employers over wages and working conditions.
- Fingerspell: U-N-I-O-N

union[2] or **labor union** (alternate sign)

- **work** Tap the heel of the right *S hand*, palm forward, with a double movement on the back of the left *S hand* held in front of the body, palm down.
- Fingerspell: U-N-I-O-N

United States attorney See signs for ATTORNEY GENERAL[1,2].

United States court of appeals One of the intermediate appellate courts in the federal judicial system.
- Fingerspell: U-S
- **complain** Tap the fingertips of the right *curved 5 hand* against the center of the chest.

- **court** Move both *F hands*, palms facing each other, up and down in front of each side of the chest with a repeated alternating movement.

401

United States district court

United States District Dourt The federal court of original jurisdiction for civil and criminal matters.

- **government** Beginning with the extended right index finger pointing upward near the right side of the head, palm facing forward, twist the wrist to touch the finger to the right temple.

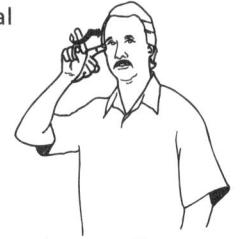

- **court** Move both *F hands,* palms facing each other, up and down in front of each side of the chest with a repeated alternating movement.

unlawful See signs for ILLEGAL[1,2].

unlawful assembly The offense of coming together as a group in public for the purpose of engaging in a riot or some other openly violent activity.

- **illegal** Hit the palm side of the right *L hand*, palm left, sharply on the palm of the left *open hand*, palm right, and off again.

- **meeting** Beginning with both open hands in front of the chest, palms facing forward and fingers pointing up, close the fingers with a double movement into *flattened O hands* while moving the hands together.

use tax A state tax on goods purchased outside the state from a vendor who does business in the state and intended for use within the state.

- **sell** Beginning with both *flattened O hands* held in front of each side of the chest, palms down and fingers pointing down, swing the fingertips forward and back by twisting the wrists upward with a double movement.

- Fingerspell: T-A-X

- **other** Beginning with the right *10 hand* in front of the chest, palm down, flip the hand over, ending with palm up.

---- [sign continues] -->

usury

- **use** With the heel of the right *U hand* on the back of the left *S hand*, move the right hand in a small circle.
- Fingerspell: T-A-X

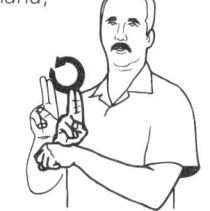

- **here**¹ Beginning with both *curved hands* in front of each side of the body, palms facing up, move the hands toward each other with short repeated movements.

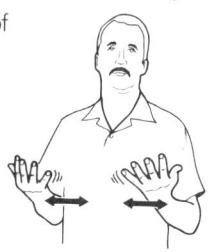

usury The crime of charging a higher rate of interest for a loan than is allowed by law.

- **take-advantage** With a double movement flick the bent middle finger of the right *5 hand* upward off the heel of the upturned left *open hand*.

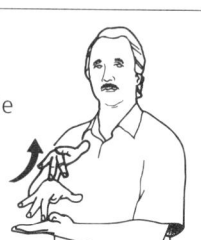

- **borrow** With the little-finger side of the right *V hand* across the index-finger side of the left *V hand*, bring the hands back, ending with the right index finger against the chest.

- **interest** Rub the little-finger side of the right *I hand*, palm facing the chest, in a repeated circle on the back of left *S hand*, palm facing down.

- **high** Move the right *H hand*, palm facing left and fingers pointing forward, from in front of the right side of the chest upward to near the right side of the head.

403

vacate See sign for SET ASIDE.

vague Uncertain in meaning or scope.
- **vague** With the palms of both *5 hands*, move the right hand in a circular movement on the left palm.

value-added tax A tax levied upon the increase in value of a product at each stage of production or distribution.
- **price** Tap the fingertips of both *F hands* together, palms facing each other, with a repeated movement.

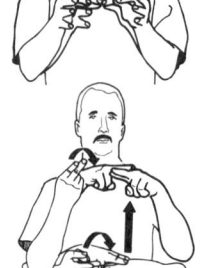

- **increase** Beginning with the right *H hand*, palm up, slightly lower than the left *H hand*, palm down, flip the right hand over, ending with the right fingers across the left fingers. Repeat as the hands move up.

- **cost** Strike the knuckle of the right *X hand*, palm facing in, down on the palm of the left *open hand*, palm facing right and fingers pointing forward.

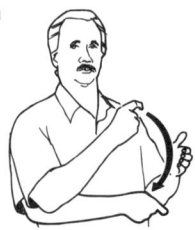

variance In zoning law, permission to use property in a particular way that is not generally allowed in that zone, granted to an individual property owner to prevent undue hardship.
- **allow** Beginning with both *open hands* in front of the waist, palms facing each other and fingers pointing down, bring the fingers forward and upward by bending the wrists.

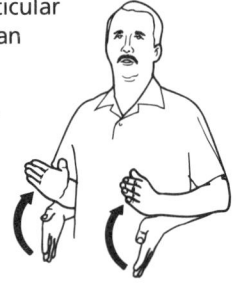

---- [sign continues] ----

verdict

- **use** With the heel of the right *U hand* on the back of the left *S hand*, move the right hand in a small circle.

venue The country or judicial district where a case is maintained.
- **place** Beginning with the middle fingers of both *P hands* touching in front of the body, palms facing each other, move the hands apart in a circular movement back until they touch again near the chest.

verbal act Words having legal effect, such as a verbal contract.
- **say**² Move the extended right index finger in a repeated upward circular movement in front of the chin, palm facing in and finger pointing left.

- **happen** Beginning with both extended index fingers in front of the body, palms facing up and fingers pointing forward, flip the hands over toward each other, ending with the palms facing down.

verdict The jury's decision in a case.
- **jury** Beginning with the little-finger sides of both *bent V hands* together in front of the chest, palms facing up, move the hands apart to each side.

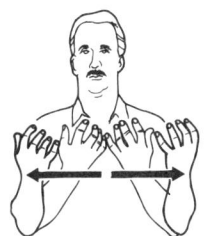

- **decide** Move the extended right index finger from the right side of the forehead, palm left, down in front of the chest while changing into an *F hand*, ending with both *F hands* moving downward in front of the body, palms facing each other.

405

verify

verify To swear or to affirm the authenticity of a document, or the truth of the statements it contains.

- **testify** While holding the left *open hand* in front of the left side of the body, palm down and fingers pointing forward, move the right extended index finger from in front of the mouth, palm left, forward while opening to an *open hand*.

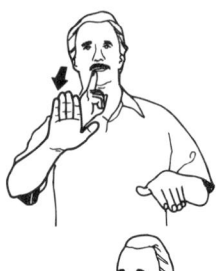

- **proof** Move the right *open hand* downward, ending with the back of the right hand on the palm of the left *open hand*, both palms facing up in front of the chest.

vested Describing an interest in property that confers a present right to possession, use, or enjoyment of the property. See sign for JOIN.

victim impact statement A report on the impact a crime had on its victims, given to the judge for consideration in sentencing.

- **person** Move both *P hands*, palms facing each other, downward along the sides of the body.

- **happen** Beginning with both extended index fingers in front of the body, palms facing up and fingers pointing forward, flip the hands over toward each other, ending with the palms facing down.

- **sentences** Beginning with the thumbs and index fingers of both *F hands* touching in front of the chest, palms facing each other, with a double movement pull the hands apart to in front of each side of the chest.

- **your** Push the palm of the right *open hand*, palm forward and fingers pointing up, toward the person being talked to with a double movement.

victims' rights

victimless crime Conduct not in itself harmful to a person or property, but nevertheless defined as criminal.

- **crime** Place the palm side of the right *L hand*, palm facing left, first on the fingers and then on the heel of the left *open hand*, palm facing right and fingers pointing up. Then beginning with both *S hands* in front of the body, index fingers touching and palms down, move the hands away from each other while twisting the wrists with a deliberate movement, ending with the palms facing each other.

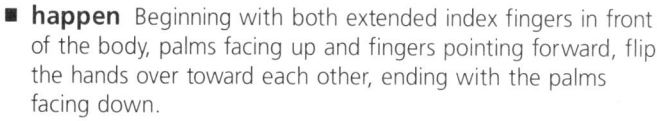

- **happen** Beginning with both extended index fingers in front of the body, palms facing up and fingers pointing forward, flip the hands over toward each other, ending with the palms facing down.

- **hurt** Beginning with the extended index fingers of both *one hands* pointing toward each other, right palm down and left palm up, twist the wrists in opposite directions, ending with the right palm up and the left palm down.

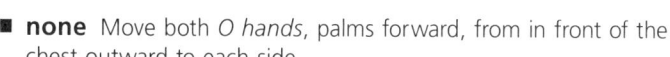

- **confess** Beginning with the palm sides of both *S hands* on the chest, move the hands forward in an arc while opening into *5 hands*.

- **none** Move both *O hands*, palms forward, from in front of the chest outward to each side.

victims' rights Rights of the victims of crime to be informed of various stages of prosecution and to present their views to the judge before sentencing and to the parole board at hearings.

- **person** Move both *P hands*, palms facing each other, downward along the sides of the body.

---- [sign continues] -->

victims' rights

- **happen** Beginning with both extended index fingers in front of the body, palms facing up and fingers pointing forward, flip the hands over toward each other, ending with the palms facing down.

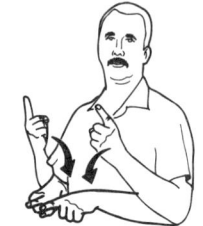

- **your** Push the palm of the right *open hand*, palm forward and fingers pointing up, toward the person being talked to with a double movement.

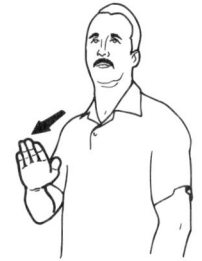

- **law** Place the palm side of the right *L hand*, palm facing left, first on the fingers and then on the heel of the left *open hand*, palm facing right and fingers pointing up.

- **allow** Beginning with both *open hands* in front of the waist, palms facing each other and fingers pointing down, bring the fingers forward and upward by bending the wrists.

violation A breach, infringement, or transgression of any rule, law, or duty.

- **illegal** Hit the palm side of the right *L hand*, palm left, sharply on the palm of the left *open hand*, palm right, and off again.

- **break** Beginning with both *S hands* in front of the body, index fingers touching and palms down, move the hands away from each other while twisting the wrists with a deliberate movement, ending with the palms facing each other. See signs for CRIME, INFRACTION.

voluntary manslaughter

visa Written authorization to enter a country, issued to an individual from another country.
- Fingerspell: V-I-S-A

visitation A visit by a child's noncustodial parent.
- **visit** With both *V hands* in front of the face, palms facing in and fingers pointing up, move the hands in alternating forward circles.

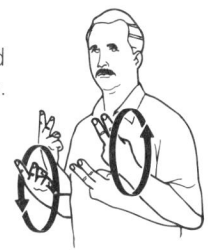

- **children** Beginning with the index-fingers of both *B hands* touching in front of the body, palms down and fingers pointing forward, move the hands outward to each side with a bouncing movement.

void Having no legal force or effect; not enforceable. See sign for NULL, SET ASIDE.

voluntary Done without compulsion or obligation.
- **volunteer** Pinch a piece of clothing on the right side of the chest with the bent index finger and thumb of the right *5 hand* and pull forward with a short double movement.

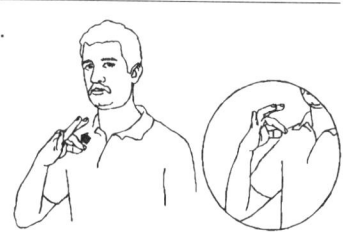

voluntary manslaughter or **manslaughter** Causing the death of another person under circumstances that are considered extenuating and therefore fall short of murder.
- **kill** Push the side of the extended right index finger, palm down, across the palm of the left *open hand*, palm right, with a deliberate movement.

- **not** Bring the thumb of the right *10 hand* forward from under the chin with a deliberate movement.

---- [sign continues] ----

409

voluntary manslaughter

- **plan** Move both *open hands* from in front of the left side of the body, palms facing each other and fingers pointing forward, in a long smooth movement to in front of the right side of the body.

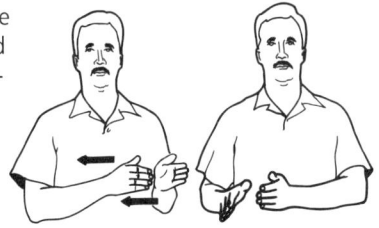

- **before** Beginning with the back of the right *open hand*, palm in and fingers pointing left, touching the back of the left *open hand*, palm forward, move the right hand in toward the chest.

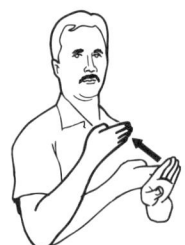

voter qualification A legal requirement for eligibility to vote in a public election, such as age or residence.

- **vote** Insert the fingertips of the right *F hand*, palm down, with a double movement in the opening of the left *S hand*, palm right.

- **person marker** Move both *open hands*, palms facing each other, downward along the sides of the body.

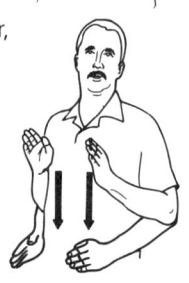

- **law** Place the palm side of the right *L hand*, palm facing left, first on the fingers and then on the heel of the left *open hand*, palm facing right and fingers pointing up.

waive[1] To abandon a right, privilege, or claim, with knowledge of what you are giving up.
- **give-up** Beginning with both *open hands* in front of the body, palms facing down, flip the hands upward in large arcs while opening into *5 hands,* ending in front of each shoulder, palms facing forward.

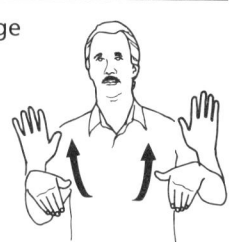

waive[2] See sign for RECALL[2].

waiver The voluntary, intentional relinquishment of a right, privilege, or claim that you know you have.
- **paper** Brush the heel of the right *open hand* with a double movement on the heel of the left *open hand*, palms facing each other.

- **say**[2] Move the extended right index finger in a repeated upward circular movement in front of the chin, palm facing in and finger pointing left.

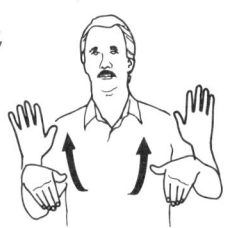

- **give-up** Beginning with both *open hands* in front of the body, palms facing down, flip the hands upward in large arcs while opening into *5 hands,* ending in front of each shoulder, palms facing forward.

ward of the court *Informal.* Any minor or incompetent person involved in legal proceedings, in which case the judges have a duty to make sure the ward's interests are adequately represented and well protected.
- **court** Move both *F hands,* palms facing each other, up and down in front of each side of the chest with a repeated alternating movement.

[sign continues]

411

ward of the court

- **order** Move the extended right index finger, palm forward and finger pointing up, from in front of the mouth forward and down, ending with the finger pointing forward and the palm down.

- **supervise** With the little-finger side of the right *K hand* on the thumb side of the left *K hand*, palms facing in opposite directions, move the hands in a flat circle in front of the body.

- **person marker** Move both *open hands*, palms facing each other, downward along the sides of the body.

warning In lieu of a ticket. See signs for ADMONITION[1,2].

warrant, arrest warrant, or **bench warrant** A formal document issued by a court authorizing an official to take specific action, such as arresting or searching an individual.

- **court** Move both *F hands*, palms facing each other, up and down in front of each side of the chest with a repeated alternating movement.

- **order** Move the extended right index finger, palm forward and finger pointing up, from in front of the mouth forward and down, ending with the finger pointing forward and the palm down.

- **arrest** Move the right *C hand* from in front of the right side of the chest, palm facing left, to the left to close around the extended left index finger held up in front of the chest, palm facing right.

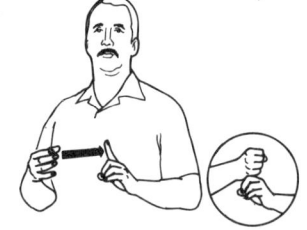

whole life insurance

warranty A legally binding representation made in connection with a sale of goods making the manufacturer liable if the product fails to perform according to what is promised. See sign for AFFIRM.

weapon Anything designed or used to cause bodily injury.
- Fingerspell: W-E-A-P-O-N

whistleblower An employee who reports dangerous or illegal conduct of an employer to the authorities.
- **tattle** Beginning with the thumb side of the right *S hand* near the right side of the mouth, palm forward, flick the index finger upward with a deliberate movement.
- **person marker** Move both *open hands*, palms facing each other, downward along the sides of the body.

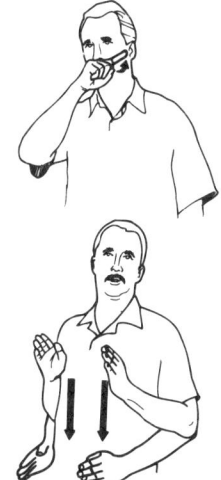

white-collar crime Any business or financial crime of a type typically engaged in legally by executives and professional people.
- **business** Brush the base of the right *B hand*, palm forward, with a repeated rocking movement on the back of the left *open hand*, palm down.
- **crime** Place the palm side of the right *L hand*, palm facing left, first on the fingers and then on the heel of the left *open hand*, palm facing right and fingers pointing up. Then beginning with both *S hands* in front of the body, index fingers touching and palms down, move the hands away from each other while twisting the wrists with a deliberate movement, ending with the palms facing each other.

whole life insurance or **straight life insurance** Life insurance for which the annual premium never increases, and which remains in effect as long as the insured person lives.
- **life** Move both *L hands*, index fingers pointing toward each other, upward on each side of the chest.

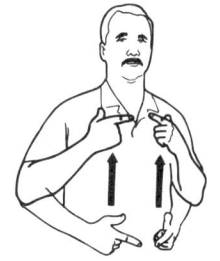

---- [sign continues] ---------------------------------→

whole life insurance

- **insurance** Move the right *I hand*, palm forward, from side to side with a repeated movement in front of the right shoulder.

- **full** Push the palm side of the right *open hand*, palm down, back across the thumb side of the left *S hand*.

wildcat strike A spontaneous strike not officially authorized by a union.

- **final** Bring the little finger of the right *I hand*, palm in, downward, striking the little finger of the left *I hand*, palm right, as it passes.

- **minute** Keeping the palm side of the right *one hand* on the palm of the left *open hand*, rotate the right hand downward a short distance.

- **work** Tap the heel of the right *S hand*, palm forward, with a double movement on the back of the left *S hand* held in front of the body, palm down.

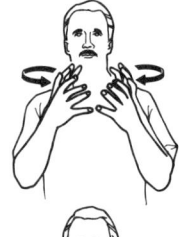

- **group** Beginning with both *claw hands* in front of the chest, palms facing each other, bring the hands away from each other in outward arcs while turning the palms in, ending with the little fingers near each other.

- **protest** Beginning with the right *S hand* in front of the right shoulder, palm facing back, twist the hand sharply forward.

with prejudice

will, last will and testament, or **testament** A person's declaration of how she wants her property to be distributed when she dies. Same sign used for **bequest, legacy.**
- Fingerspell: W-I-L-L

wiretap Any interception or recording of conversations or data transmissions by electronic or other artificial means without the consent of the participants.
- **secret** Tap the thumb side of the right *A hand*, palm left, against the mouth with a repeated movement.

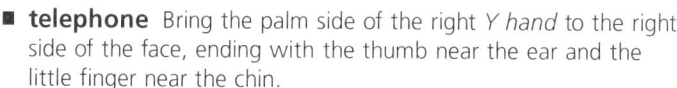

- **telephone** Bring the palm side of the right *Y hand* to the right side of the face, ending with the thumb near the ear and the little finger near the chin.

- **splice-lines** Bring the right *H hand* up to cross under the left *H hand*, both palms down.

- **eavesdrop** Bring the thumb of the right *bent 3 hand* to the right ear, palm facing forward, and bend the middle and index fingers up and down with a double movement.

with prejudice Having the effect of denying a party the right to contest a particular issue in the future.
- **decide** Move the extended right index finger from the right side of the forehead, palm left, down in front of the chest while changing into an *F hand*, ending with both *F hands* moving downward in front of the body, palms facing each other.
- **later**[2] Beginning with the right *L hand*, palm facing left and index finger pointing up, in front of the right shoulder, twist the hand forward, ending with the right index finger pointing forward.

---- [sign continues] ----

415

with prejudice

- **complaint** With a double movement, tap the fingertips of the right *curved 5 hand* against the center of the chest.

- **can't** Bring the extended index finger of the right *one hand* downward, hitting the extended index finger of the left *one hand* as it moves.

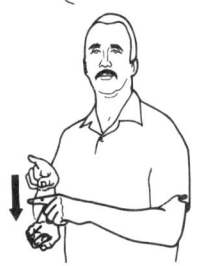

withholding tax A sum of money required to be held back from an employee's wages and sent directly to taxing authorities as an advance on future taxes.

- **work** Tap the heel of the right *S hand*, palm forward, with a double movement on the back of the left *S hand* held in front of the body, palm down.
- Fingerspell: T-A-X

without prejudice Preserving the right to contest a particular issue in the future.

- **decide** Move the extended right index finger from the right side of the forehead, palm left, down in front of the chest while changing into an *F hand*, ending with both *F hands* moving downward in front of the body, palms facing each other.

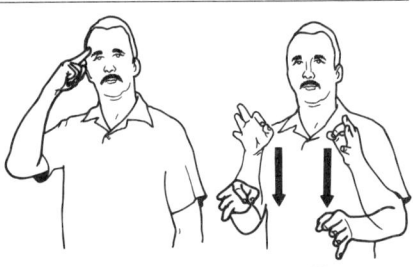

- **later**[1] With the thumb of the right *L hand*, palm facing forward, on the palm of the left *open hand*, palm facing right and fingers pointing forward, twist the right hand forward, keeping the thumb in place and ending with the right palm facing down.

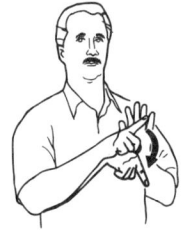

- **complain** Tap the fingertips of the right *curved 5 hand* against the center of the chest.

---- [sign continues] ----→

416

witness

- **can** Move both *S hands,* palms facing down, downward simultaneously in front of each side of the body.

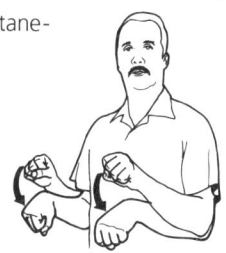

witness[1] A person who has seen or heard something relevant to a case or an investigation.

- **person** Move both *P hands*, palms facing each other, downward along the sides of the body.

- **see** Bring the fingers of the right *V hand* from pointing at the eyes, palm facing in, forward a short distance.

- **proof** Move the right *open hand* downward, ending with the back of the right hand on the palm of the left *open hand,* both palms facing up in front of the chest.

witness[2] (alternate sign)

- **witness** With the index finger of the right *X hand* pull down slightly on the cheek near the outside corner of the right eye.

- **person marker** Move both *open hands*, palms facing each other, downward along the sides of the body.

417

witness stand

witness stand or **stand** In a trial, the place where a witness sits while testifying.

- **testify** While holding the left *open hand* in front of the left side of the body, palm down and fingers pointing forward, move the right extended index finger from in front of the mouth, palm left, forward while opening to an *open hand*.

- **sentences** Beginning with the thumbs and index fingers of both *F hands* touching in front of the chest, palms facing each other, with a double movement pull the hands apart to in front of each side of the chest.

- **sit** Place the fingers of the right *H hand*, palm facing down, across the extended fingers of the left *H hand* held in front of the chest, palm facing down and fingers pointing right.

work for hire See sign for WORK MADE FOR HIRE.

work made for hire or **work for hire** Any of a certain class of copyrightable works, to which copyright is not owned by the creator of the work, but by the company that hired the creator to do the work.

- **work** Tap the heel of the right *S hand*, palm forward, with a double movement on the back of the left *S hand* held in front of the body, palm down.

- **for-for** With a questioning expression and beginning with the extended right finger touching the right side of the forehead, twist the hand forward with a double movement, turning the index finger forward each time.

- **money** Tap the back of the right *flattened O hand*, palm facing up, with a double movement against the palm of the left *open hand*, palm facing up.

418

wrongful death

workers' compensation Payment to a worker as compensation for on-the-job injury as covered by state or federal laws.

- **work** Tap the heel of the right *S hand*, palm forward, with a double movement on the back of the left *S hand* held in front of the body, palm down.

- **person marker** Move both *open hands*, palms facing each other, downward along the sides of the body.
- Fingerspell: C-O-M-P

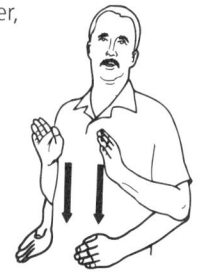

wrong The violation of or failure to perform a legal duty, or the infringement upon another's legal rights.

- **wrong** Bring the middle fingers of the right *Y hand*, palm in, back against the chin with a deliberate movement.

wrongful death Criminal action, brought by close relatives or beneficiaries of someone who has died, alleging that the death was caused by a wrongful act of the defendant, such as medical malpractice, reckless driving, etc.

- **accidental** With the middle fingers of the right *Y hand* against the chin, twist the hand with a deliberate movement.

- **die** Beginning with both *open hands* in front of the body, right palm down and left palm up, flip the hands to the right, turning the right palm up and the left palm down.

X A mark traditionally used as a signature by people who cannot write their names.

- **put-down** Touch the fingertips of the right *flattened O hand*, palm down, to the palm of the left *open hand*, palm up. Then slap the palm of the right *open hand* against the left palm.

- **x** Place the extended right index finger across the extended left index finger to form an *X*.

X-rated Material having sexually explicit or obscene content, such as movies, books, etc. See signs for PORNOGRAPHY[1,2].

year-and-a-day rule The common-law rule that one cannot be found guilty of homicide if the victim lives for a year and a day after the act.

- **try** Beginning with both *T hands* in front of the chest, palms in, simultaneously twist the wrists forward, ending with the palms facing forward.

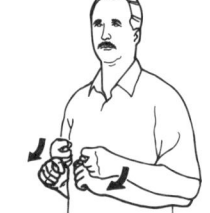

- **kill** Push the side of the extended right index finger, palm down, across the palm of the left *open hand*, palm right, with a deliberate movement.

---- [sign continues] ---->

year-and-a-day rule

- **person marker** Move both *open hands*, palms facing each other, downward along the sides of the body.

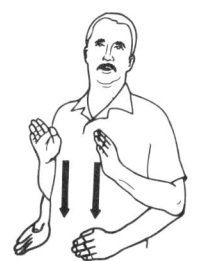

- **continue** Beginning with the thumb of the right *10 hand* on the thumbnail of the left *10 hand,* both palms facing down in front of the chest, move the hands downward and forward in a double arc.

- **live** Move both *10 hands*, thumbs pointing up, upward on each side of the chest.

- **one-year** Hold up the extended right index finger. Then beginning with the little-finger side of the right *S hand*, palm left, on top of the index-finger side of the left *S hand*, palm right, move the right hand forward around the left hand, ending with the right *S hand* on the left *S hand*.

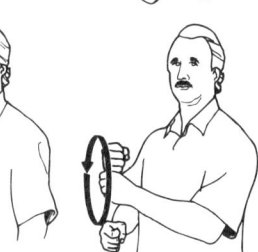

- **one-day** Beginning with the bent right elbow resting on the back of the left hand held across the body, palm facing down, bring the extended right index finger from pointing up in front of the right shoulder, palm facing left, downward toward the left elbow.

- **file** Move the fingers of the right *V hand*, palm facing forward, downward on each side of the extended left index finger, which is pointing up in front of the chest.

---- [sign continues] ---->

year-and-a-day rule

- **against** Hit the fingertips of the right *bent hand* into the left *open hand*, palm right and fingers pointing forward.

- **can't** Bring the extended index finger of the right *one hand* downward, hitting the extended index finger of the left *one hand* as it moves.

Your Honor See sign for HONORABLE.

youthful offender See sign for DELINQUENT.

zoning The division of a locality into geographic zones, pursuant to a plan that designates the kinds of uses and structures.
- Fingerspell: Z-O-N-E